AF574506

CATCHING THE LIGHT

BRUCE MUNRO

To Judy, Brian, Mac (my parents), Matthew (my brother), Jane (my sister),
Serena (my wife), Millie, Florrie, Tink, Tom (our children),
Ludo (dog), Duck (duck), and the Chooks (chickens)

Library of Congress Control Number: 2013944044
ISBN 978-1-937720-17-9

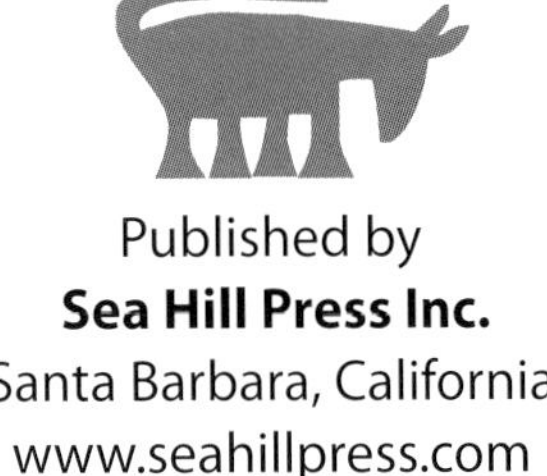

Published by
Sea Hill Press Inc.
Santa Barbara, California
www.seahillpress.com

Printed in Hong Kong

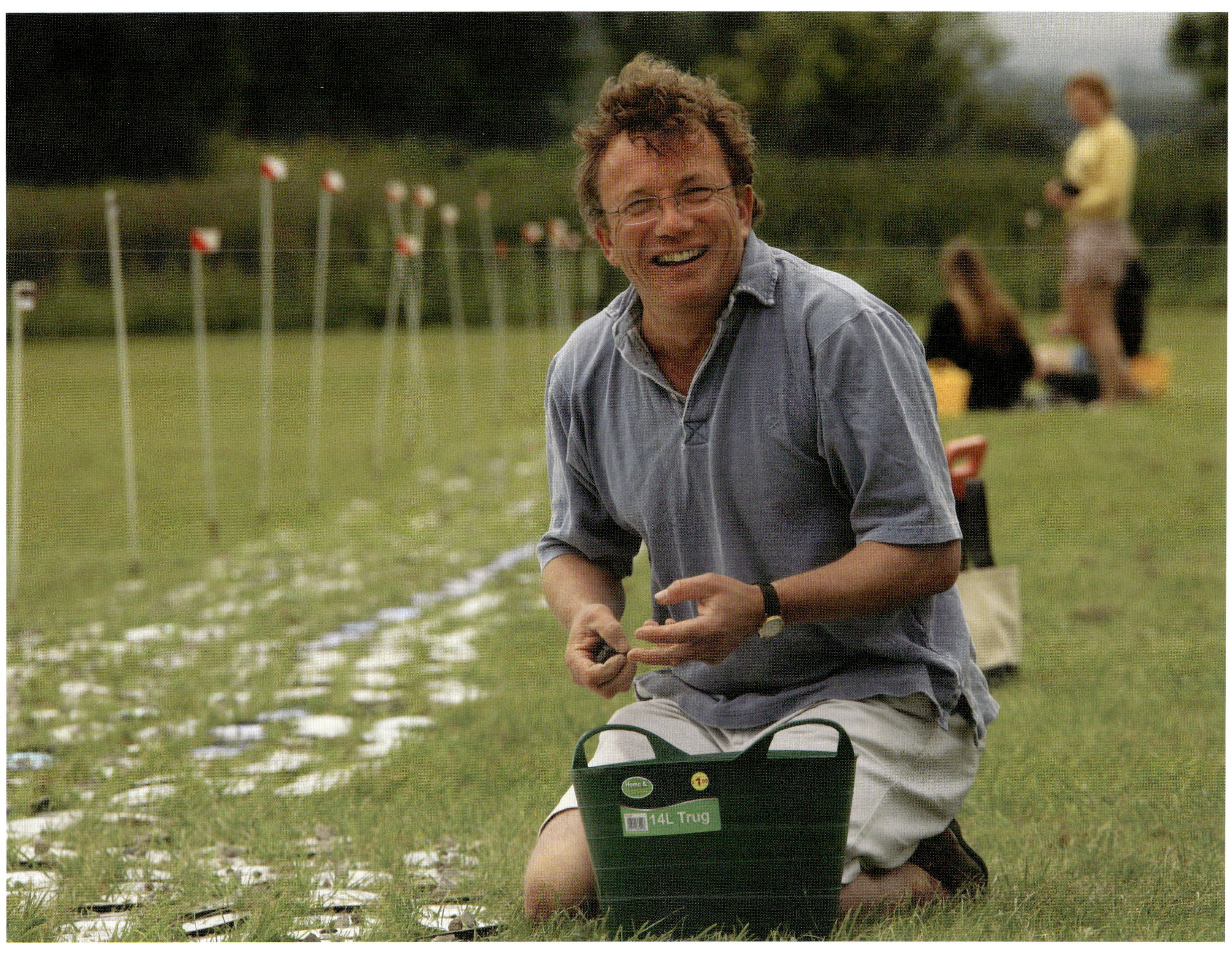
14L Trug

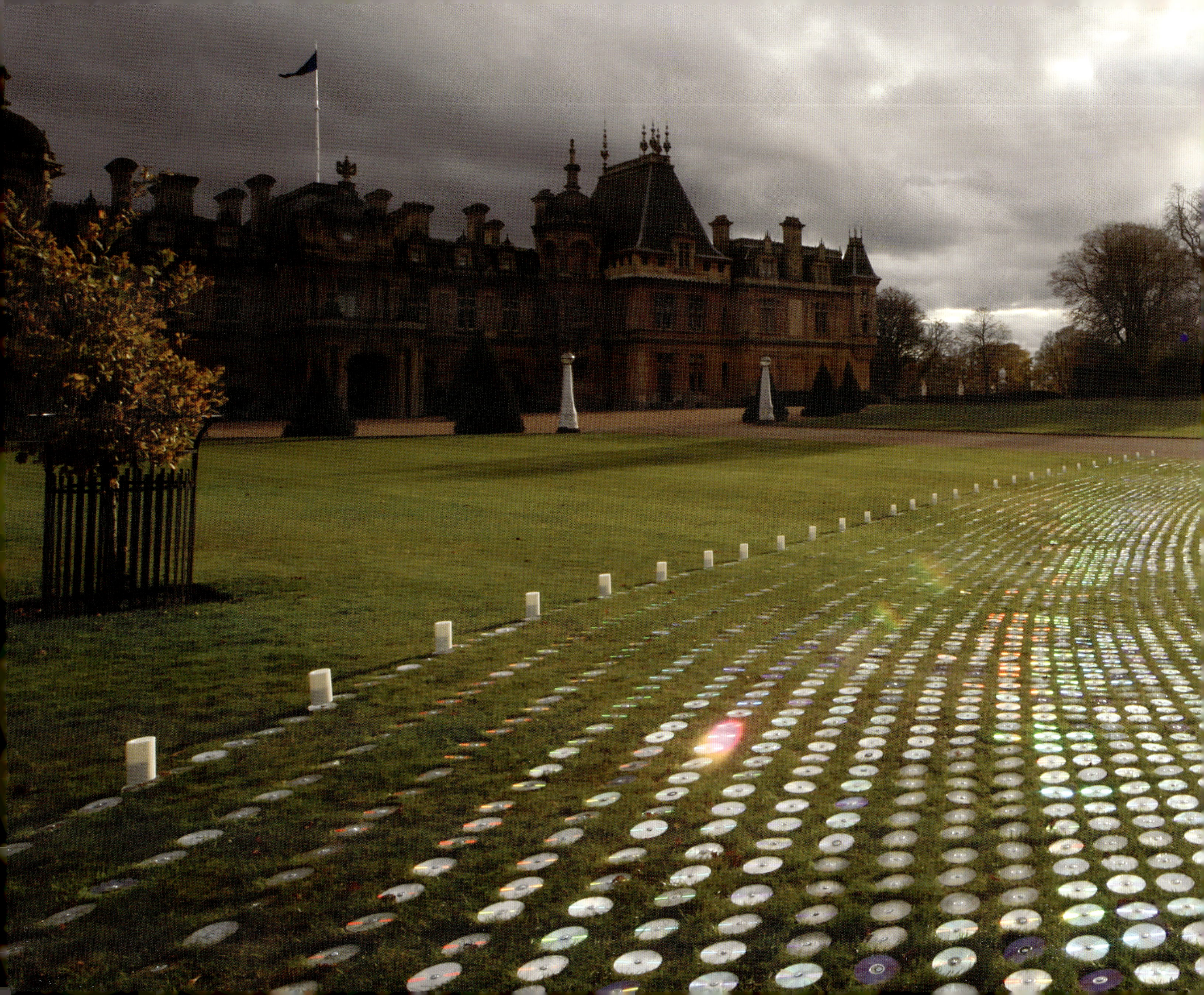

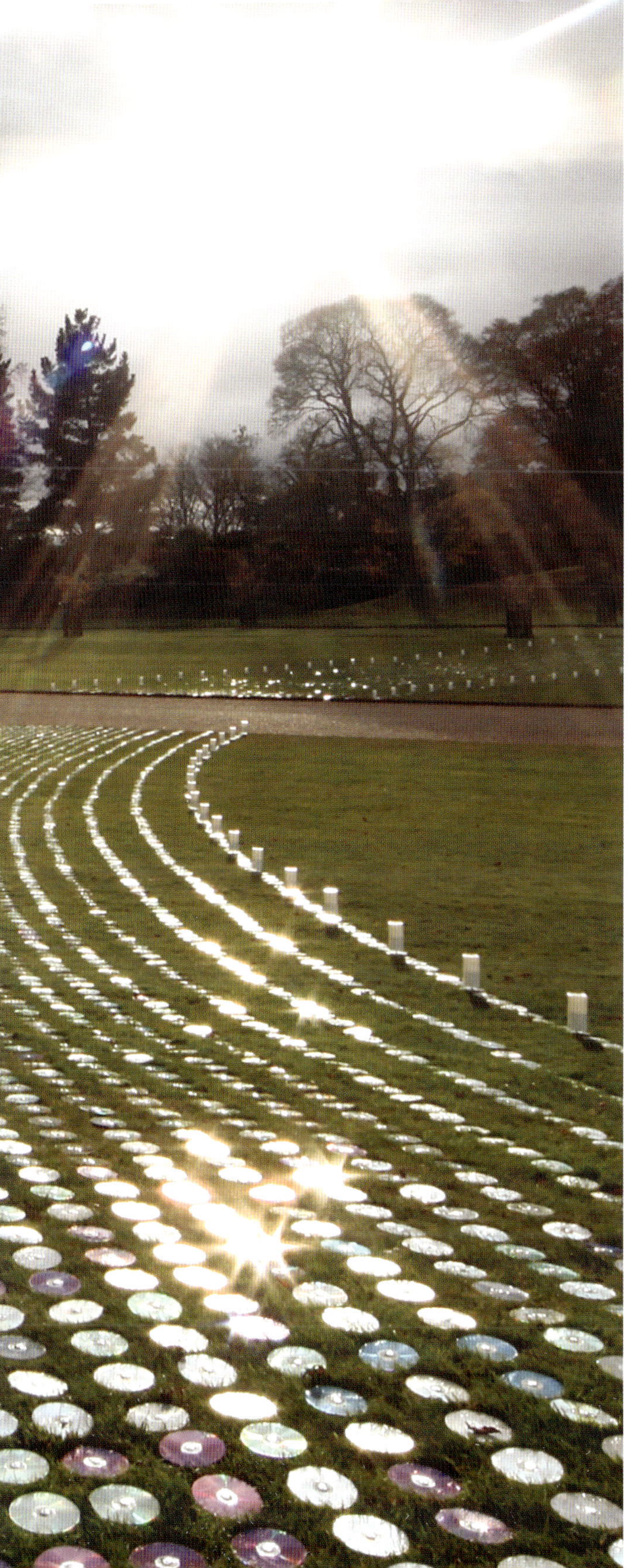

FOREWORD
LORD ROTHSCHILD

Light, and its management, has long been a subject of debate and discussion at Waddesdon Manor, the great Rothschild house in Buckinghamshire, which has been my pleasure and privilege to steer for the last twenty-five years. Historically, it should be said, this debate largely concerned the control of light, which, in conservation terms at least, was considered the enemy of the inlaid marquetry furniture, delicate textiles, and eighteenth-century drawings, so much so that rules were introduced to protect them by drawing down the blinds and covering everything up when the house was not in use. Now, of course, our views are rather different. Although we continue to manage light in the Manor with great care, we are becoming increasingly interested in its power and potential as an artistic medium in its own right. Waddesdon Manor has launched a major initiative to celebrate light art for our public, both national and international, bringing artists and installations to the Manor to explore and enhance our uniquely beautiful building and its landscape, highlighting the dramatic effects of light on the architecture, sculpture, fountains, and trees. The innovative technological aspects of light-based art and the way in which it blends art and science also strike a chord with my family's long-standing interest in the scientific and environmental worlds. Our collaboration with Bruce Munro is an exciting beginning to this initiative.

The Manor has always existed as a place to celebrate the best in art and design. Baron Ferdinand, from the Viennese branch of the Rothschild banking dynasty, built the Manor to entertain the

Angel of Light, *Waddesdon Manor, Buckinghamshire, UK, 2012.*

fashionable world and to display his matchless collection. He acquired the hilltop site and the surrounding estate from the Duke of Marlborough in 1874. Over the next six years, an astonishing creation took shape: a French Renaissance-style chateau designed by Parisian architect Gabriel-Hippolyte Destailleur was set off by one of the most important nineteenth-century gardens in Britain. Guests including Queen Victoria, Edward VII, and the Shah of Persia enjoyed legendary hospitality, but the house was built with not only entertaining in mind. Ferdinand was one of the most discerning collectors in a family renowned for their activities in this field. Fascinated by the culture and history of the *Ancien Règime* court, he assembled a collection—eighteenth-century French furniture and porcelain, eighteenth-century English portraits, Dutch Golden Age paintings, Renaissance works of art, textiles, books, and gold boxes—that marches in certain areas alongside those of the Wallace Collection, the V&A, and the Louvre. The antiquarianism of the Manor's interiors belied the modernity of its structure. Indeed, the Manor has always embraced new technology. It was one of the first houses of its generation in Britain to install electricity. When Queen Victoria visited in 1890, she was reportedly so delighted by the innovation that she spent some time turning the lights on and off.

Later generations of the family, notably Ferdinand's sister, Alice, and her great-nephew and heir, James de Rothschild, and his English wife, Dorothy, added to the collections, in James's case mainly through inheritance from his father, Baron Edmond. After the death of James in 1957, the house and the majority of its contents were bequeathed to the National Trust, but continued to be managed with immense skill and dedication by my cousin Dorothy, a role which now falls to me, as chairman of the Rothschild Foundation. In recent years, we have started to explore a number of different avenues of Rothschild history and interest, including contemporary art. The Rothschild Foundation has made a number of important acquisitions for the permanent collections, and the property is also home to several significant loans. These include pieces by Lucian Freud, Richard Long, David Hockney, Anish Kapoor, Sarah Lucas, Stephen Cox, and Xavier Veilhan. The exhibitions programme has included a major show of contemporary sculpture in collaboration with Christie's, an exhibition of Andy Warhol prints, and a retrospective of the work of Angus Fairhurst. One of the earliest expressions of this new direction was the commission of a light work from the Munich-based designer Ingo Maurer, who in 2004 was invited to create a chandelier for the Blue Dining Room upstairs at the Manor.

It is against this background of a tradition of collecting at the highest level and the development of the contemporary art programme that our

Blue Moon on a Platter, *Waddesdon Manor, Buckinghamshire, UK, 2012.*

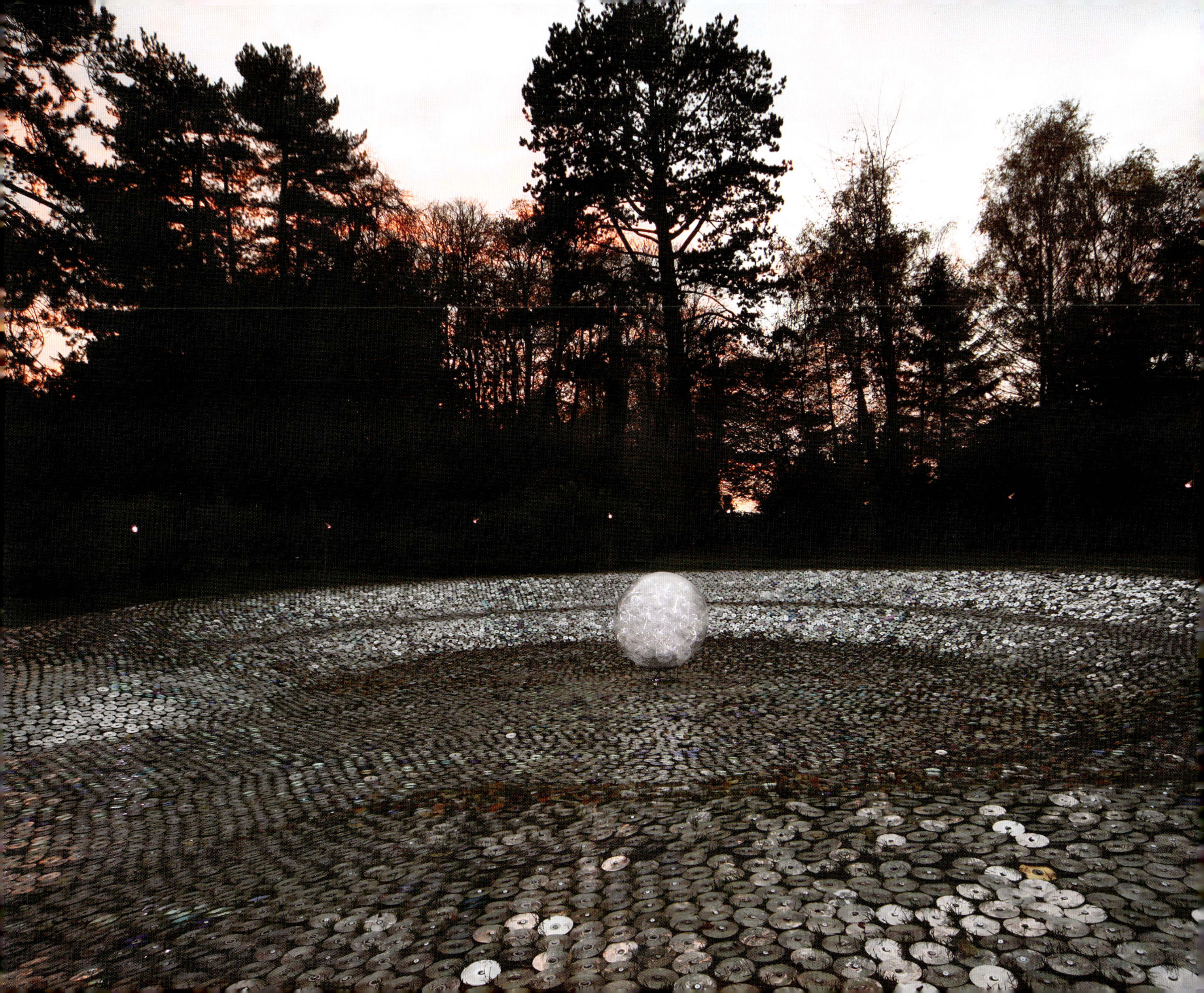

collaboration with Bruce Munro should be seen. We became aware of Munro's work in 2011 through the extraordinary impact of his commission *Field of Light* at the Holburne Museum in Bath and his subsequent work at Longwood Gardens, near Philadelphia. This led to the invitation for him to come to Waddesdon, from which came the proposal for a pair of artworks for the Winter Season of 2012. Both of these employed second-use CDs, a favourite material for Munro. He first used them for *CDSea* at Long Knoll Field, Wiltshire, in 2010. At the Manor they made a shimmering base for a glowing globe of coiled optic fibres for *Blue Moon on a Platter*, and over five thousand of them were laid out to form a vast, circular halo in front of the Manor for *Angel of Light*. They refract ambient light beautifully—splitting the light beams and giving a true reflection of colour. There are no permanently bonded elements, and the CDs are recycled at the end of the installation. This is partly born of environmental concerns but ephemerality is also an artistic choice.

The theme of light art expanded in 2013 with a special commission for Waddesdon's contemporary art space at the Coach House. *Cantus Arcticus*, which evokes the Northern Lights through delicate curtains of optical fibres whose colours shift and change in a choreographed pattern, is in many ways typical of Munro's work in that it explores the immersive, deeply sensory potential of light when combined with sound and music. The work was inspired by both the landscape of the Arctic tundra and the music of the Finnish composer Einojuhani Rautavaara (b. 1928), whose orchestral composition of the same name, also known as *Concerto for Birds and Orchestra*, weaves the calls of migrating birds recorded at the Arctic Circle into a haunting orchestral score. Rautavaara's music has become particularly significant for Munro, who used his Symphony No. 7, *Angel of Light*, as the soundscape for the work at the Manor of the same name.

Bruce Munro is the first in what we hope will be a series of artists working with light who are invited to showcase their work at Waddesdon. His residency will run until 2015 with a series of changing, site-specific light installations throughout the Garden. As Waddesdon faces the future, with all that it will bring in technological and digital advancement, the ability of light and light art to celebrate the place and bring people together through shared experience and pleasure seems more relevant than ever.

Lord Rothschild

Opposite: Angel of Light, *Waddesdon Manor, Buckinghamshire, UK, 2012.*

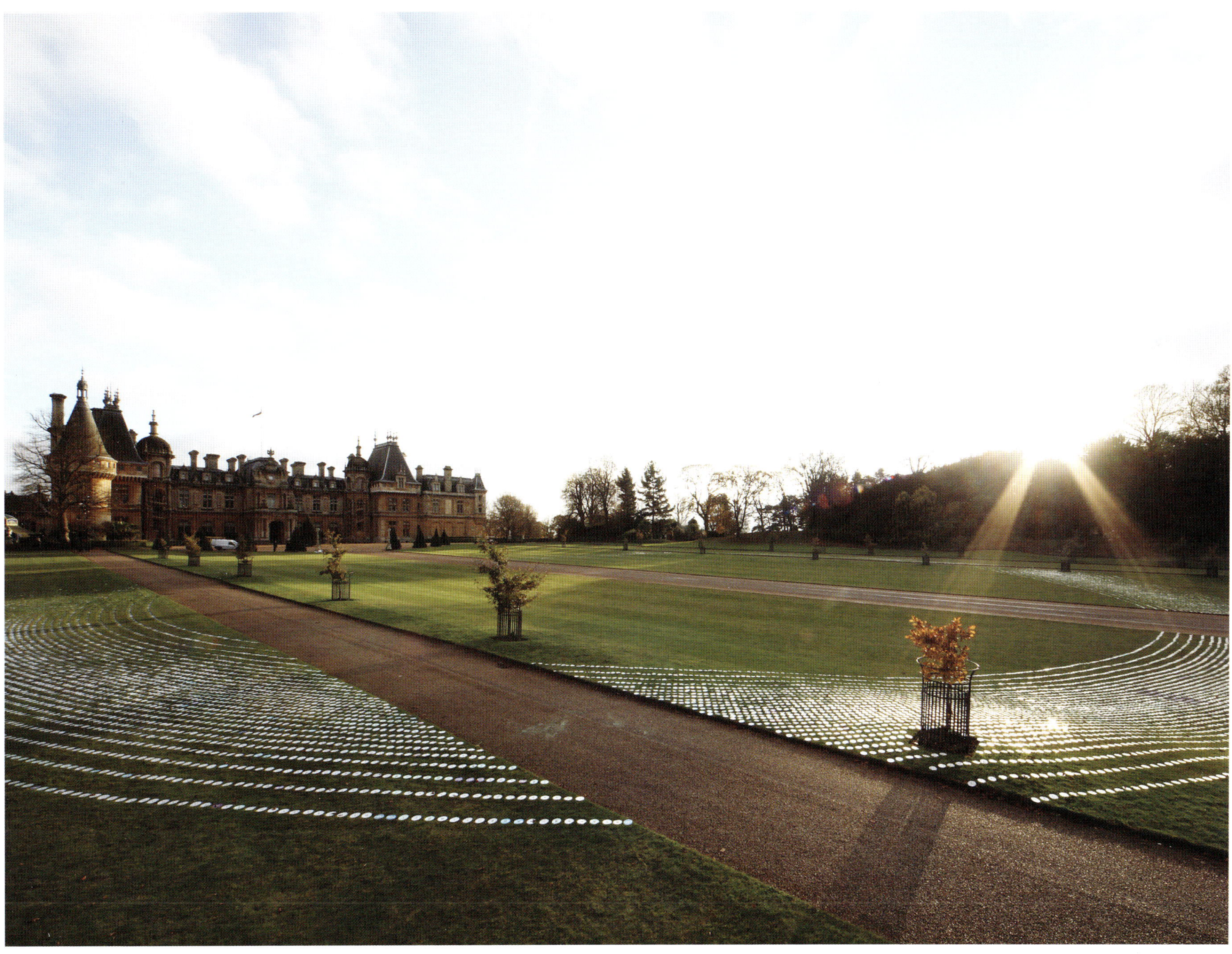

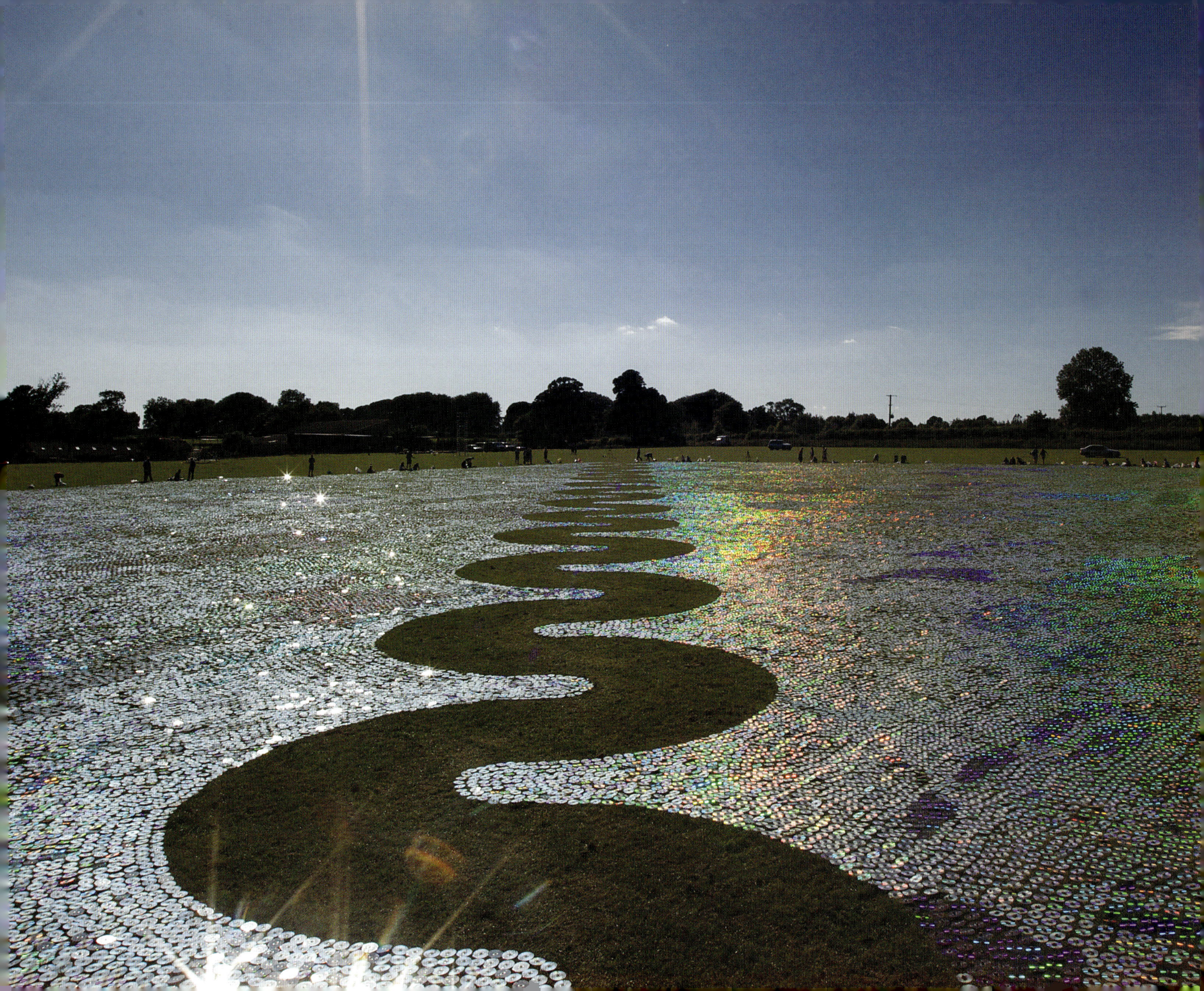

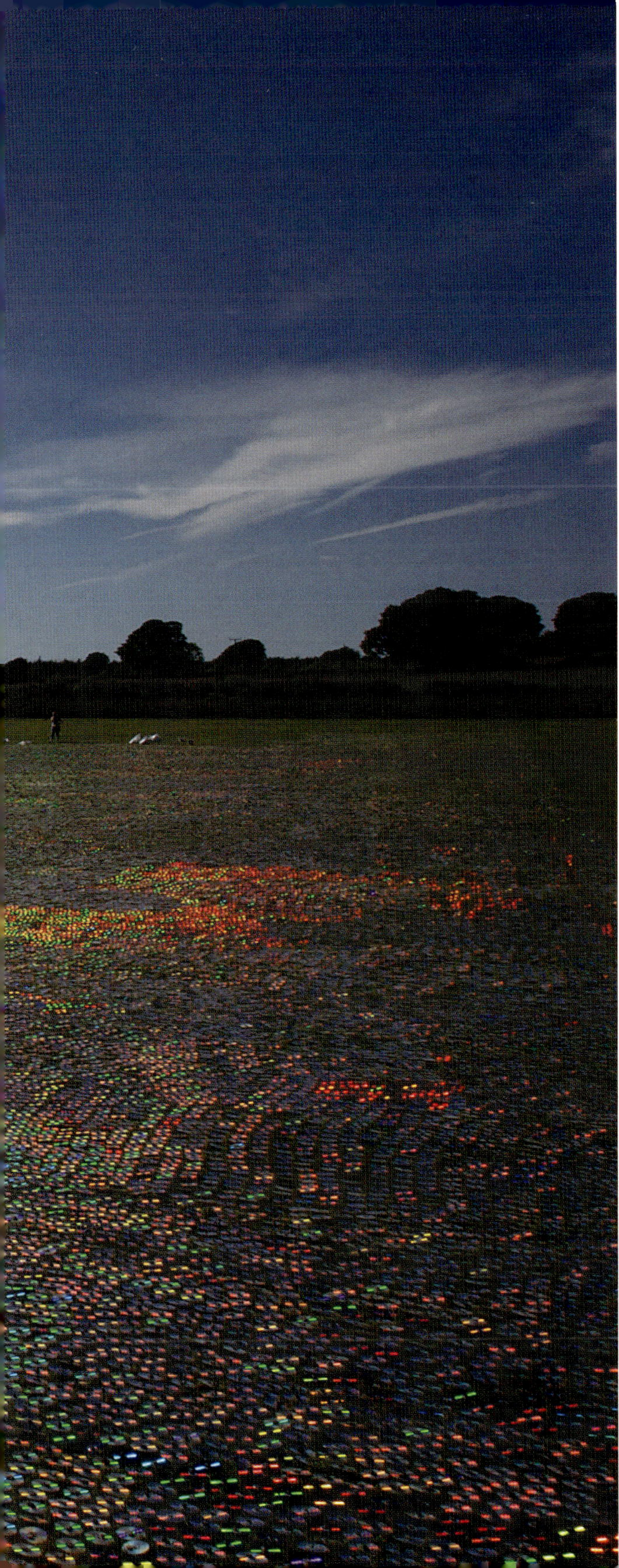

CATCHING THE LIGHT

DR RICHARD CORK

With spectacular audacity, Bruce Munro succeeded in transforming a large English field with 600,000 unwanted compact discs. Given by donors across the world, these discarded CDs were given new life by a team of volunteers walking over Long Knoll Field in Wiltshire. They included families with children, all of whom helped to lay out the discs so deftly that they ended up creating a vast blanket of silver. It emphasised the immensity encompassed by this ambitious work, which Munro called *CDSea*. And once it was complete, the entire shimmering installation was open to everyone who roamed along the public footpath bisecting Long Knoll Field. Rather than viewing it at a respectful and alienating distance, local people were able to experience *CDSea* in a very direct, visceral way. They must have felt like swimmers, poised on the edge of a glinting ocean. The ancient solidity of the field was replaced by a water-like alternative, and after its installation in June 2010, the summer sunshine often gave these discs an aura of intense optical vivacity.

In this respect, Munro was remaining true to the seminal experience which inspired *CDSea*. It happened in Australia, where he spent eight years after graduating from art school in Bristol. Munro made very little art during his Australian period, which commenced in 1984. But his subsequent work has benefited immeasurably from the stimulus provided by a few revelatory moments in the Antipodes. So far as *CDSea* was concerned, the epiphany occurred one Sunday afternoon when he escaped to Nielsen Park, a part of Sydney Harbour National Park, which provided refuge from his

CDSea, *Long Knoll Field, Wiltshire, UK, 2010.*

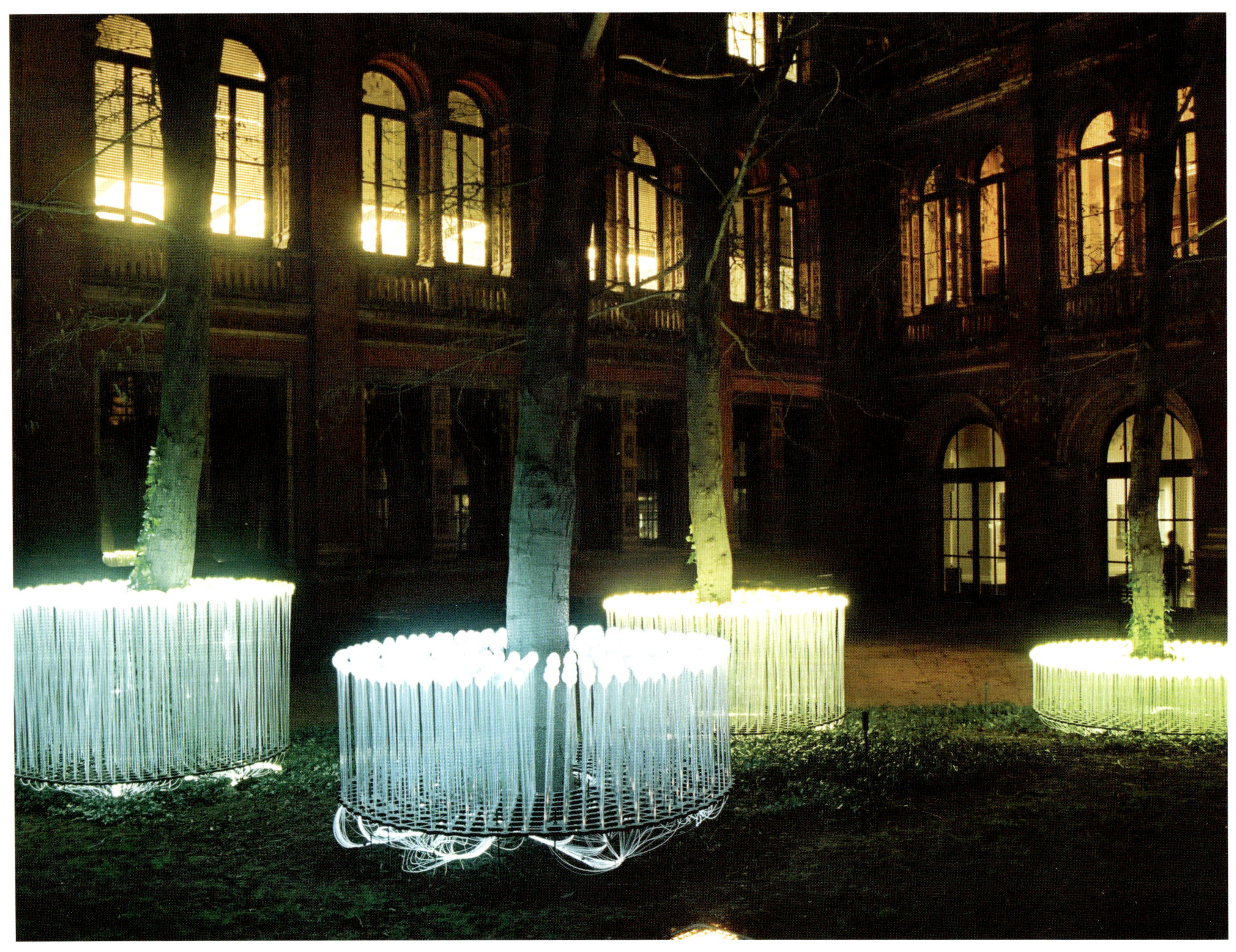

Field of Light, *Victoria & Albert Museum, London, UK, 2004.*

weekday routine. Seated on a rocky peninsula, he gazed out to sea and found himself astonished by the sheer potency of the light. Munro's longing for England, and especially Salcombe in South Devon where his father lived, was alleviated by the thought that the sun-saturated Sydney sea was linked, on a fundamental level, to the water lapping around Salcombe's coast. That is why Munro left Nielsen Park beach in a very positive mood, amazed that the play of light had changed his state of mind so profoundly. He now thinks that "it proved an unforgettable turning-point in my life." Elsewhere, the irresistible power of Australian light would also nourish another of Munro's major sculptural installations. This time it happened in 1992 when he was journeying to Uluru through the barren red desert of central Australia. By a paradox, the extraordinary heat and brightness gave him a sustained energy. Every evening he would pull off the Stewart Highway and spend the night in a campsite. There, meditating quietly before sleep, Munro made on the pages of his ever-present sketchbook the first drawings for a work which has now undergone several fascinating permutations: *Field of Light*. As its title suggests, this installation comes alive at the onset of dusk. Suddenly, when the field grows dark and almost invisible, the stems of light which Munro planted there in thousands burst into bloom. He originally imagined them, during his epic 1992 expedition, flowering in the red desert as if nourished by a miraculous shower of rain.

During the first decade of the present century, when Munro's art reached maturity, *Field of Light* finally emerged in London. It made an arresting appearance in the "Brilliant" exhibition at the Victoria & Albert Museum in summer 2004. And during the same year, a ten-acre version containing more than 15,000 individual stems of light was "planted" in Long Knoll Field. Through the seasons, he was able to scrutinise it from his nearby studio workshop until summer 2005, and thereafter Munro was given the opportunity to recreate *Field of Light* at the Eden Project in Cornwall. Here, between the Mediterranean and Rainforest "biomes," he installed 6,000 acrylic stems capped by frosted glass spheres. Laced with optic fibre, they were planted in the grass roof sheltering the visitors' centre. All through the Cornish winter of 2008–09, *Field of Light* provided an affirmative and, at times, revelatory spectacle for people who encountered it. And in 2011 Munro installed a 5,200-stem *Field of Light* behind the Holburne Museum in Bath, where a major extension had just been designed with great success by the architect Eric Parry. Munro is now hoping to take *Field of Light* back to its immense heartland at Uluru in central Australia, where no less than 250,000 stems illuminated by custom-made solar power projectors will be installed.

He has also been busy making pieces for landmark outdoor locations in the United States. Early in 2010 Munro was invited to create a solo exhibition

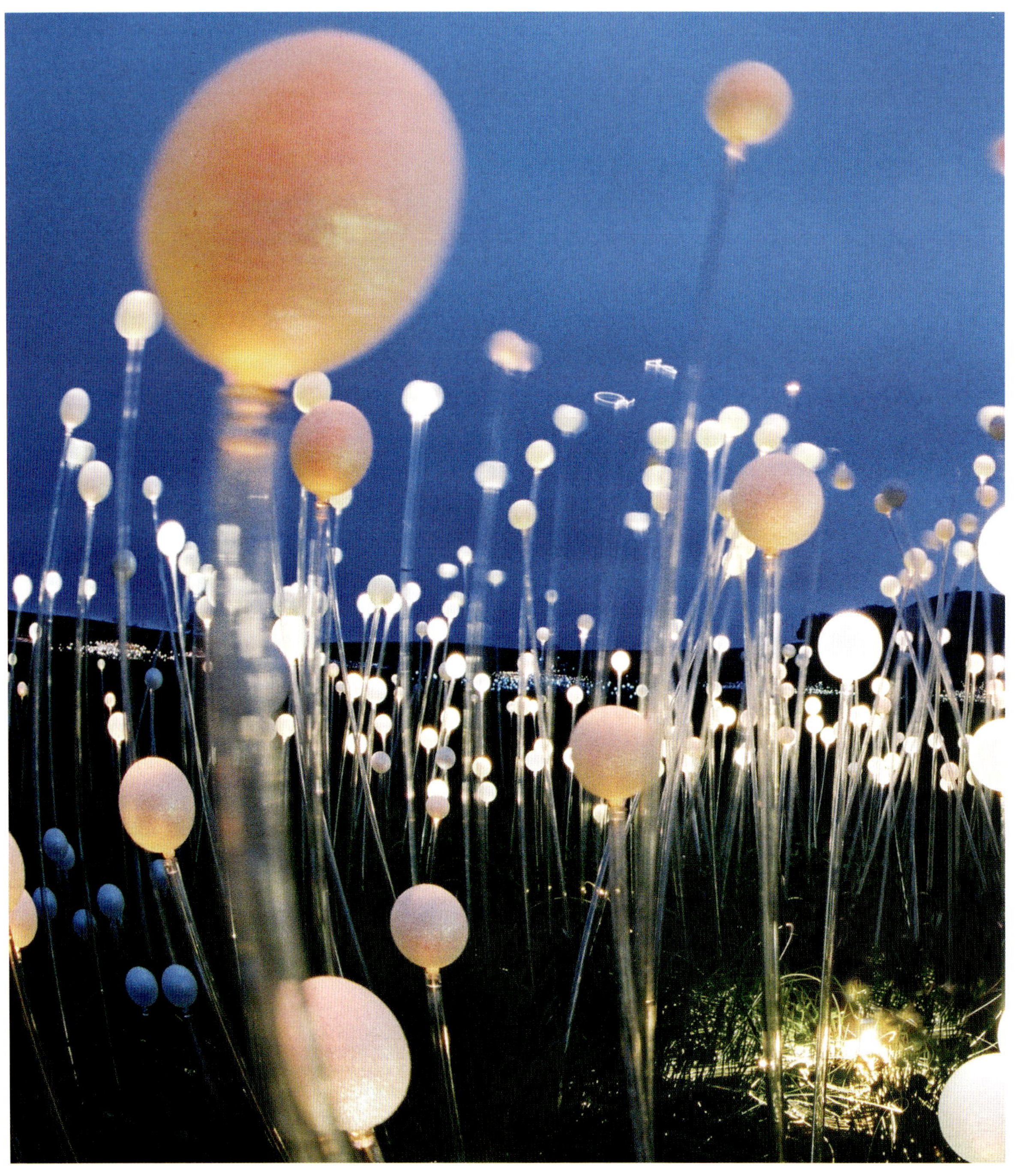

for Longwood Gardens near Philadelphia, founded by Pierre S. du Pont. It opened two years later, and *Field of Light* played an important part in the show when it was spread across five acres of Longwood's Forest Walk to create *Forest of Light*. Subsequent exhibitions at Cheekwood Botanical Garden and Museum of Art in Nashville, Tennessee, and Franklin Park Conservatory in Columbus, Ohio, were quickly proffered. At night, the garden visitors who discovered his sparkling assertion of multicoloured growth and luminosity had no difficulty understanding why Munro once declared, "Light is my passion." The origins of this central obsession can be traced back to a very early stage in his development. Munro's parents split up when he was six years old, and subsequently he always looked forward to visiting his father down on the coast at Salcombe. The exceptional allure of the natural surroundings enthralled him, and he still remembers "when I was about

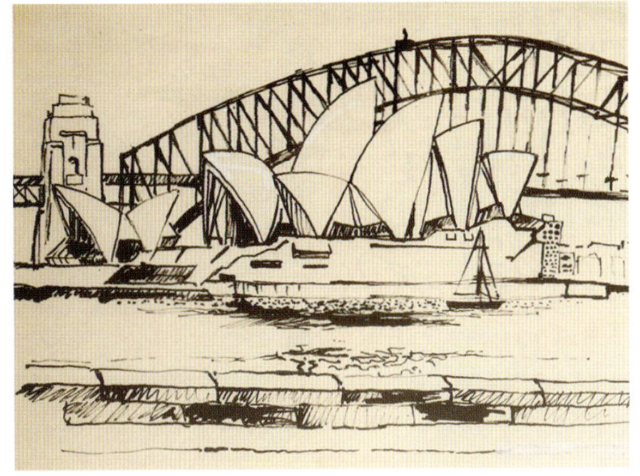

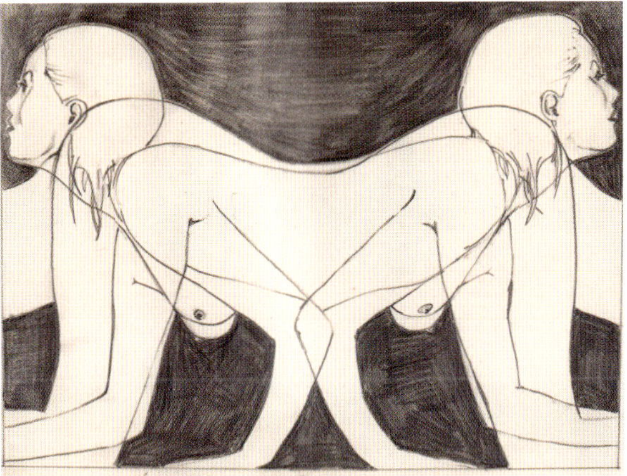

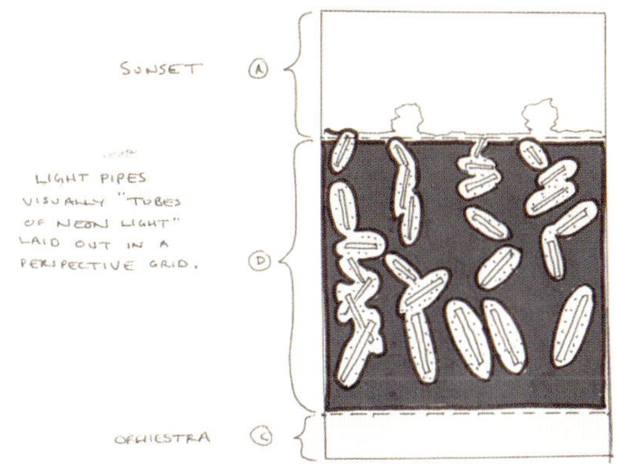

eight walking from my father's house into Salcombe and thinking: 'When is the secret going to be revealed?' Because I thought there was an essence which was mysterious." As a teenager, Munro got into trouble for his penchant for daydreaming, and he created his own private world in the pages of sketchbooks. Although they were often dismissed as mere escapism, the truth is that Munro's persistent dreams were all inspired by his alert, hungry response to the world around him. He recalls how "at the age of twenty-one, I was running down a path at home and smelling wild apricots on a beautiful autumn evening. Then I disappeared, and felt as if I were floating across the ground. It was a magic moment, being at one with the world." But he was not yet ready to give these visions a sculptural form. Munro had spent much of his adolescence trying to paint his nightly dreams, and he was haunted by "images of a shark in a pool, big waves, and a mushroom cloud." Although he is now pursuing some of these nightmarish images, they led him nowhere during his teenage years. Even at art school Munro did not realise that sculpture was the prime area he should explore. Several painters commanded his particular respect as a student. He remembers admiring Matisse "because I

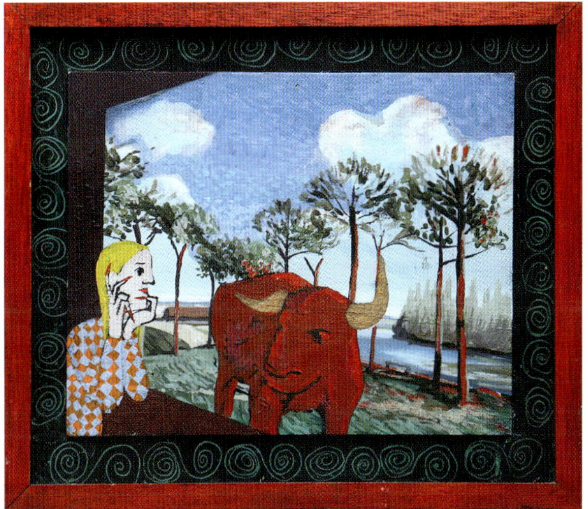

Above, from left to right: Sketches and paintings from Munro's notebooks and collection.

Opposite: Field of Light, *Long Knoll, Wiltshire, UK, 2004.*

felt he was so spiritual, and I adored Howard Hodgkin. I would love to make sculptures that have the feel of his paintings." Munro was also impressed by Georgia O'Keeffe's "beautifully haunting paintings," especially a large, late image of "clear blue sky populated by abstracted clouds that receded from the bottom to top edge of the canvas." Among the pioneering artists inspired by the land, he responded to James Turrell as well as Richard Long, who had started out studying at the same art school in Bristol. And Munro has never forgotten watching a mesmeric film of a road, *Last Chants for a Slow Dance*, by the independent American filmmaker Jon Jost.

Book-reading likewise played a significant part in nourishing Munro's emergent imagination. Although he was "a late and slow reader, and never found it easy," his cousin brought books by C. S. Lewis to the family house. Munro's boyhood memories of the Narnia Chronicles were still alive enough in his mind to trigger a work called *Parliament of Owls*. His first thoughts for this piece were stimulated by a glass lens which reminded Munro of a caricatured owl's eye. But then he recalled that in *The Silver Chair*, of the Narnia Chronicles, a collection of owls was called a "parliament." Hence his decision to mount a whole collection of glass eyes on a telegraph pole which he had removed from the Long Knoll Field before burying the power lines underground. Munro always relishes finding new uses for discarded materials, and the telegraph pole was triumphantly restored to an upright position for its new role in *Parliament of Owls*, finally to be executed at Waddesdon Manor in 2013.

Another important source of literary inspiration was Lyall Watson's book *Gifts of Unknown Things*. Munro read this radical text when he was twenty-one, and became captivated by the young girl Tia who lives on an island in the Indonesian archipelago. Very mysteriously, she can respond to sounds by seeing them in colour. And Tia's magical ability gave Munro the crucial starting-point for an elaborate, maze-like work called *Water-Towers*. In 2011 this dramatically illuminated sequence of 69 monumental structures, each containing 252 recycled water bottles, was installed in the Cloisters at Salisbury Cathedral, one of the most aspirant gothic buildings in Britain. Munro stacked the bottles and lit them with optic fibres, which responded to the sound of choral music. Visitors were invited to make their way through this dazzling maze, and found themselves caught up in the synchronised rainbow of colours. They irradiated the people as well as the architecture, while inside the Cathedral a breathtaking *Light Shower* installation cascaded from the Spire Crossing. Munro succeeded in transforming the place where the transepts intersect with the nave, sending no less than 2,000 optic fibres floating downwards before they terminated in clear diffusers shaped like teardrops. The piece was illuminated to herald the beginning of Advent, when a

Water-Towers, *Salisbury Cathedral, Wiltshire, UK, 2010.*

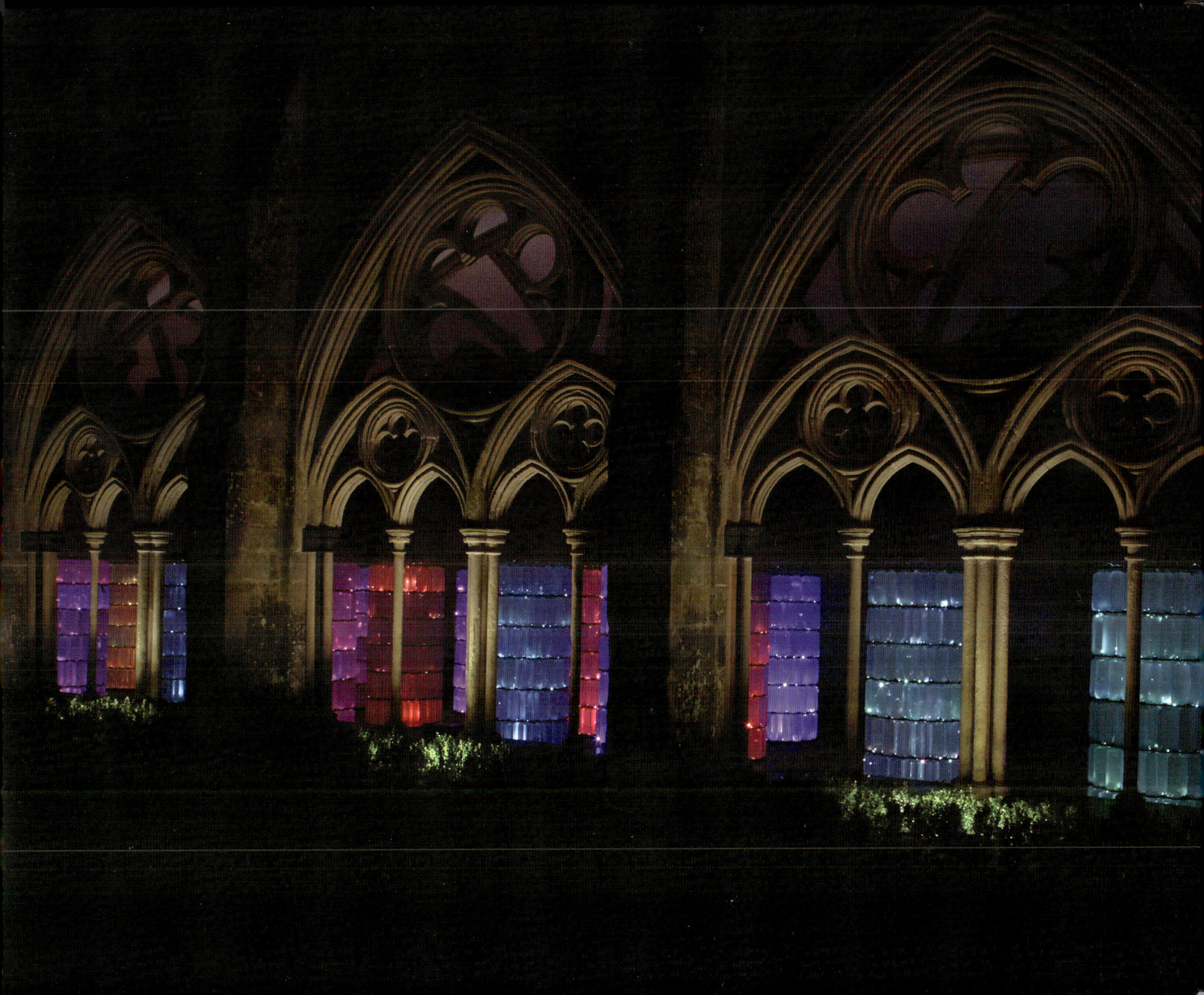

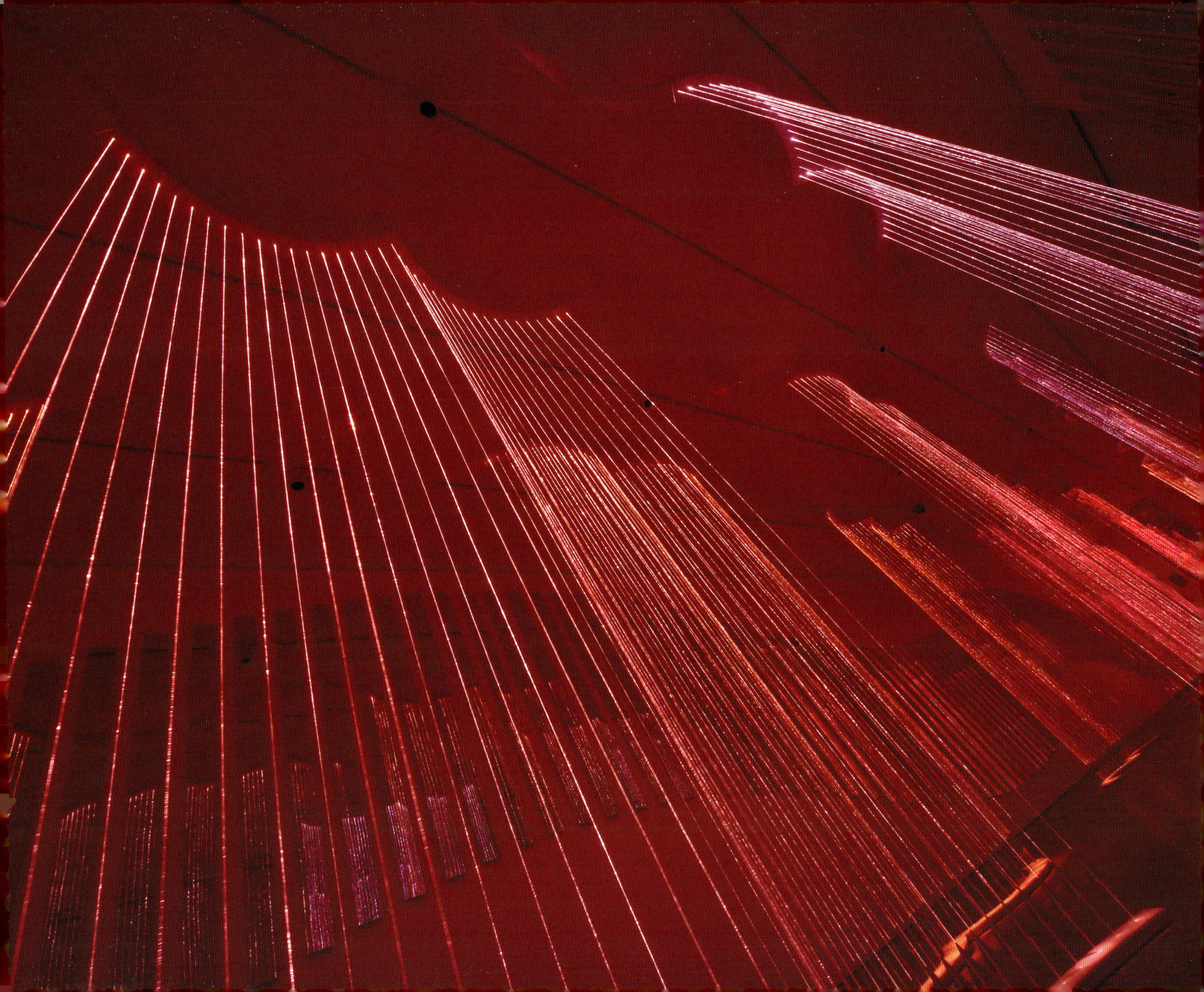

candle-lit procession moved through the Cathedral celebrating the significance of the Advent Procession "From Darkness to Light." By no means are all Munro's recent works as affirmative in mood. Like everyone, he has been affected by the pessimism and fear plaguing a Western world still shaken by military aggression and, above all, economic gloom. In a project for the future called *Last Charge*, he brings together 600 wooden clothes horses with 3,365 fencers and 6,730 discarded fluorescent tubes to create an outdoor area of stroboscopic light. Its flashing urgency evokes the appalling tragedy of the Light Brigade's futile charge in the Battle of Balaclava. Lord Cardigan led this doomed cavalry assault during the Crimean War of 1854, and Munro's soundtrack of thundering hooves encourages everyone to visualise the riders hurtling to their tragic destination. Seen in its entirety, *Last Charge* looks like a flickering graveyard of fallen hopes.

An even more ominous future project is *The Last Wave*, a traumatic image which can be traced back to Peter Weir's film of the same name. Munro saw it on BBC television in 1984, just before he left his native country and moved to Australia. Eight years later, while making a farewell trip around Australia with his fiancée, Serena, Munro was still so haunted by memories of the film that he dreamed about a tsunami-like wall of water curving high over Sydney. Now he is determined to recreate its impact, using 2.5 million black mussel-shell casts suspended in mid-air and glowing with fibre-optic cables. This looming apparition would clearly be an unnerving spectacle, and sum up the apocalyptic anxieties which often invade twenty-first-century consciousness today.

Ultimately, however, Munro is sustained by an obstinate and fundamental spirit of optimism. At Waddesdon Manor, the magnificent property built in Buckinghamshire by Baron Ferdinand de Rothschild, he has made an evocative installation in 2013 called *Cantus Arcticus*. Music once again played a major role in bringing this work to the forefront of Munro's imagination. He heard on the radio a symphony with this title by the Finnish composer Einojuhani Rautavaara. Its sublime soundscape captivated him, and after downloading a copy of the music, he listened to it time and again. Such obsessive concentration led Munro to create, for the capacious interior of Waddesdon's Coach House at the Stables, an evocation of the Northern Lights and the frozen landscape of the Arctic tundra. Abstracted forms inspired by seabirds can be found here, suspended in a space where curtains of fibre-optic strands are fortified by steel cone bells. Veils of light cascading from above create an all-pervasive luminosity and cast soft pools of colour which alter in response to the unfolding drama of Rautavaara's symphony. *Cantus Arcticus* testifies to the enduring power of music in Munro's current work,

Cantus Arcticus, *Waddesdon Manor, Buckinghamshire, UK, 2013.*

but he also regards the Waddesdon installation as an act of homage to Kama, the Hindu god of love. Munro is convinced that Rautavaara's music is "a holistic interpretation of the beauty and wonder of life itself, in this instance the lives of humans and birds."

After the death of Munro's father in 1999, Munro suffered a crisis and then benefited from the healing power of meditation. It enabled him to realise the importance of focusing above all on being at one with the world, and this sense of unity finally helped him to develop his mature vision as an artist. Although most of his outdoor works are temporary, one of his most ambitious projects centres on the creation of a building called *Mettabhavana*. It originated in a Barbados beachside house, where he was staying with his family in 1997. On the first night, Munro dreamed that he saw a mysterious building from which light softly emanated, generating an aura of peacefulness. Now he has completed the design of just such an elemental structure, reassuring in mood and accompanied on all sides by water in elliptical pools. During the day this building will be illuminated by the sun, and at night by beeswax candles. He sees it essentially as a place where Metta Bhavana, the loving-kindness meditation, can be practised by everyone who enters its calm, luminous interior.

While riding his bicycle in 2009, Munro remembered the undulating pathway in *CDSea* and realised that it linked up with the spiritual river which appears in two of the books he most admires. In *Kim*, Rudyard Kipling describes an arrow passing "far beyond sight" before falling and creating a river of limitless beneficence. In the other book, *Siddhartha* by Herman Hesse, "The river looked at him with a thousand eyes: green ones, white ones, crystal ones, sky-blue ones." It sounds uncannily like a description of Munro's glinting installations, and when Siddhartha "listened attentively to the thousand-fold song of the river . . . to all of them, the whole, when he perceived the unity," then at last he "ceased to struggle with fate, ceased to suffer. On his face bloomed the cheerfulness of wisdom that is no longer opposed by will, that knows perfection, that is in harmony with the river of what is, with the current of life." Of all the connections across music, science, and literature which feed Munro's multi-faceted art, these heartfelt words sum up the essence of his vision with disarming eloquence.

Dr Richard Cork

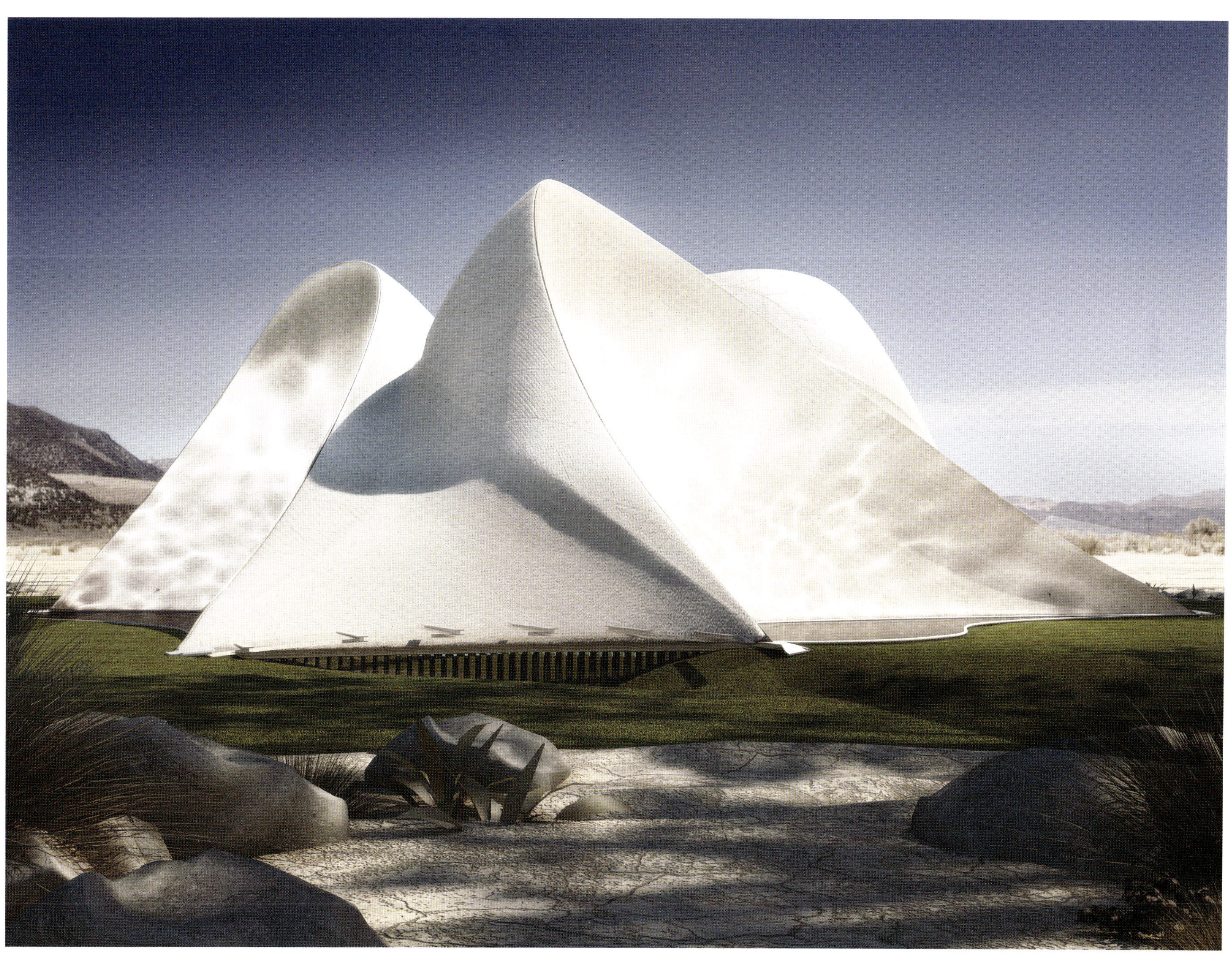

Above: Mettabhavana, *concept drawing. Overleaf:* Field of Light, *Cheekwood Botanical Garden and Museum of Art, Tennessee, USA, 2013.*

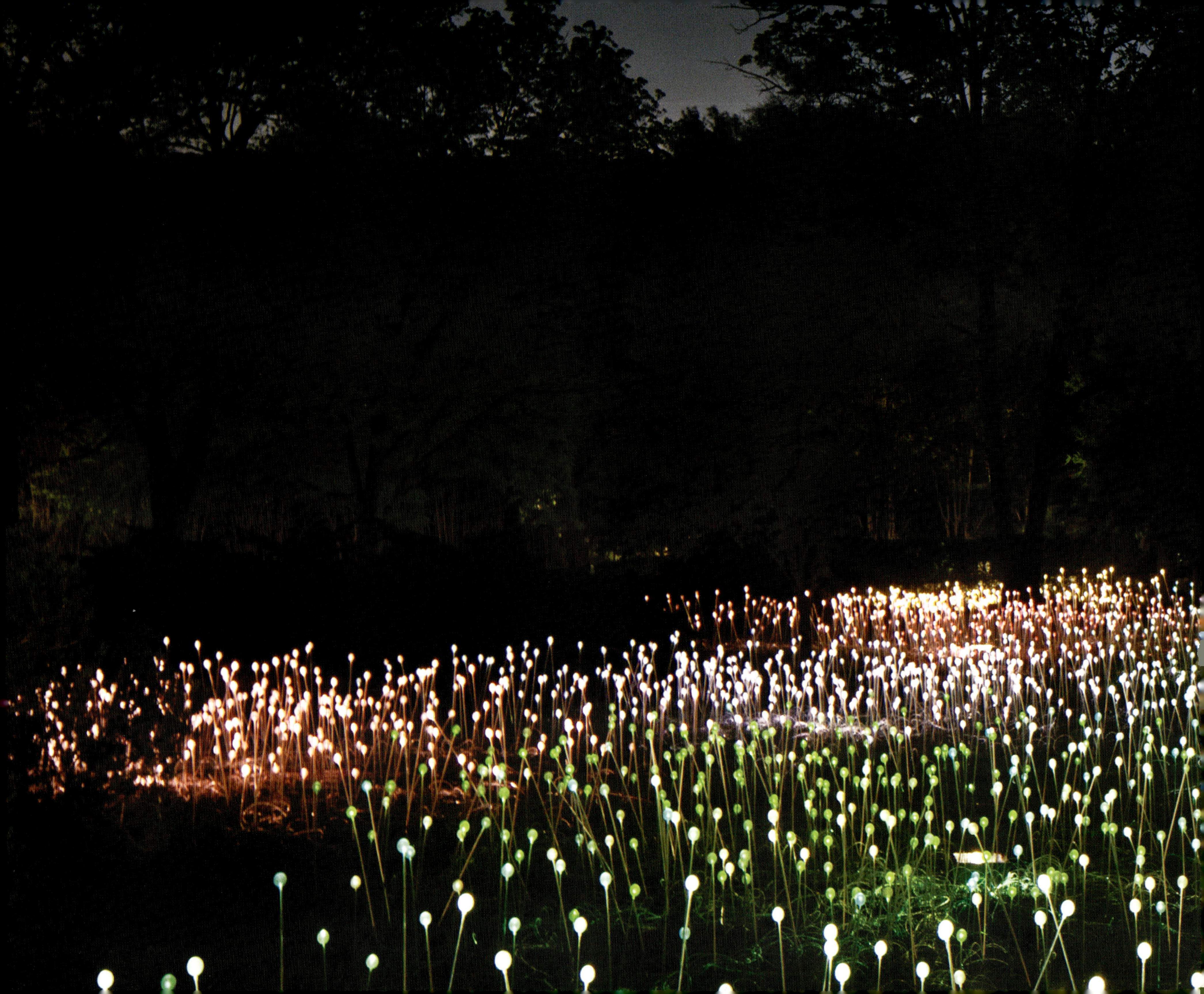

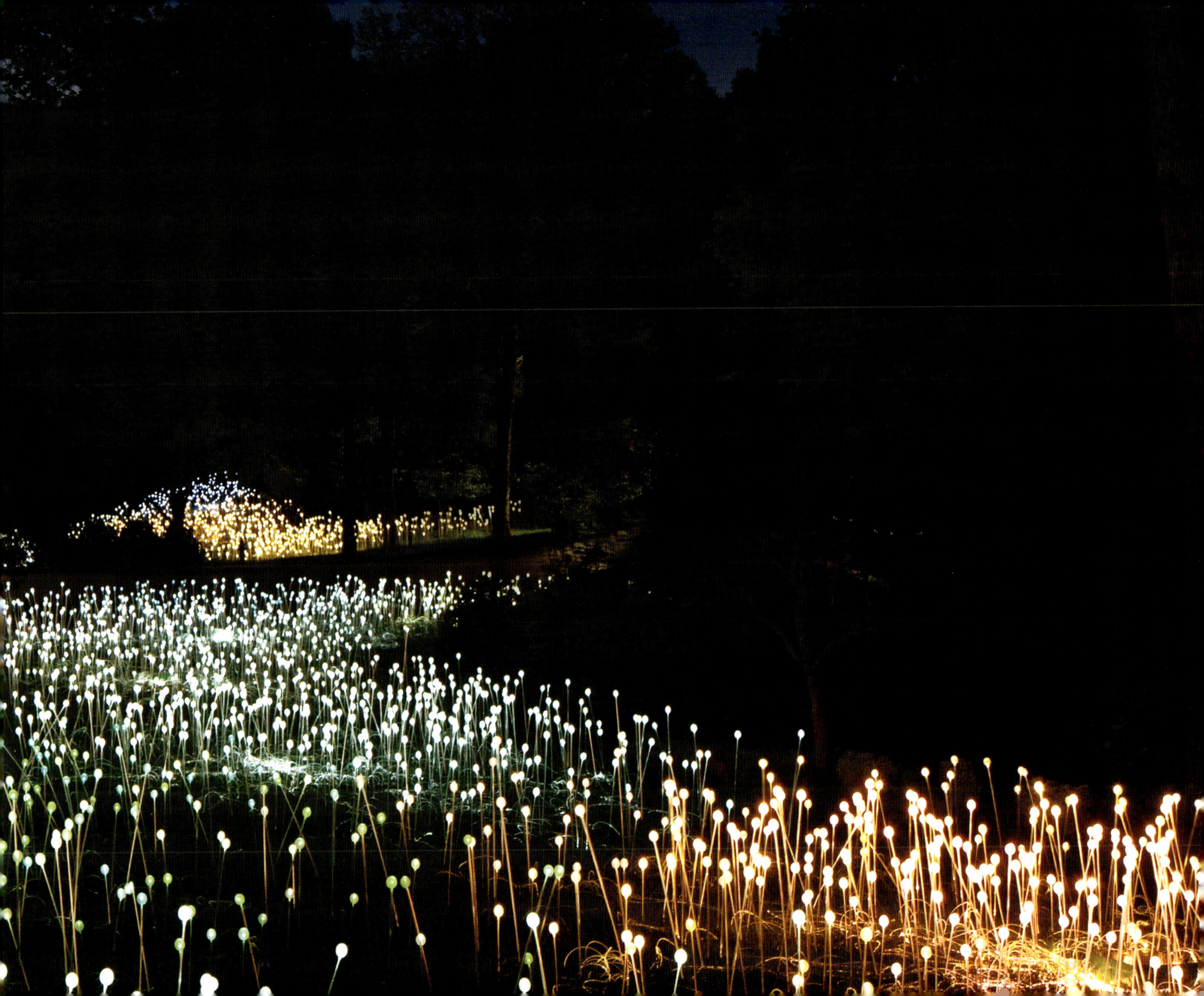

INSTALLATIONS

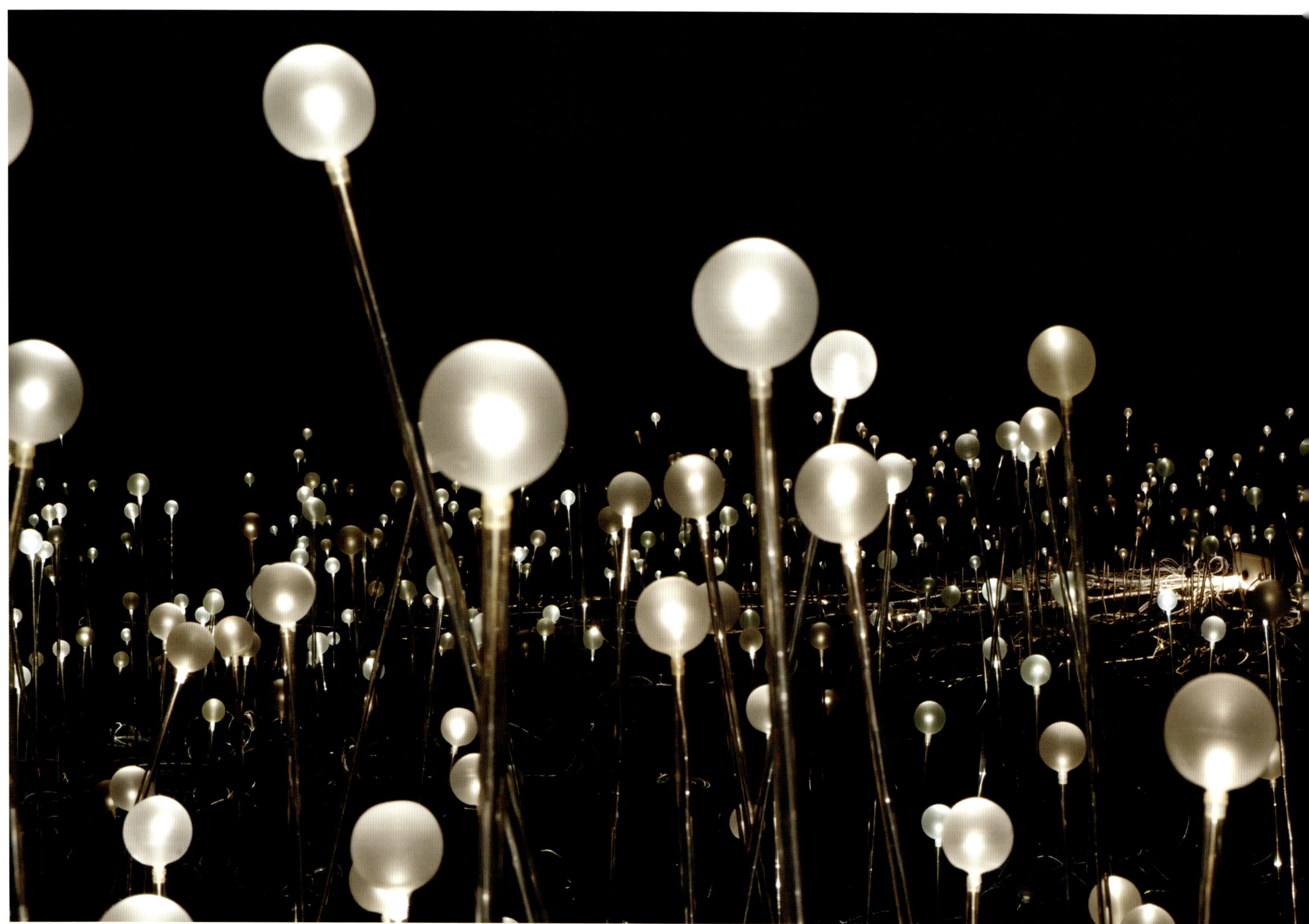

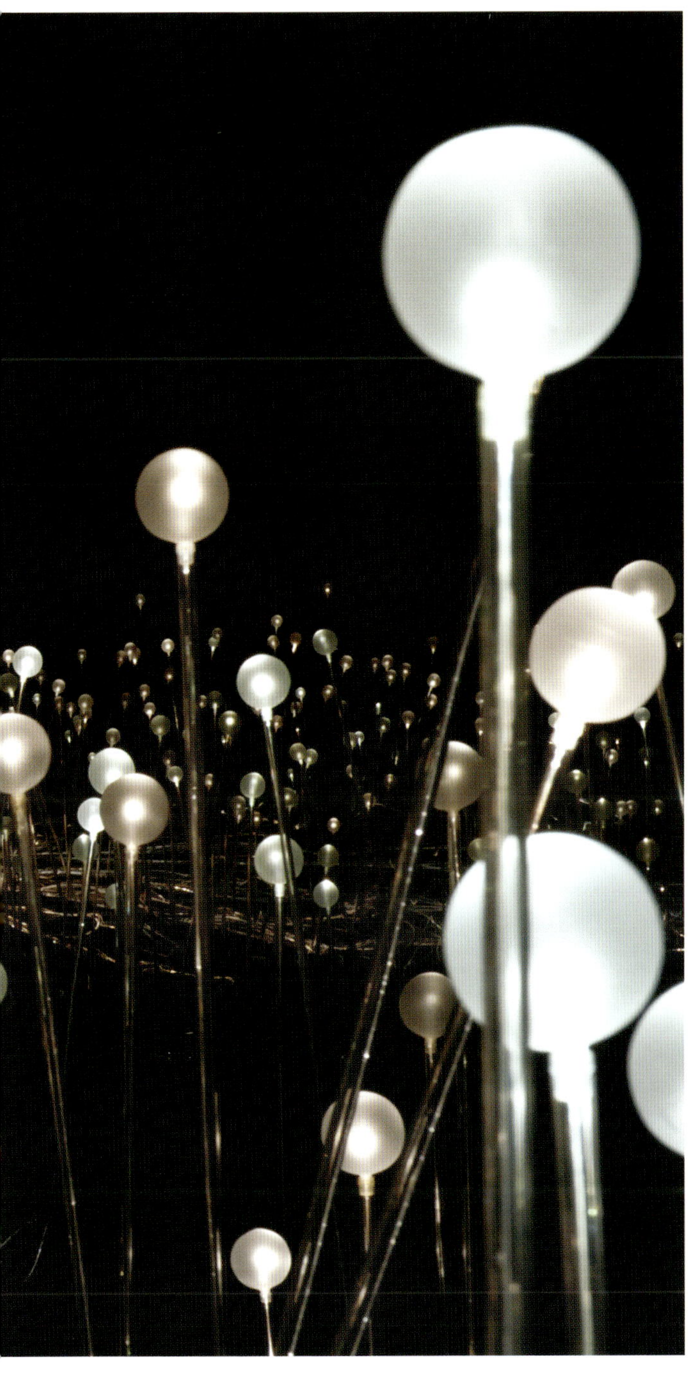

INSPIRATIONS

BRUCE MUNRO

I discovered light as a medium first in my professional career, outside of fine art. I had studied painting during my school and degree education in Britain, but I needed to earn a living and found myself doing that in Australia, manufacturing display signs using a glowing ultraviolet plastic whose properties I loved. When I decided to work in light, I chose it very carefully because I felt that I had too many thoughts and ideas about everything and I needed some kind of focus. I thought that by working in a medium that was very pure and true I could then have the opportunity to express lots of different ideas that filled my head.

In my early forties, I began making things that were personal using repurposed manufacturing components and light. I realised that I had always been striving to be so different—to make my art different—but starting then, I began looking for shared experience. I've kept sketchbook journals for the last forty years and had recorded moments and memories of feeling connected with the world, and I realised that a lot of that could be expressed by light. Our experiences of being connected to the world in its largest sense, of being part of an essential pattern, became my subject matter.

Above: Field of Light, *Longwood Gardens, Pennsylvania, USA, 2012. Pages 6–9:* Field of Light, *Eden Project, Cornwall, UK, 2008–09.*

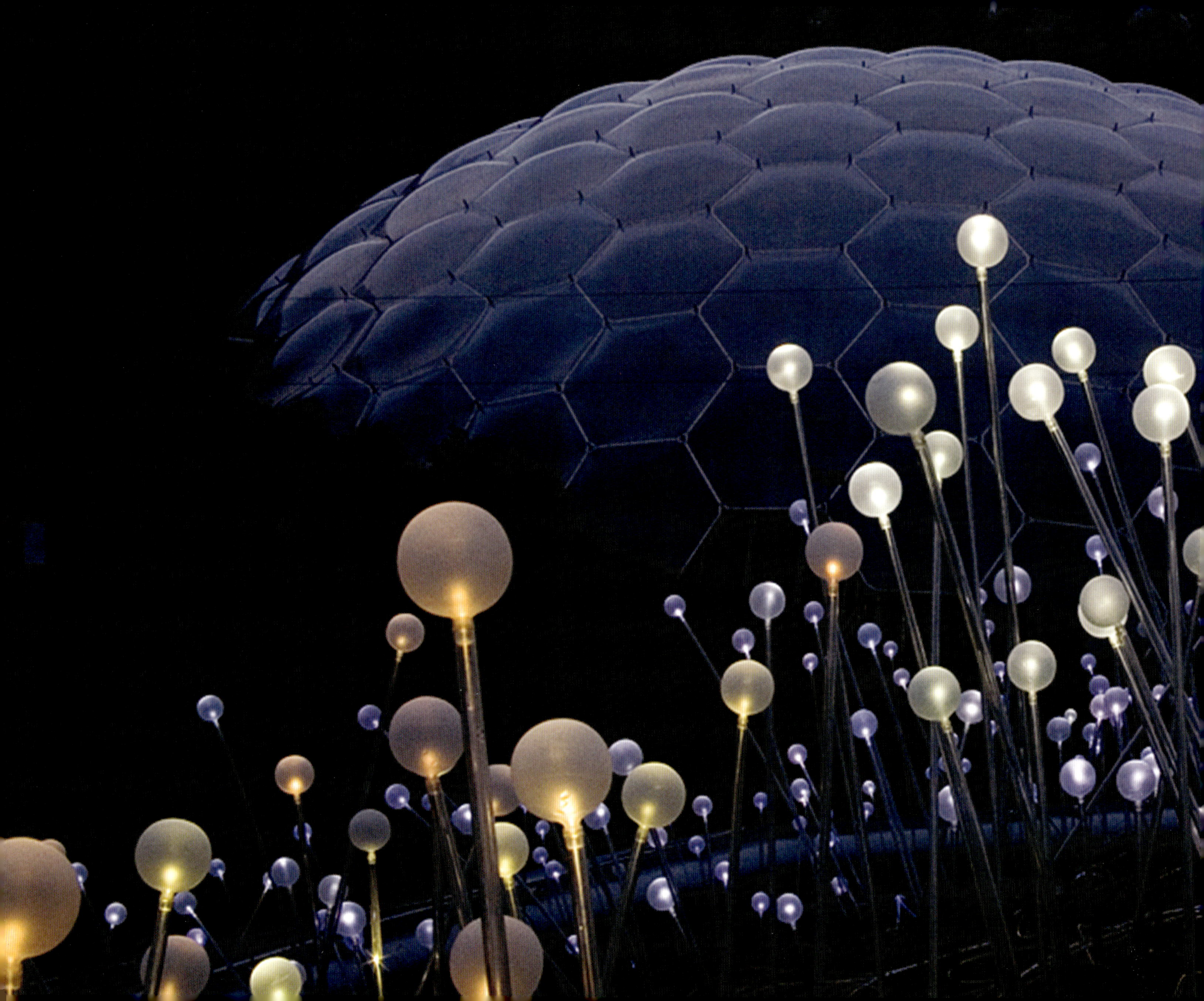

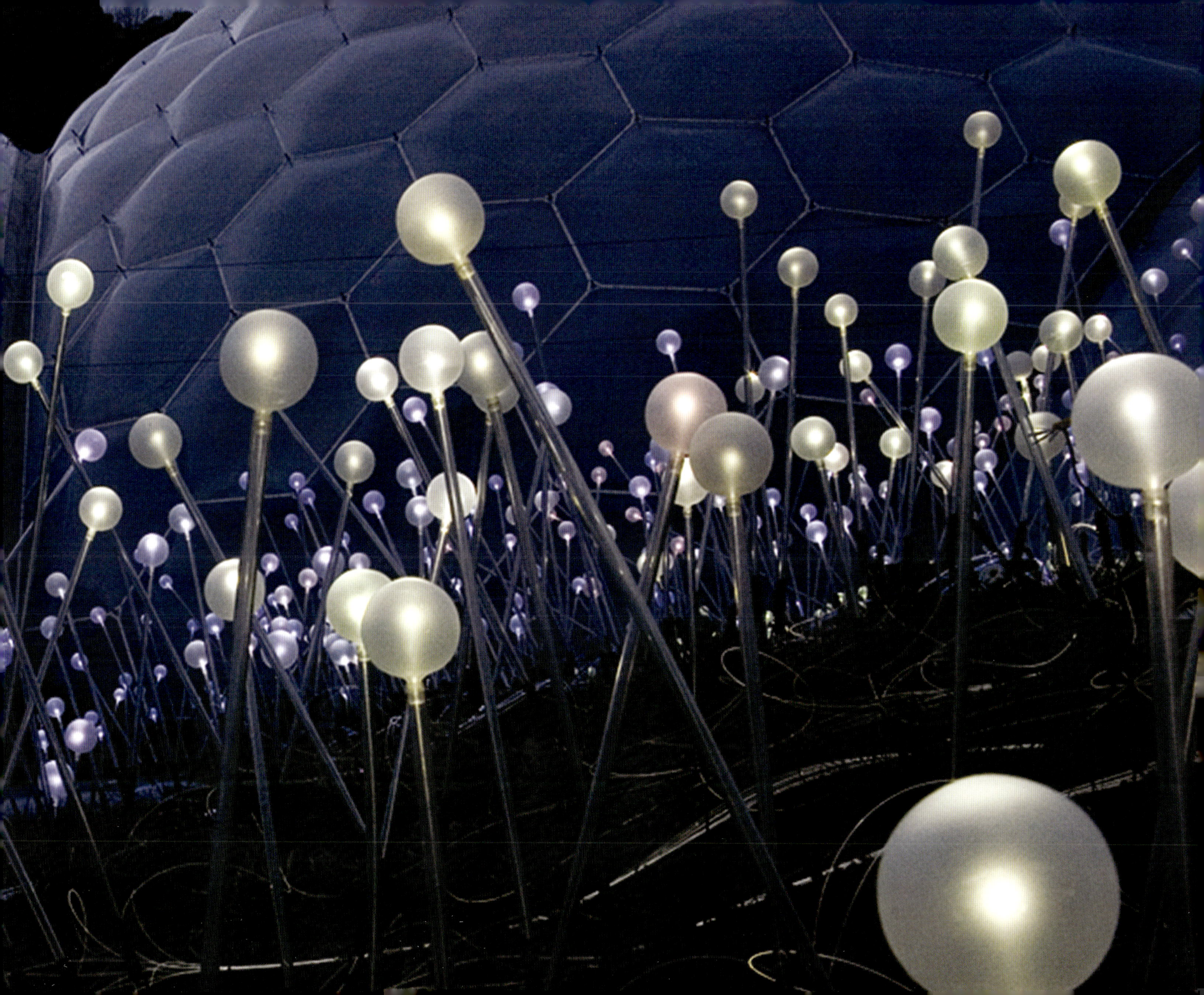

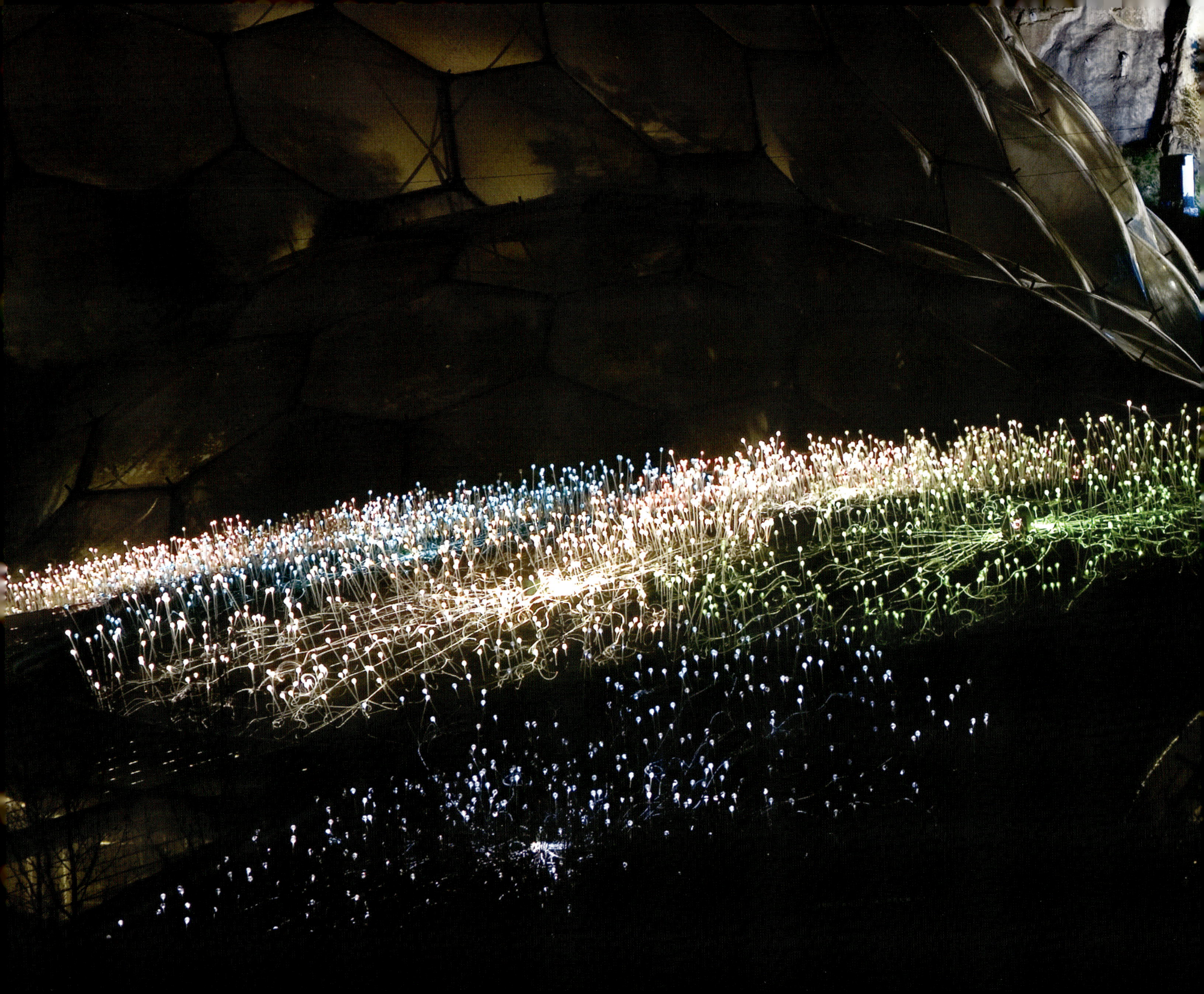

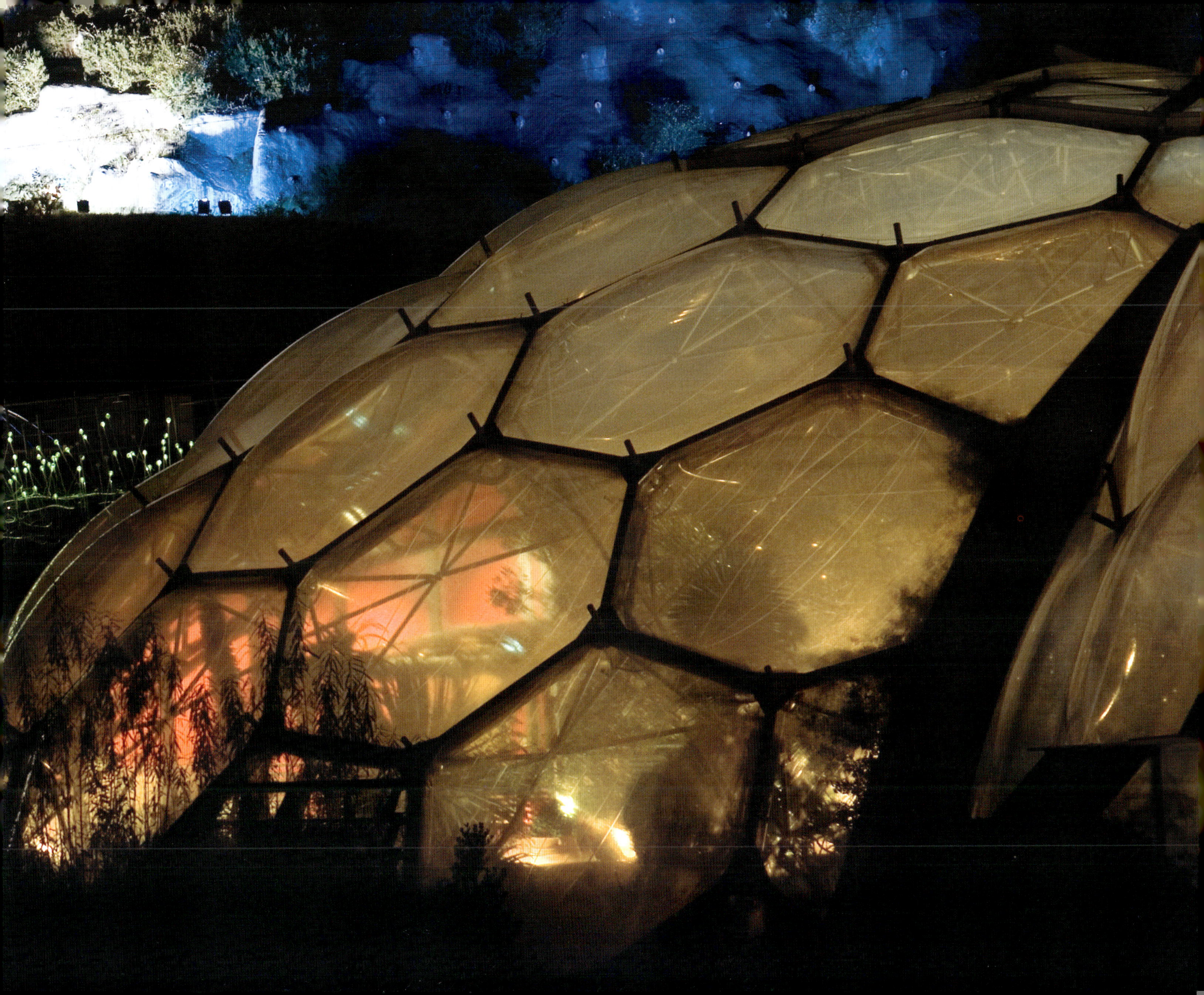

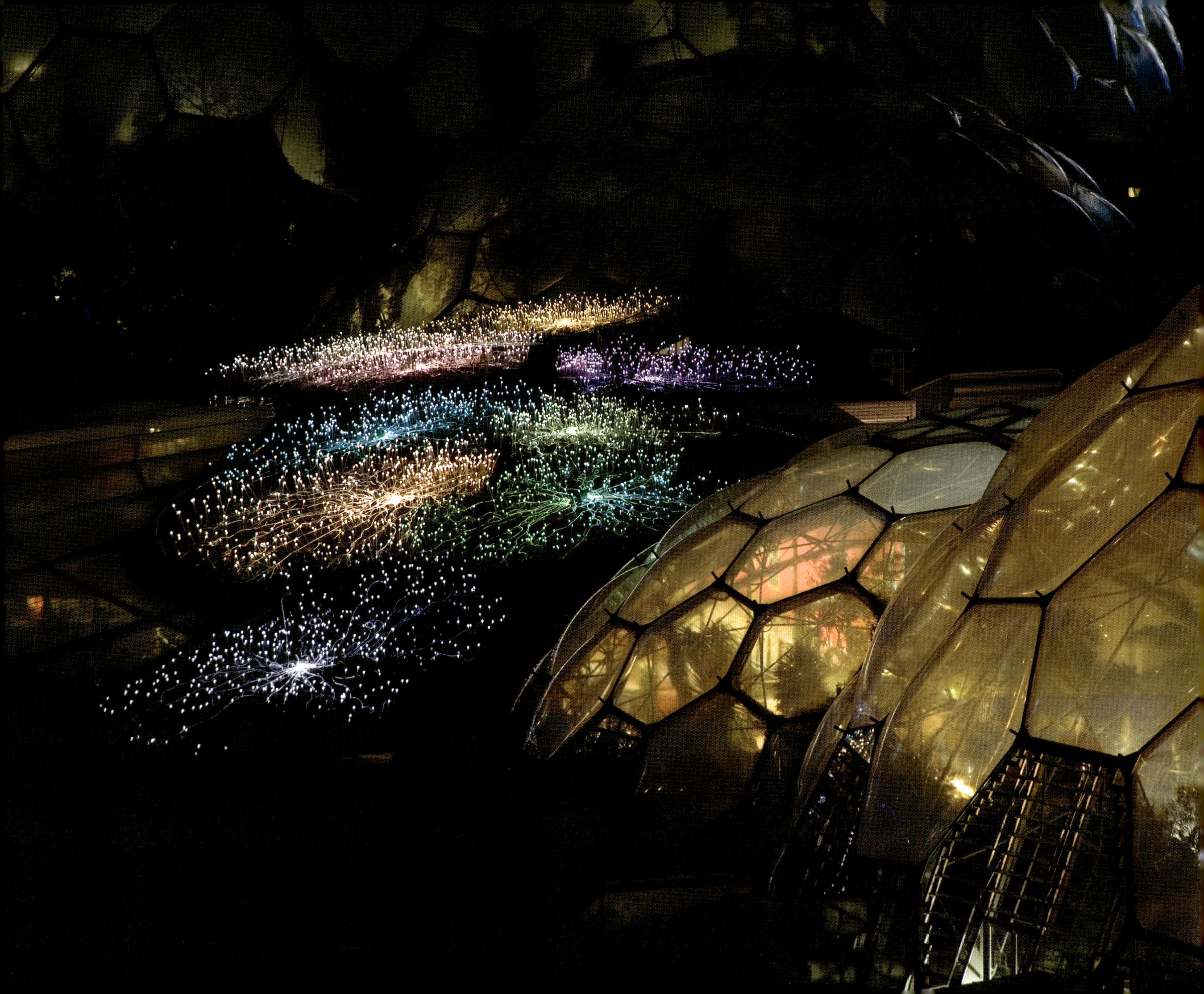

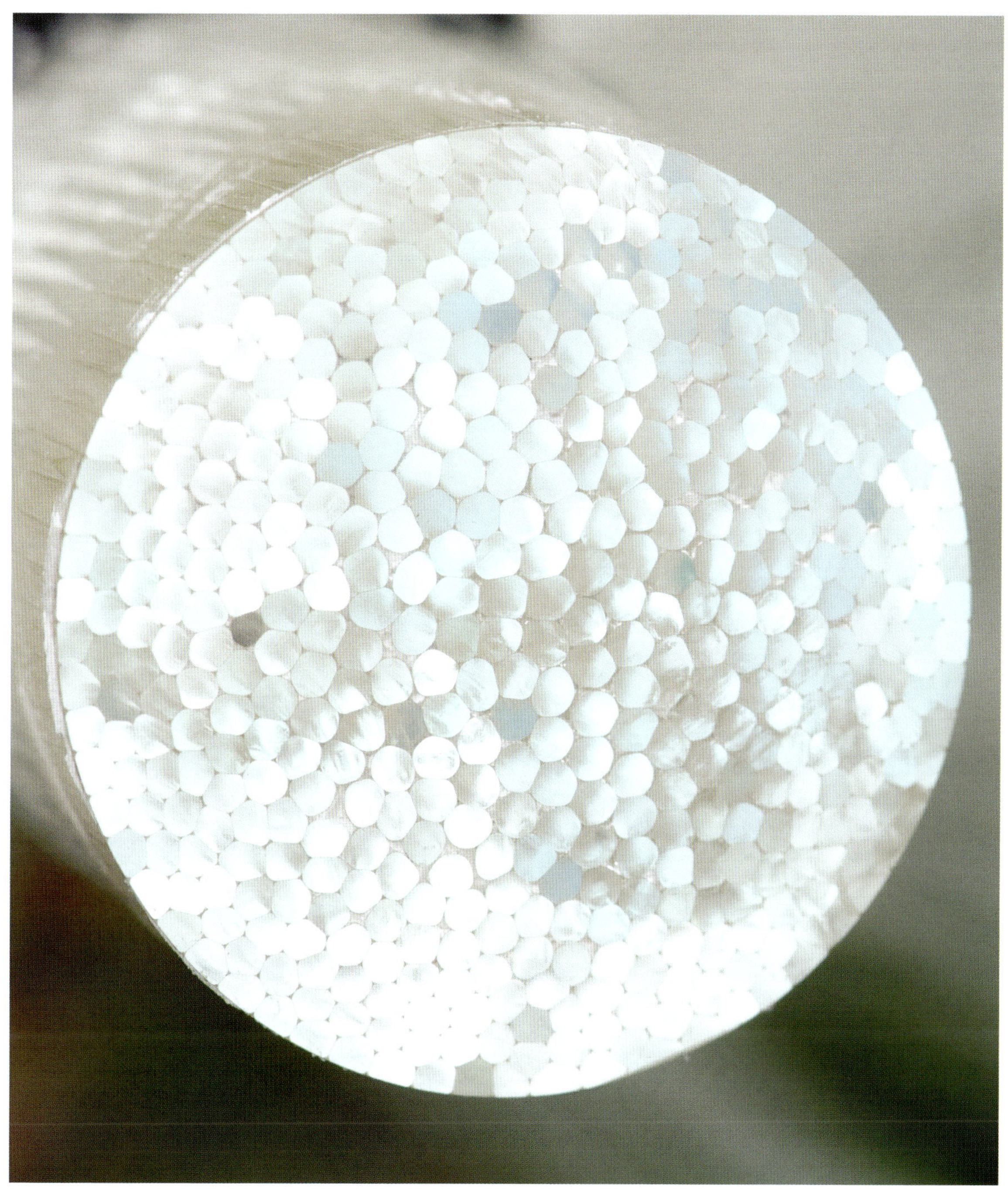

FIELD OF LIGHT

The *Field of Light* was originally conceived in 1992 during a trip through central Australia. The red desert had an incredible feeling of energy; ideas radiated from it along with the heat. The *Field of Light* installation was one idea that landed in my sketchbook and kept on nagging at me to be done.

Deserts have many incongruities. Travelling along the Stewart Highway, aside from brief fuel, food, and beverage stops in the day, one tends to pull off the road at dusk, moving on at sunrise. Often, the campsites are a total contrast to the barren red desert that surrounds them, green oases doused at dusk by the stammer of artesian-fed sprinklers. Some campsites displayed a larger-than-life sculpture/sign of surreal design and proportion: the big pineapple, the banana, and the Merino sheep!

I was also struck by the transformative nature

Opposite: Field of Light, *Eden Project, Cornwall, UK, 2008–09. Above: Fibre-optic cable used in* Field of Light.

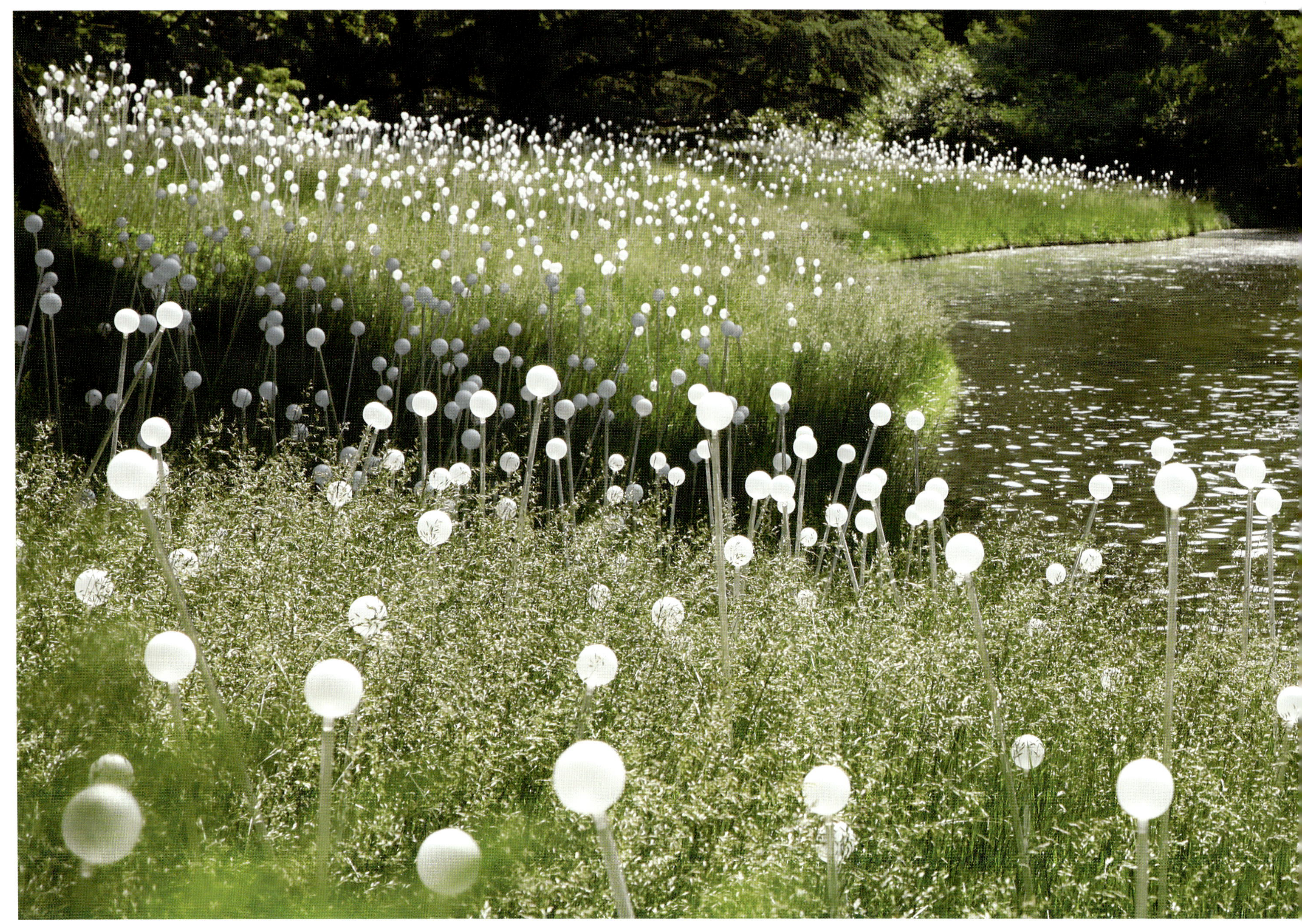

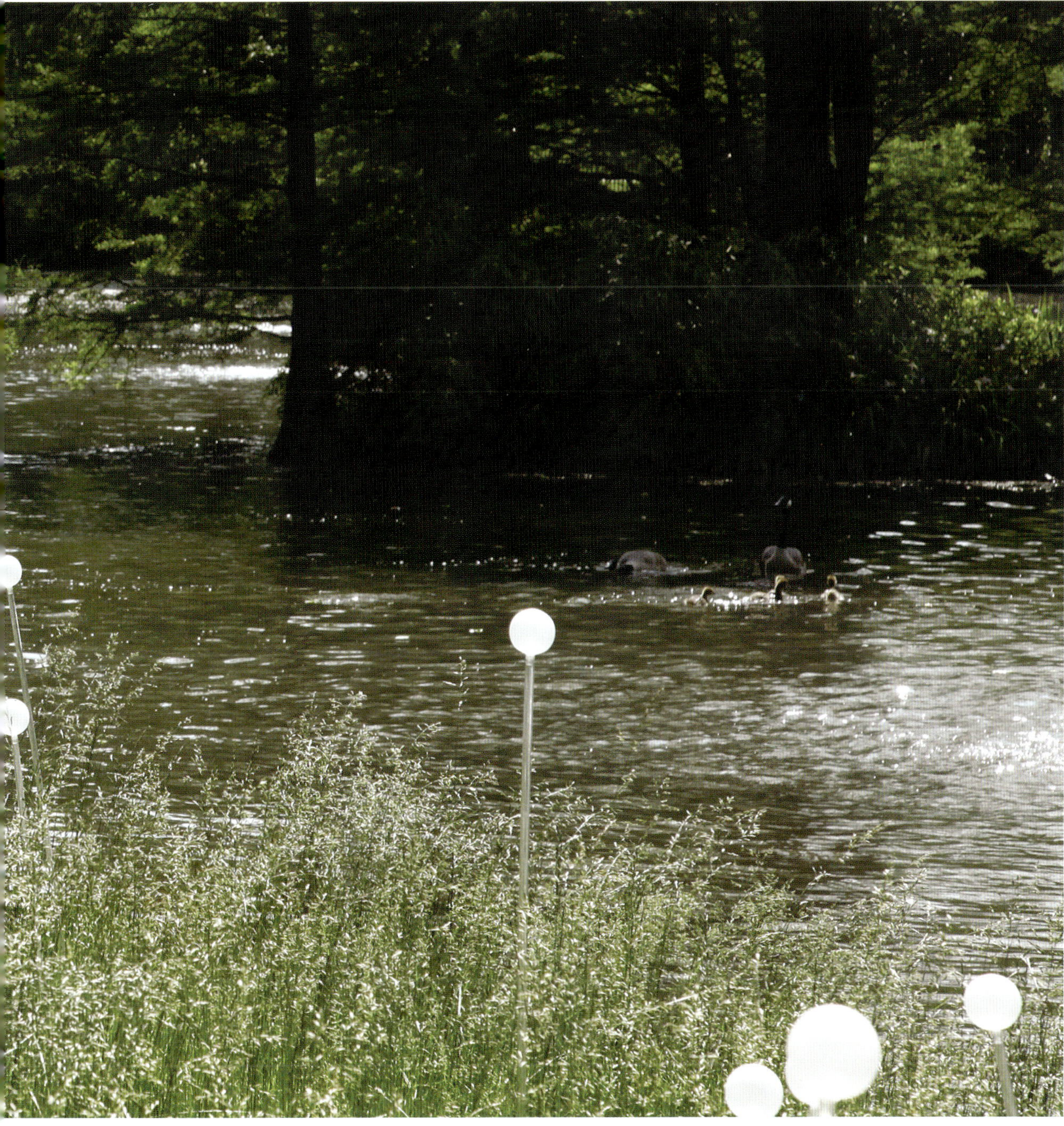

Above and pages 14–21: Field of Light, *Longwood Gardens, Pennsylvania, USA, 2012.*

of the desert landscape. On the one hand it was an infertile, barren place; until the rain came, and then it burst into life and bloomed like a veritable Eden.

I recorded thoughts of creating a sculpture on a landscape scale, incongruous in size and location, and experienced by the transient visitors who happened upon it as they set up camp. I saw in my mind a landscape of illuminated stems that, like the dormant seed in a dry desert, quietly wait until darkness falls, under a blazing blanket of southern stars, to bloom with gentle rhythms of light.

Over the next decade, these thoughts stayed in my mind. The original concept was seen as a series of light pipes that would emerge from the ground and move in a dance. Gradually I started to experiment with fibre optics and the form of the piece solidified into that which is seen today.

The very first *Field of Light* was sown under the shadow of an ancient hill behind my home in

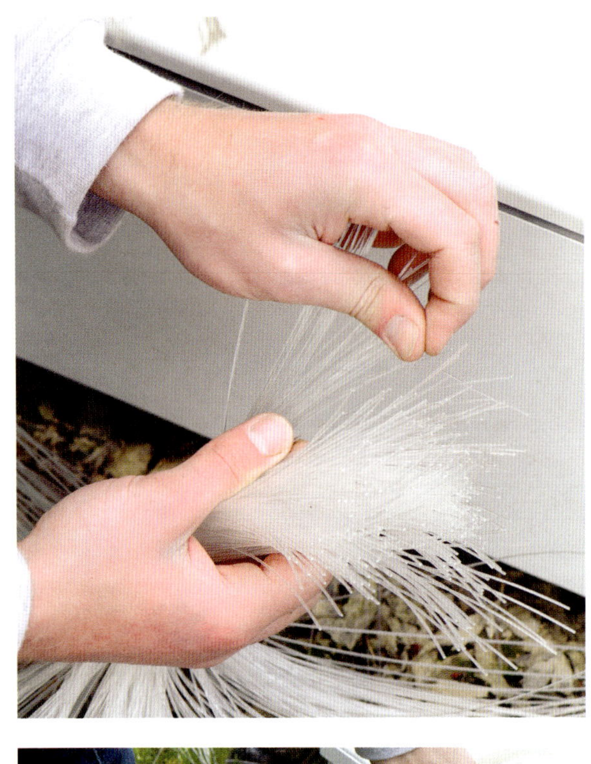

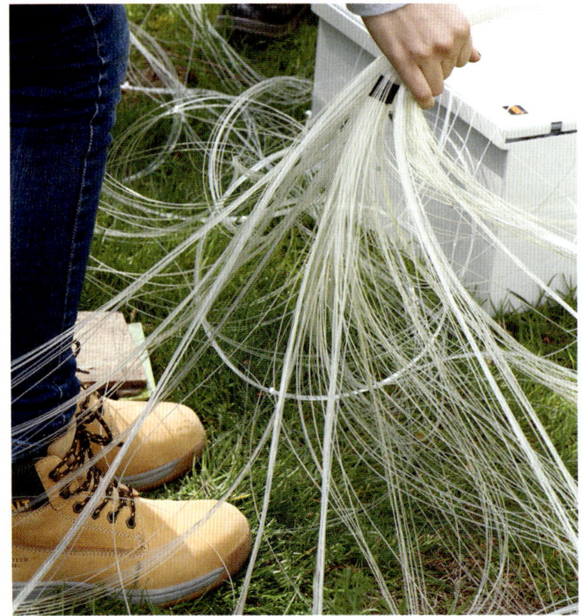

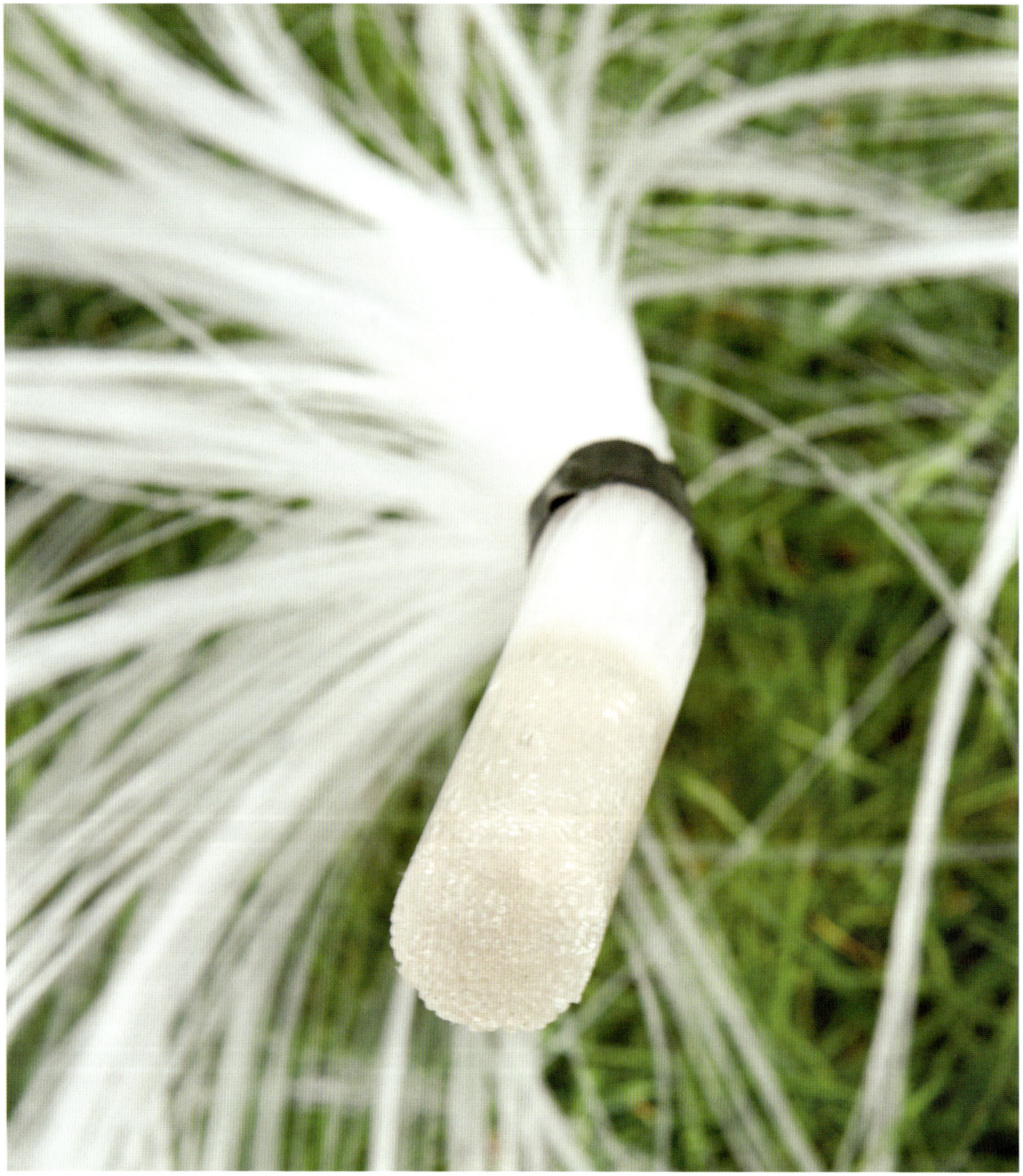

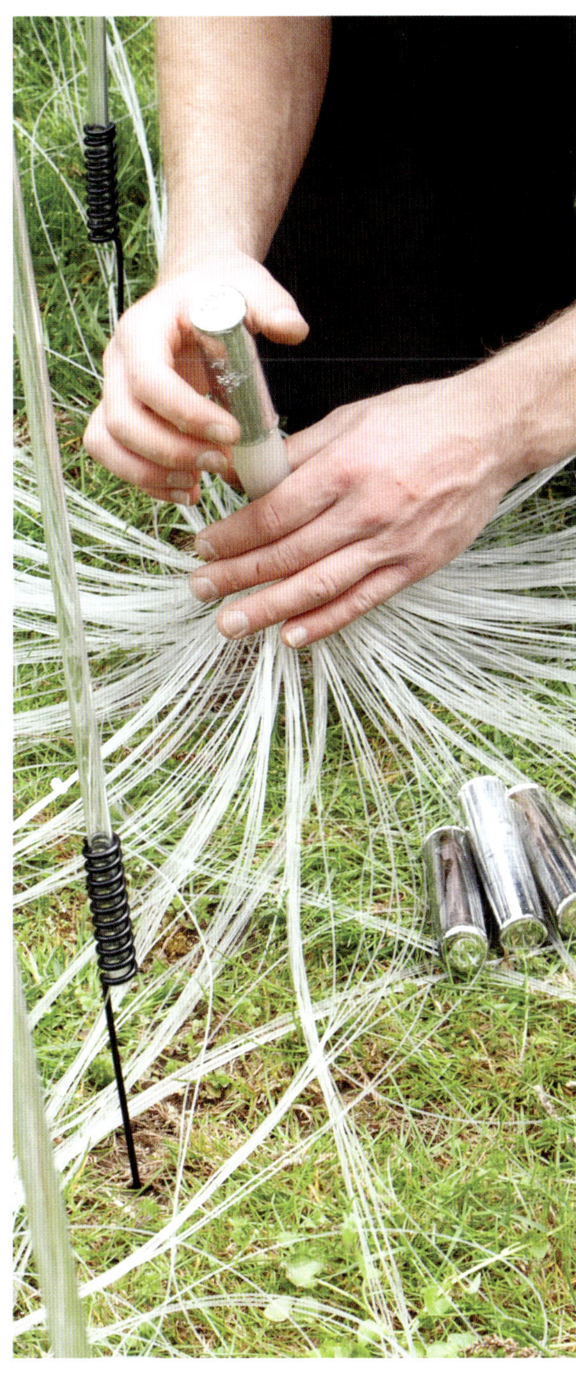

southwest England in 2004. By placing an alien installation in the midst of nature, the enormous contrast created allows one to literally see the wood from the trees. One's attention is thus drawn to the nature that surrounds the installation as well as to the *Field of Light* itself. This contrast has always been an important focus since the idea germinated.

Laid out across a field of clover bisected by a public footpath, the first *Field of Light* shimmered its way through the seasons, presenting a myriad of opportunities for passersby to catch glimpses of the piece interacting with nature in all her guises. I am hopeful that every iteration of the *Field of Light* will inspire both young and old to take from it and create something of their own to pass on to others.

In recent years, I have had many more ideas about the meaning of the *Field of Light* and an equal number of ways to express these thoughts, but my instinct tells me that that is not what I am meant to do, other than say the *Field of Light* is a personal symbol for the good things in life. My job is to make it happen and inspire those around me to join the project. I hope that it will gather its own momentum, and like the proverbial snowball, take on a life of its own when it reaches critical mass.

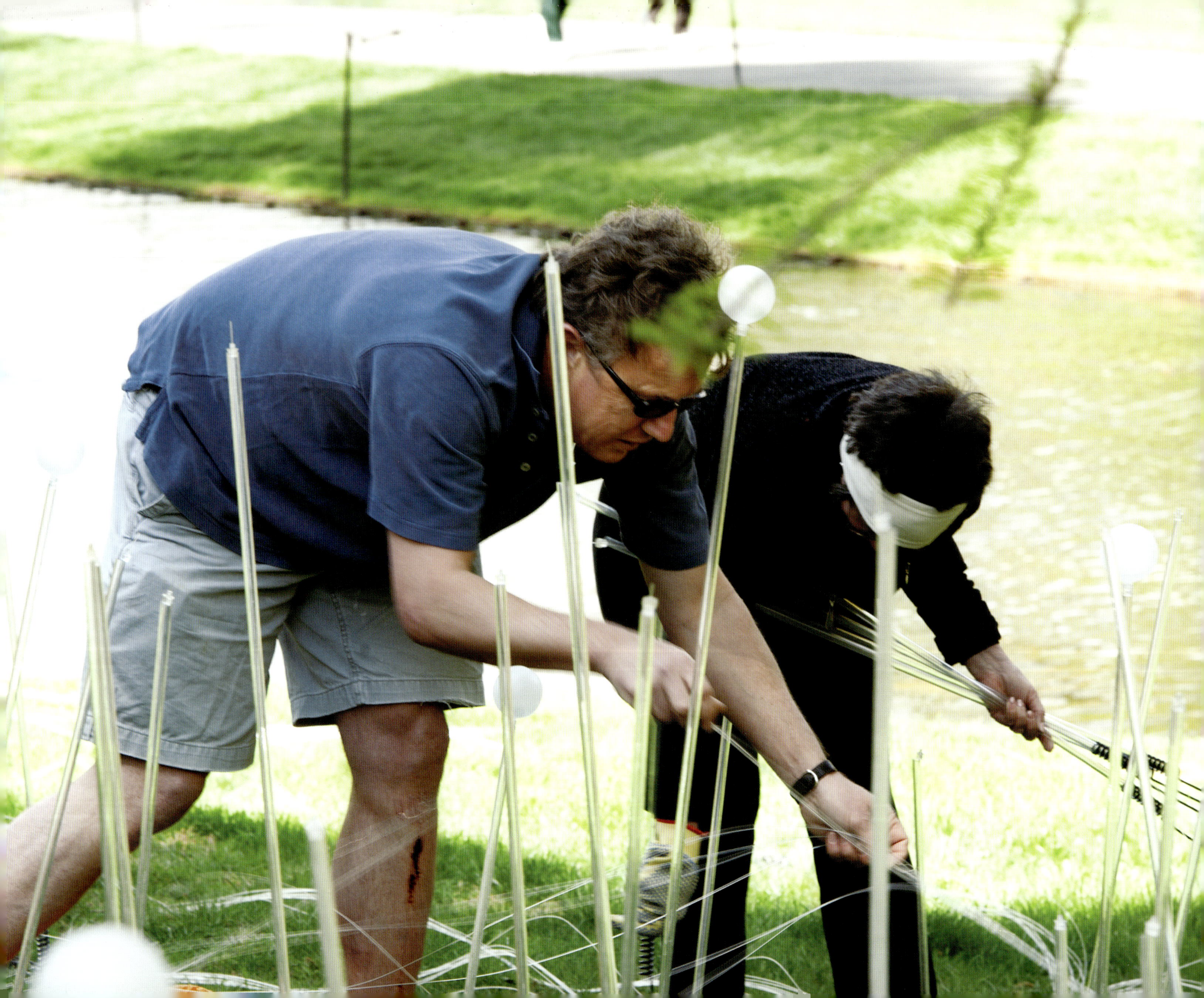

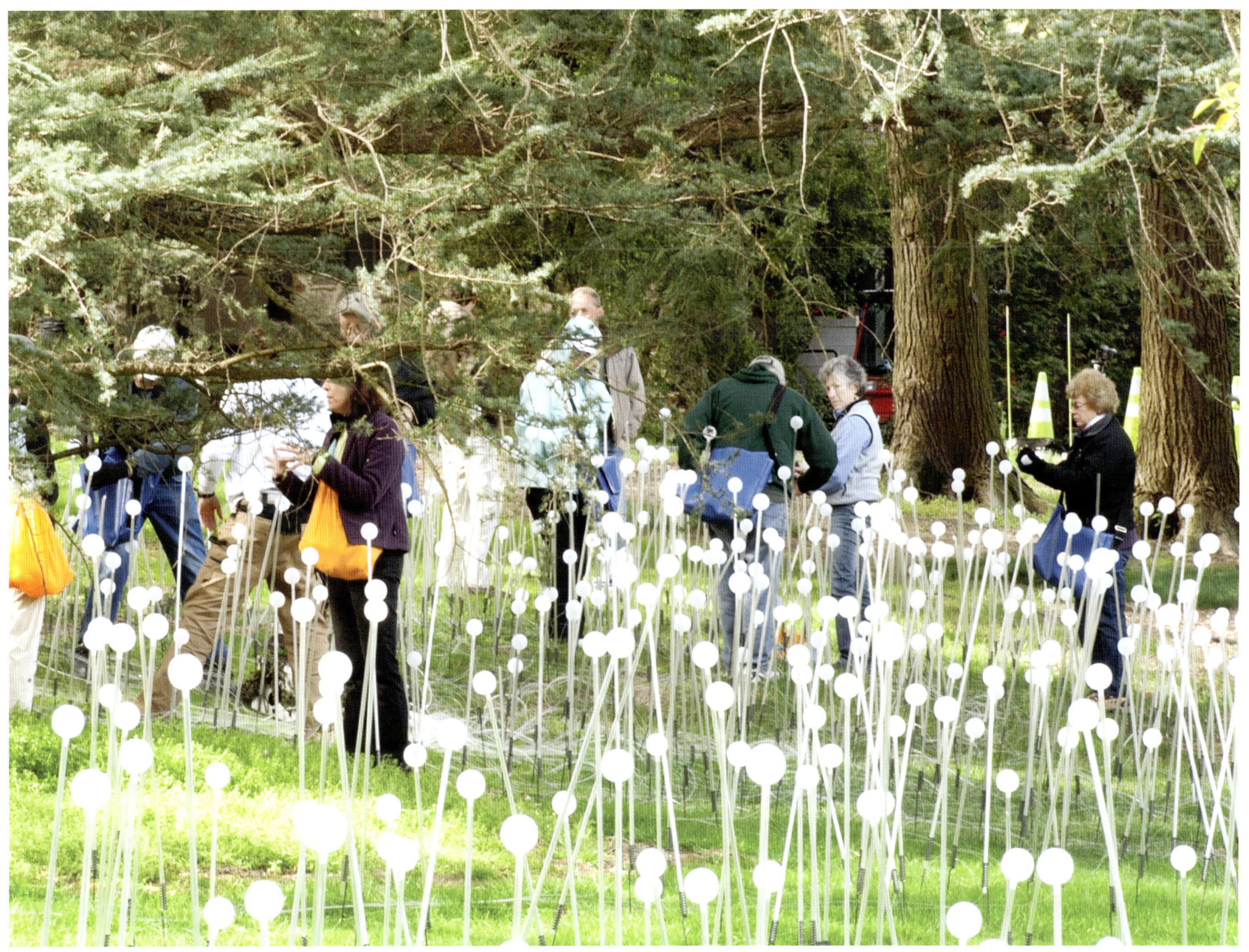

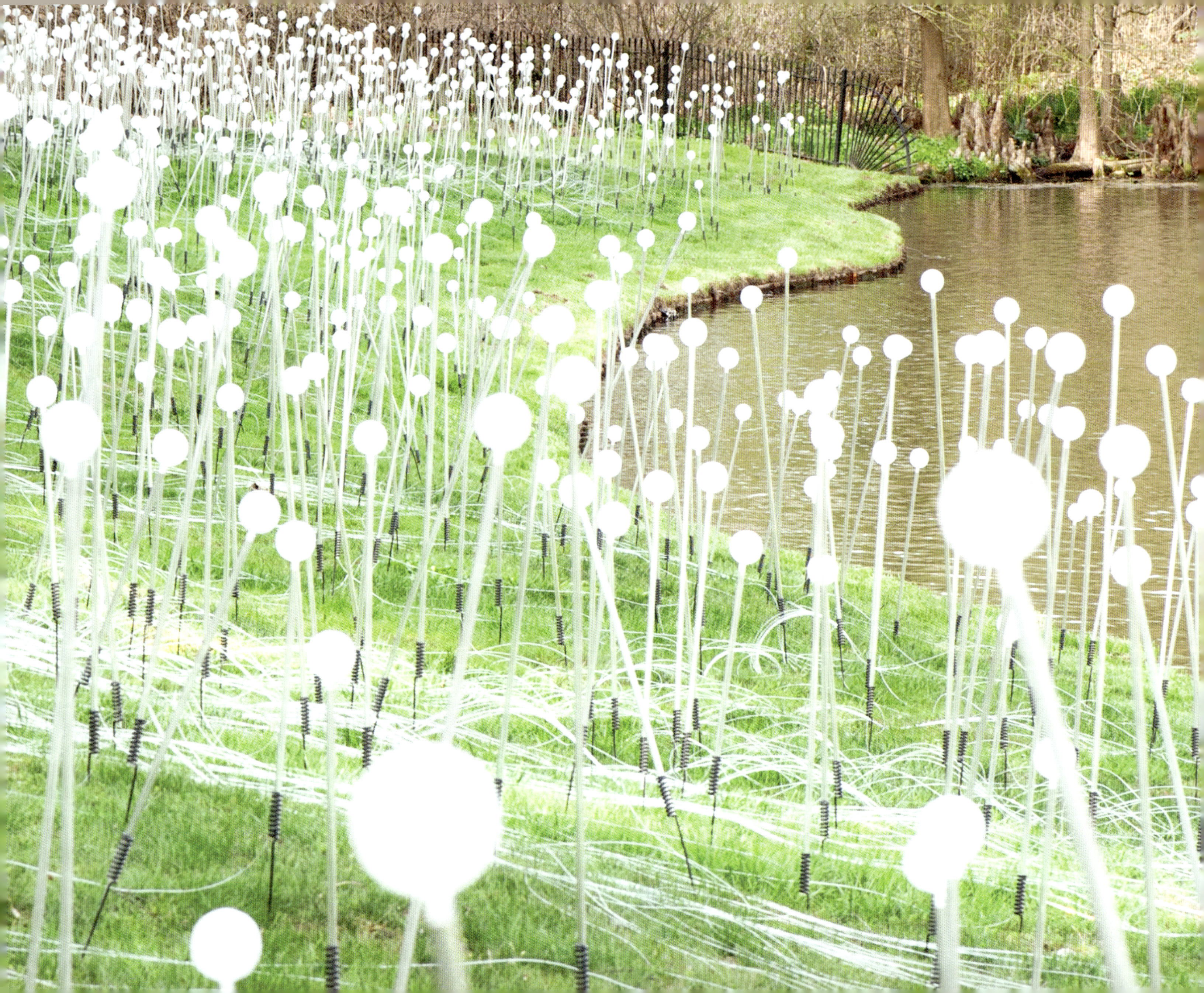

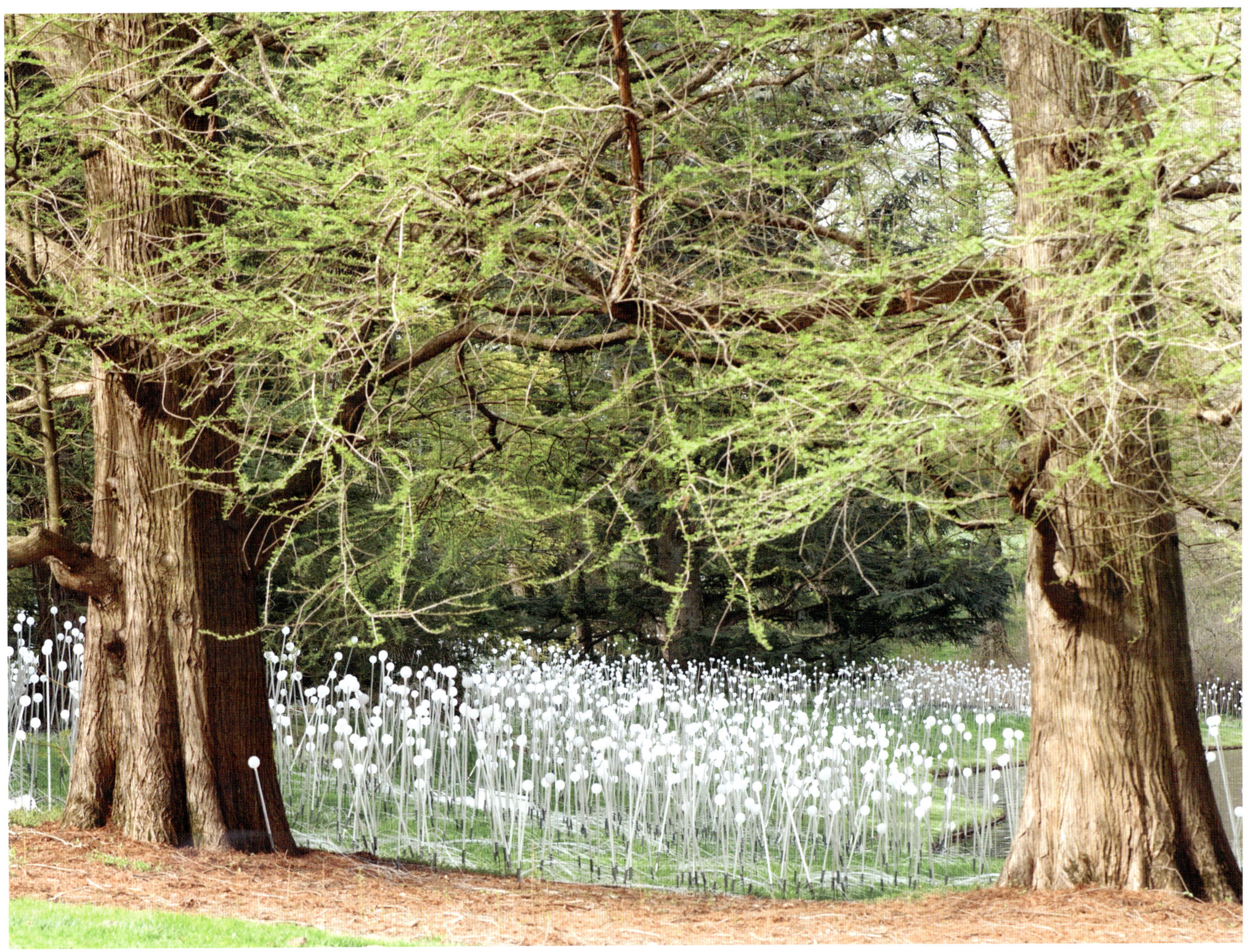

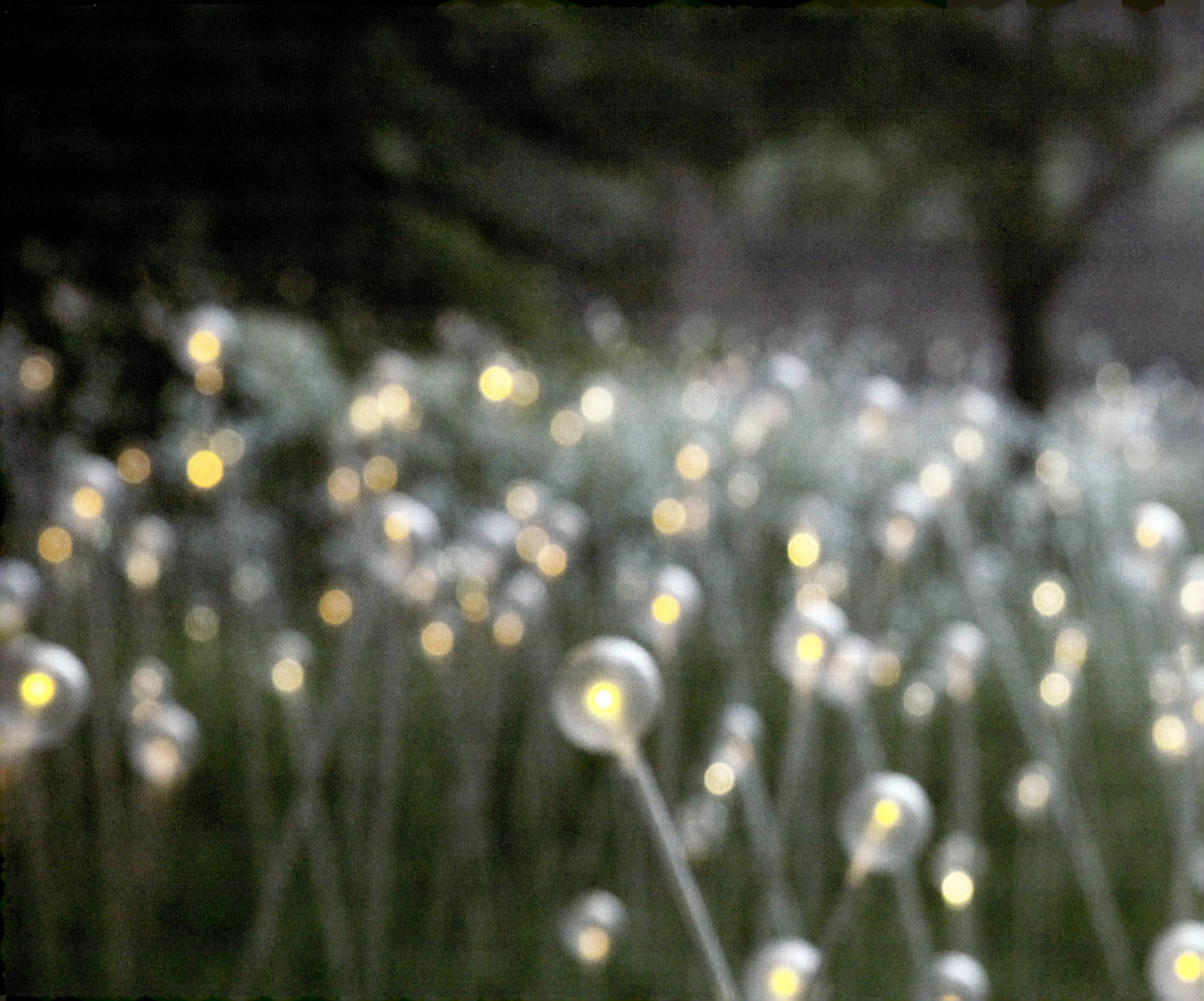

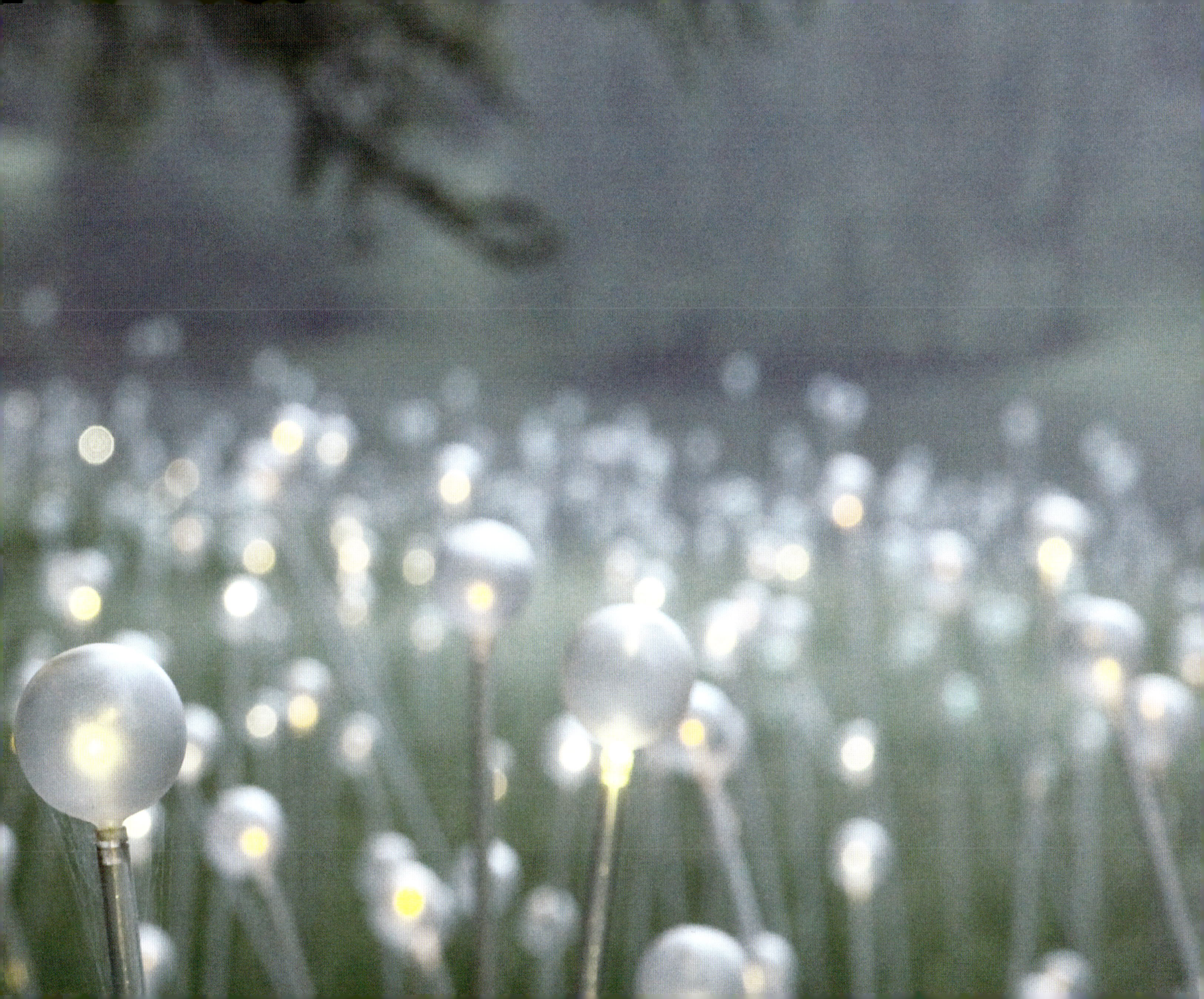

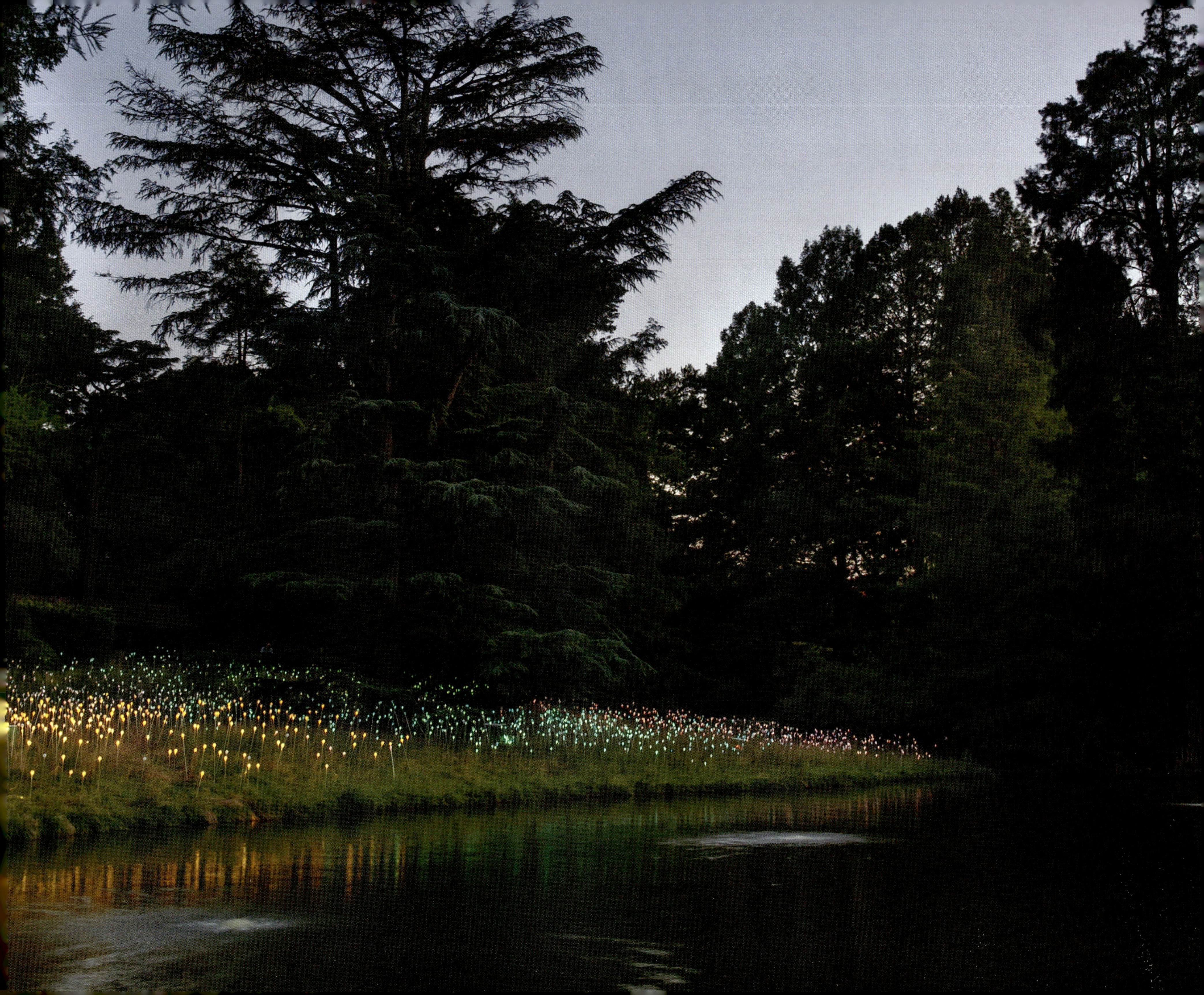

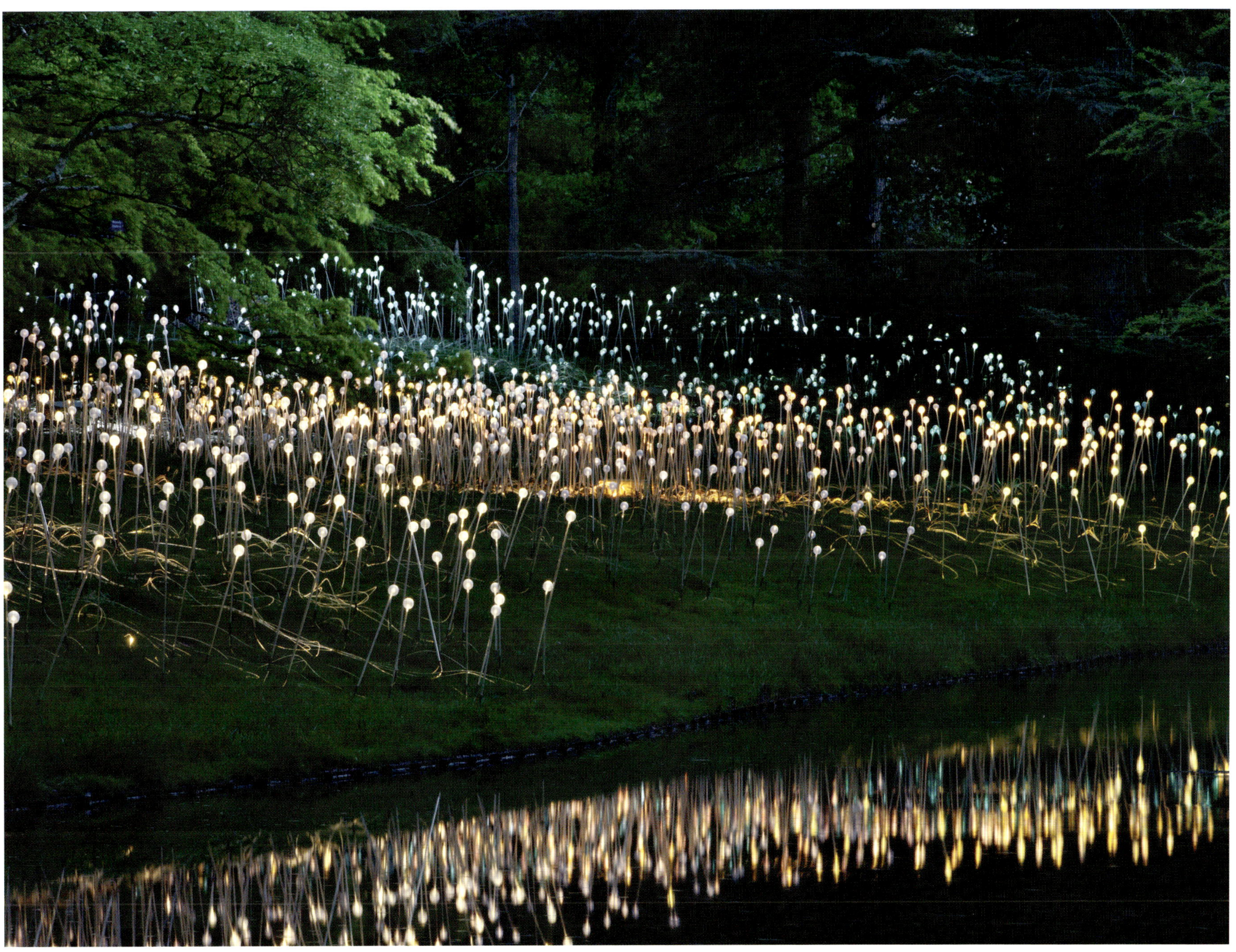

Opposite, above, and pages 24–25: Field of Light, *Longwood Gardens, Pennsylvania, USA, 2012.*

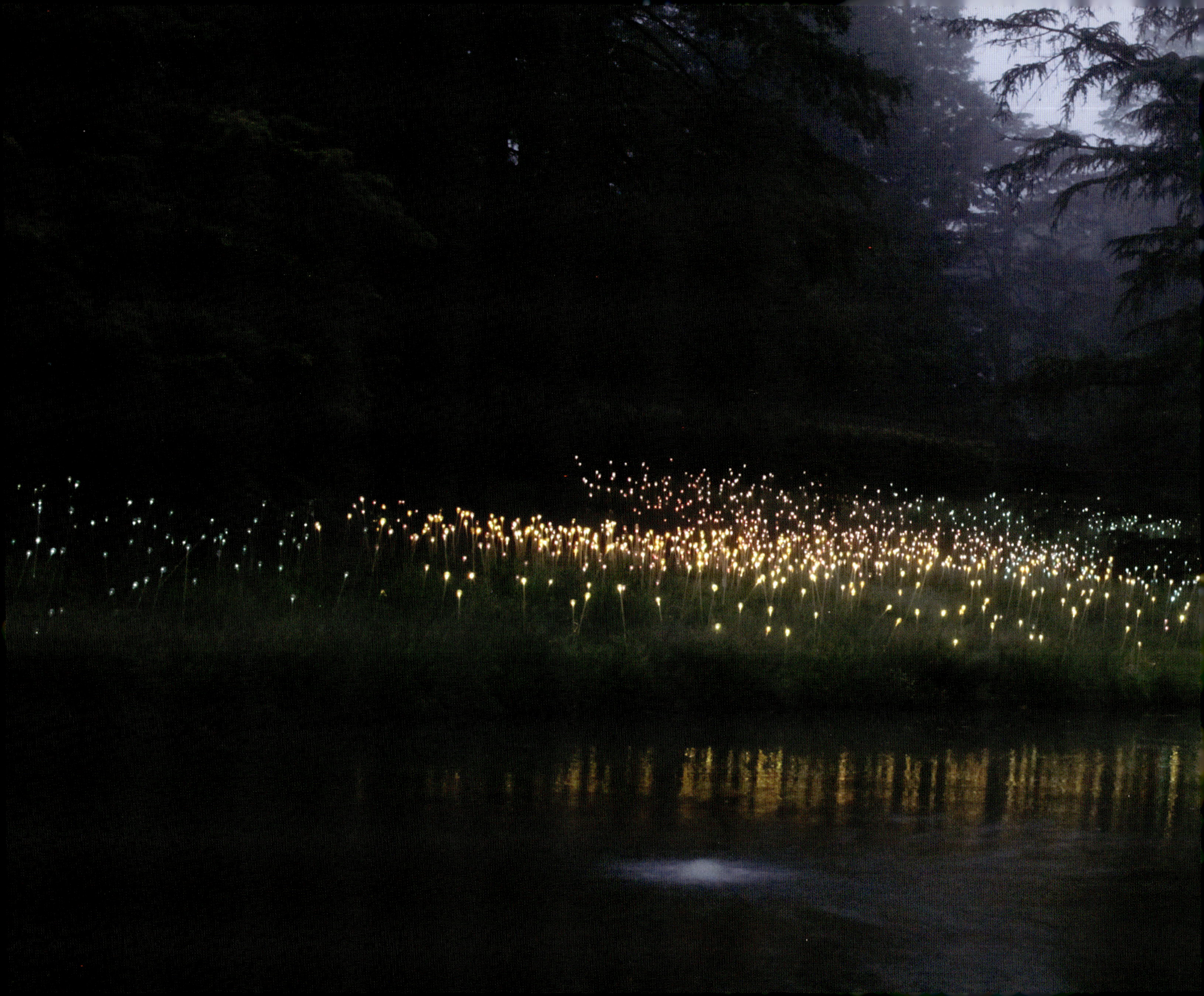

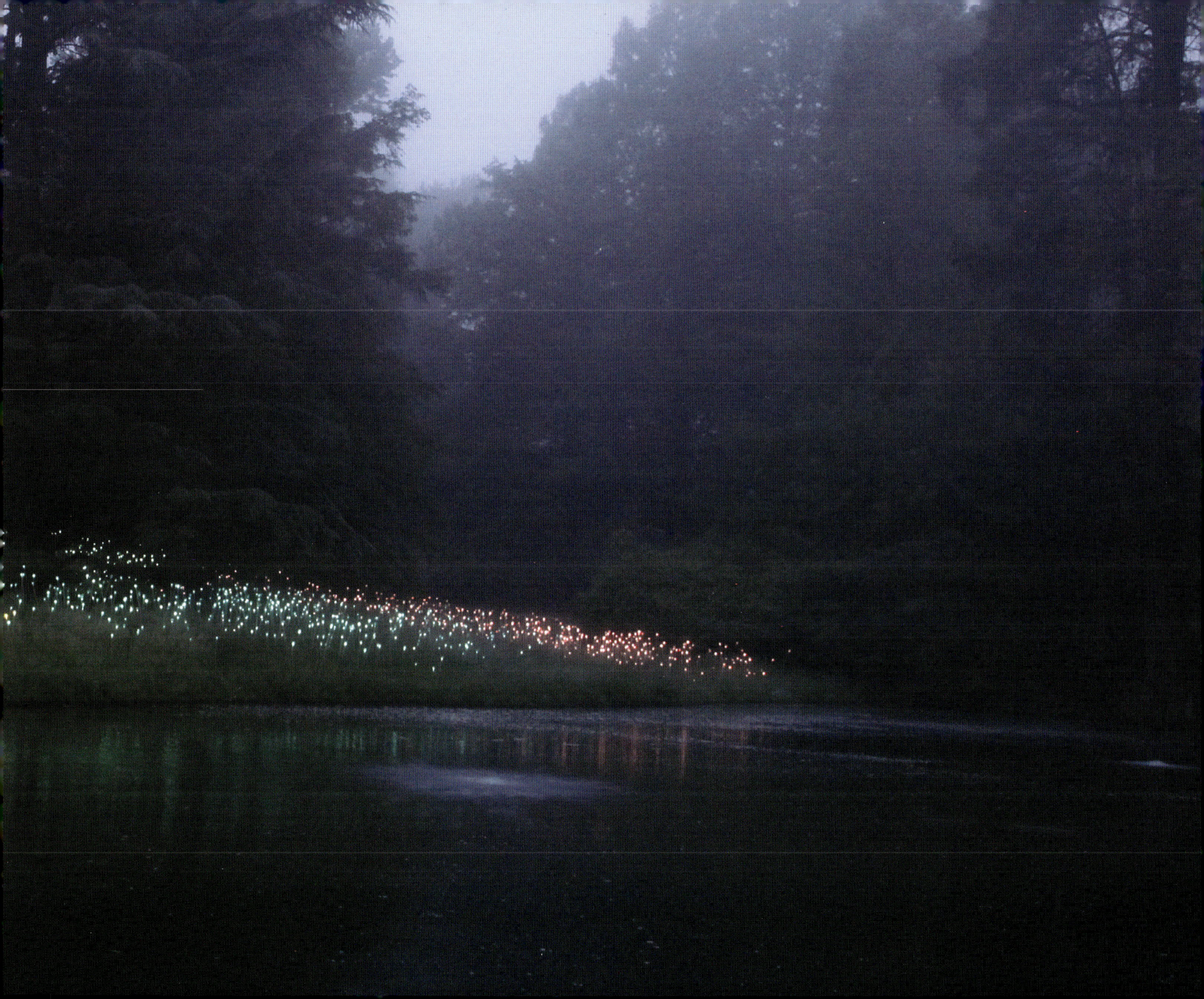

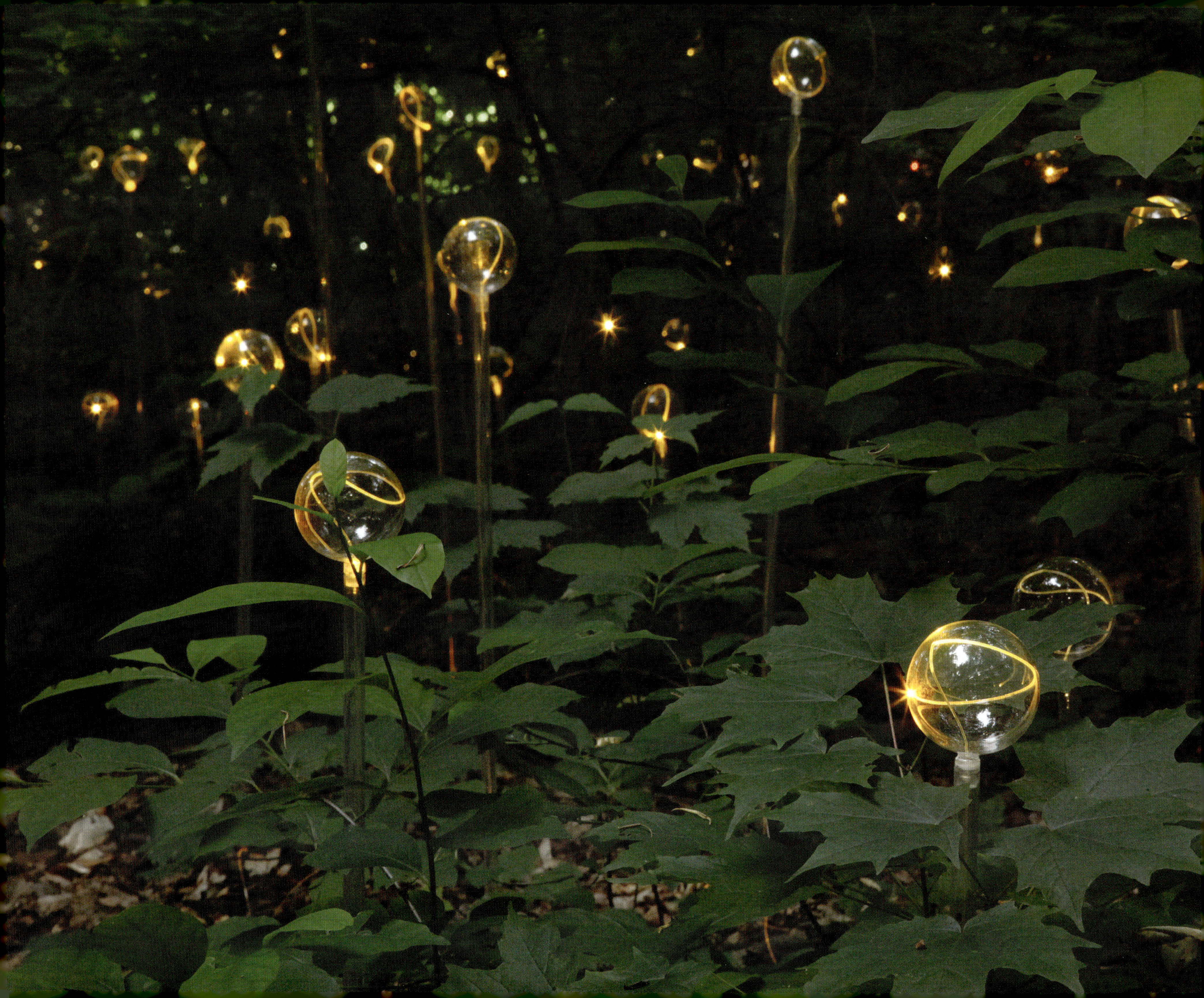

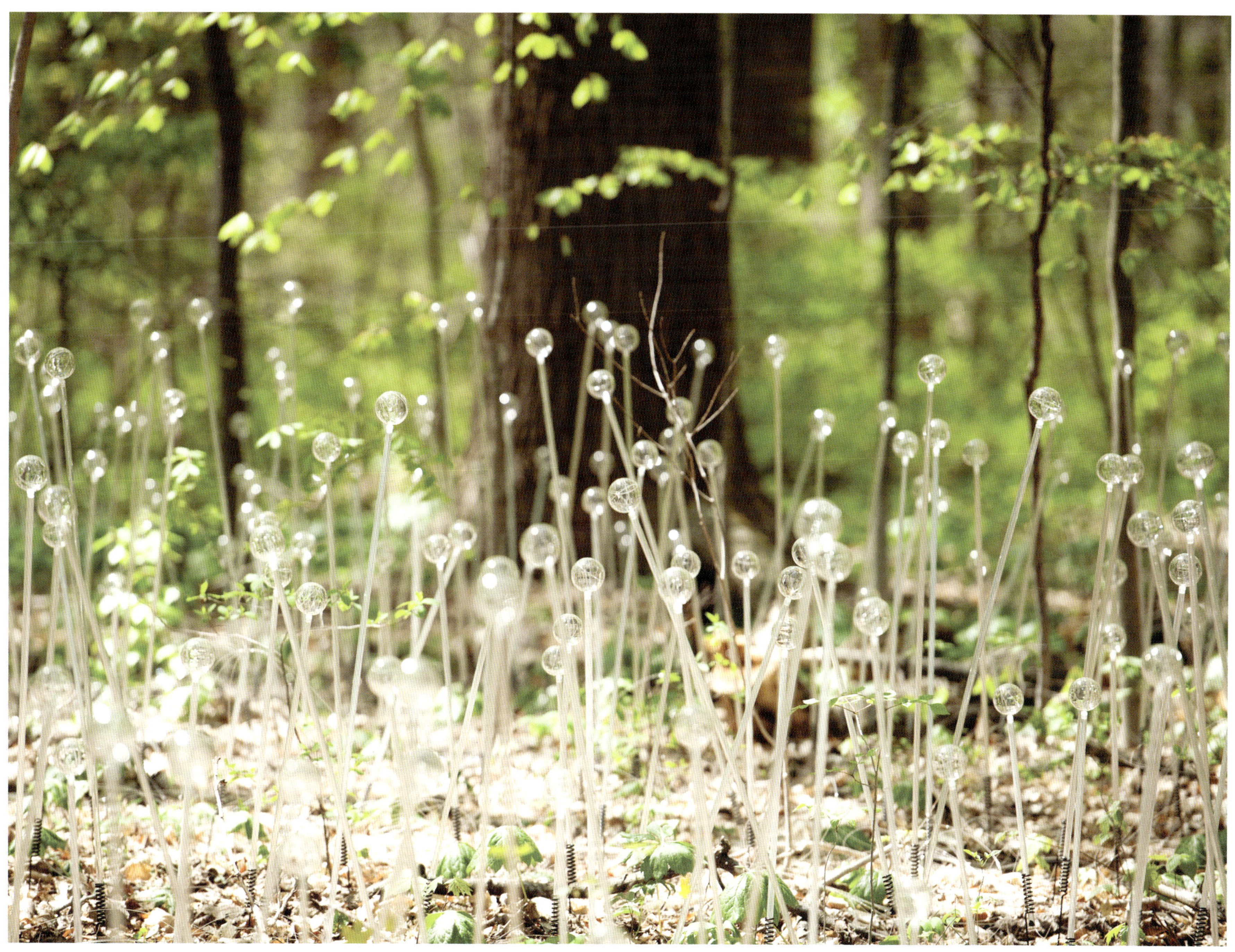

Pages 26–29: Forest of Light, *Longwood Gardens, Pennsylvania, USA, 2012.*

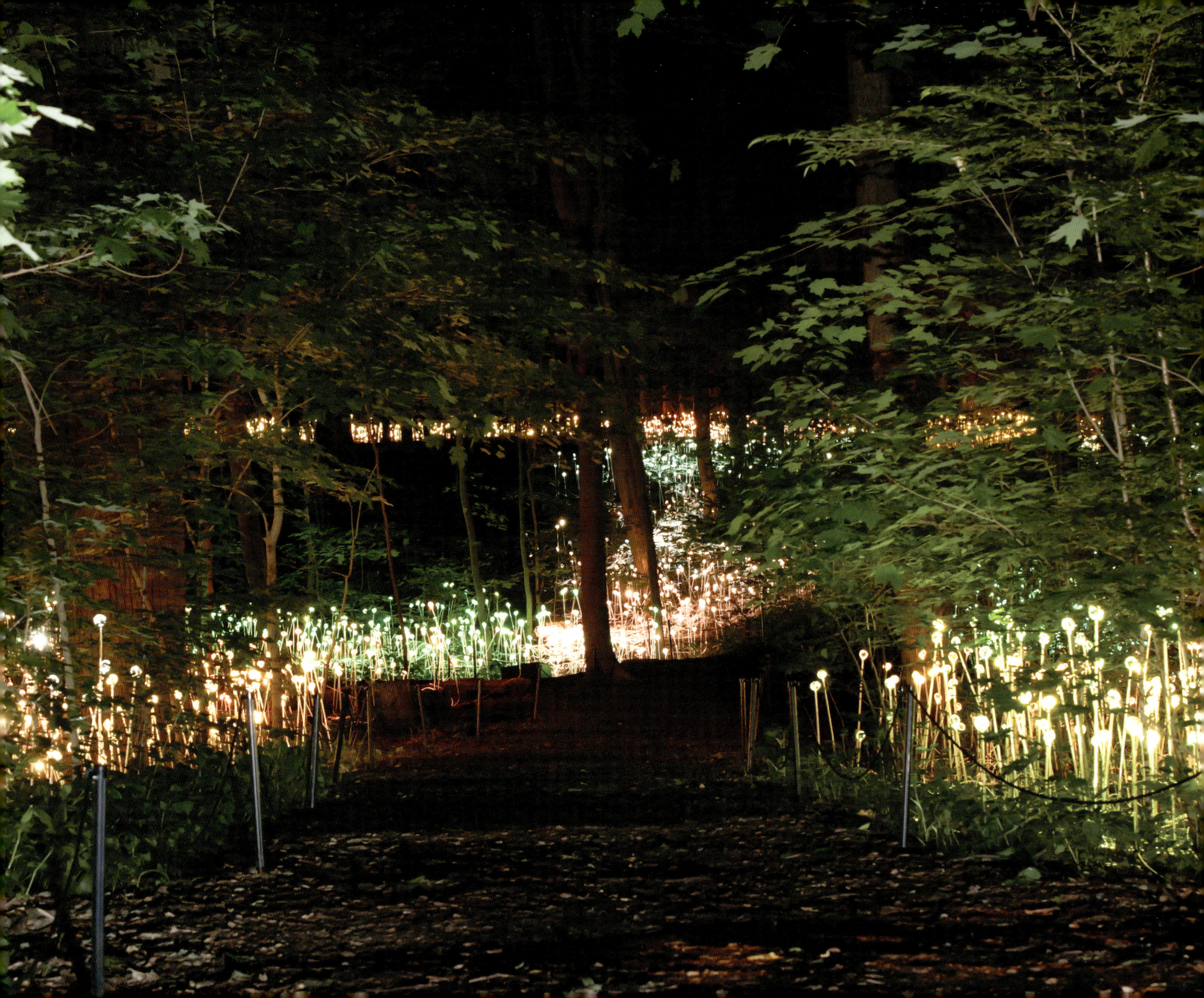

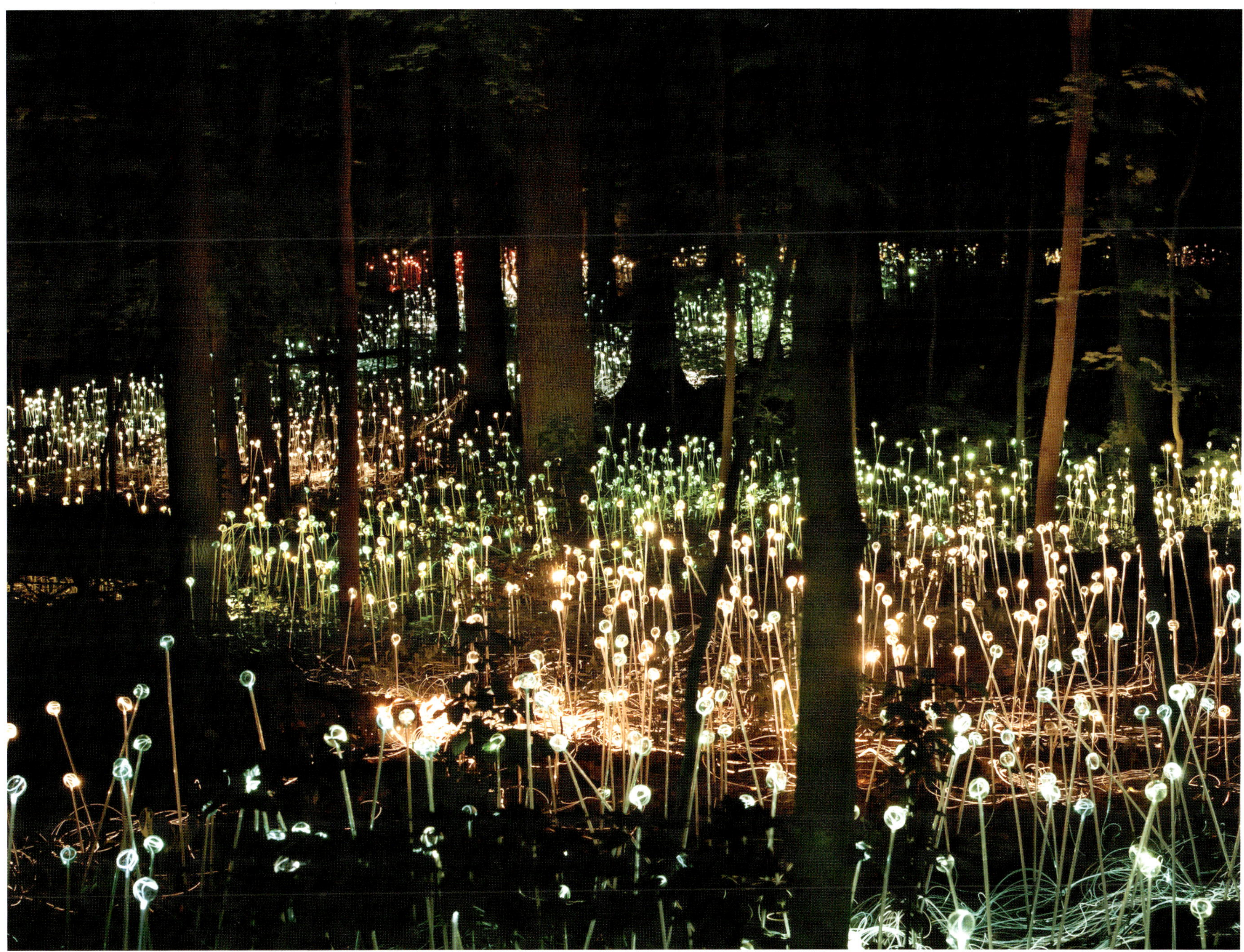

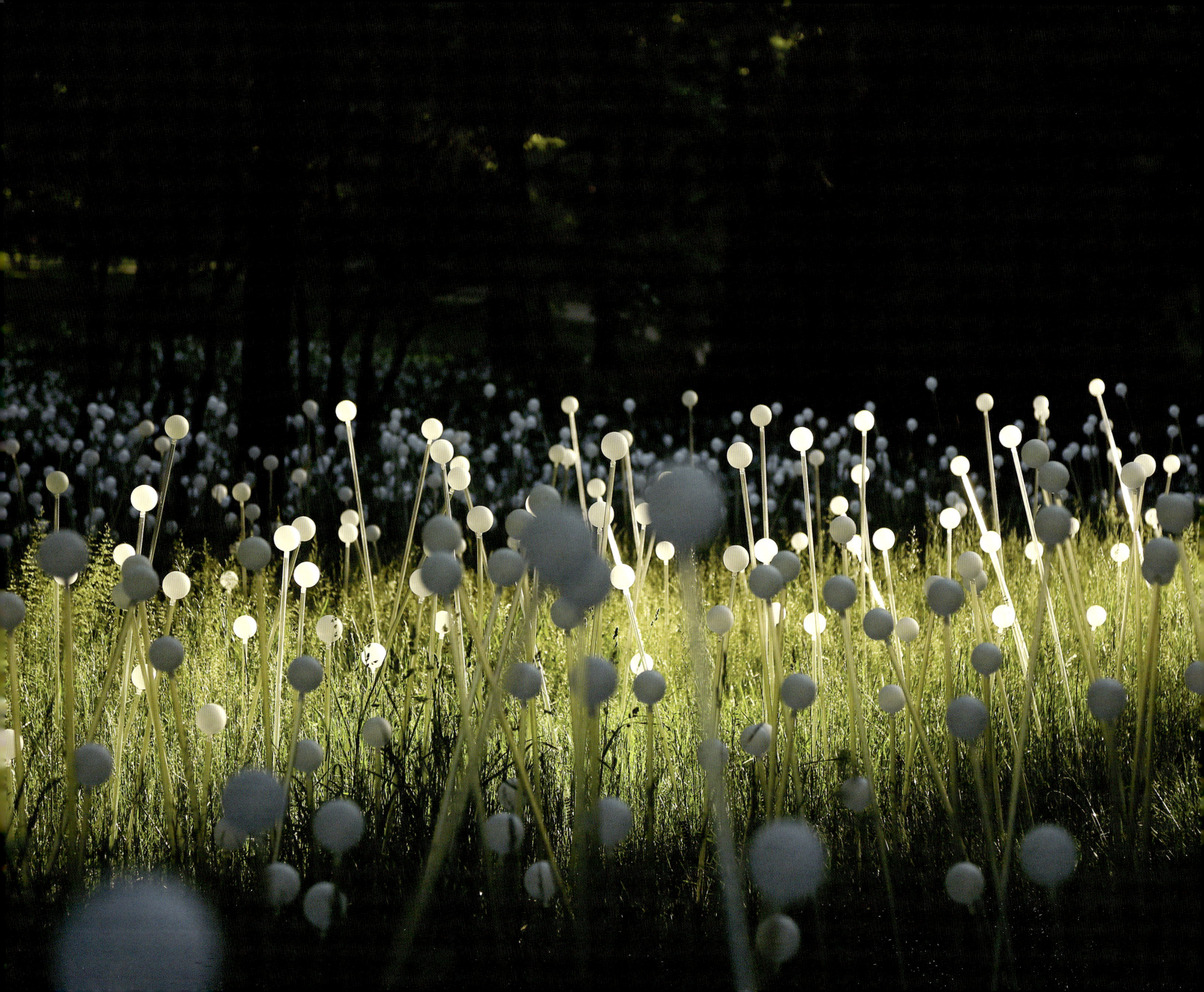

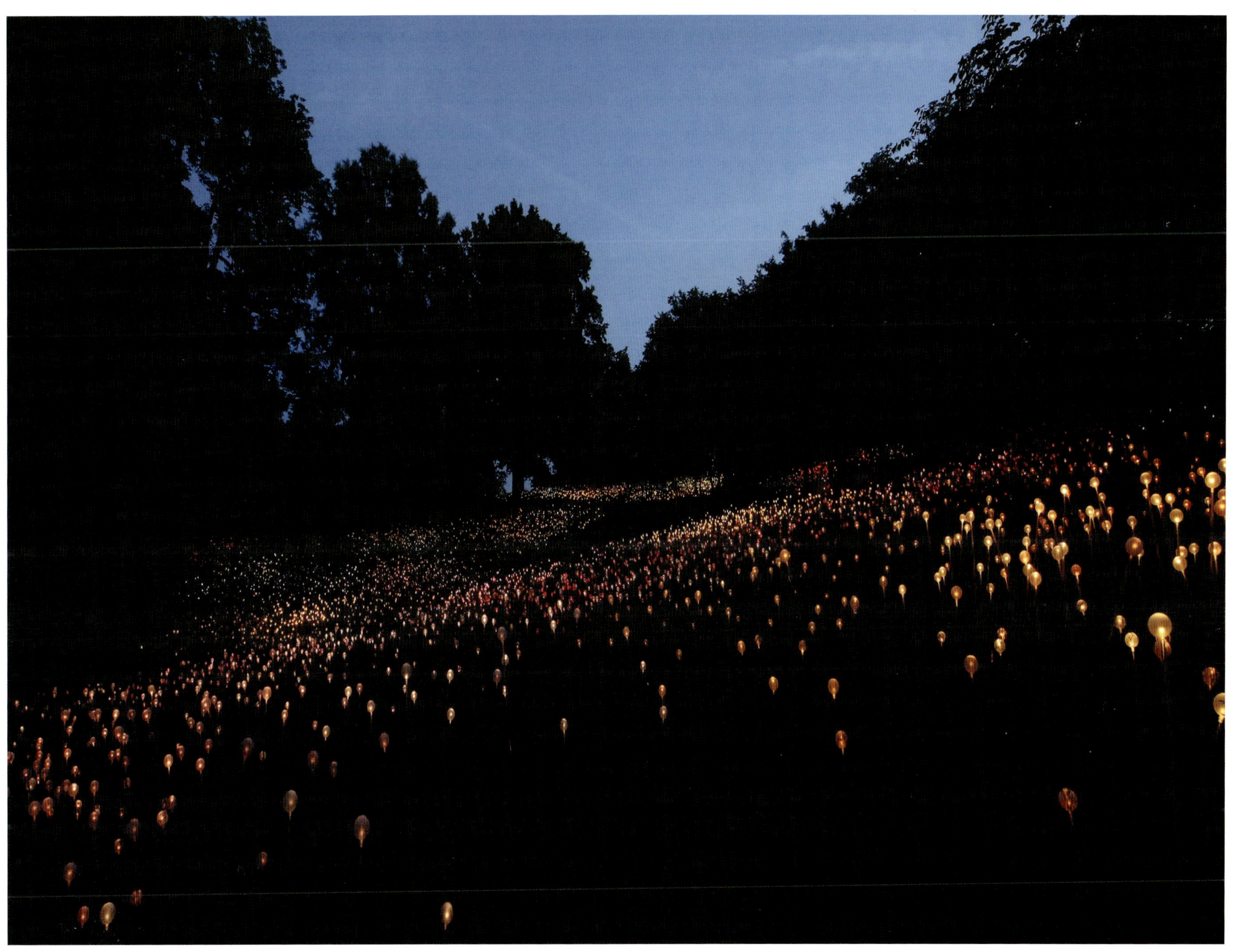

Pages 30–39: Field of Light, *Cheekwood Botanical Garden and Museum of Art, Tennessee, USA, 2013.*

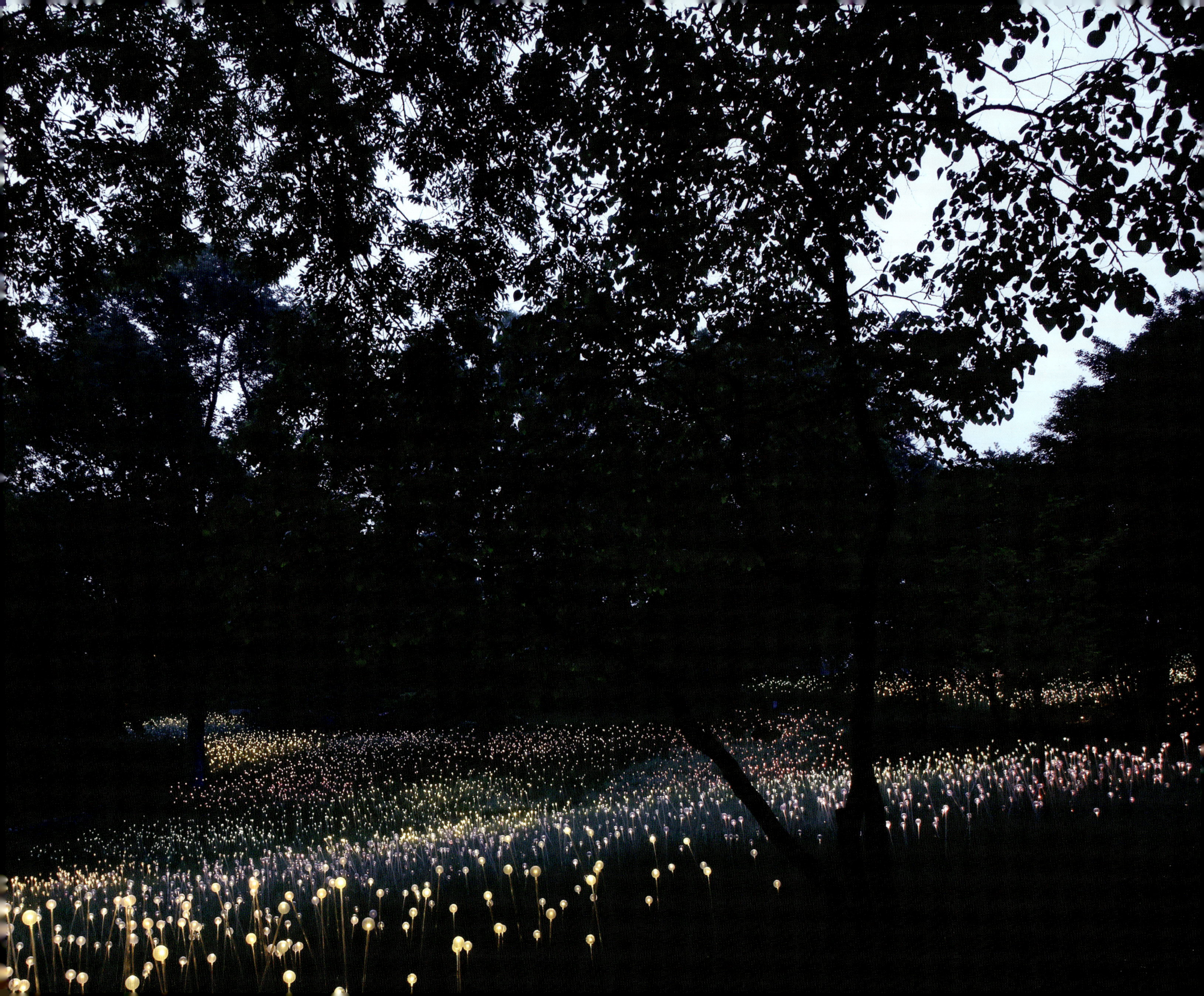

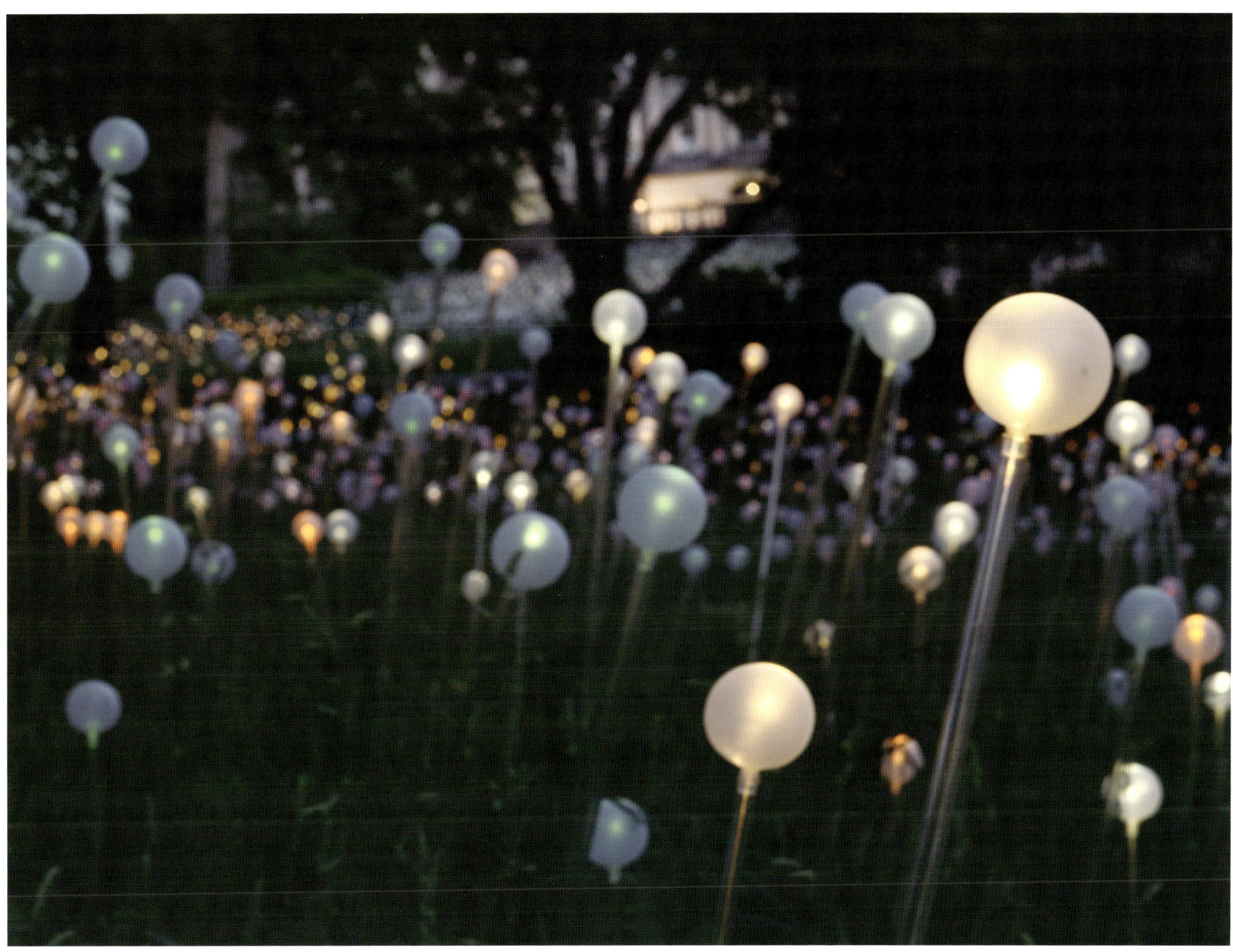

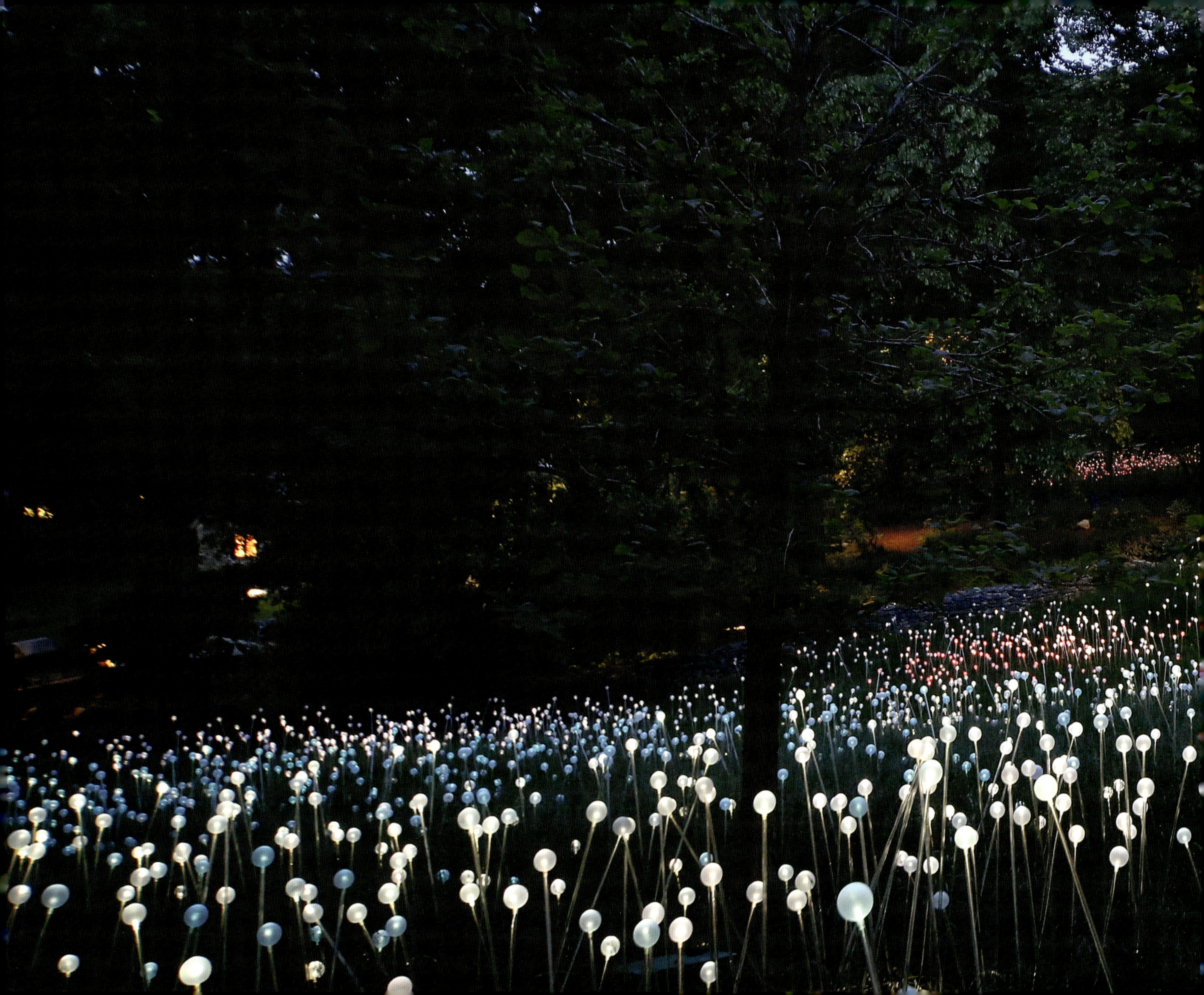

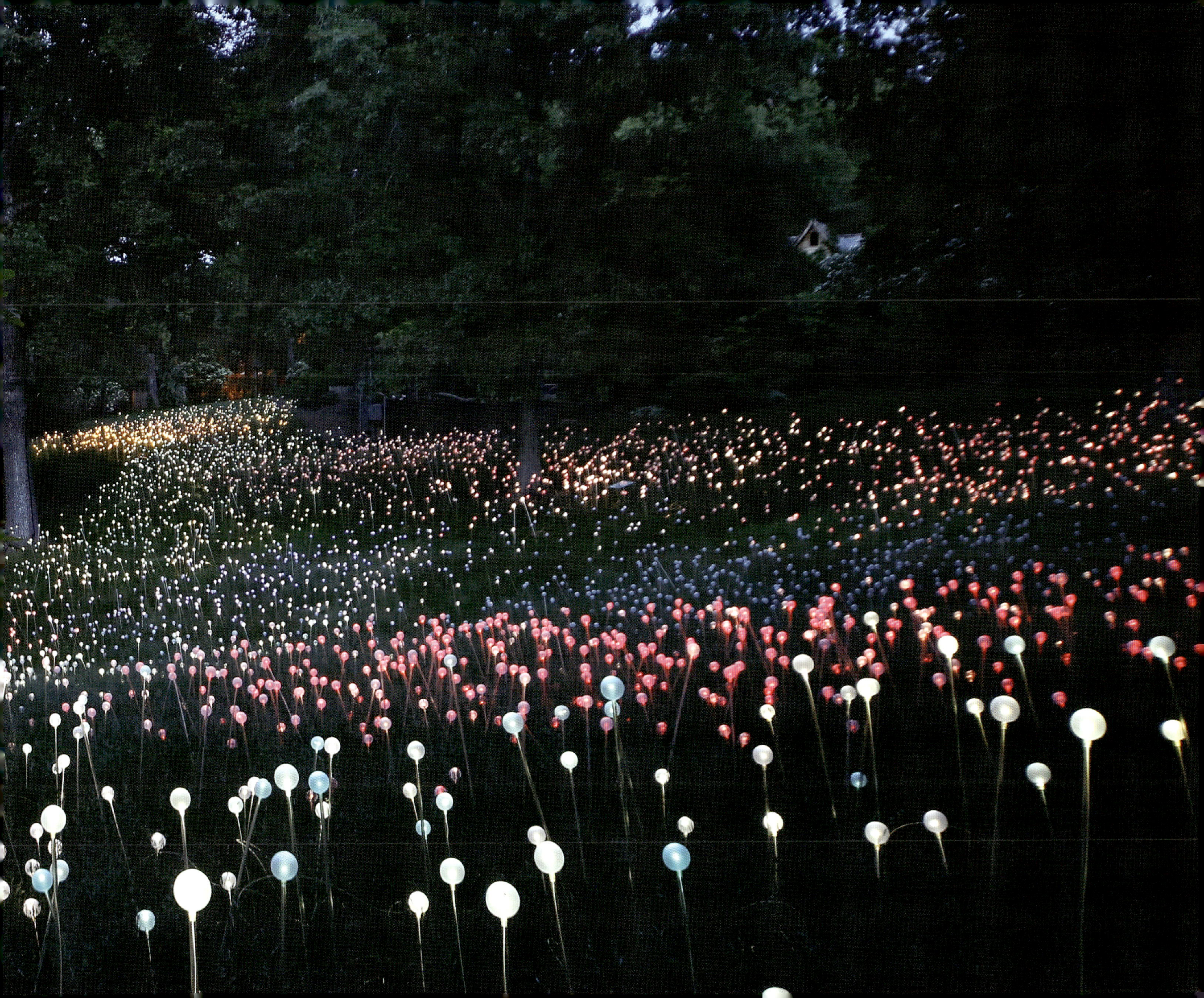

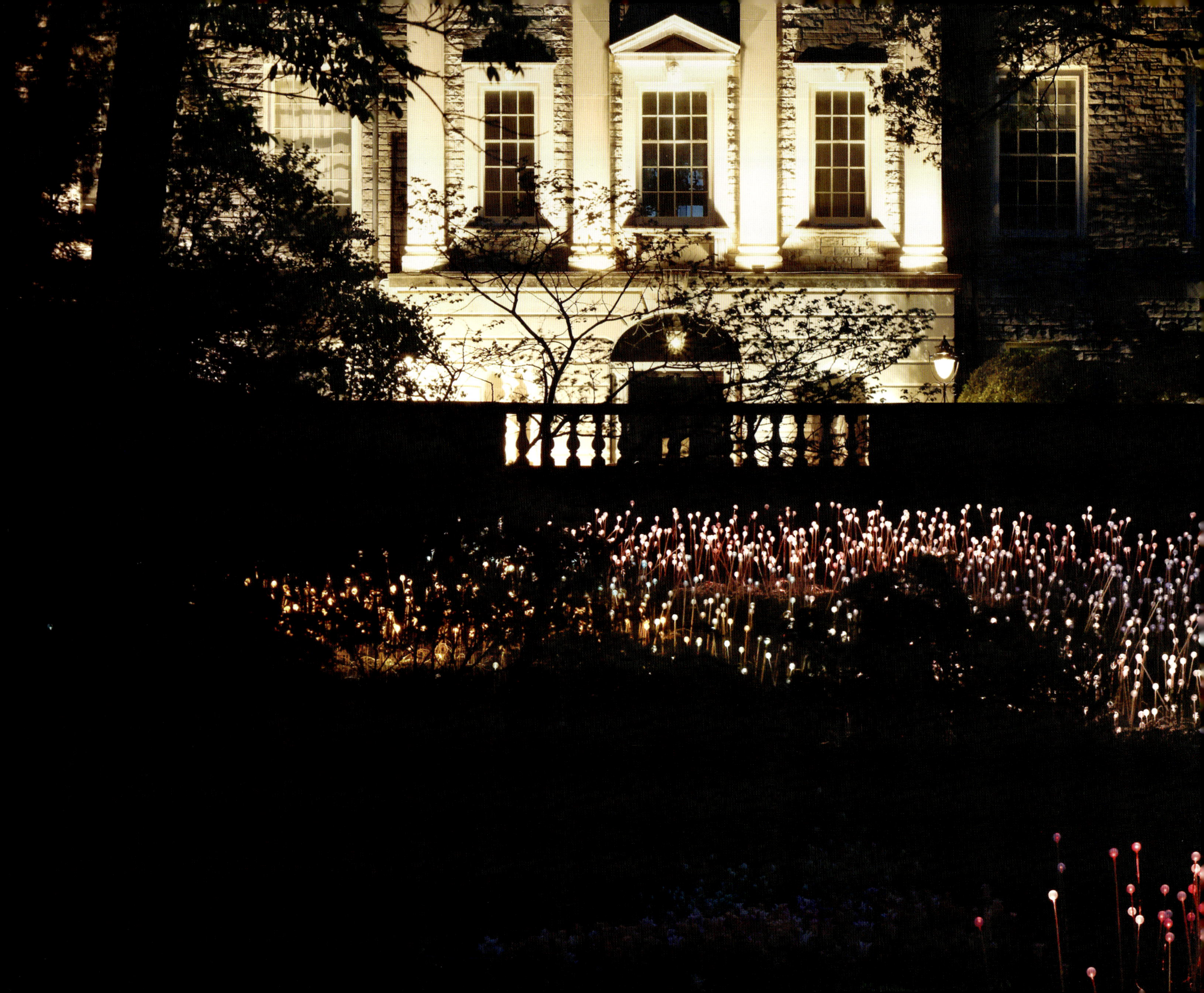

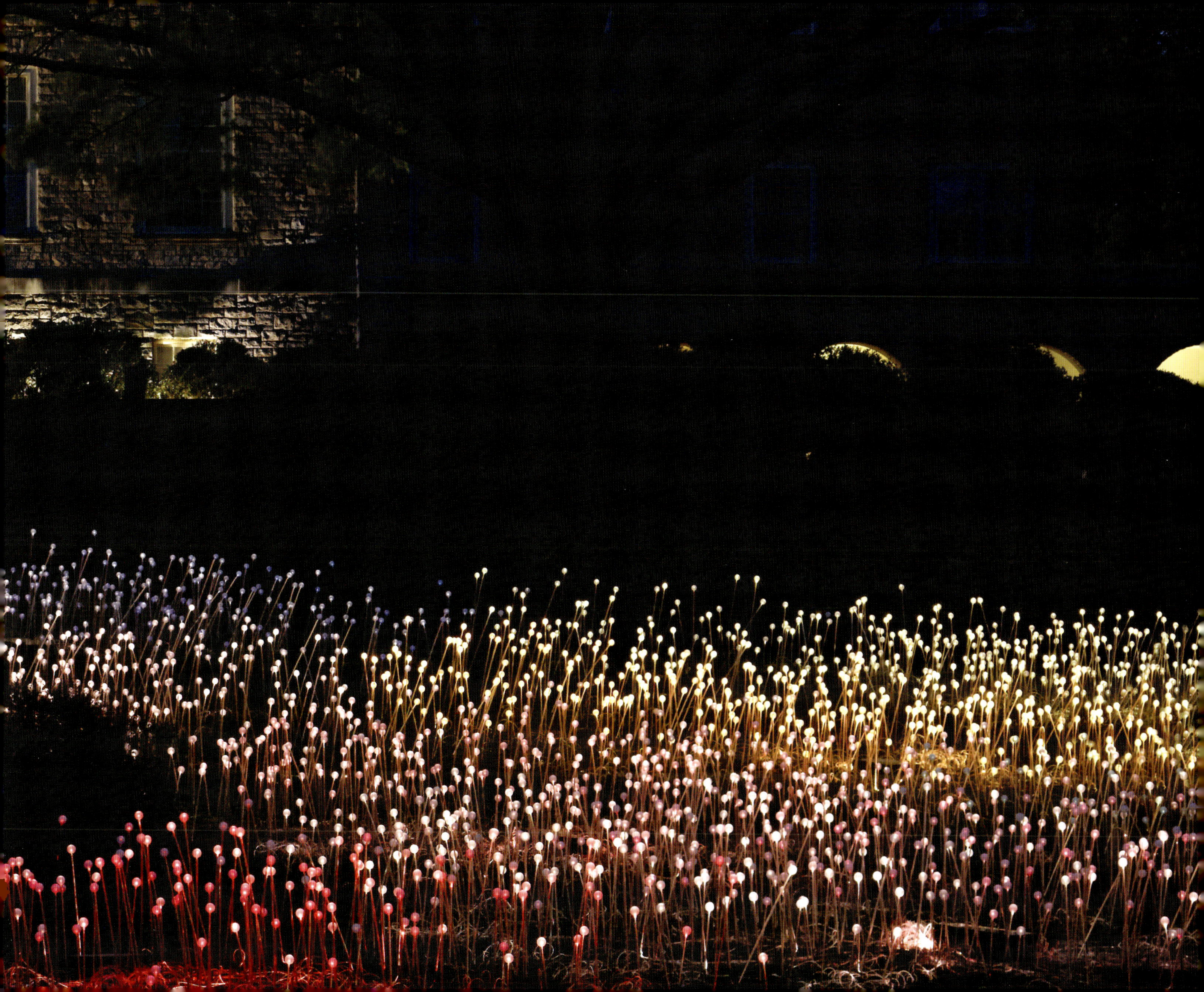

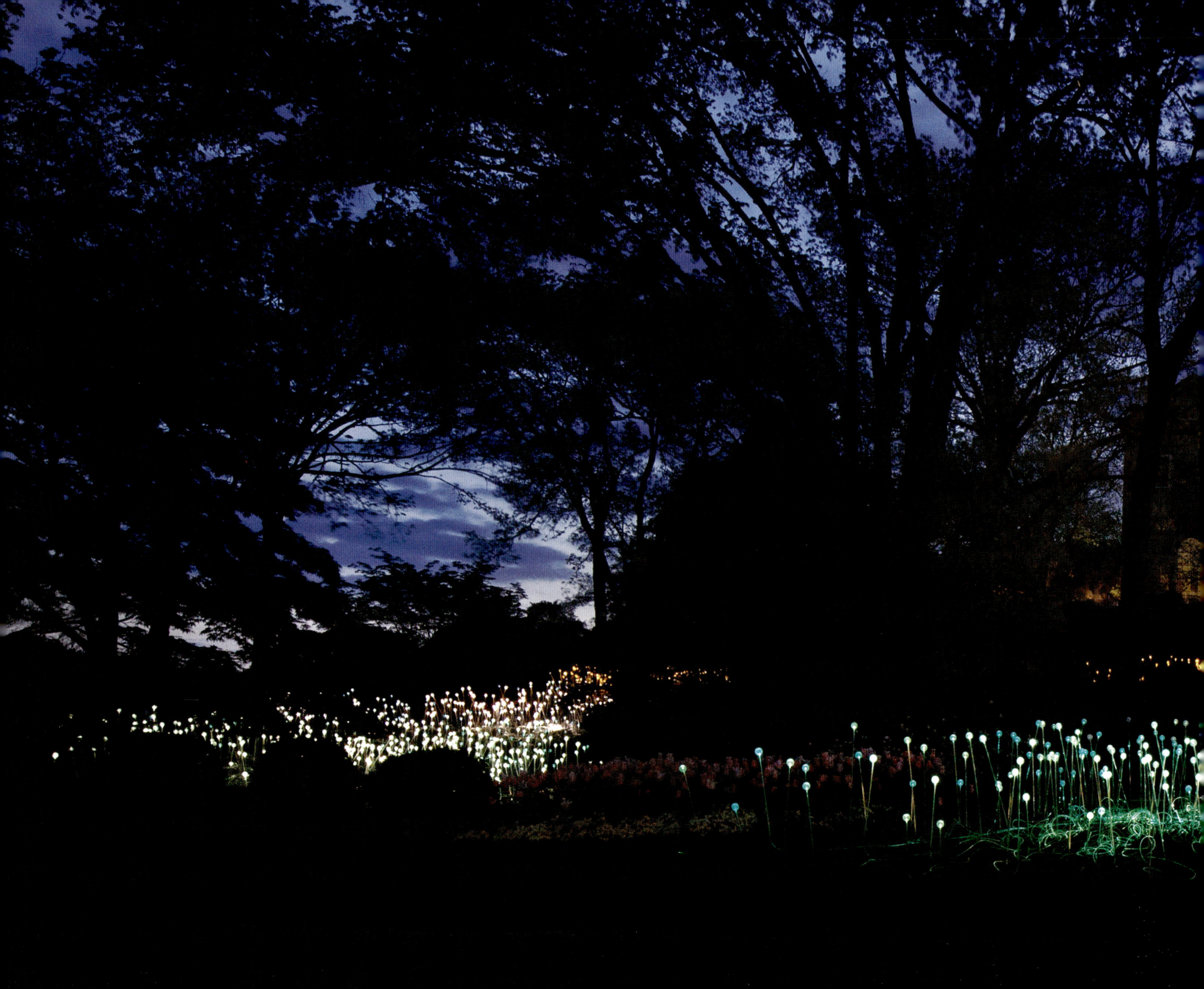

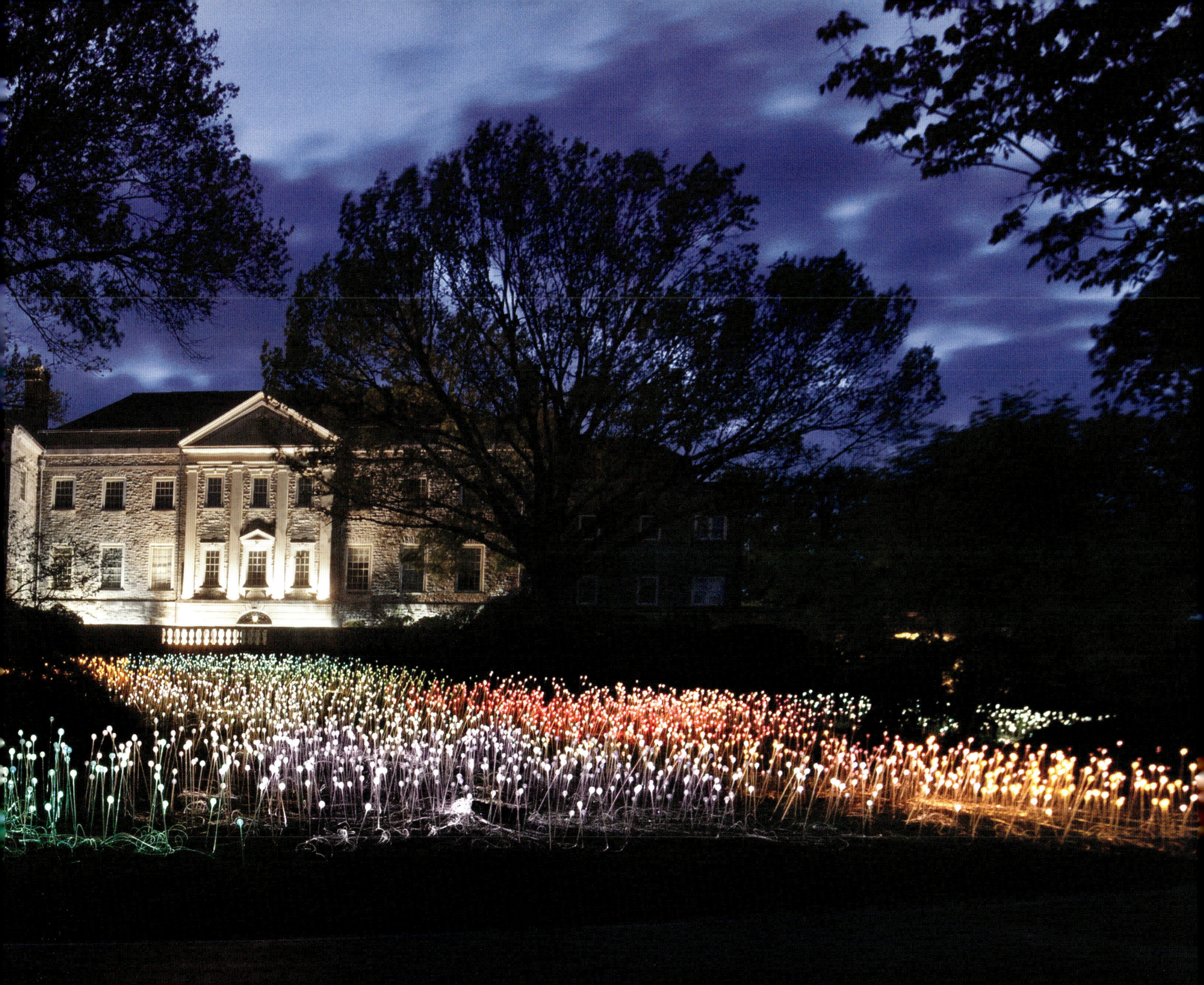

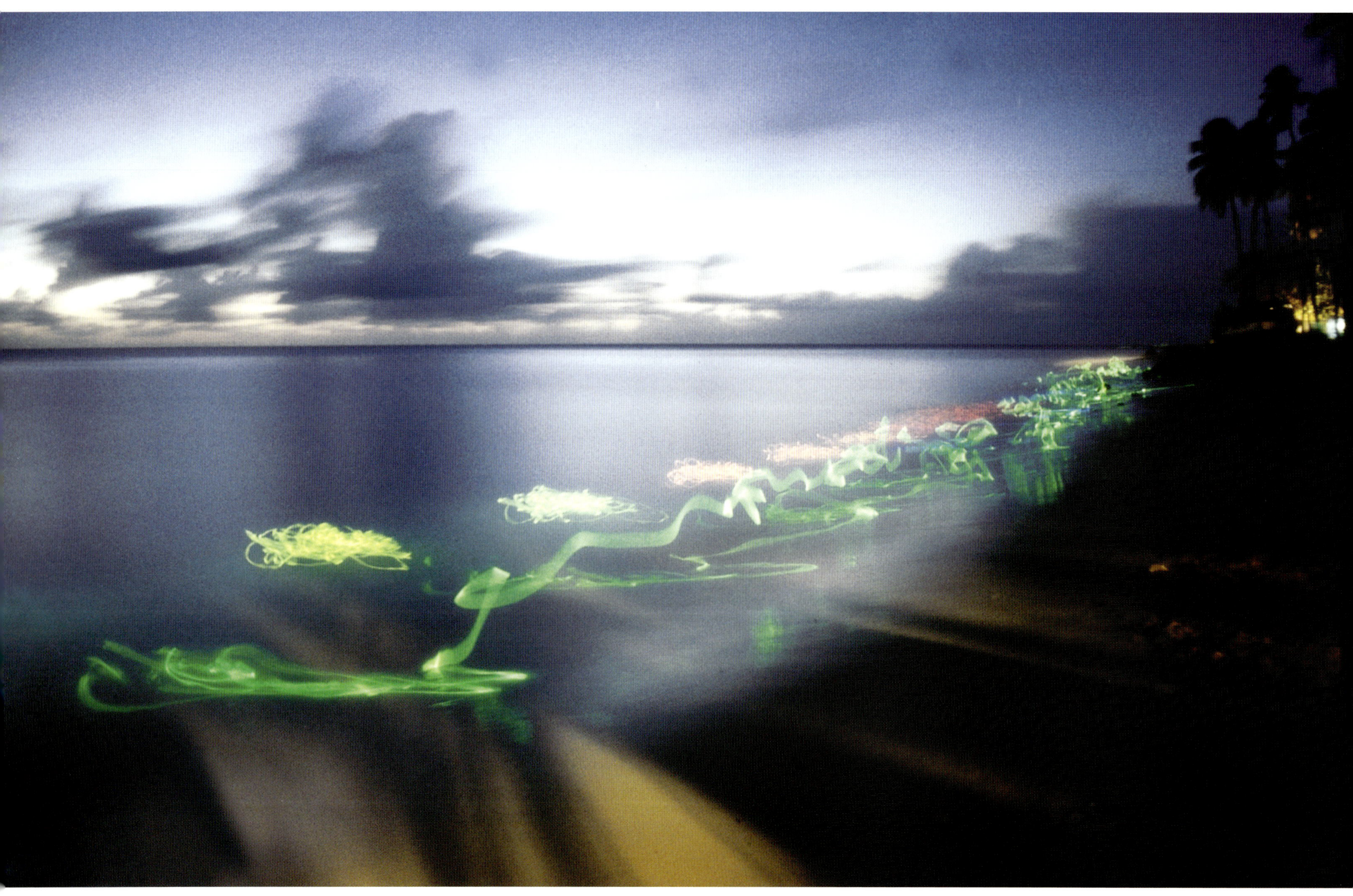

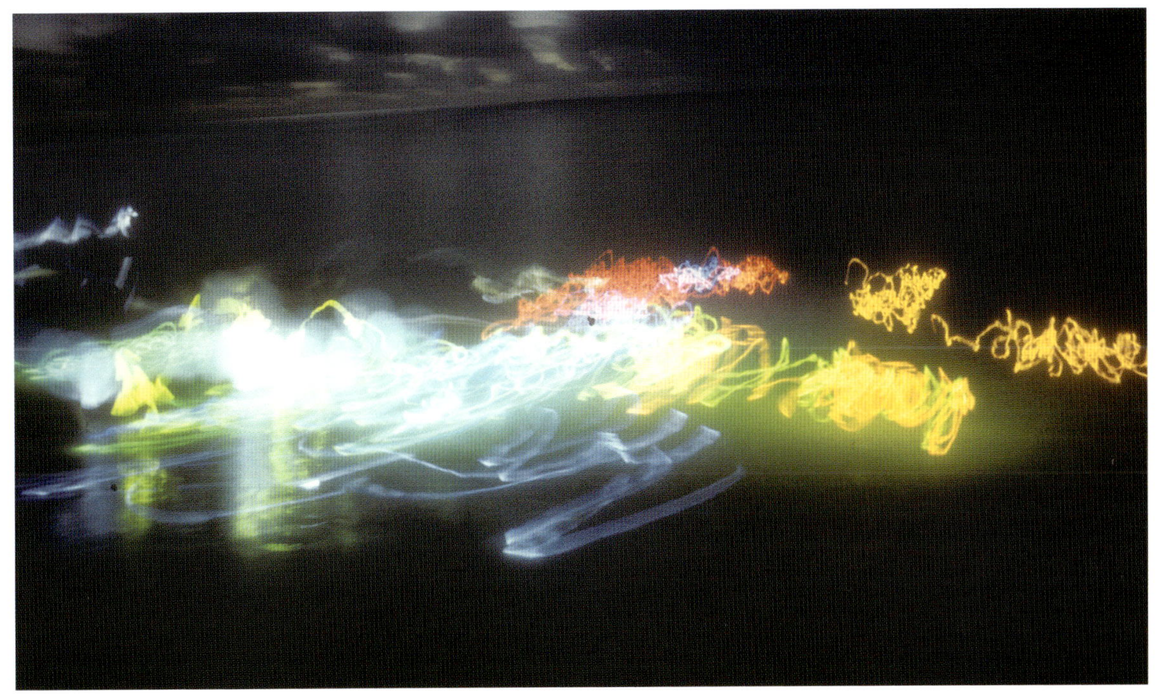

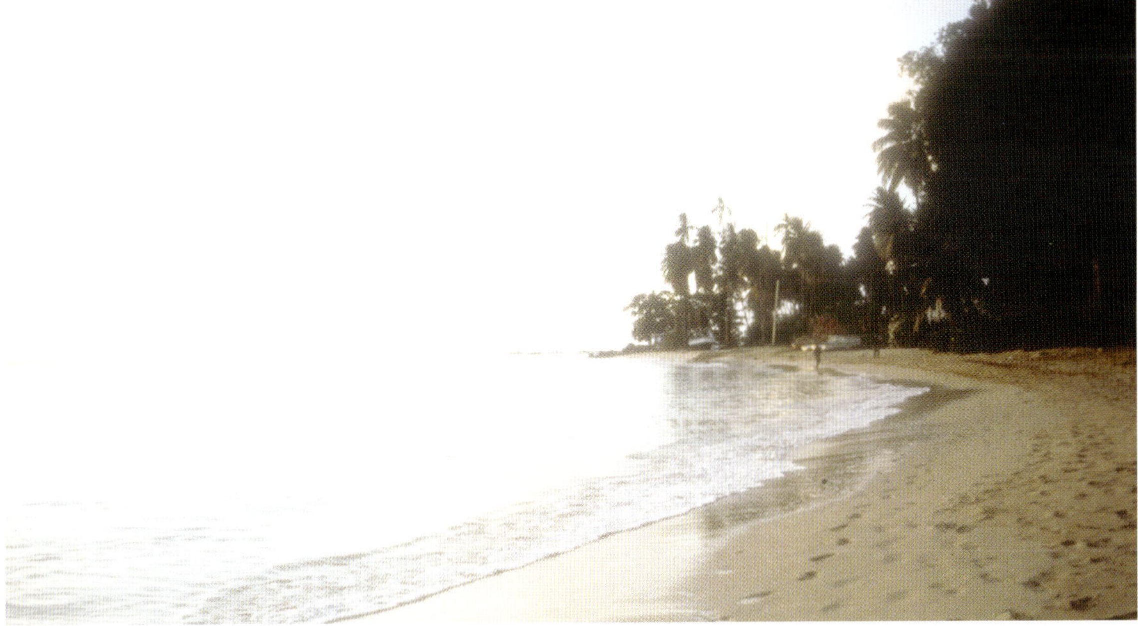

LIGHT WAVE

Light Wave was created in 1999. I was designing a lighting scheme for the beautiful beach house "Greensleeves" in the parish of St Peter's on the west coast of Barbados, West Indies. The project required me to fly fairly frequently to the island, and I often found that I had some spare time on my hands at the end of a day. *Light Wave* was an idea that popped into my head one evening while I was strolling along the beach. It was not a unique idea, and really quite simple to set up.

I actually organised the installation to coincide with a family holiday, so my children were able to help me set it up; this added to the fun.

Aside from one or two lucky snaps on my manual 35mm camera, it was all done by guess work. I realised that I really wanted to do more of this kind of thing; so in a way it was the forerunner of the larger, more complex installations such as the *Field of Light* and *CDSea*.

Opposite and above: Light Wave, *Gibb's Beach, St Peter's, Barbados, WI, 1999.*

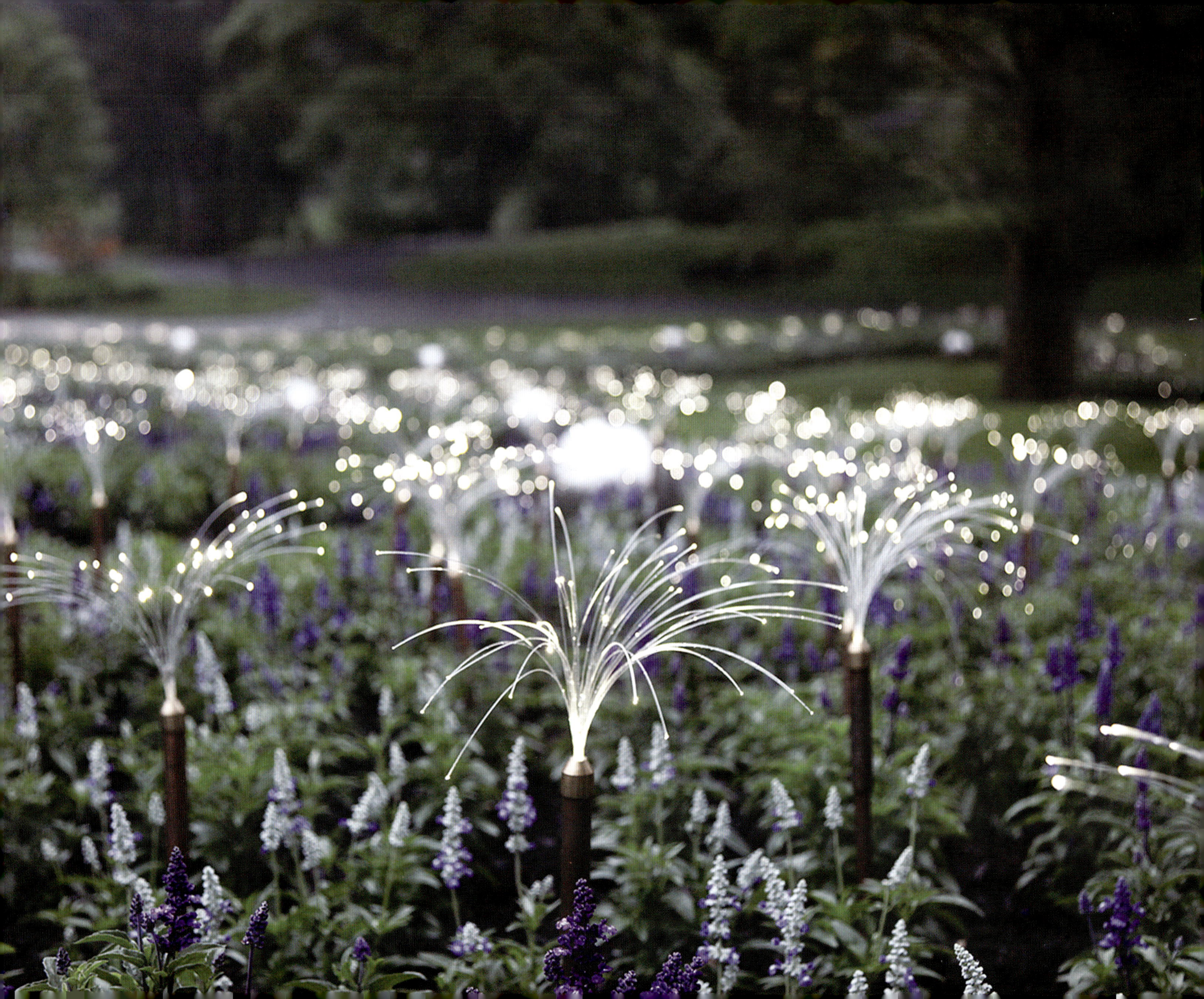

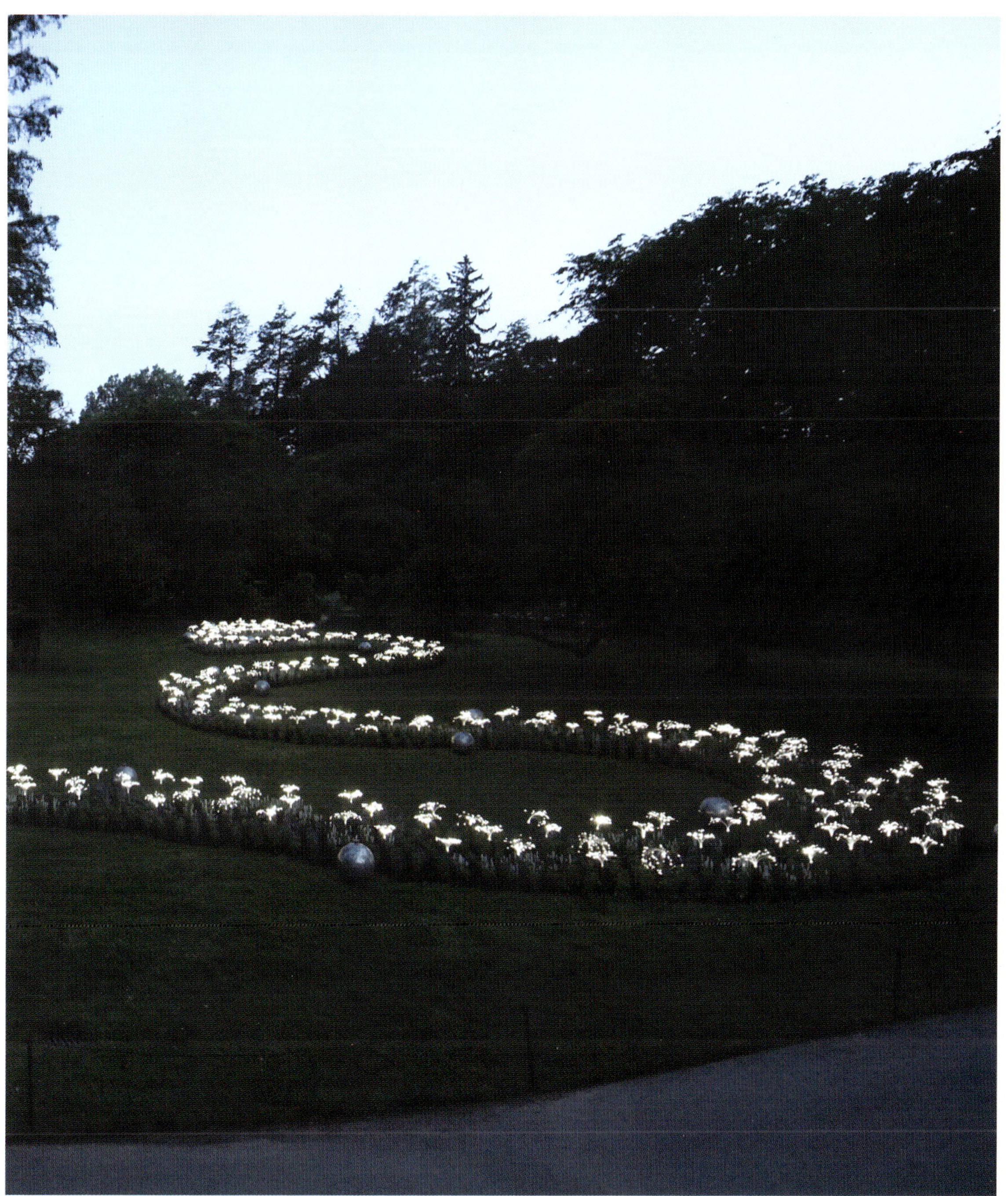

FIREFLIES

I first came up with the form of the *Fireflies* for a residential commission. Then, an idea came to me on a bike ride in 2010—I was thinking about the meandering pathway through an installation I had just made called *CDSea*, and I realised there was a personal connection with the spiritual river described in two of my favourite books, *Kim* by Rudyard Kipling and *Siddhartha* by Herman Hesse. This then became the installation *Arrow Spring*, which was shown at Longwood Gardens, inspired in part by the River Arrow in *Kim*.

What I wanted was to make a meandering spring/stream/river of light, illuminated both gently and by natural means, so I designed a number of spherical lanterns, each to be illuminated with candlelight. Sadly the naked flame proved to be too subtle, so our chosen source of light became the humble battery powered torch (flashlight) placed inside a stainless-steel sphere.

Opposite and above: Arrow Spring, *Longwood Gardens, Pennsylvania, USA, 2012.*

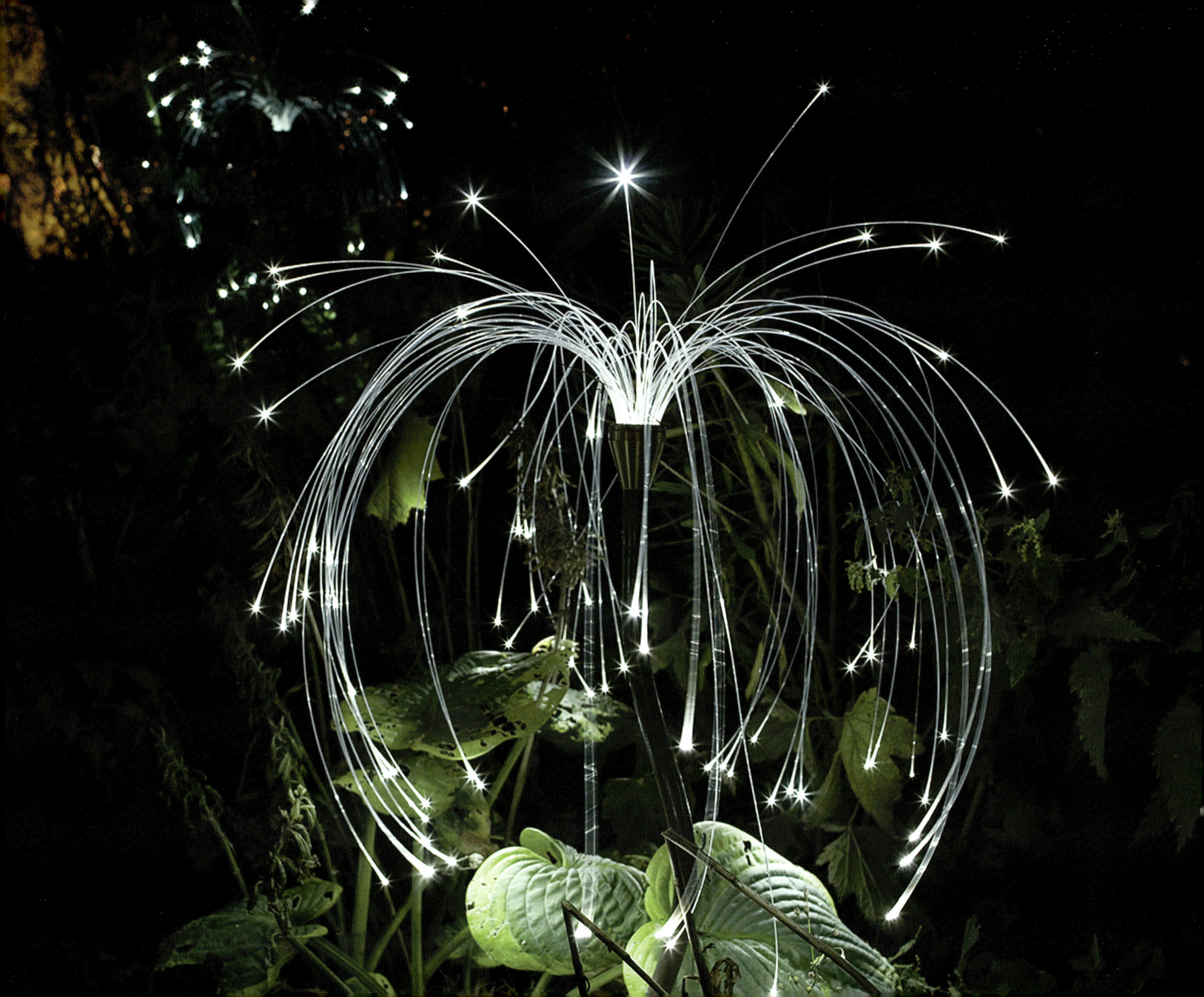

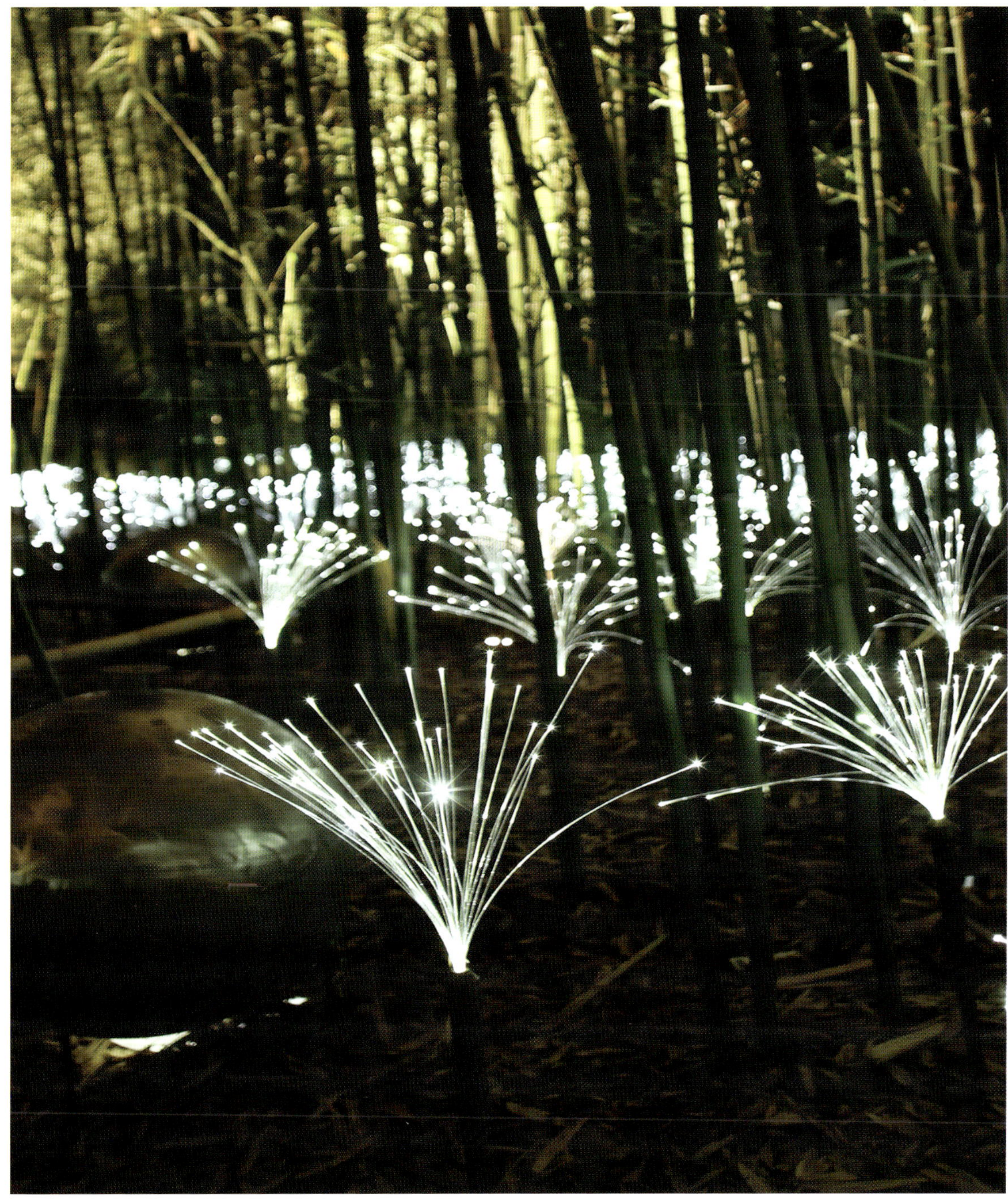

The torches illuminated 328 fibre-optic sprigs of light planted amongst the deep blue salvia. In total, *Arrow Spring* consisted of 15,000 flickering points of light.

For my exhibition at Cheekwood, I realised that the *Fireflies* were the right companion to the walled bamboo forest, which is intended to turn the mind inward as part of the progression into the Japanese Shomu-en pine-mist garden. Their low presence, coupled with the impressive height of the bamboo branches that meet above, emphasises the vertical boundaries which enclose the path, and I used mirrored panels on the side walls to increase the sense of lateral space.

Opposite: Fireflies, *private installation, UK, 2008. Above:* Fireflies, *Cheekwood Botanical Garden and Museum of Art, Tennessee, USA, 2013.*

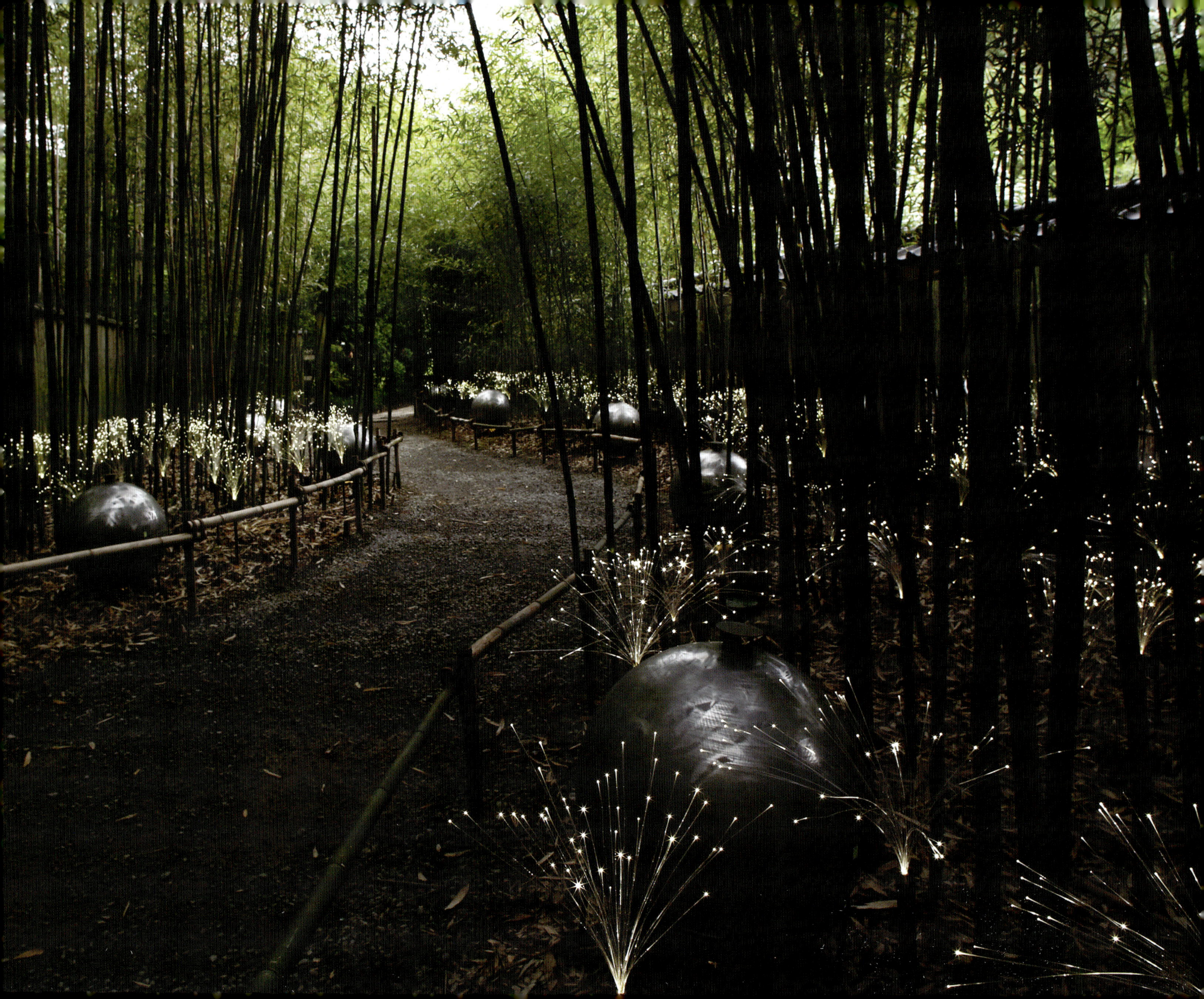

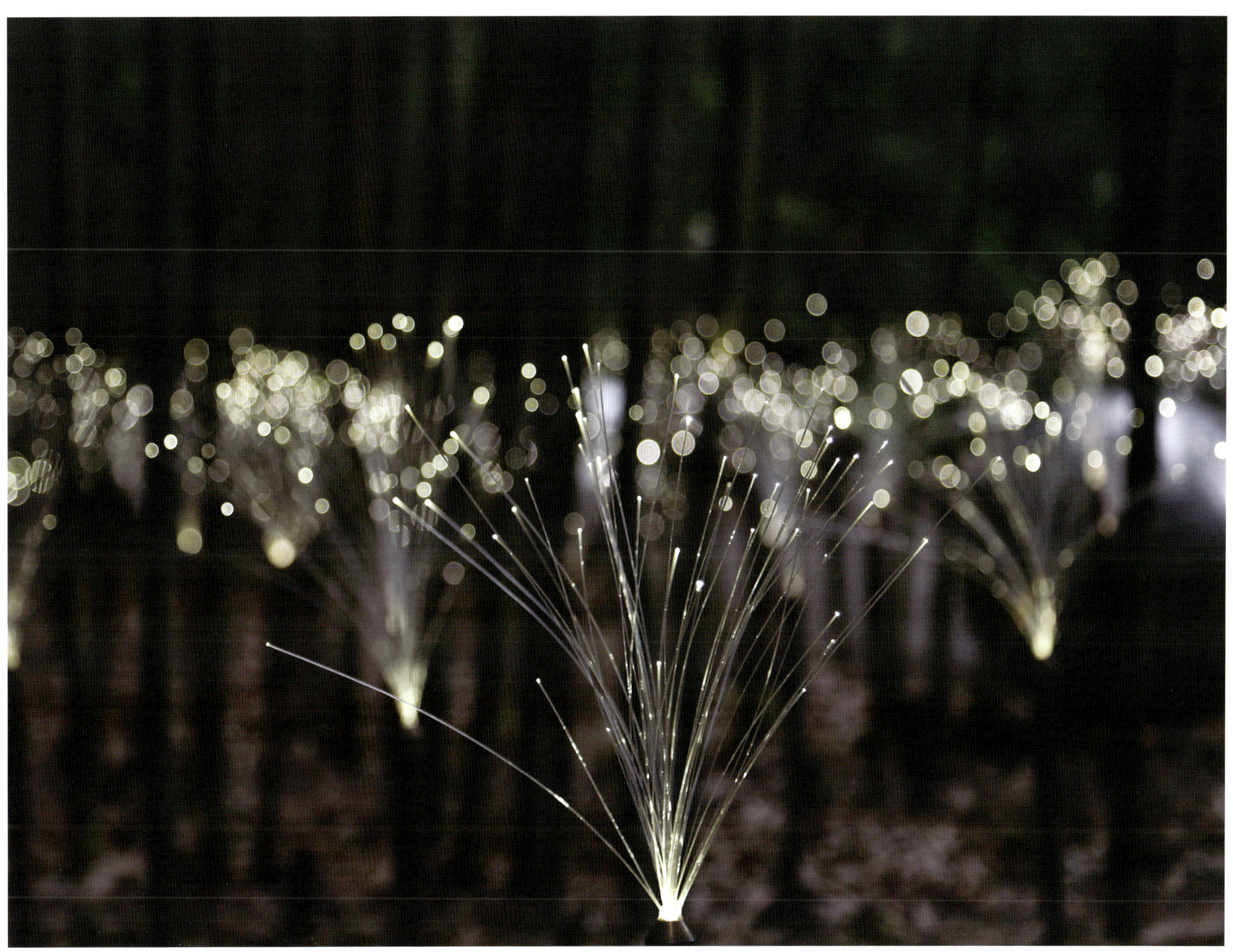

Pages 46–49: Fireflies, *Cheekwood Botanical Garden and Museum of Art, Tennessee, USA, 2013.*

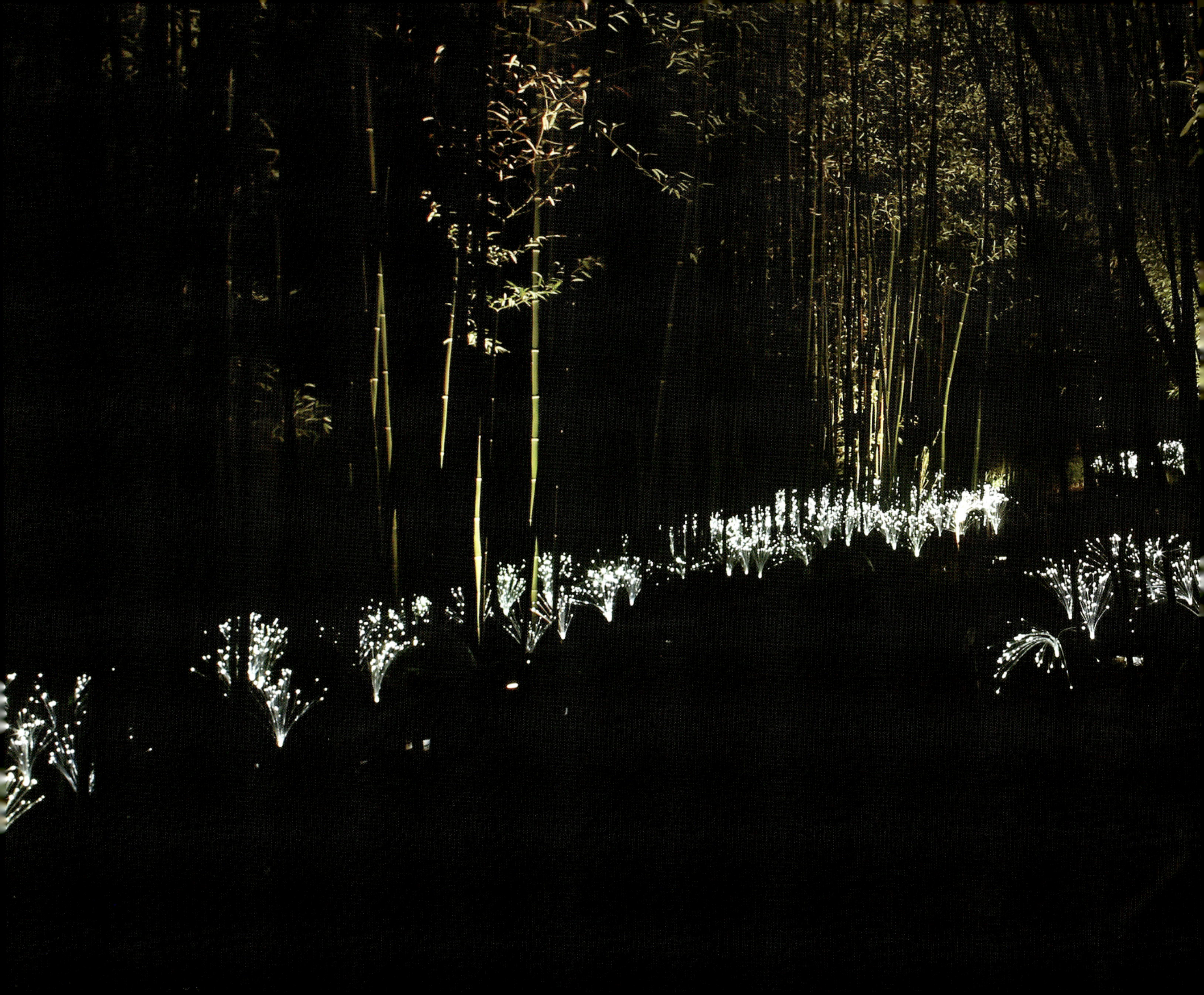

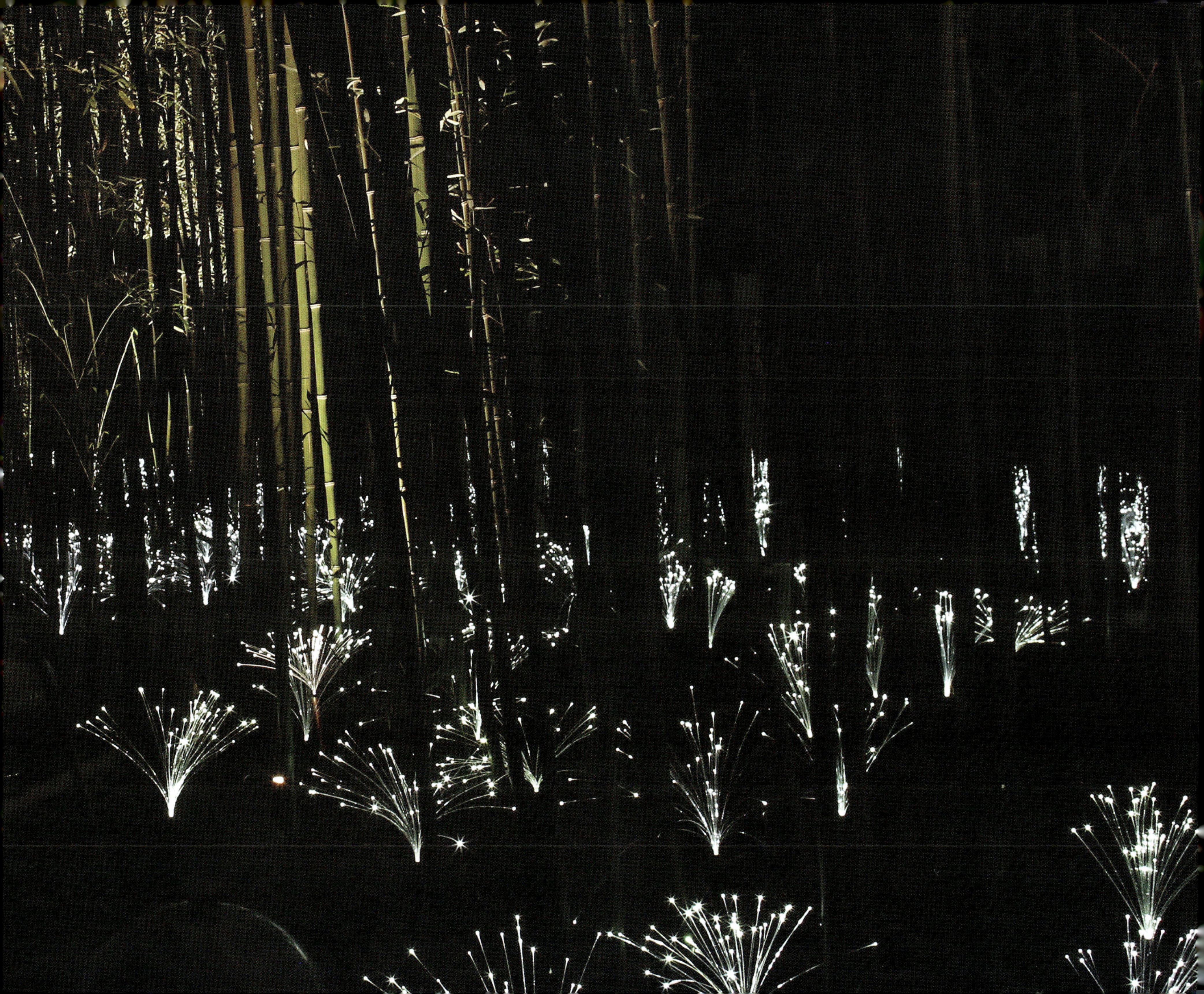

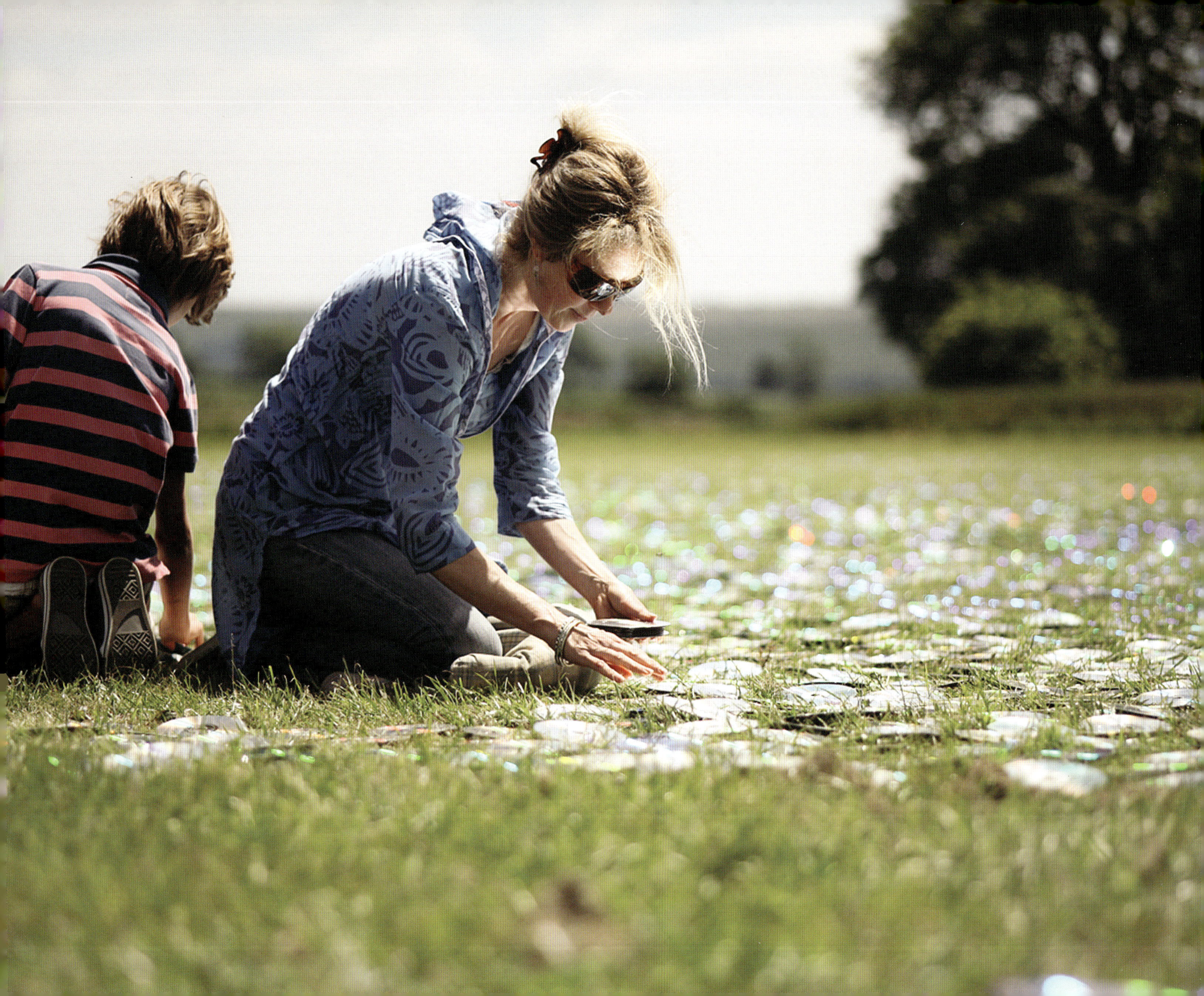

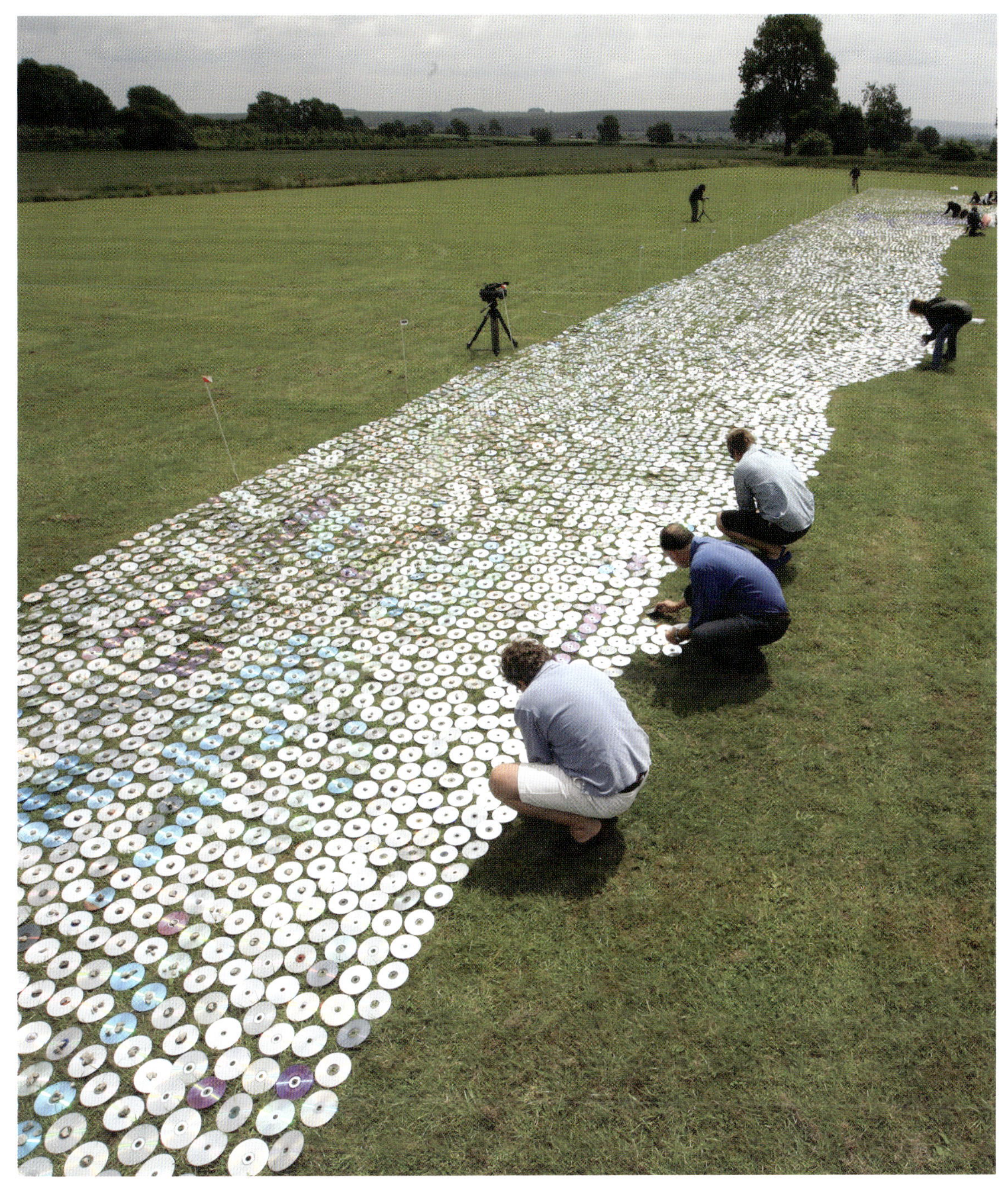

CDSEA

Entitled *CDSea*, this project was installed in June 2010 at Long Knoll Field in Wiltshire, where in 2004 we installed a prototype of the *Field of Light*. A public footpath intersects the field, and this meant that *CDSea* was on public view from the moment it was installed. Personal friends and family, including families with young children, all helped me and my team install *CDSea*.

CDSea is literally an inland sea created from 600,000 discarded compact discs, which were donated from all around the world. They created a carpet of glinting light, created by the reflections of the solstice sun. As with the *Field of Light*, the catalyst for *CDSea* was living in Australia, where eight years of exposure to the Antipodean sun left a lasting impression on me. *CDSea* was inspired one Sunday afternoon as I was sitting on a rocky peninsula at Nielsen Park, one of the beautiful Sydney Harbour beaches, where I

Pages 50–61: CDSea, *Long Knoll Field, Wiltshire, UK, 2010.*

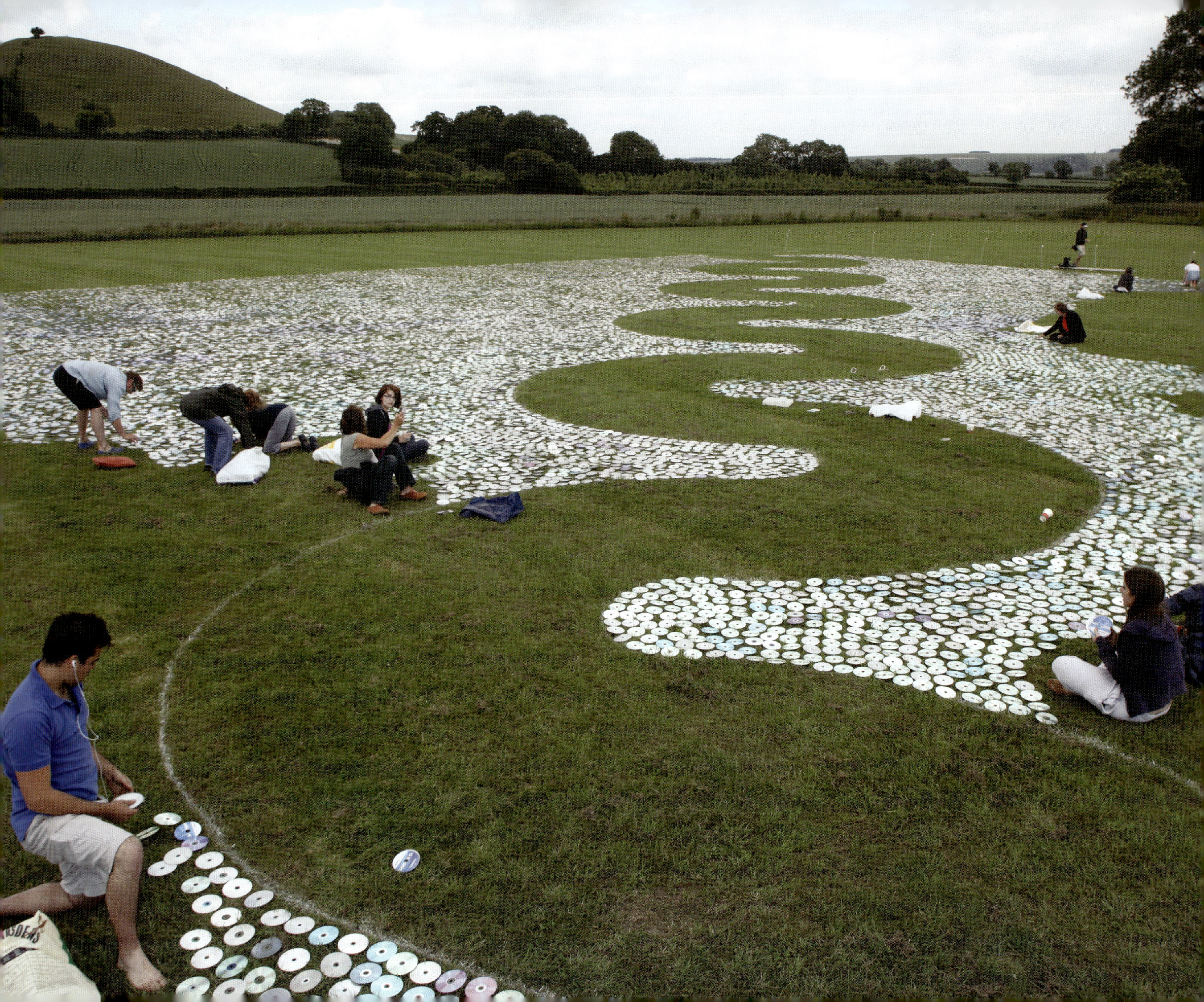

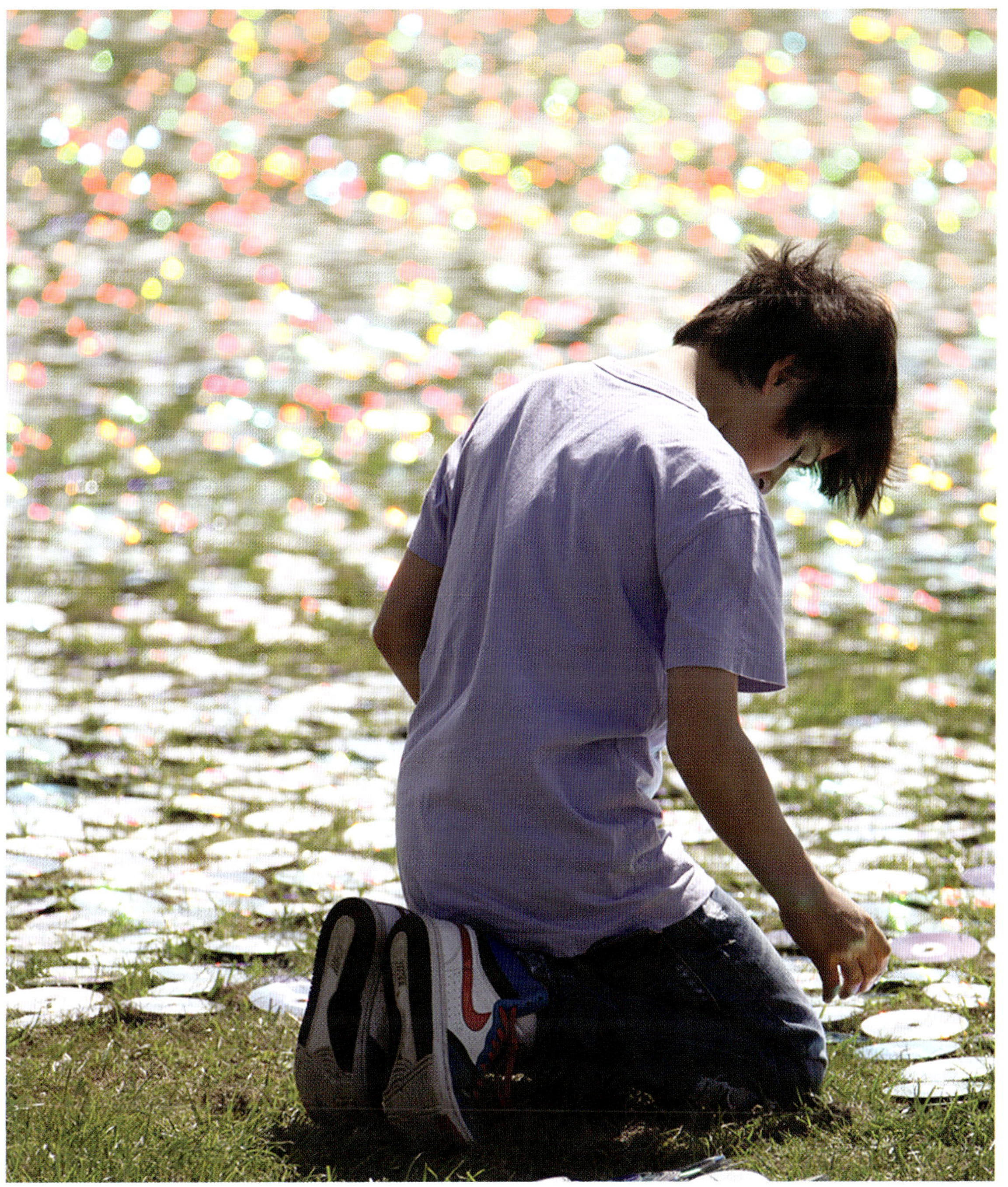

would go when I was a bit down or in the dumps. The light was still strong, like a blanket of shimmering silver light. I had this childish notion that by putting my hand in the sea I was somehow connected to my home in Salcombe, South Devon, where my father lived. I came away from the beach in a very positive at-one-with-the-world frame of mind. It was the first time I was aware that the play of light had transformed my mood, and it proved an unforgettable turning point in my life. I was astonished that something so familiar had the power to alter my emotional state. *CDSea* is a reconstruction of this event.

I do not expect visitors to feel exactly as I did, but I am certain that the materials, scale, and location, a field on top of a hill, will evoke emotions unique to each observer. If it inspires some smiling faces, then the emotional force has been successfully passed on.

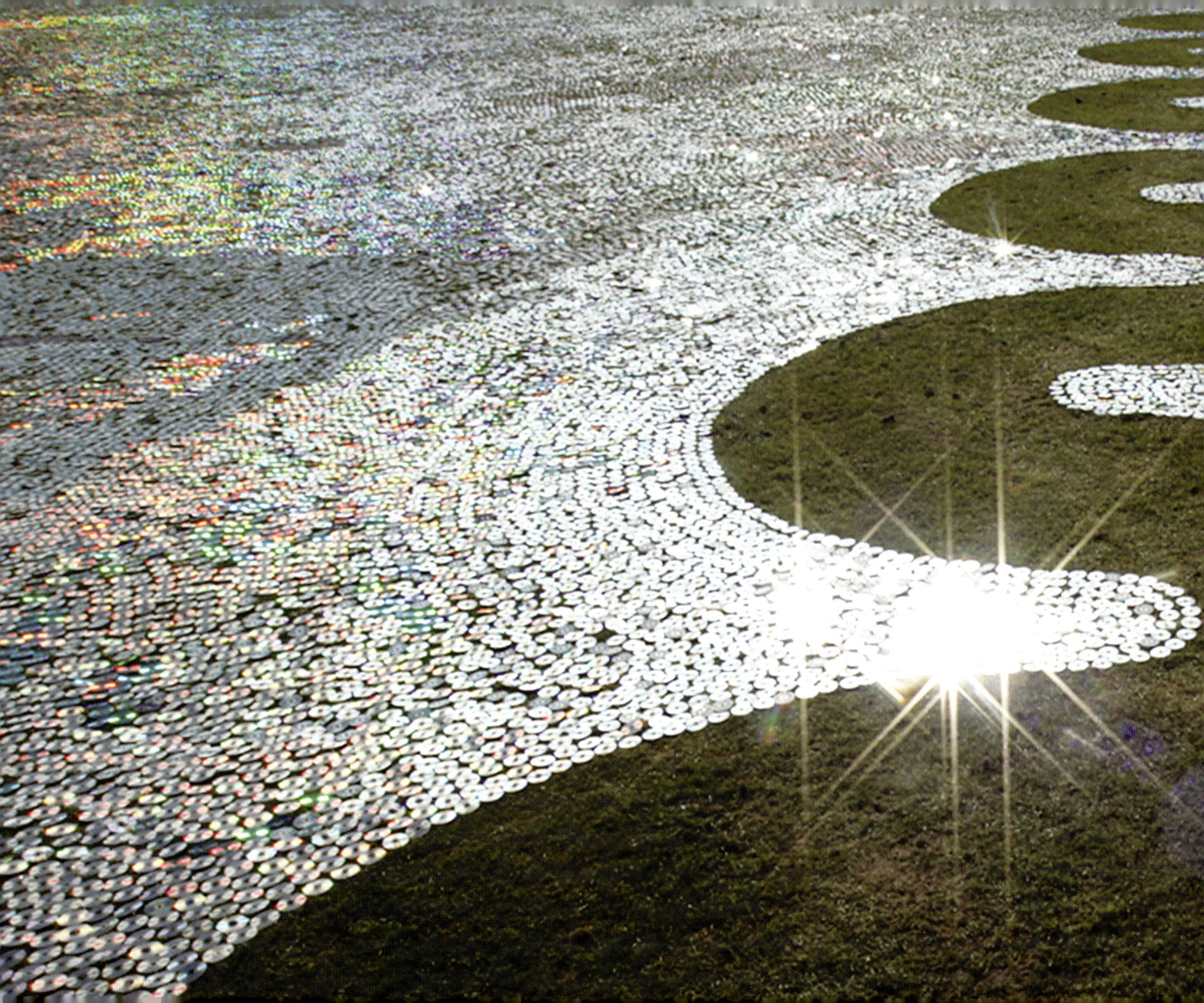

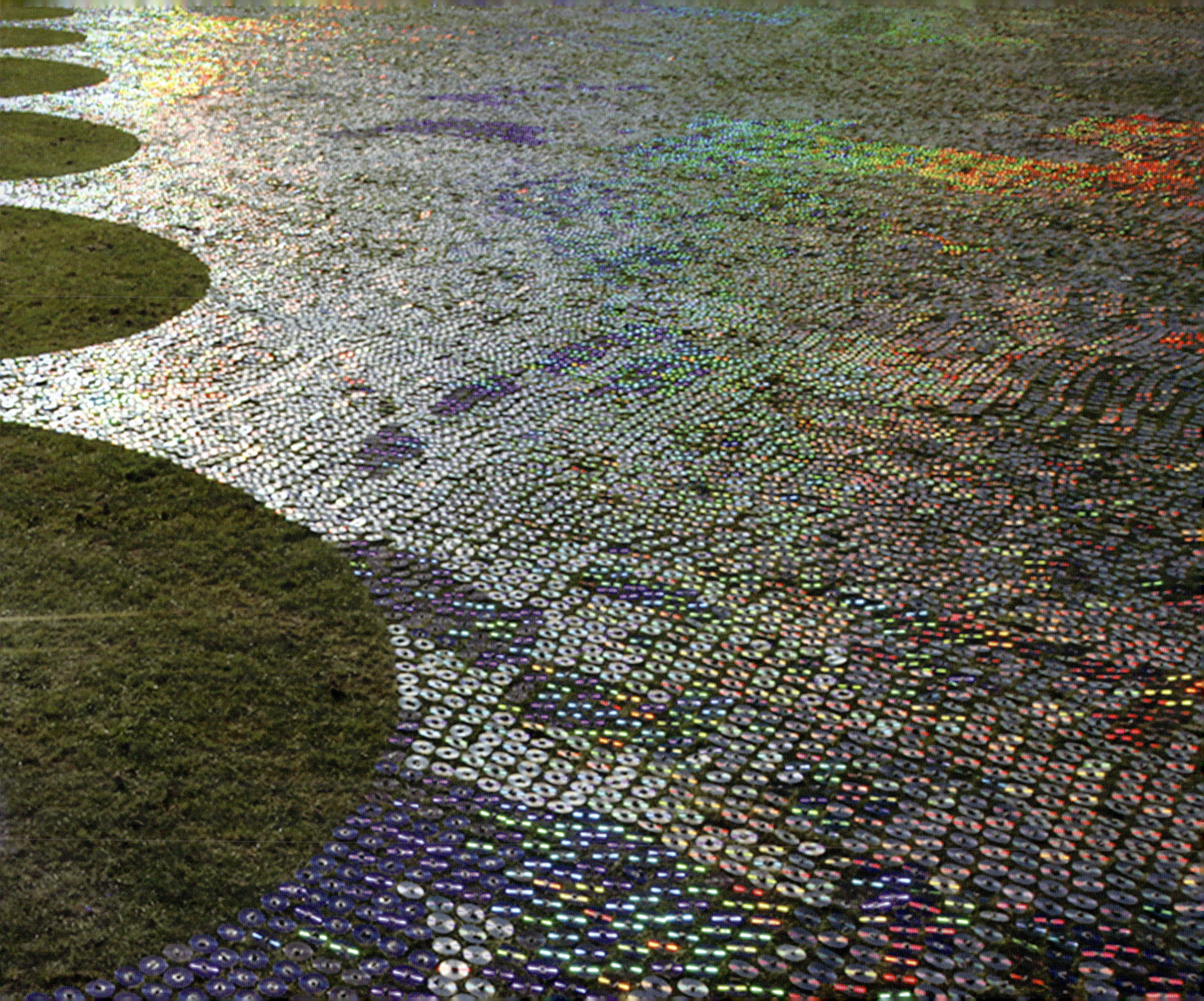

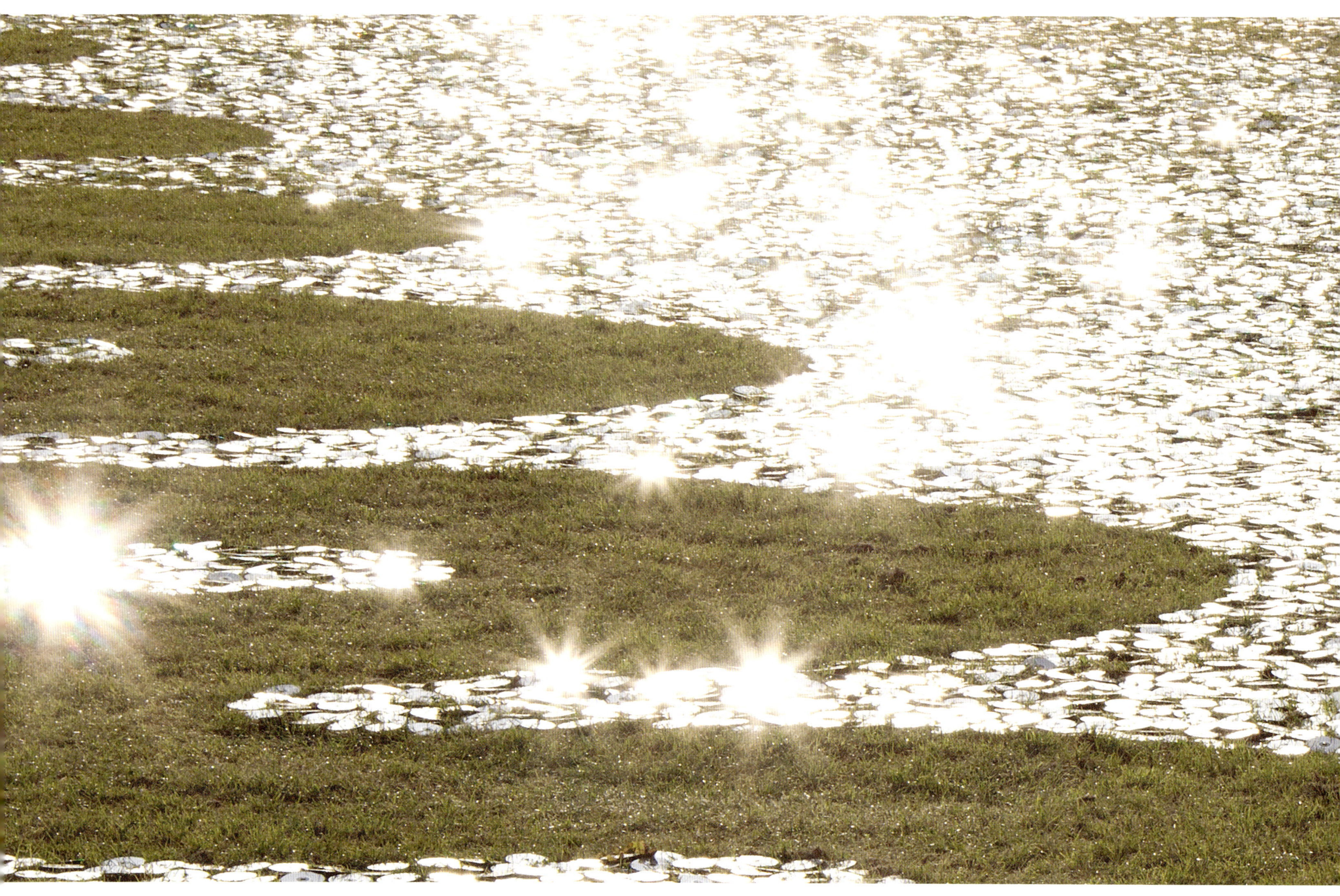

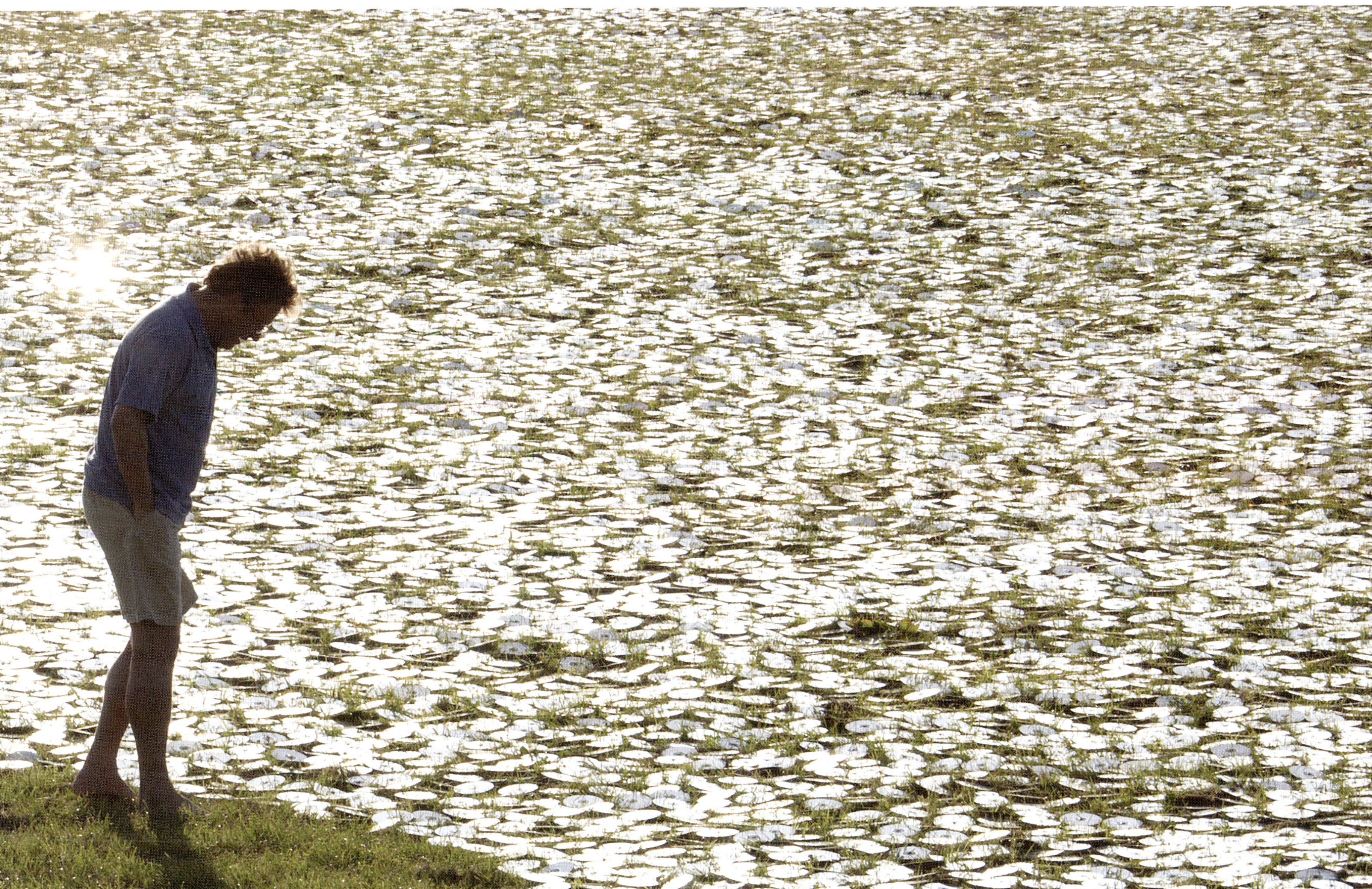

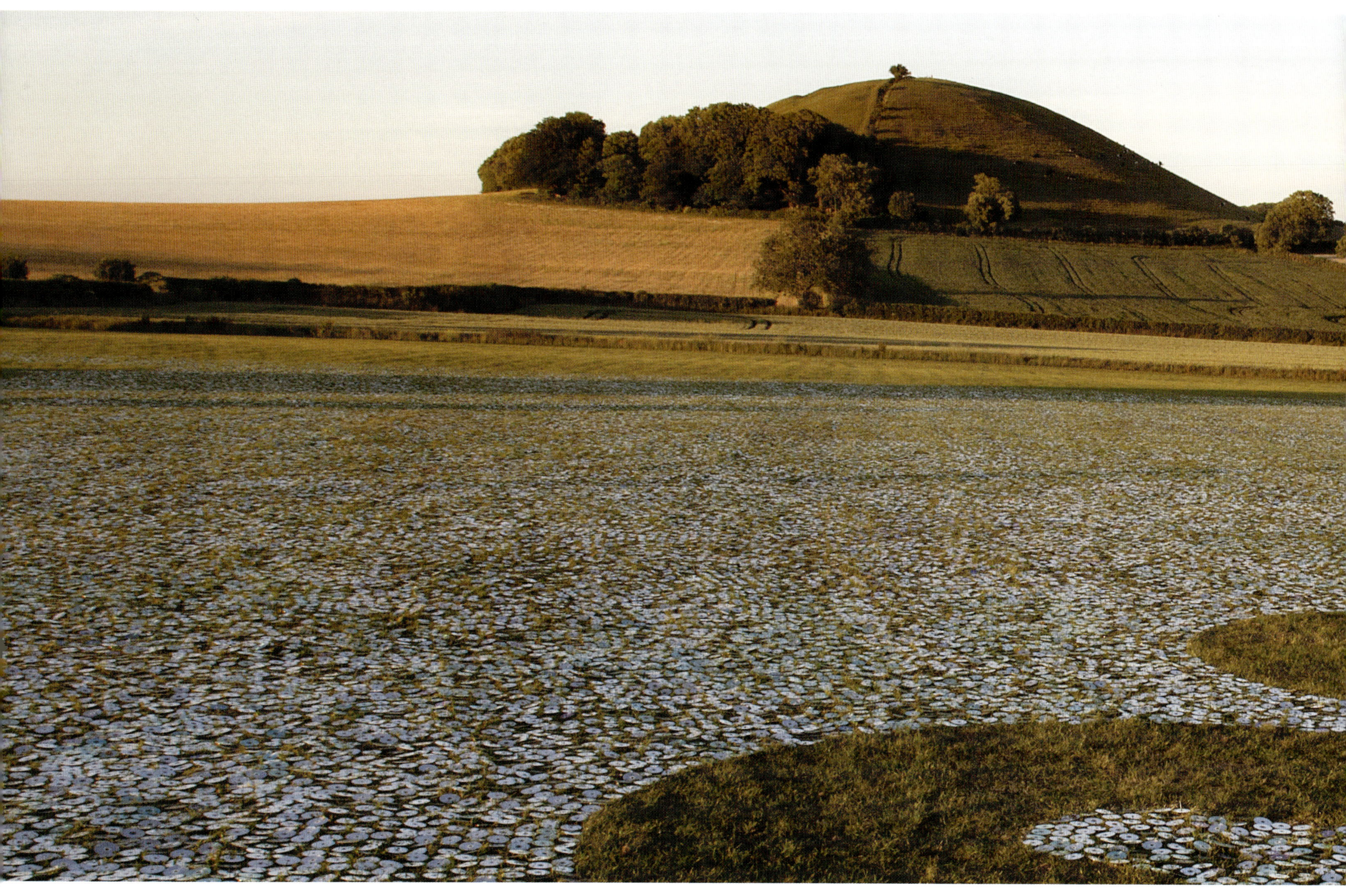

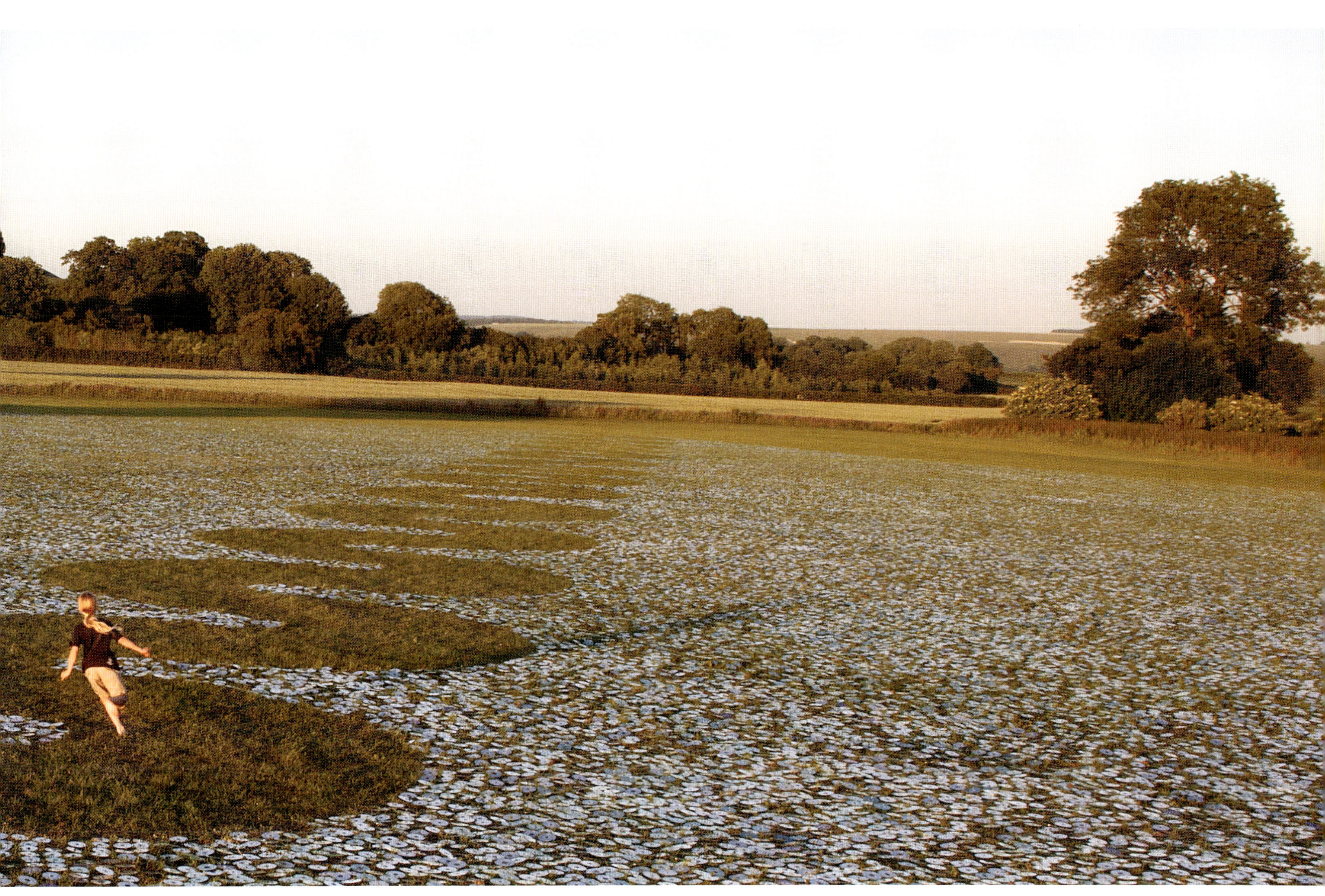

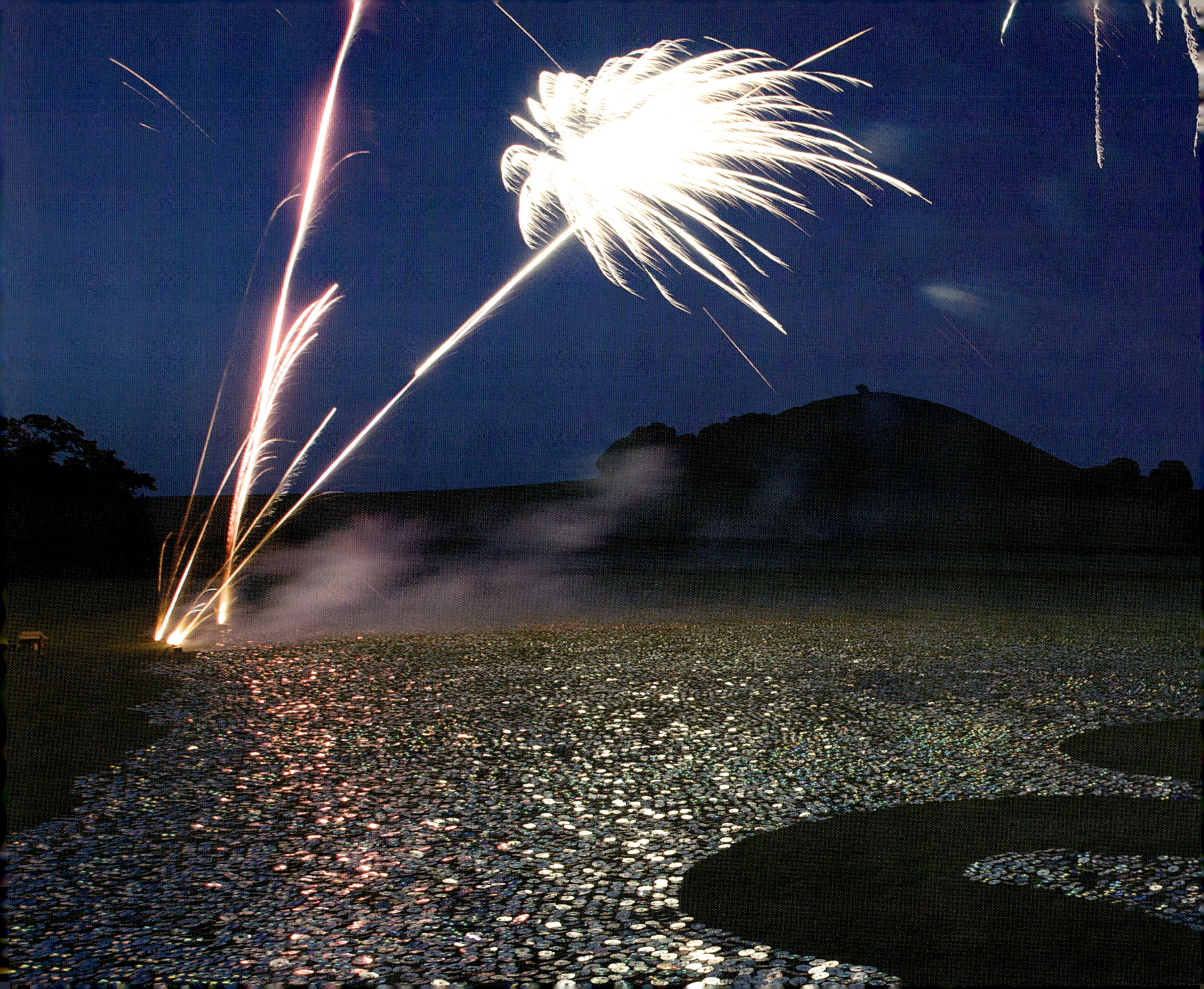

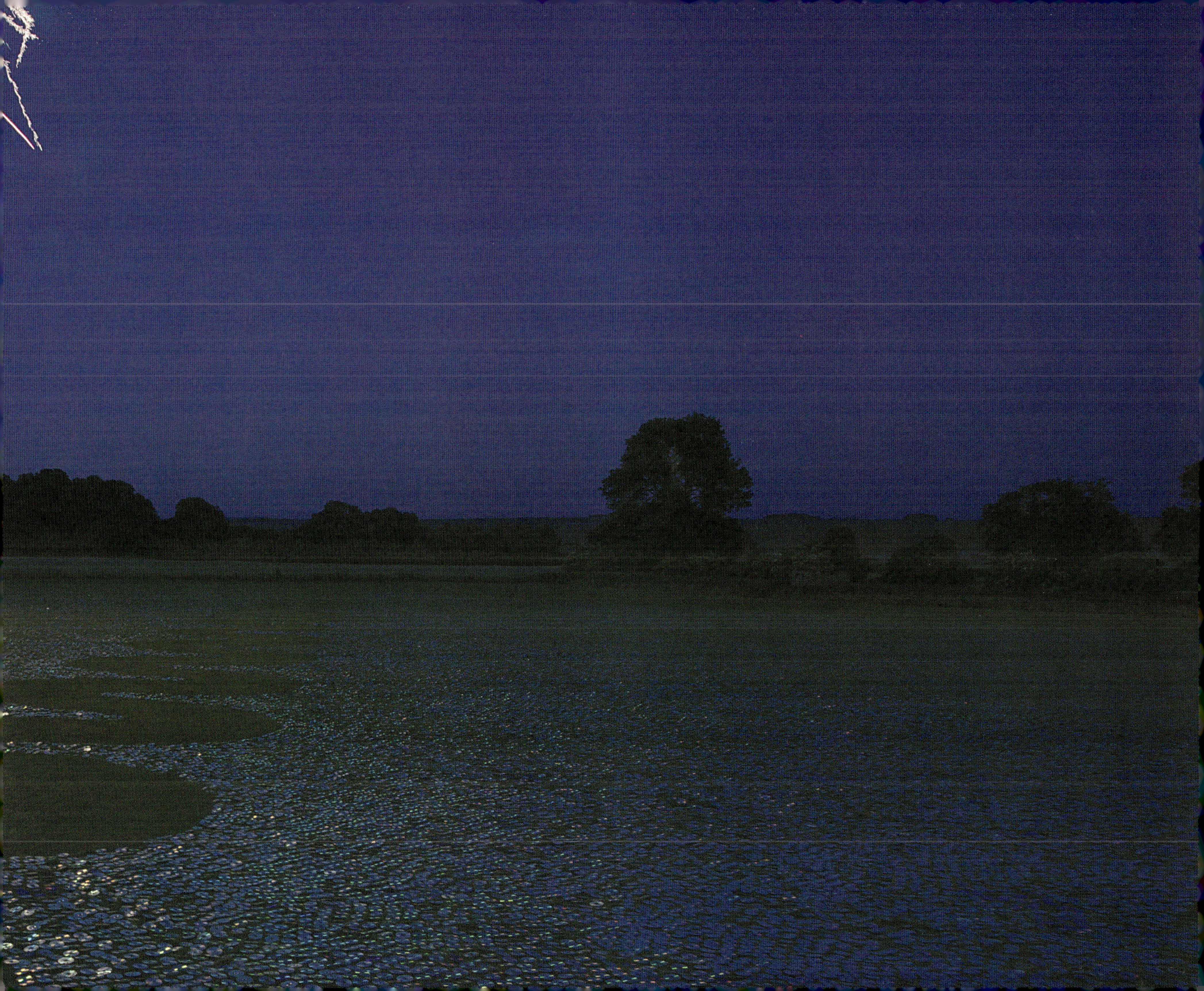

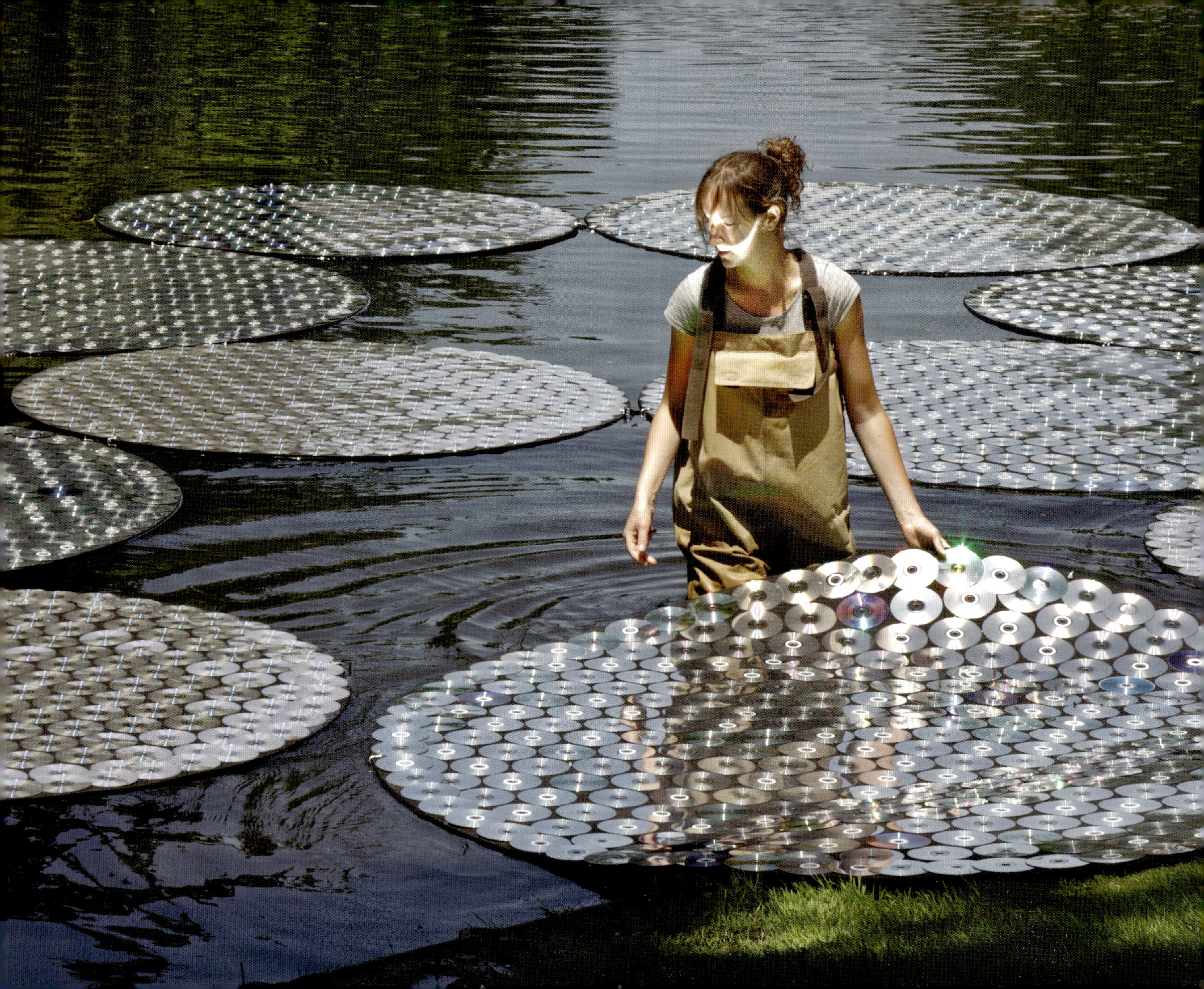

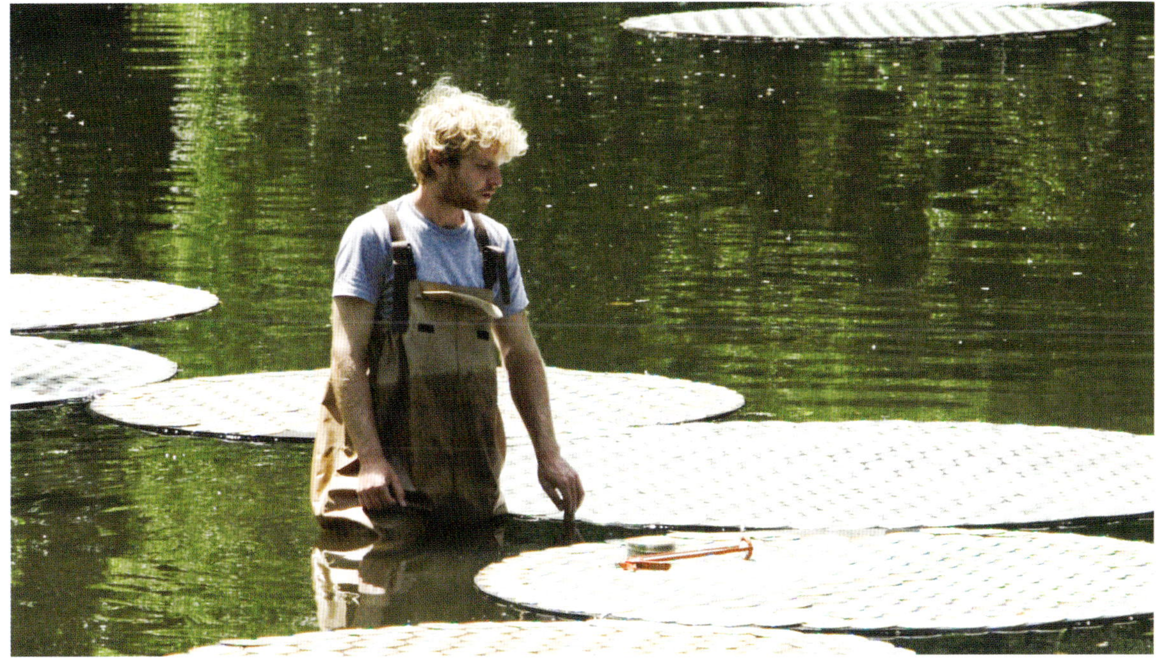

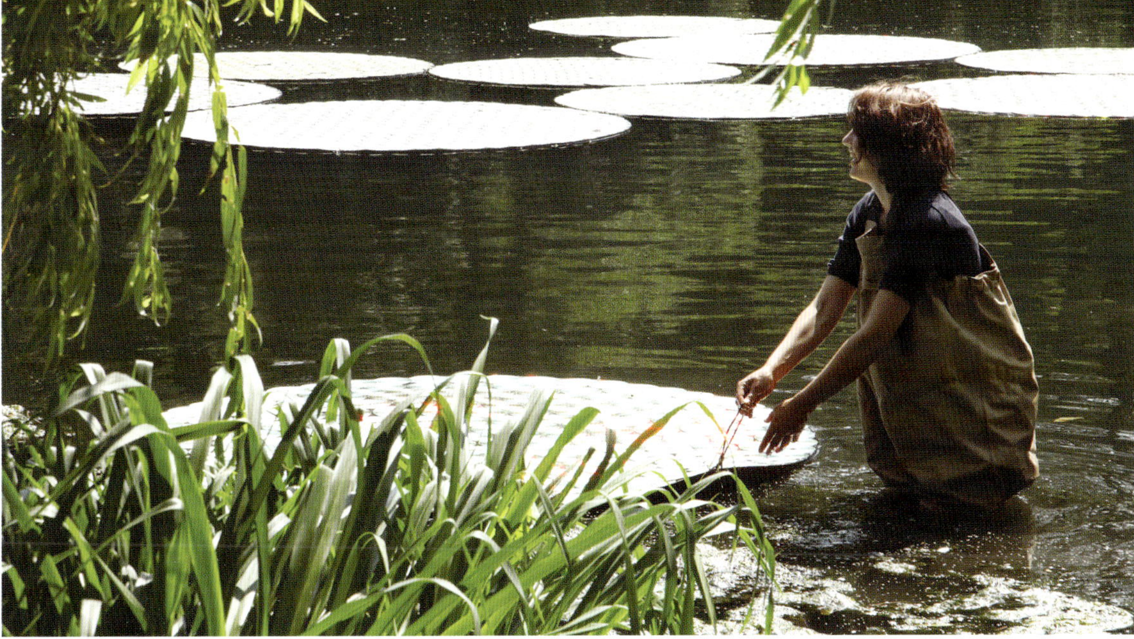

WATERLILIES

Longwood Gardens, Pennsylvania, is famous for its skillfully cultivated *Victoria amazonica* lilies. These were the catalyst behind my creation of giant water lilies made out of CDs—a material I worked with extensively in my *CDSea* installation. I also must give credit to two other inspirations. First to C. S. Lewis's book *The Voyage of the Dawn Treader*, which depicts a sea of white lilies that signifies the border between two worlds, and second to a Georgia O'Keeffe painting that shows a clear blue sky populated by abstracted clouds that receded from the bottom to the top edge of the canvas.

Pages 62–67: Waterlilies, *Longwood Gardens, Pennsylvania, USA, 2012.*

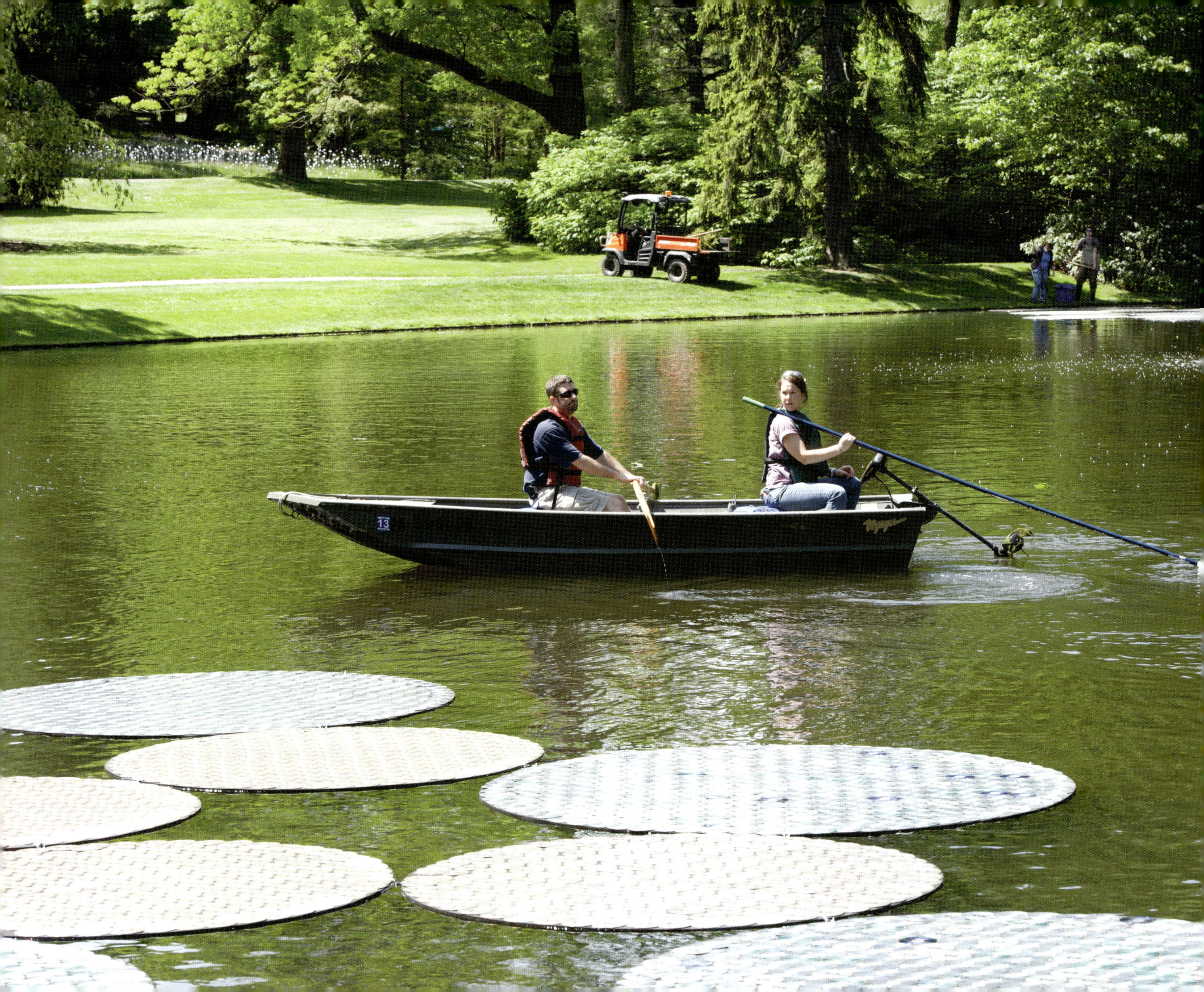
13

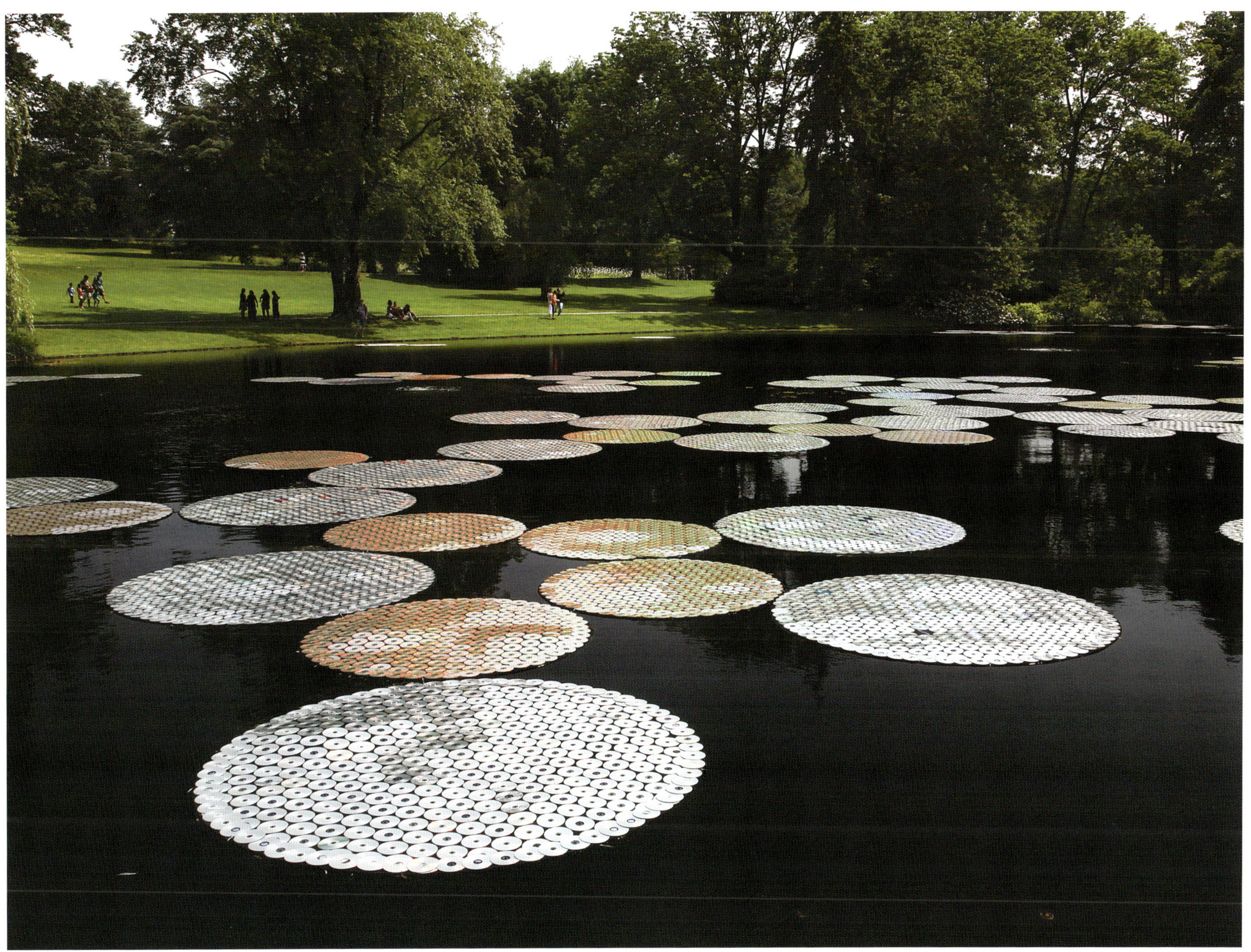

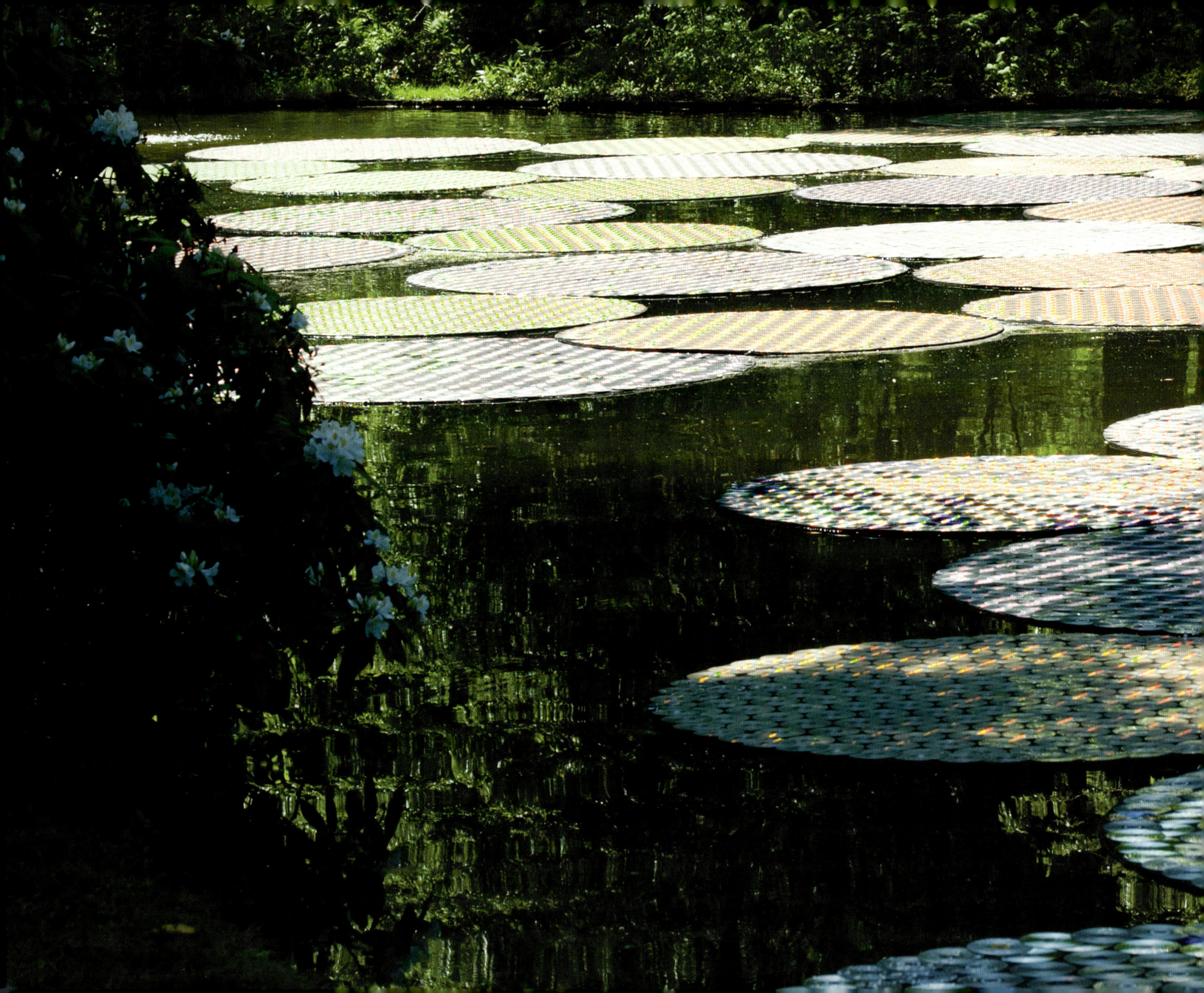

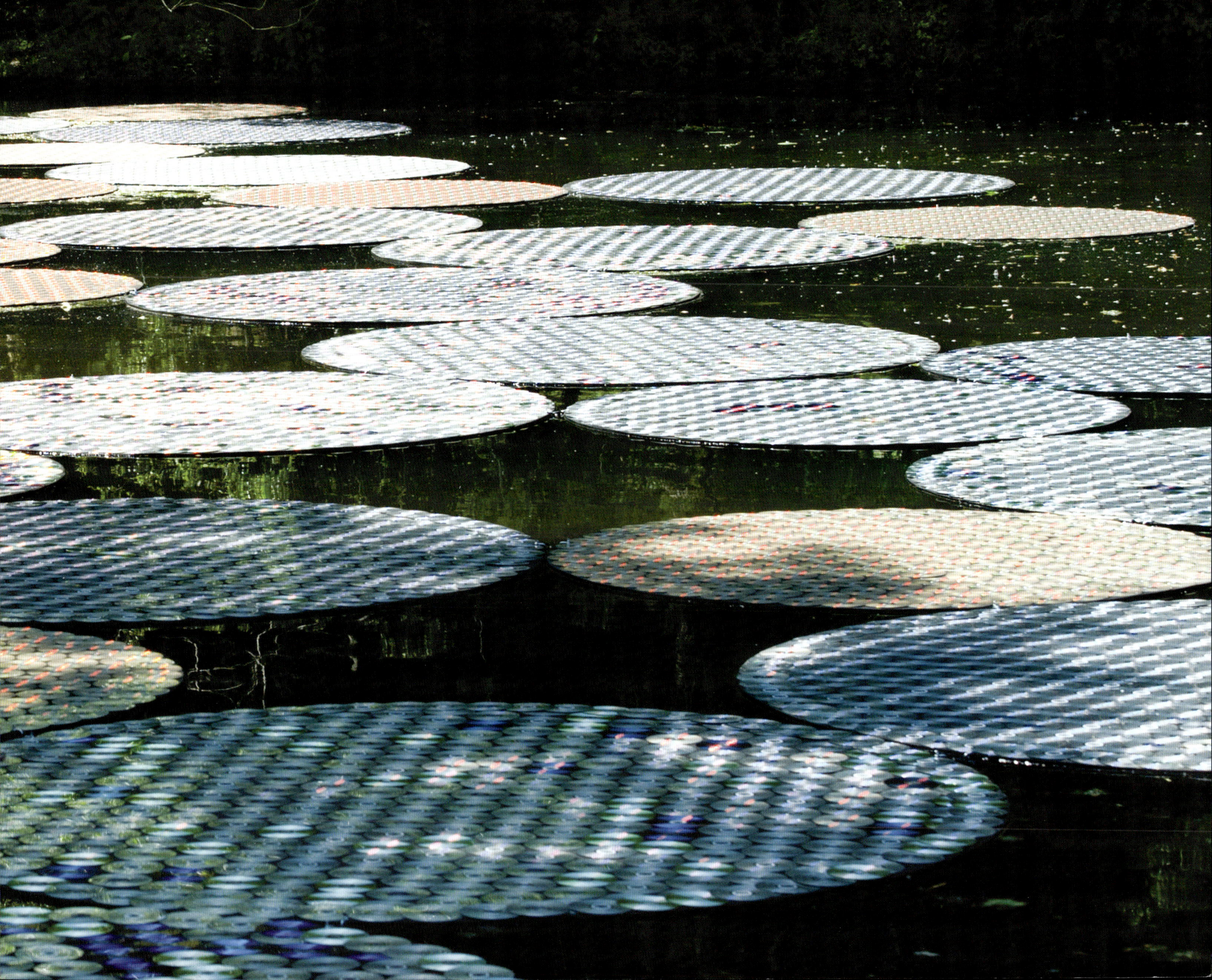

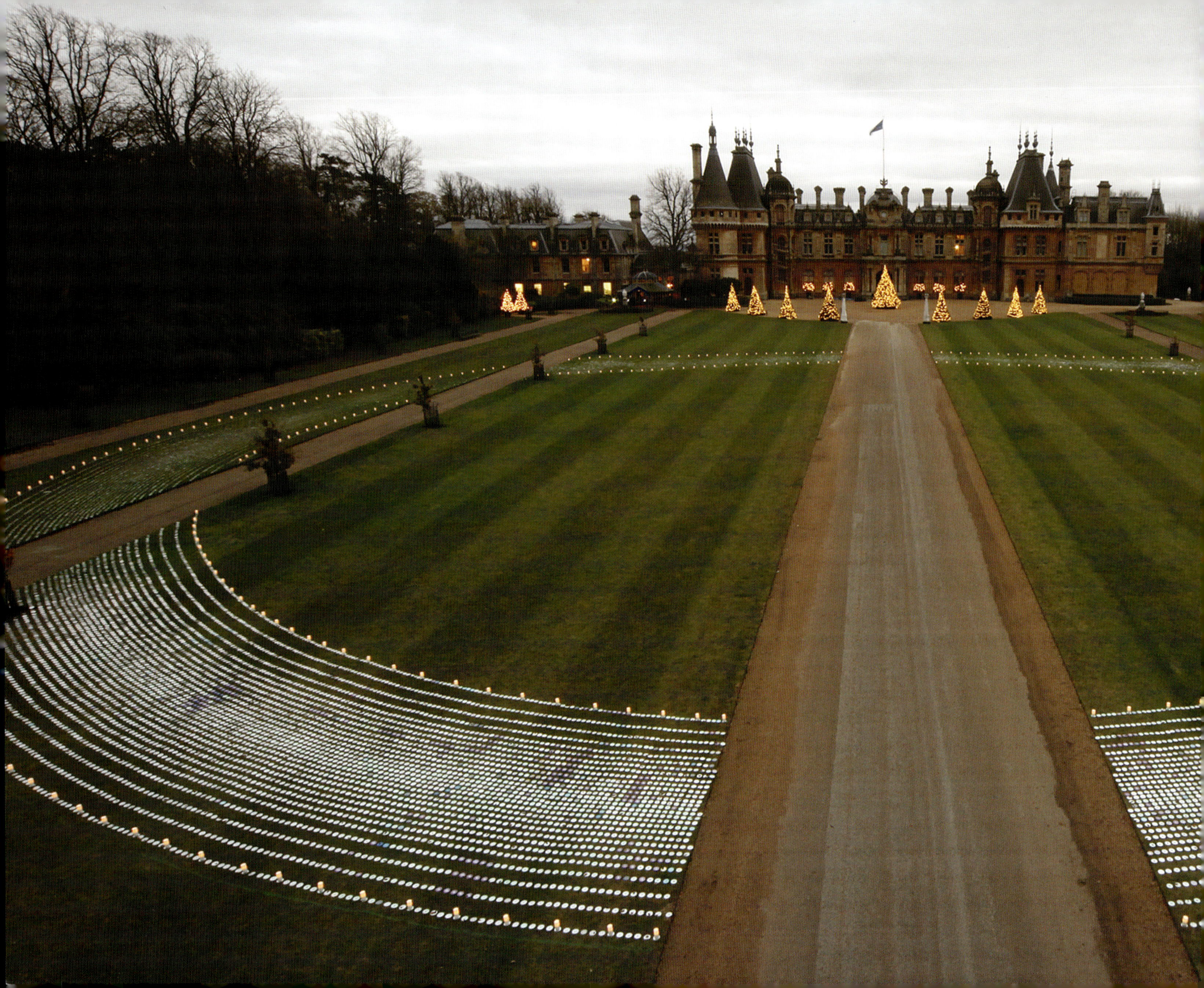

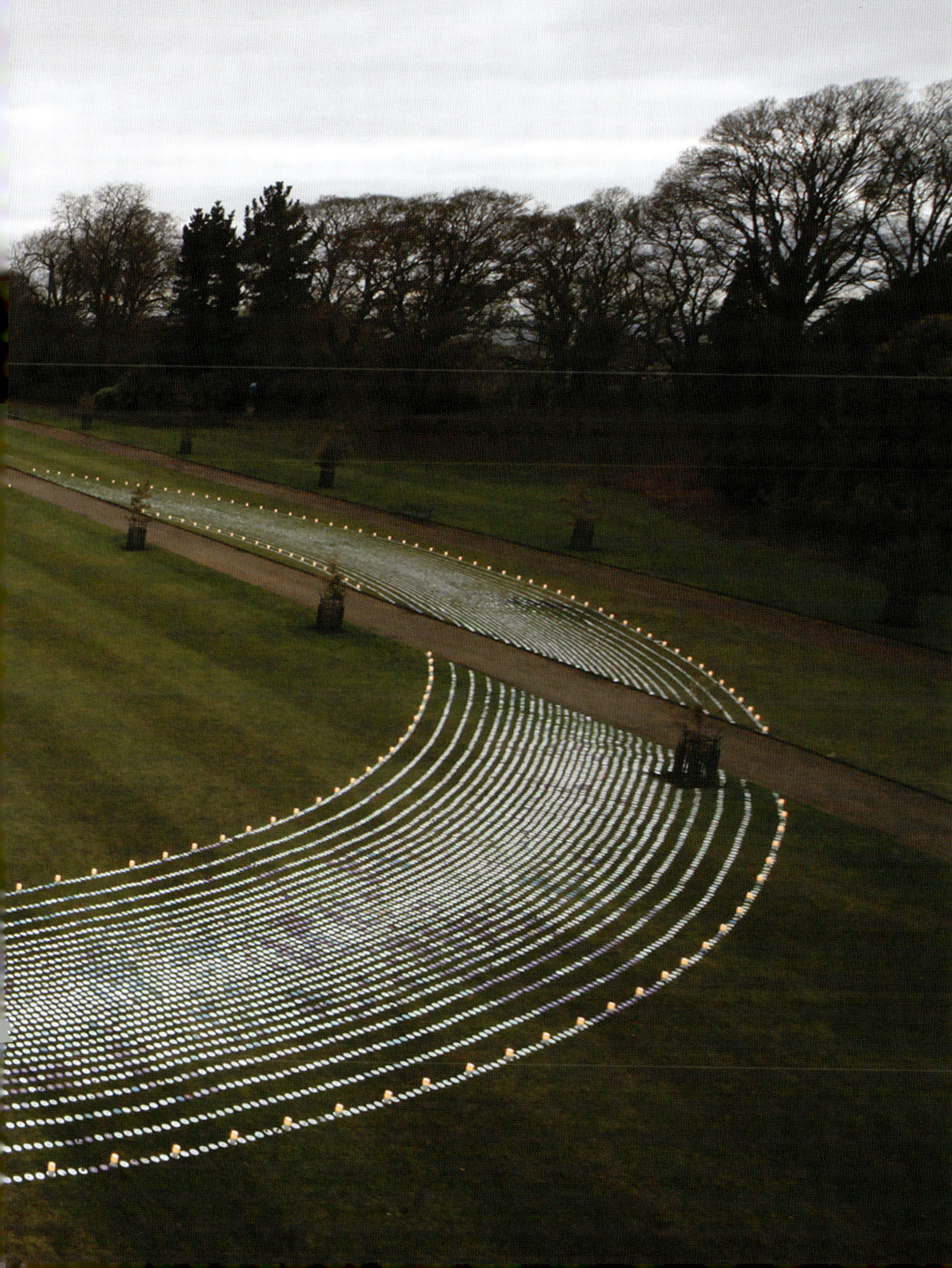

ANGEL OF LIGHT

I had just been invited to exhibit my work at Waddesdon Manor and was driving back to my studio in a euphoric mood, when I heard for the first time a number of musical compositions by the Finnish composer Einojuhani Rautavaara on the radio. His music captured my imagination, especially the seventh symphony, *Angel of Light*. In a matter of days, I had listened to it a dozen times, maybe more; and gradually a visual narrative had unfolded. Rautavaara's composition inspired a halo of light, a huge soft-edged illumination shining towards the heavens.

The North Avenue lawns in front of Waddesdon Manor were made for this installation. I created, with the help of others, an enormous halo of iridescent light from 50,000 CDs, depicted at night by 400 flickering LED candle luminaires.

Angel of Light, *Waddesdon Manor, Buckinghamshire, UK, 2012.*

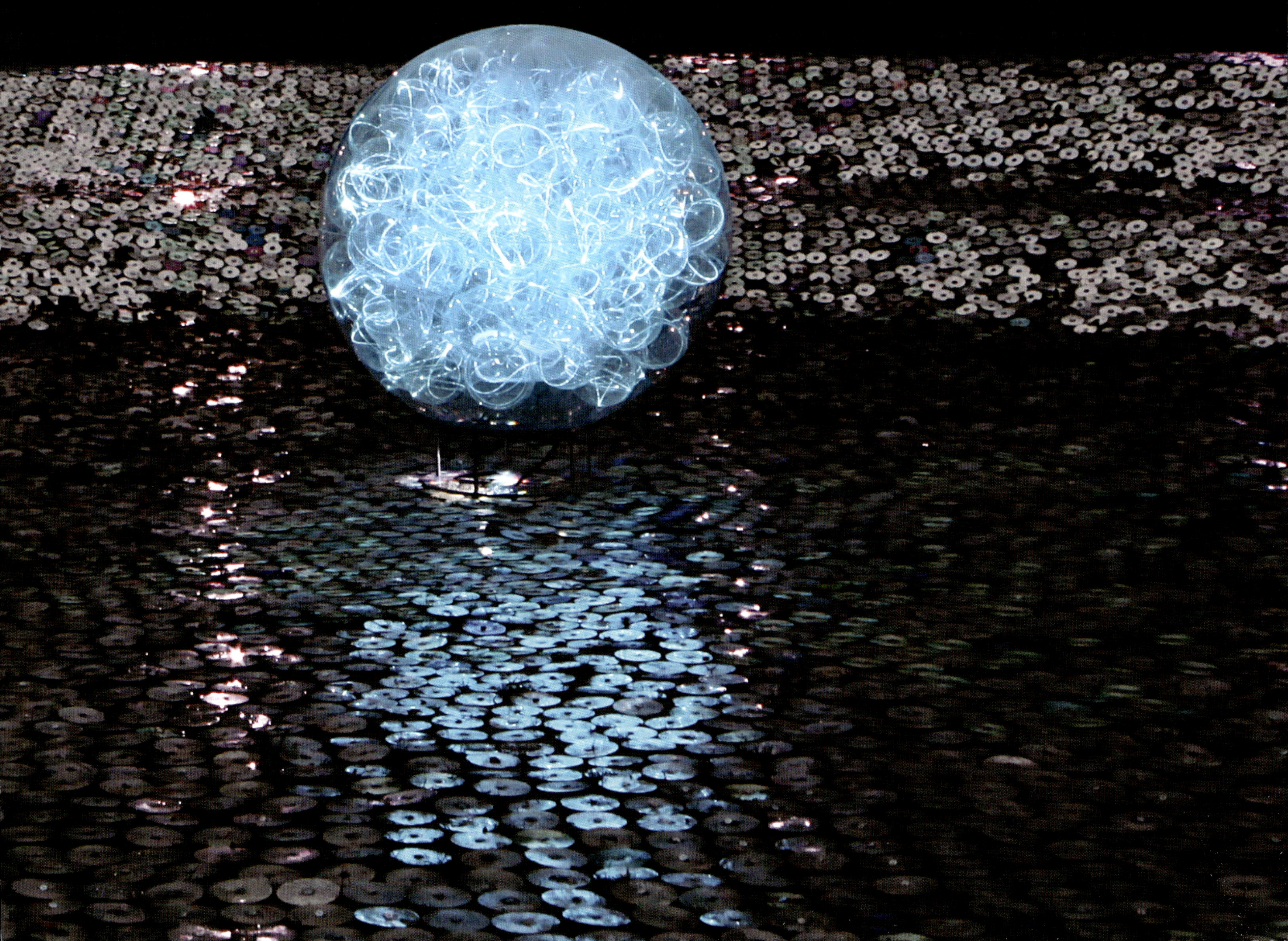

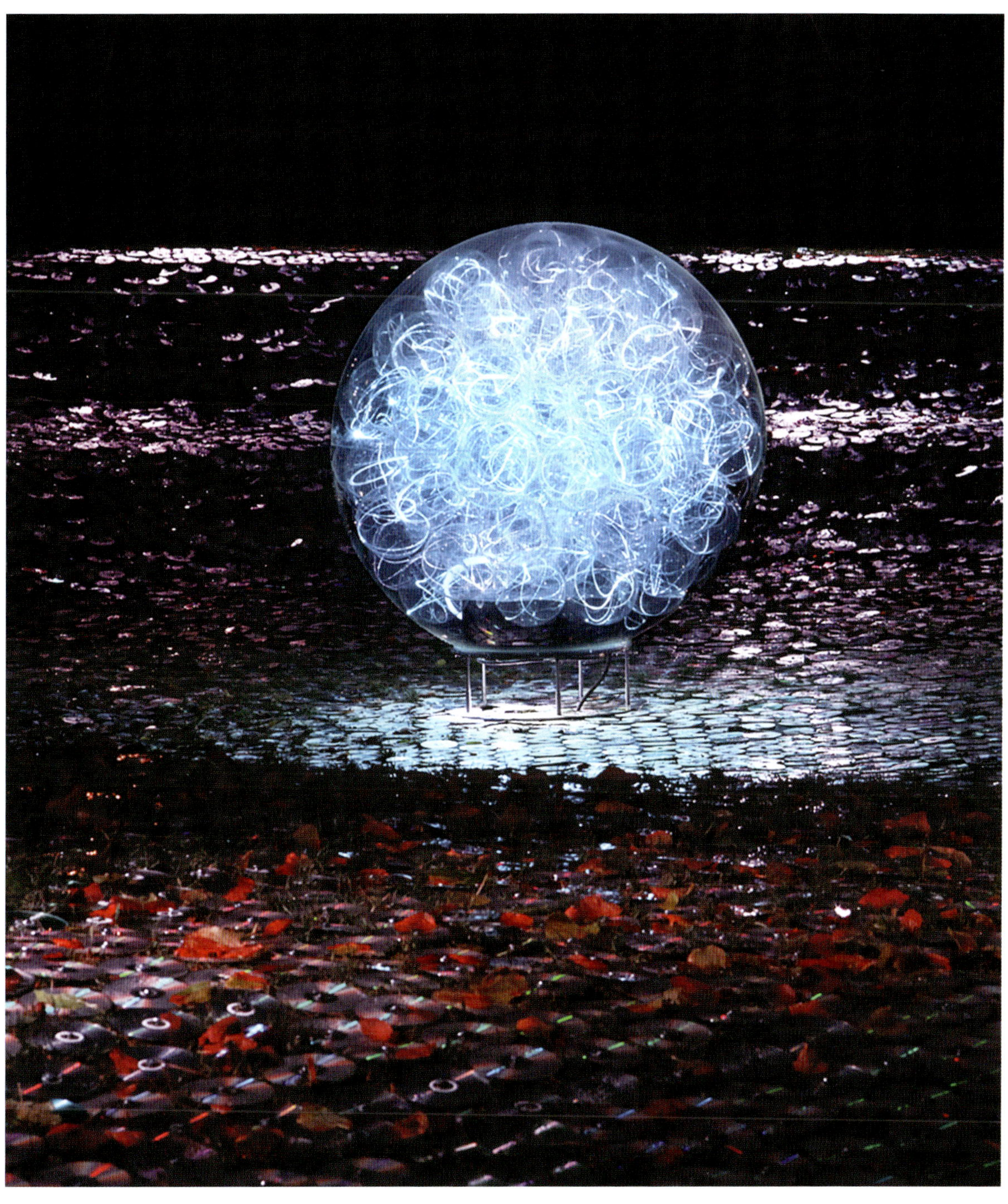

BLUE MOON ON A PLATTER

During a visit to Waddesdon Manor, I had an instinctive reaction to the sculpted lawns adjacent to the summer house. It is an intimate space, surrounded by tall trees. For some reason the landscaped lawns of the amphitheatre brought to mind a huge platter: a silver platter. Past experience has taught me that the humble CD would be an excellent material to create this effect. What was missing was a focal point; and I decided to position a large illuminated sphere to take centre stage, a moon for the silver platter: a huge icy blue one shimmering like arctic coal. Hopefully, like in the song, this moon will turn to gold, and romance will flourish at the Manor! The platter was created from about 50,000 CDs pinned to the undulating lawn. The moon glows with shades of blue light, moved through the interior of the sphere in a gentle, rhythmic pulse.

Blue Moon on a Platter, *Waddesdon Manor, Buckinghamshire, UK, 2012.*

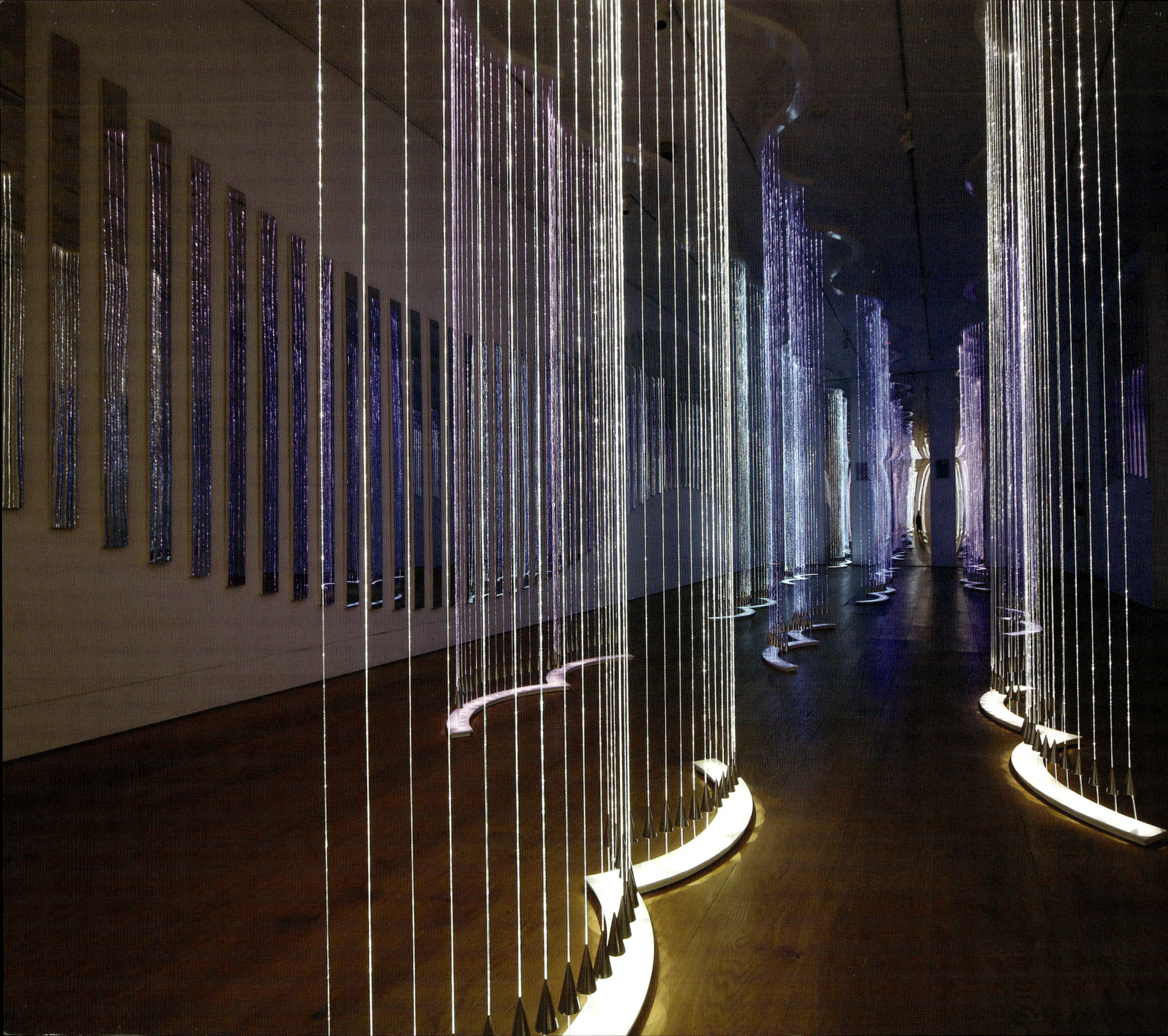

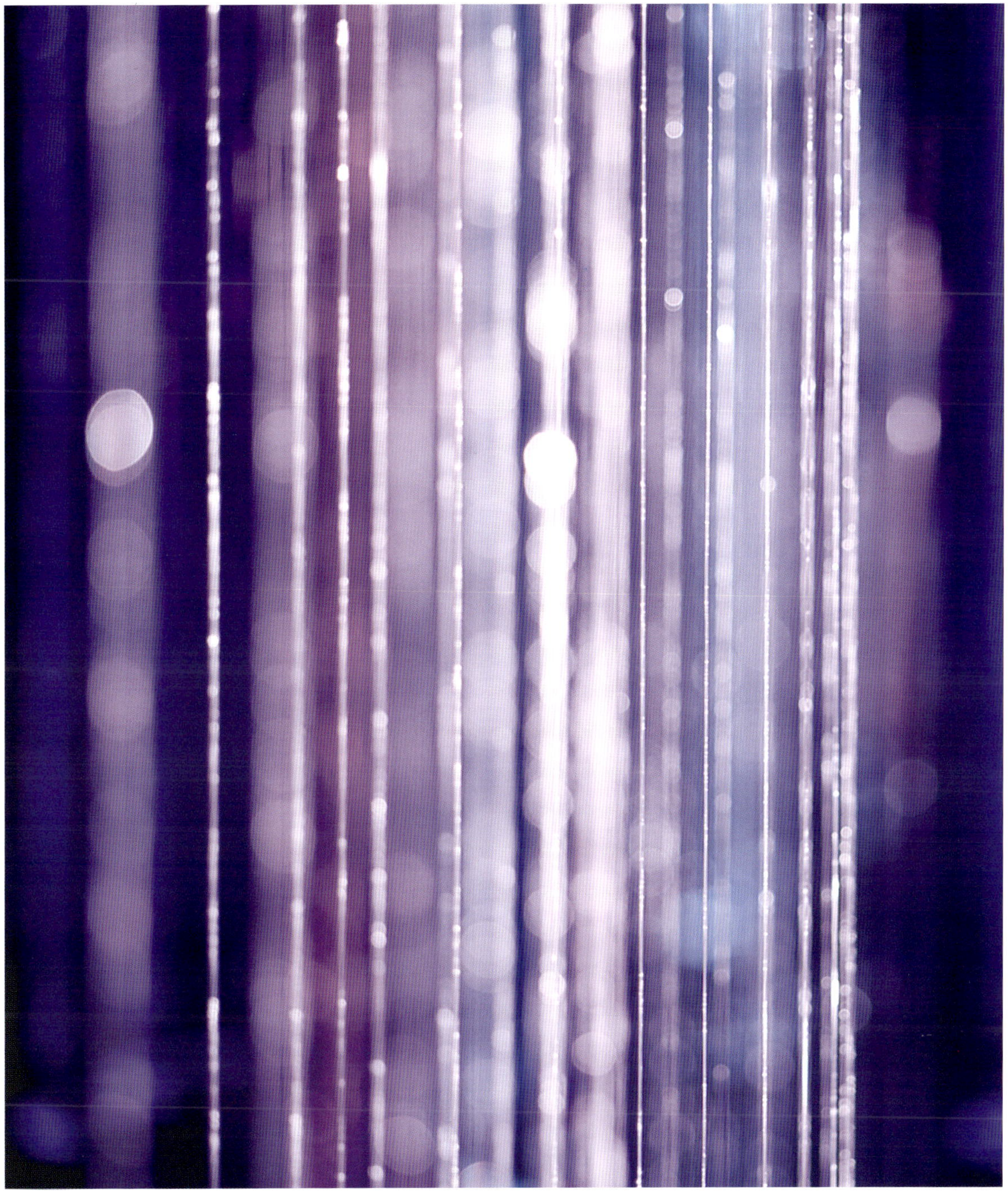

CANTUS ARCTICUS

As with *Angel of Light,* the inspiration for this piece came from the music of Finnish composer Einojuhani Rautavaara. After the chance hearing of his music on BBC Radio 3, I listened over and again to his concerto *Cantus Arcticus*.

I feel that Rautavaara's compostion is a holistic interpretation of the beauty and wonder of life itself, in this instance, the lives of humans

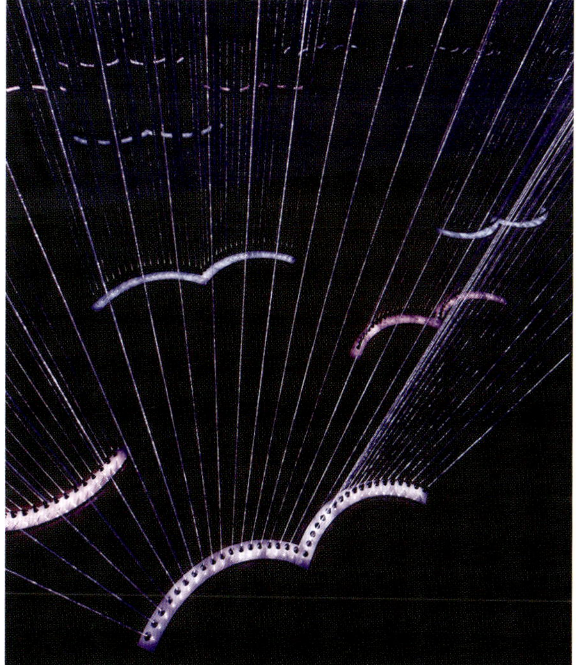

Pages 72–75: Cantus Arcticus, *Waddesdon Manor, Buckinghamshire, UK, 2013.*

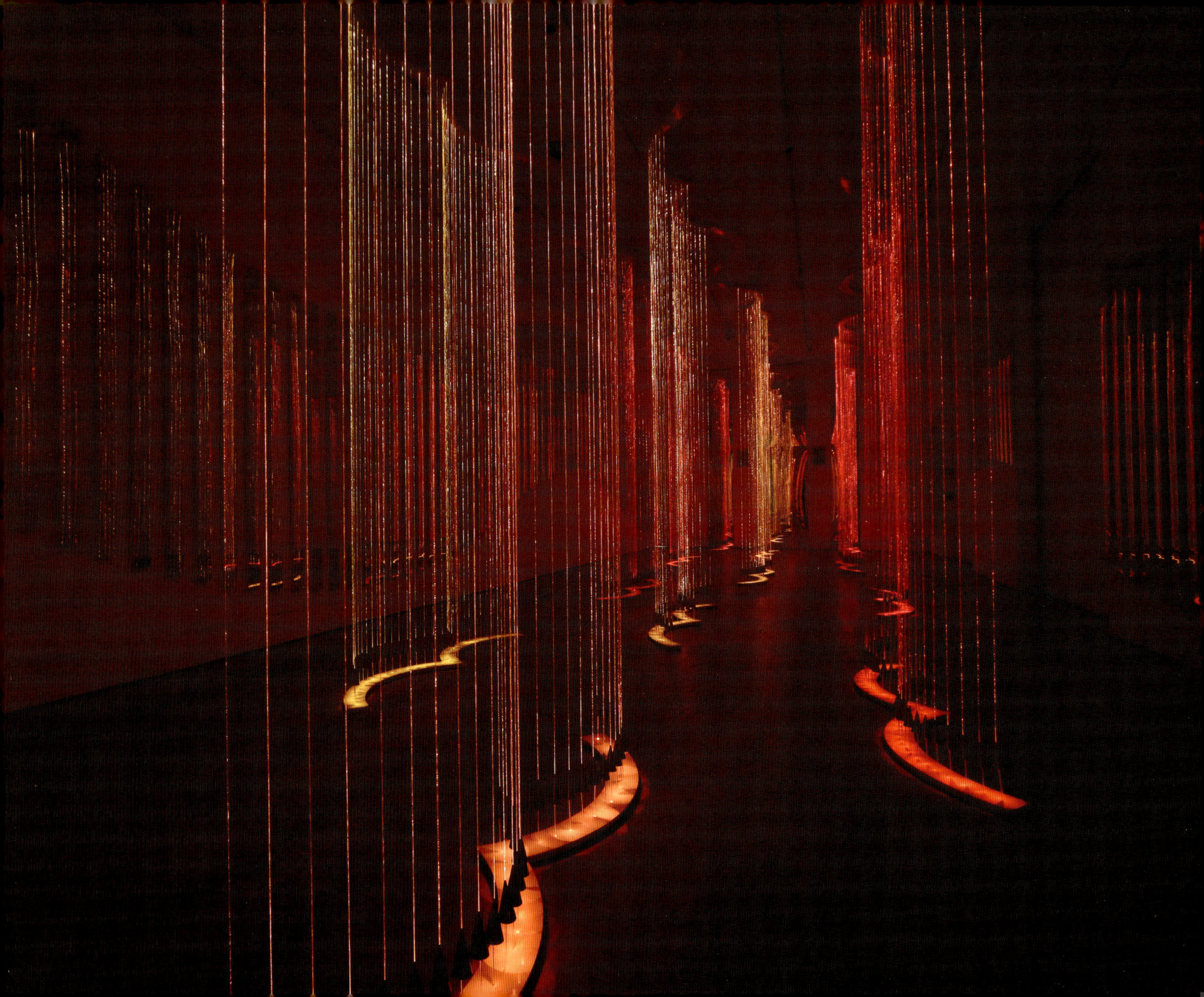

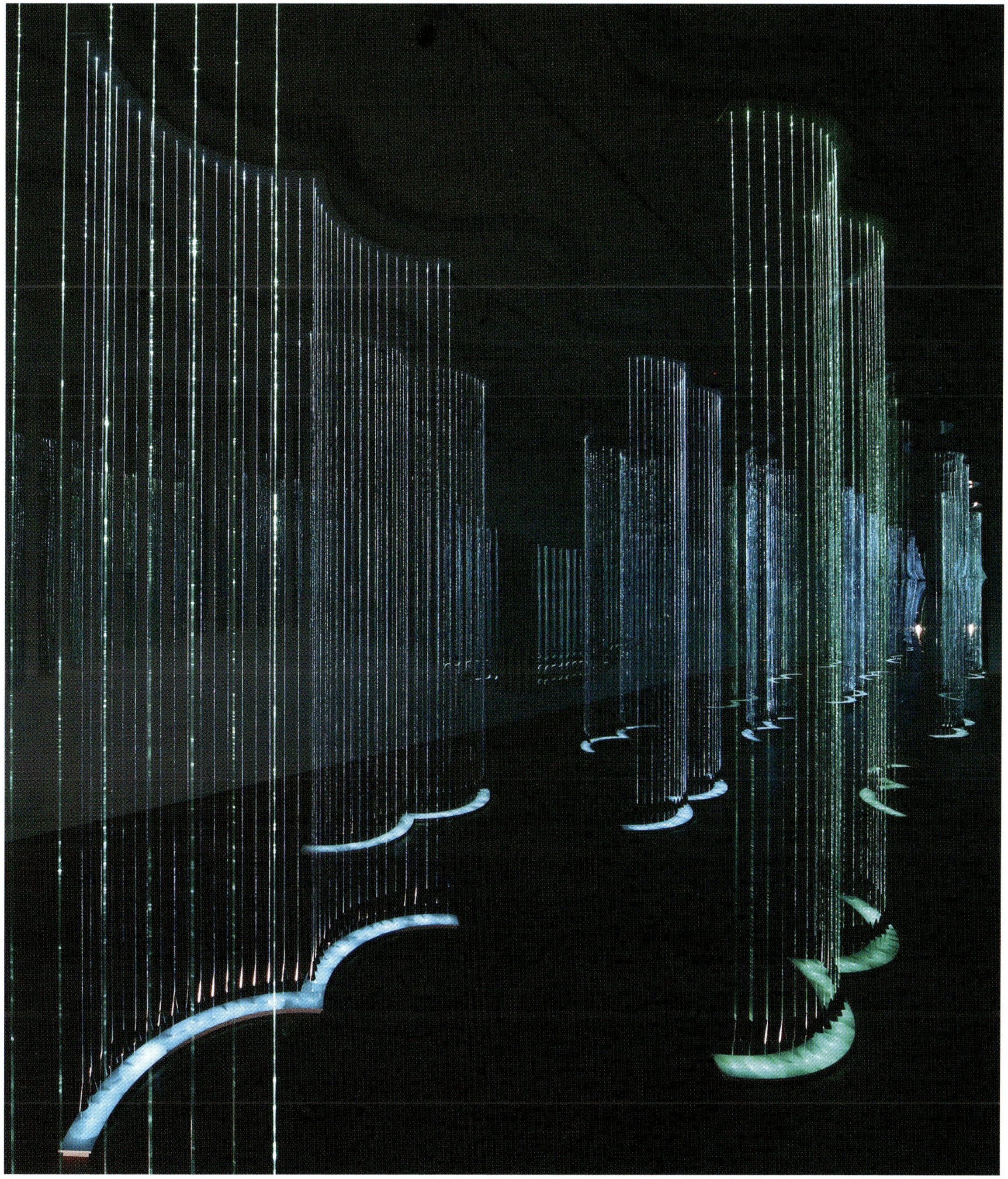

and birds. The sounds of Arctic birdsong interwoven with Rautavaara's orchestral score created a visual soundscape, which crytallised in my mind as shimmering curtains of light suggesting the Aurora Borealis interspersed with the silhouettes of circling birds. For me, the first part of the concerto describes the human being as the observer. The latter part is about man's endeavour to describe the ephemeral experience and the simple truth that everything is connected.

Truly, Rautavaara has both preserved and captured the whole experience with his music. It is my hope that I have added to his genius with the addition of this light interpretation.

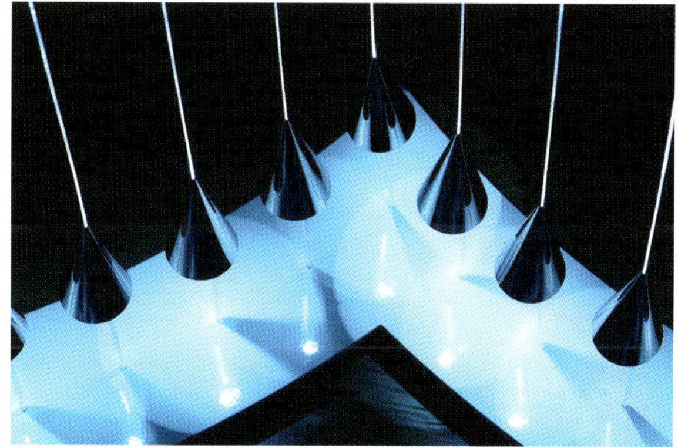

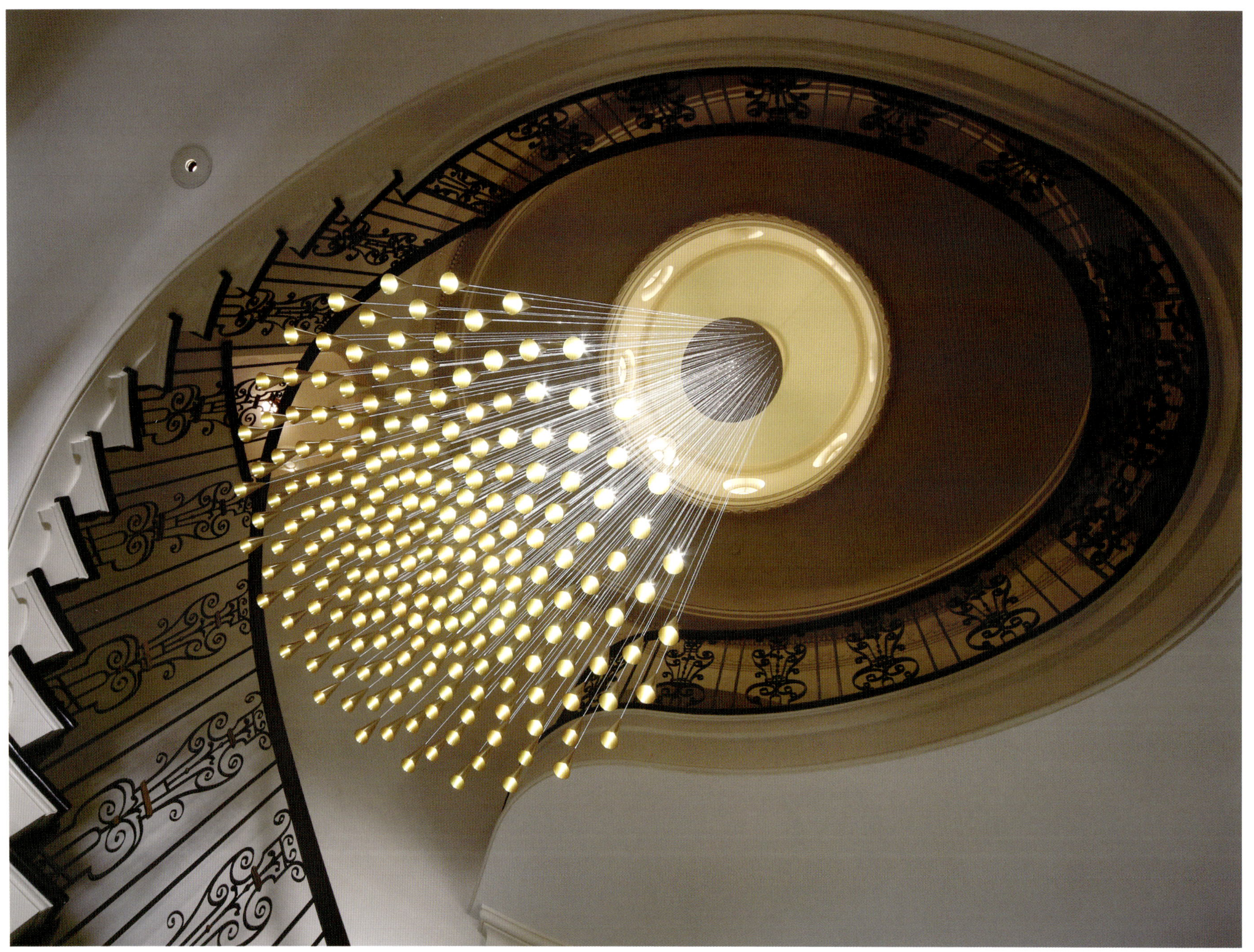

Above and opposite: Bell Chandelier, *Cheekwood Botanical Garden and Museum of Art, Tennessee, USA, 2013.*

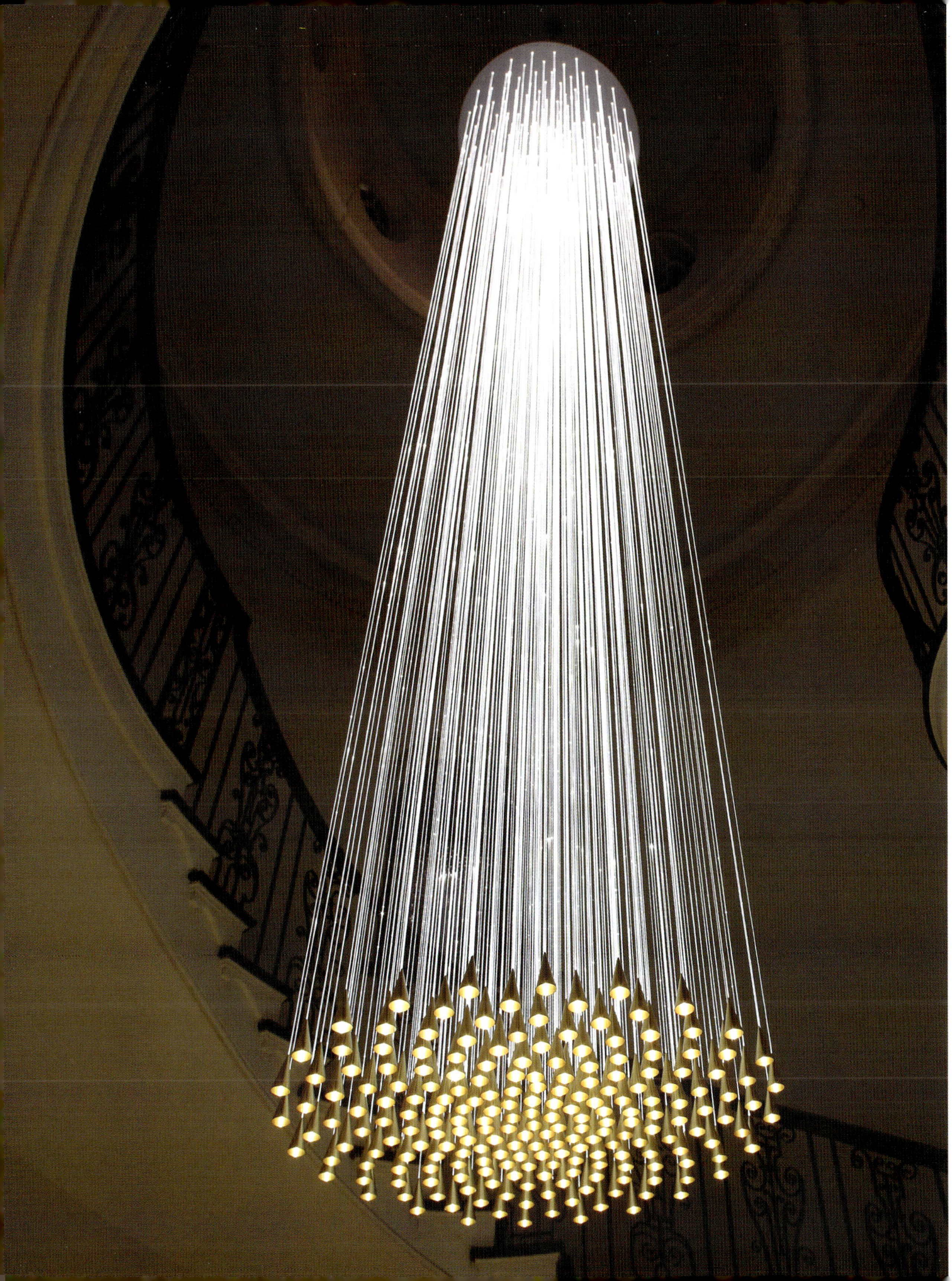

BELL CHANDELIER

Bell Chandelier is my response to the amazing space created by the spiral of the Queen Charlotte staircase and rotunda in the mansion at Cheekwood. The use of brass refers to the details of the period furniture and luminaires within the main stairwell. I wanted to make the most of the height and create a piece that linked all the elements of the space together. A favourite anachronism from my youth is KISS, Keep It Simple Stupid; consequently, the form is minimal and it works!

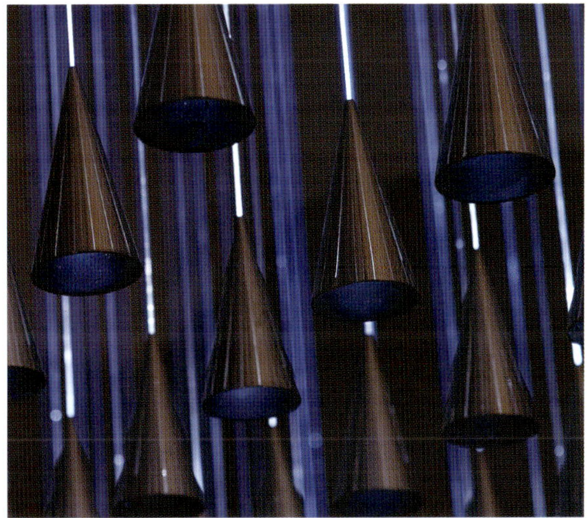

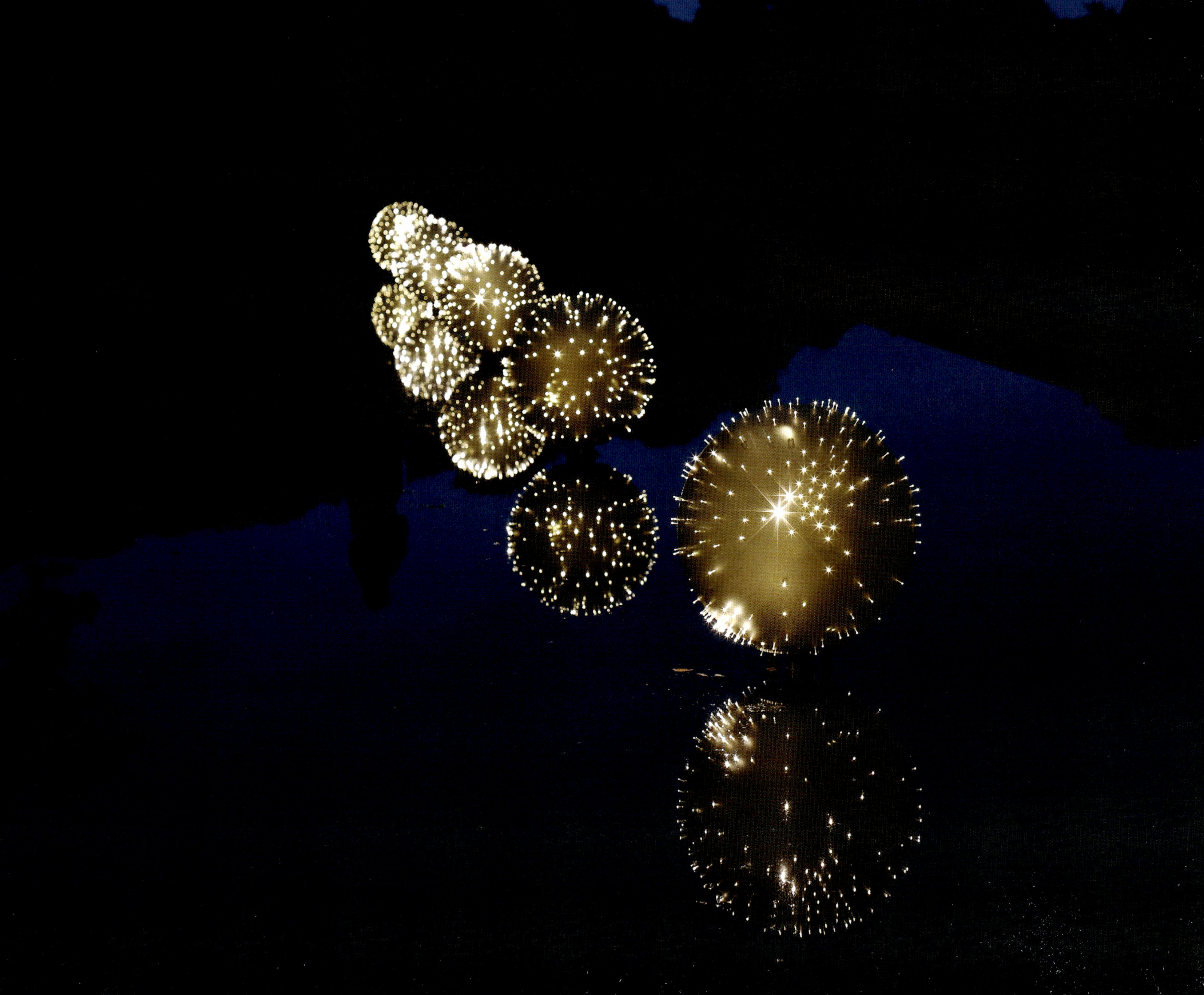

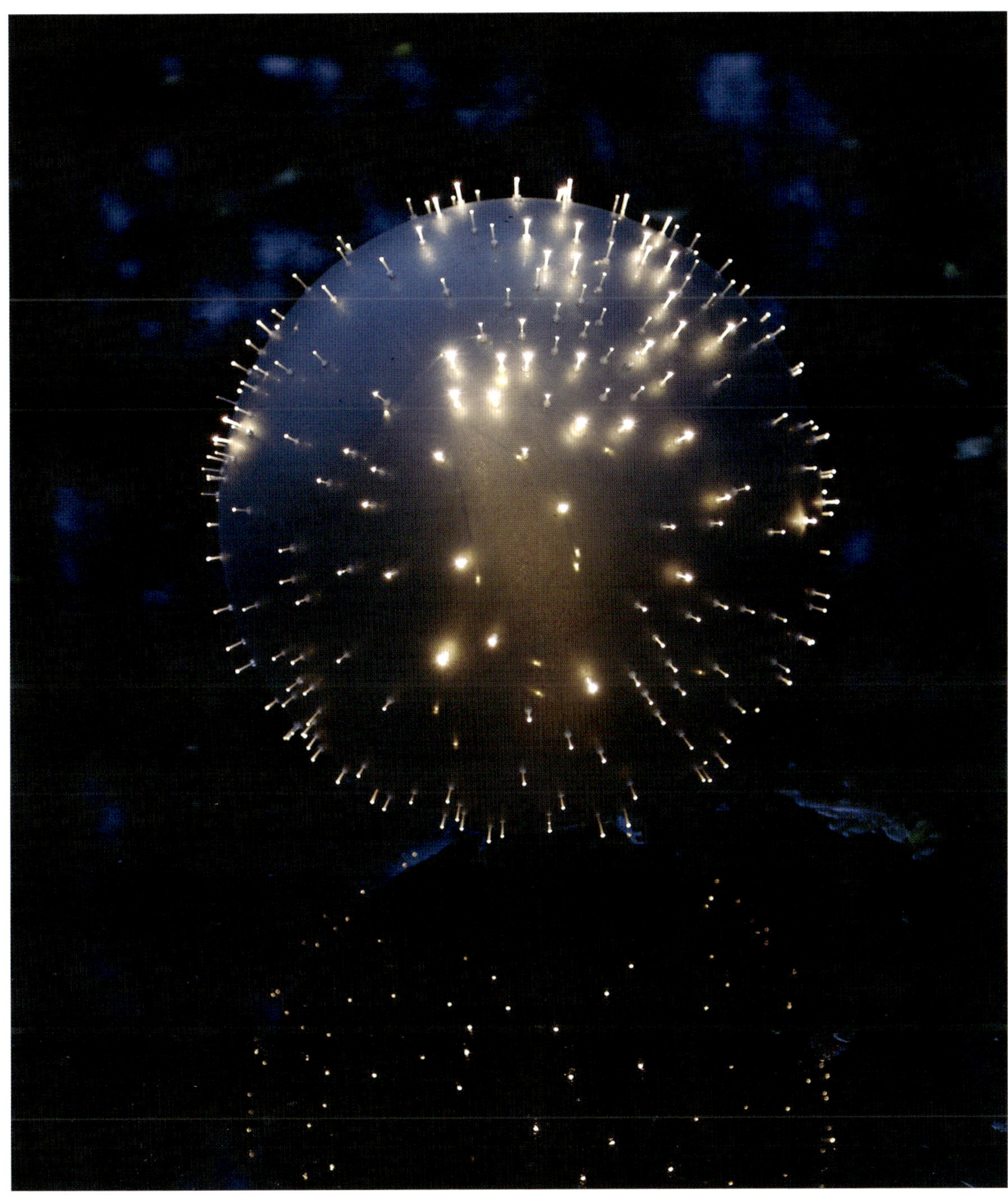

FAGIN'S URCHINS

Fagin's Urchins was created specifically for the formal Reflection Pool in the Martin Boxwood Gardens at Cheekwood. As often happens when I see a space, I had a very clear idea of what I wanted to create. The placing of the illuminated spheres close to the waterline creates the illusion of ten Lilliputian worlds at night. The name for this installation comes from my reading of *Oliver Twist* by Charles Dickens.

Opposite, above, and pages 80–81: Fagin's Urchins, *Cheekwood Botanical Garden and Museum of Art, Tennessee, USA, 2013.*

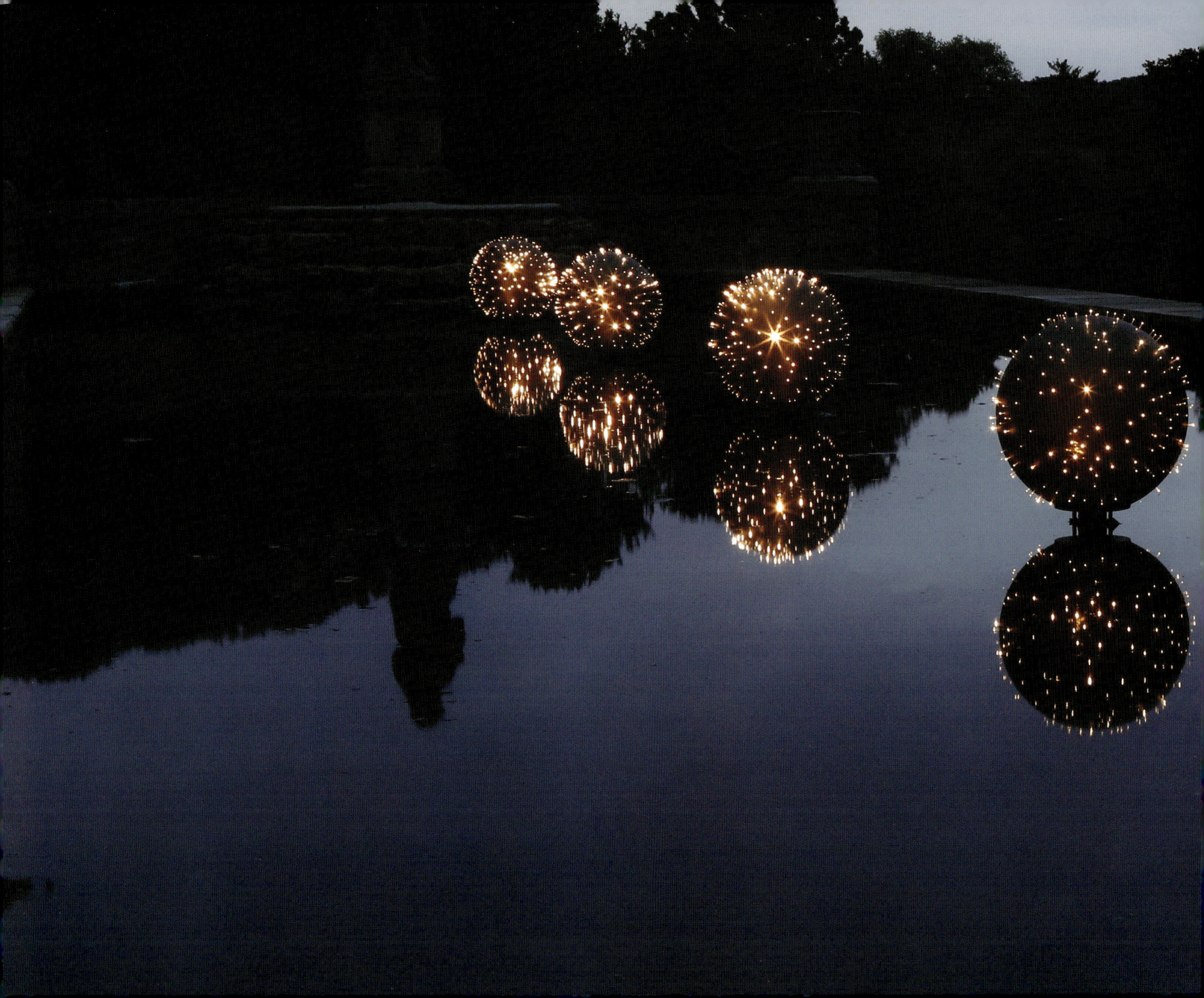

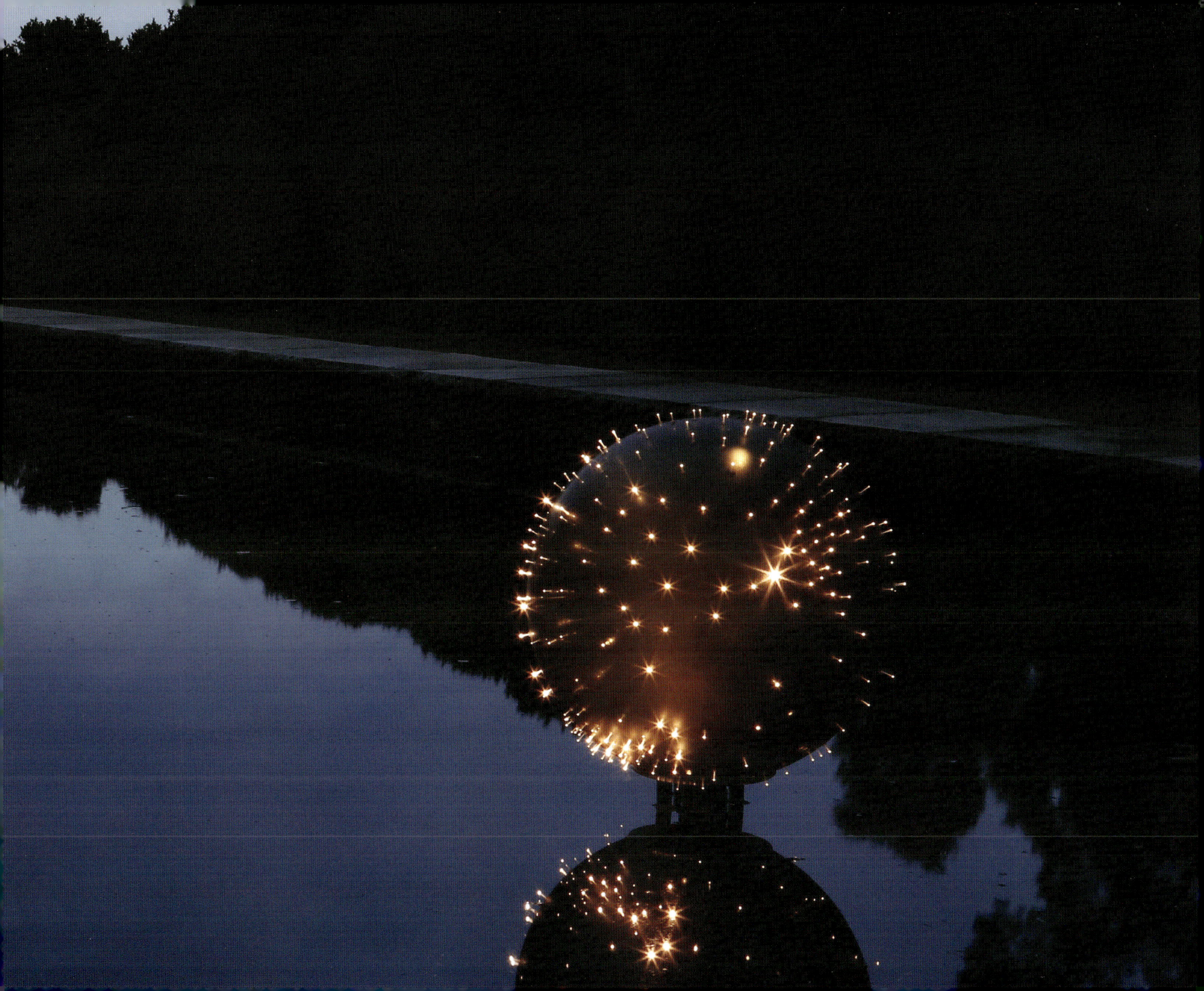

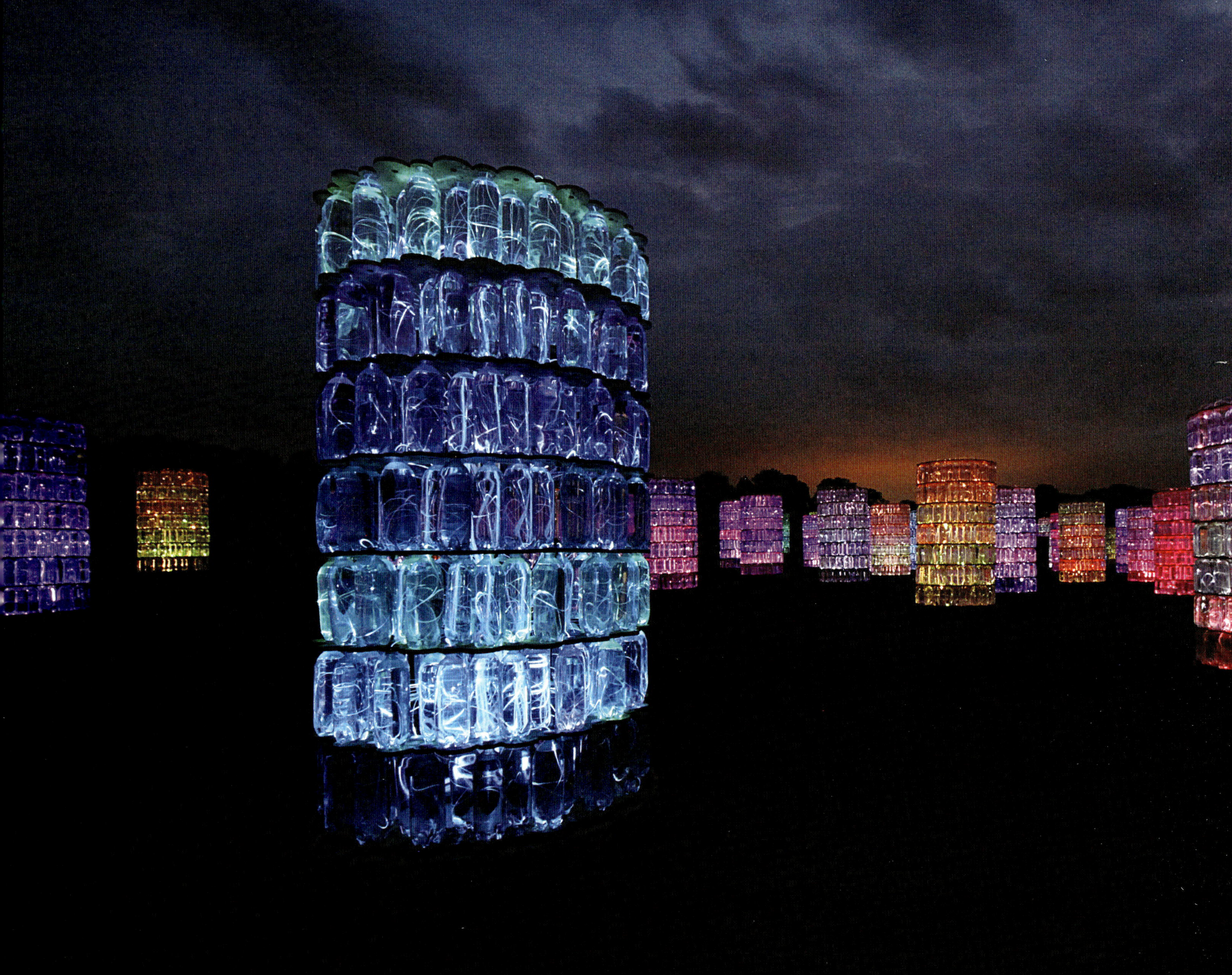

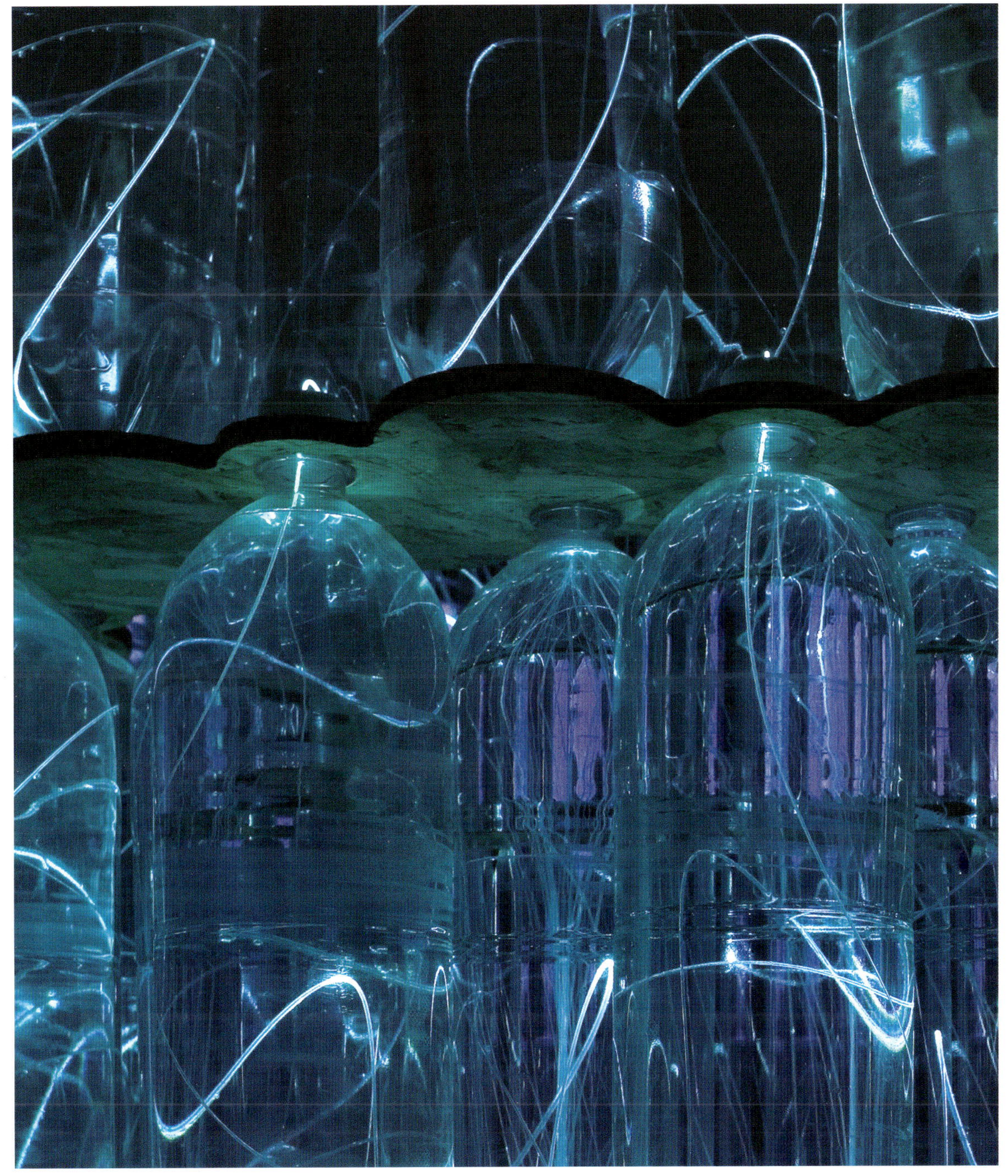

WATER-TOWERS

When I was twenty-one years old, I read a book called *Gifts of Unknown Things* by Lyall Watson, a radical thinker operating on the margins of accepted science. In it, Watson describes Tia, a young girl living on an island in the Indonesian archipelago who possesses the magical gift of seeing sounds in colour. Twenty-nine years later, Tia's gift inspired the design for a colourful, watery, musical maze.

The installation is an exercise in creating something magical from simple materials: PET plastic bottles, laser-cut wooden laminate, and water.

Watson described how the Earth has a natural pulse in the upper atmosphere, resonating at a rate of sixty-nine beats per day. The pulse forms a deep note well below human powers of hearing. This Earth pulse inspired *Water-Towers*, which originally consisted of sixty-nine towers;

Pages 82–91: Water-Towers, *Longwood Gardens, Pennsylvania, USA, 2012.*

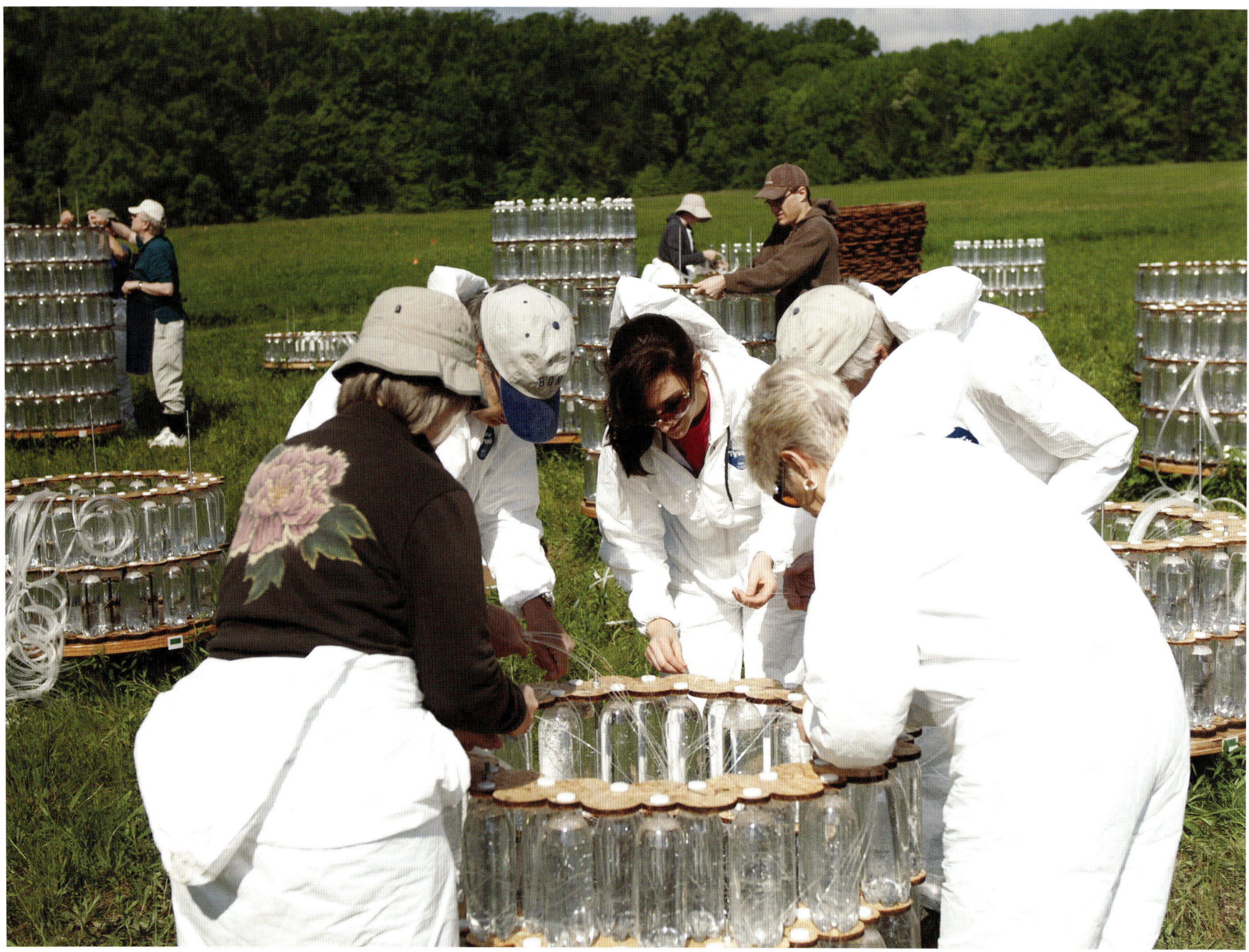

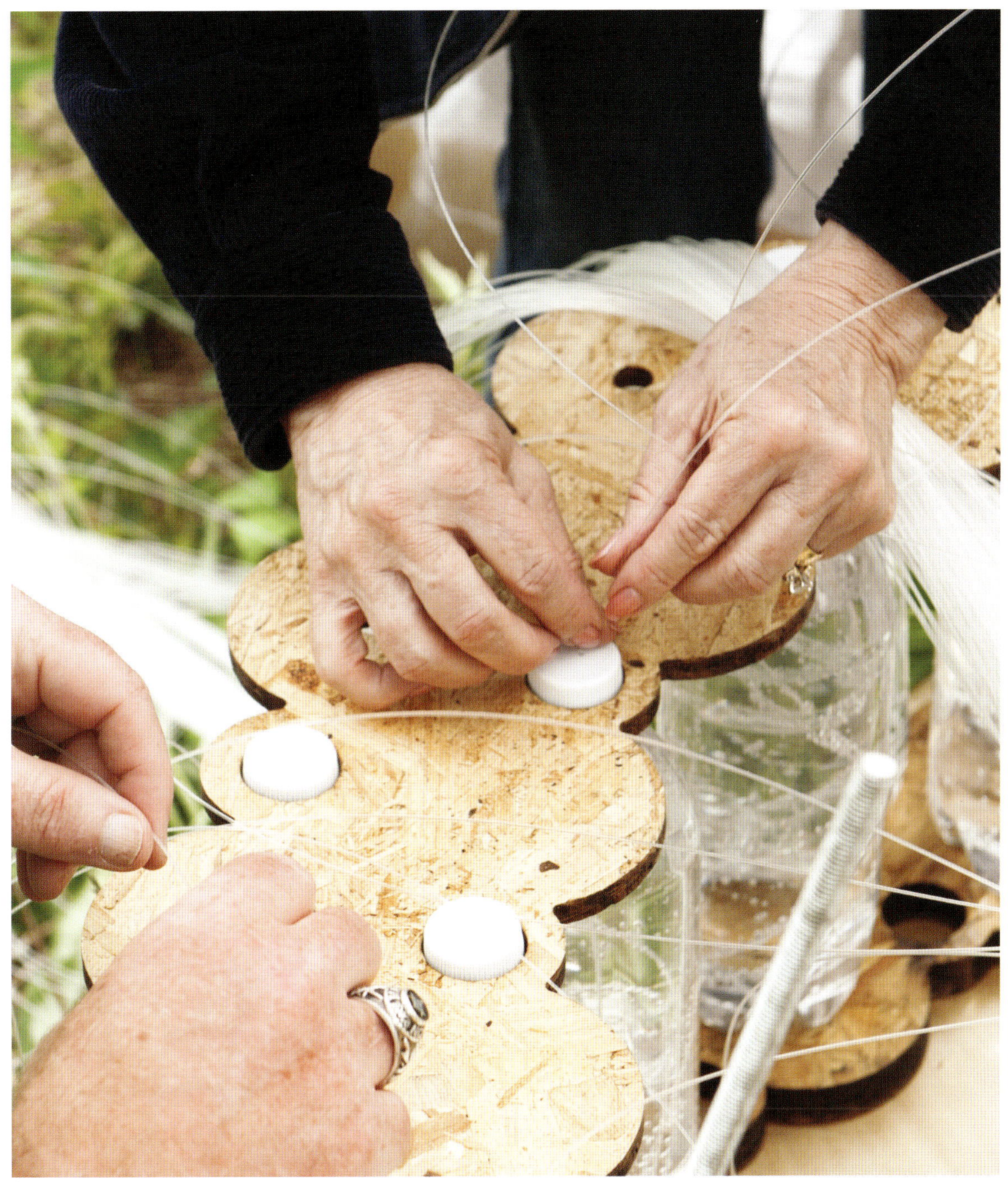

one for each pulse per day. Each tower is about two meters (six feet) tall and made from over 200 stacked water bottles illuminated by optic fibres. In their original formation the towers resembled enormous liquid batteries of light arranged in a maze formation. Music emanates from the towers; the soundtrack reflects the musical diversity of many nations.

A control system scrolls through a rainbow of colours synchronised with the soundtrack. As the towers change colour, visitors experience sound magically translated into colour, just as Tia, Lyall Watson's heroine, does. The process of creating this installation is almost as important as the end result. It is about involving other people and the community, and working on things together.

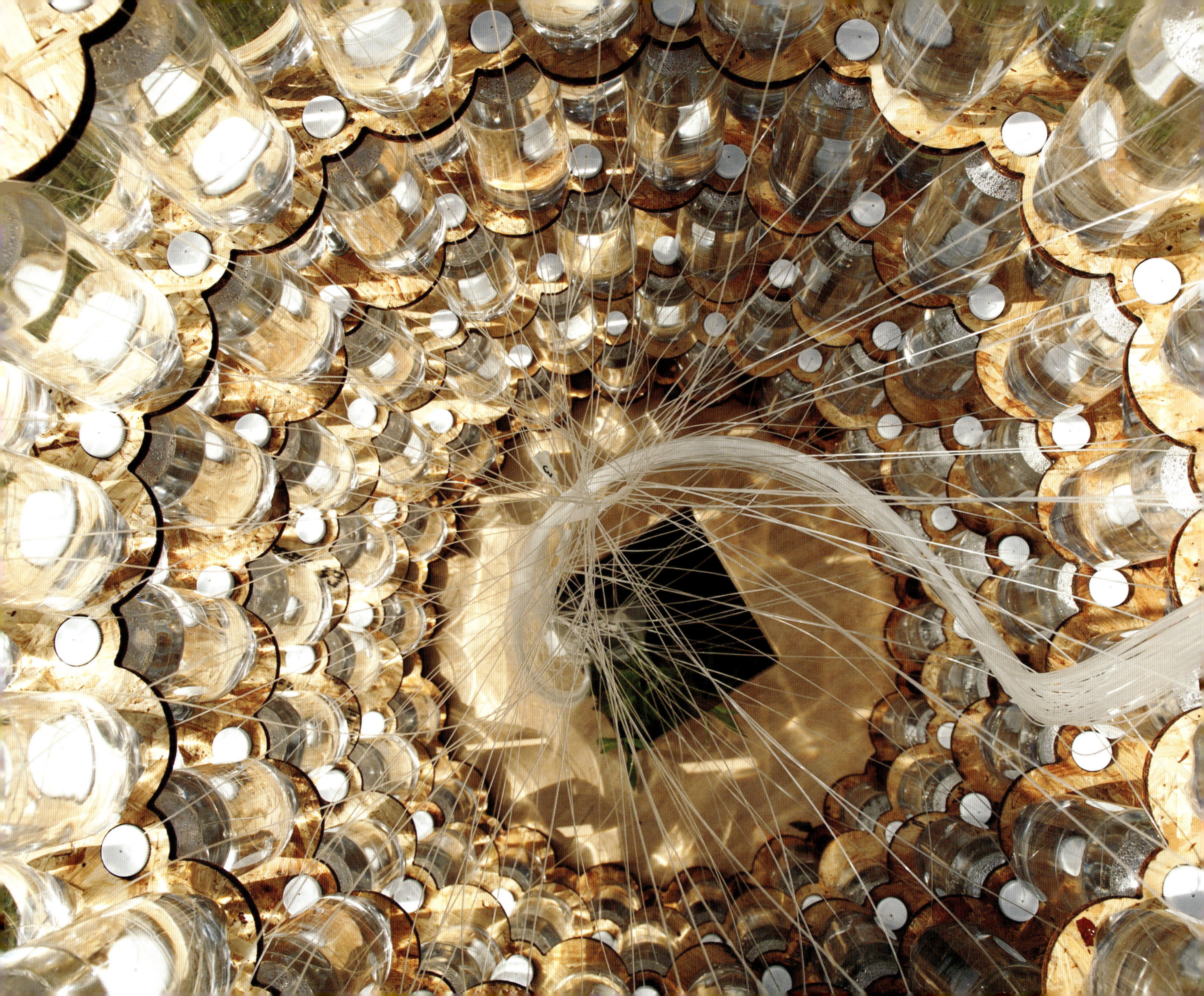

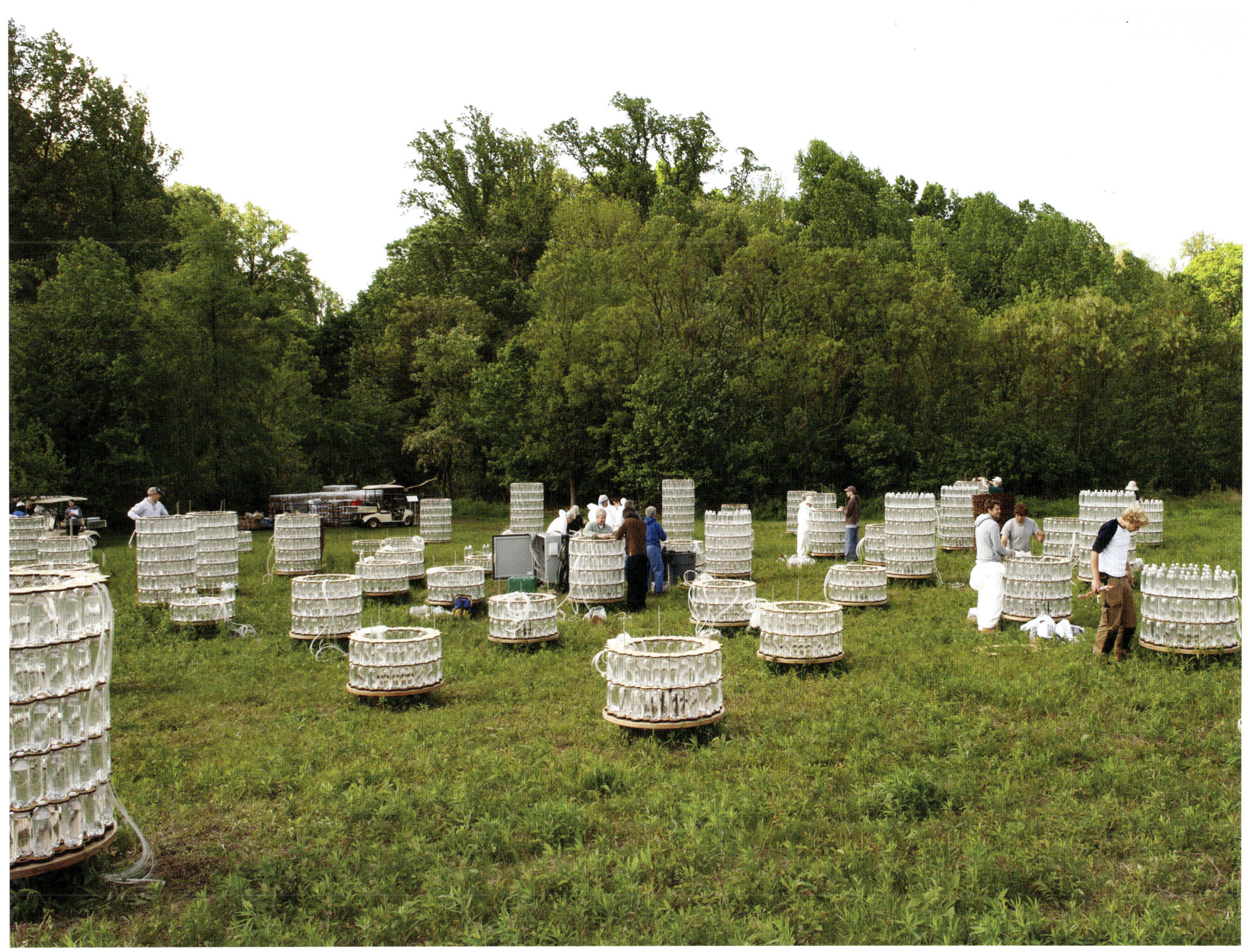

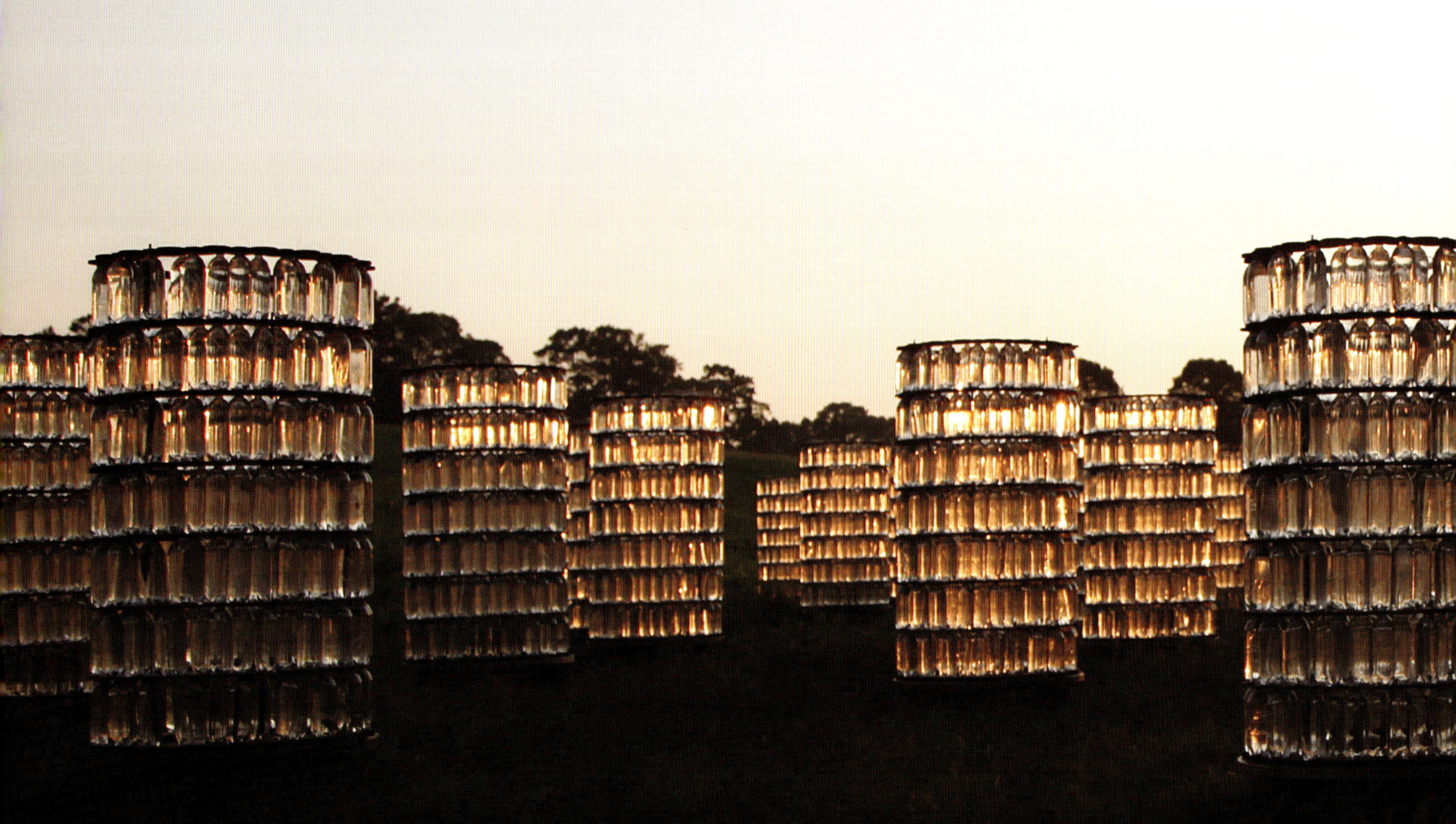

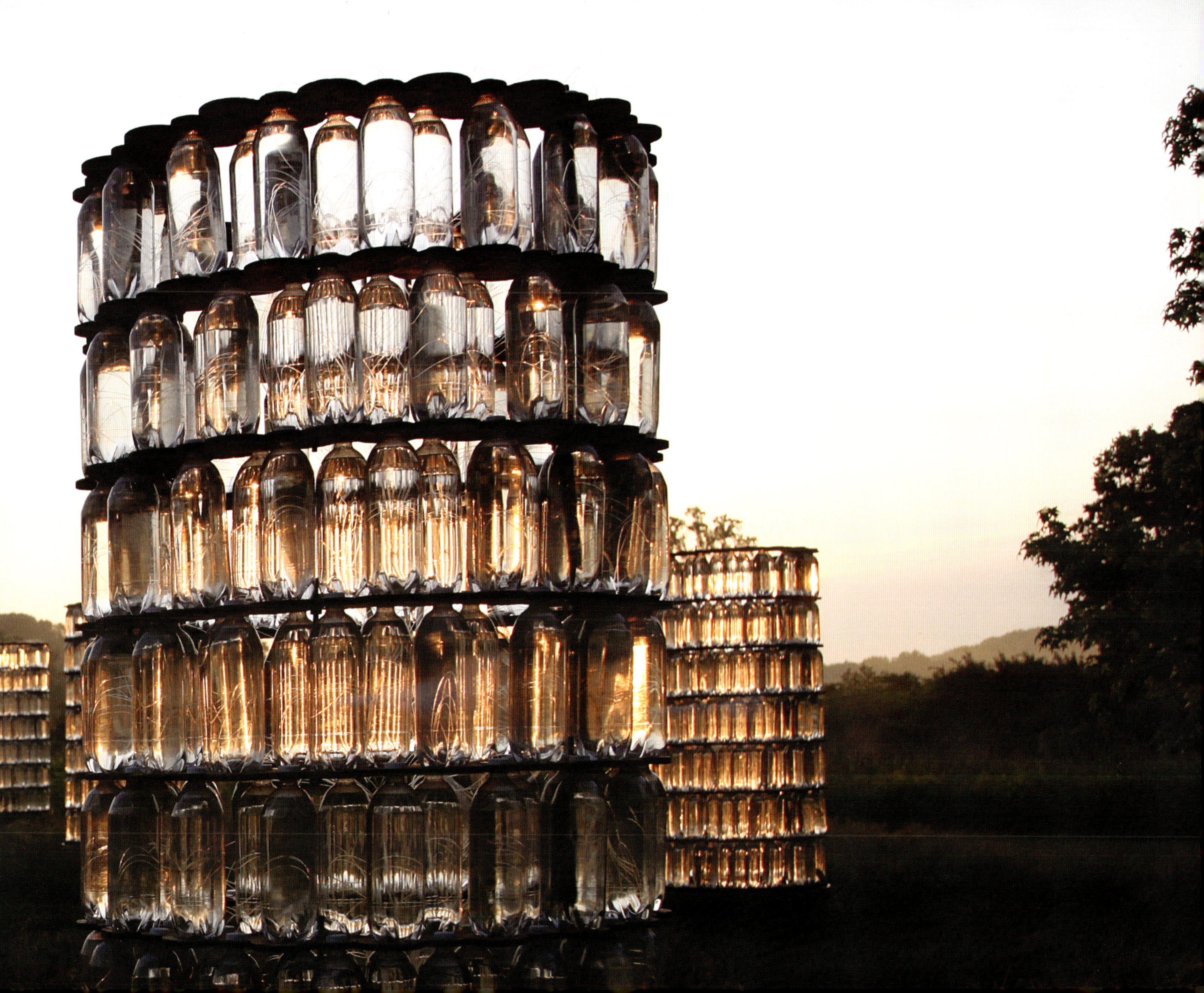

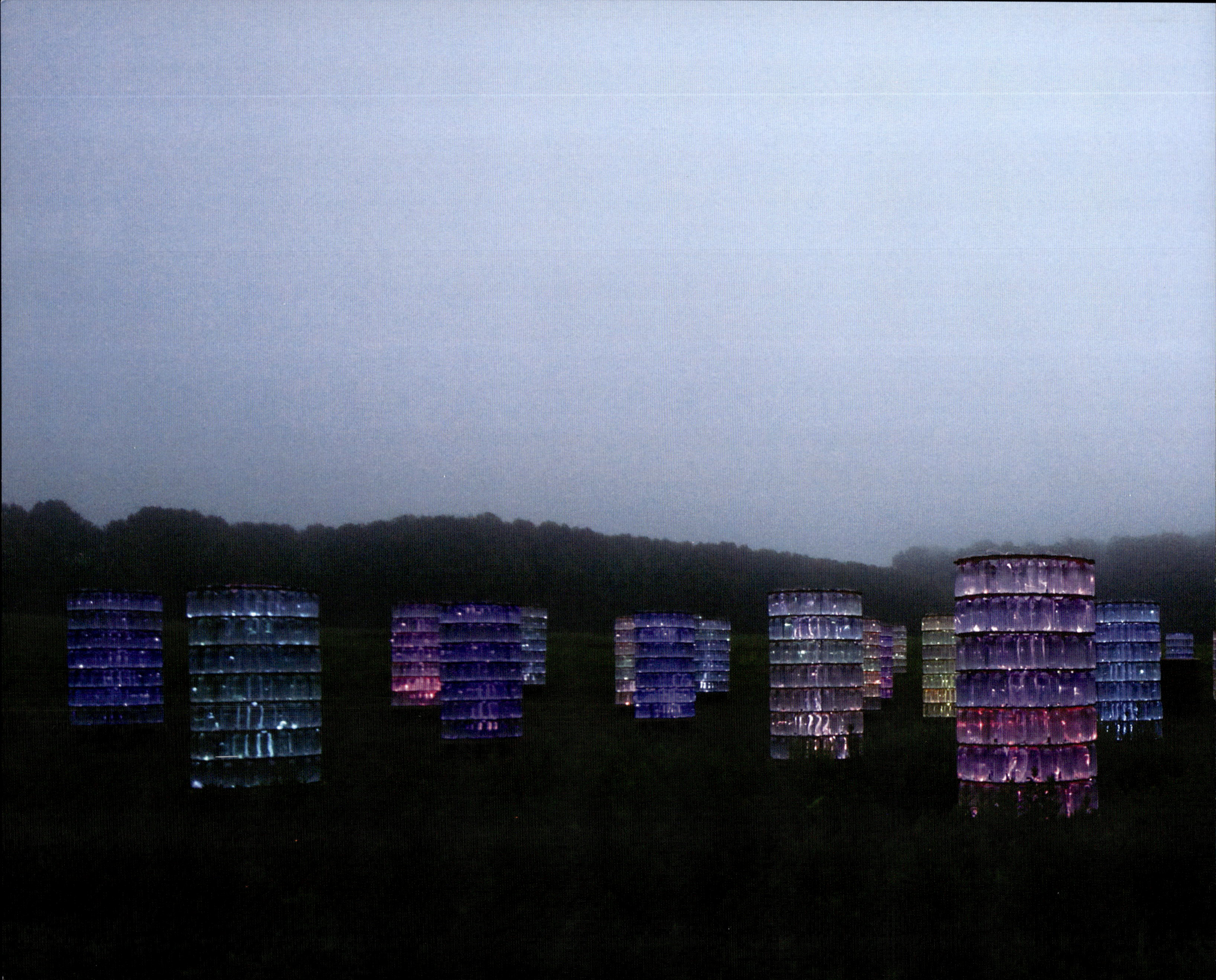

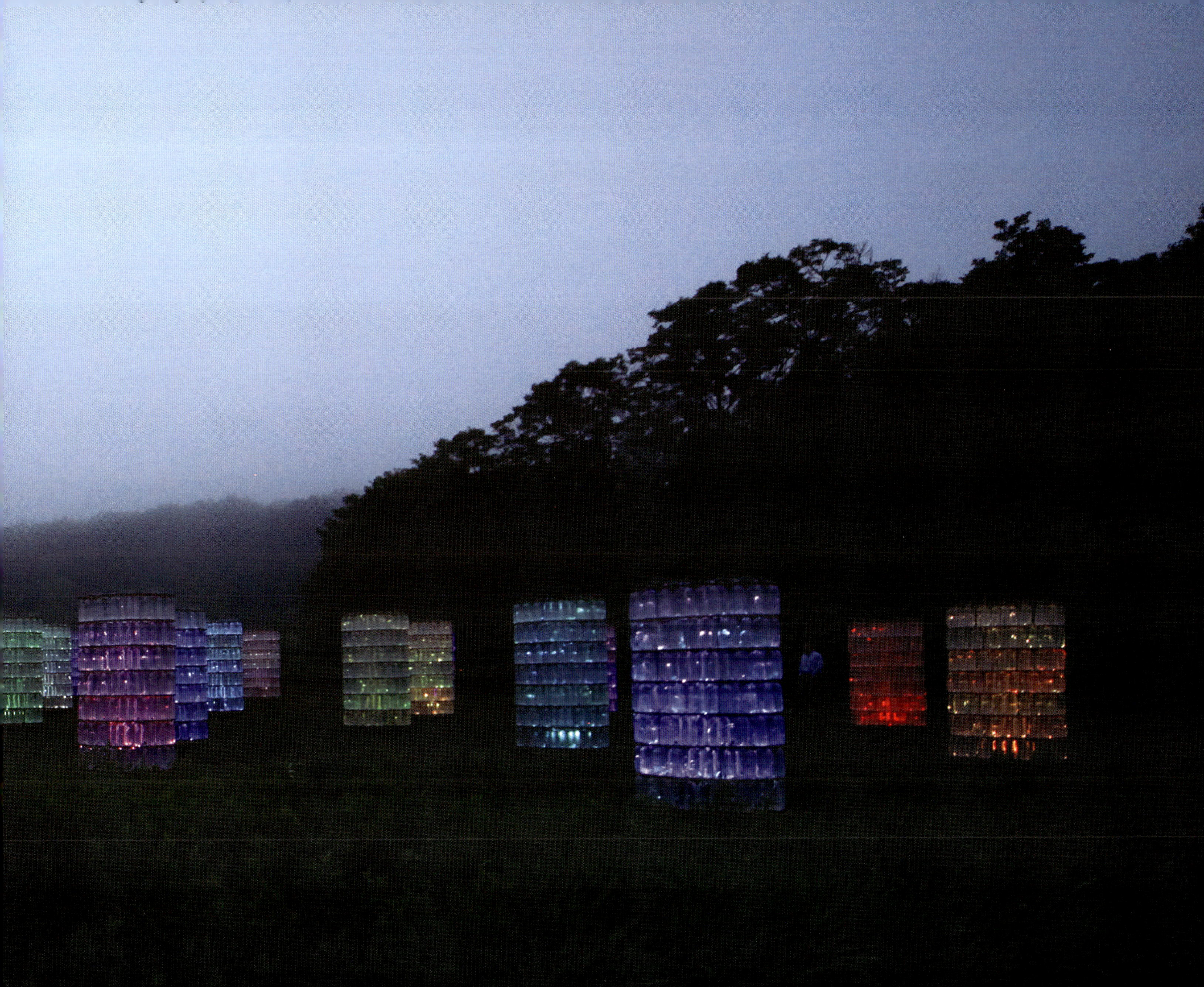

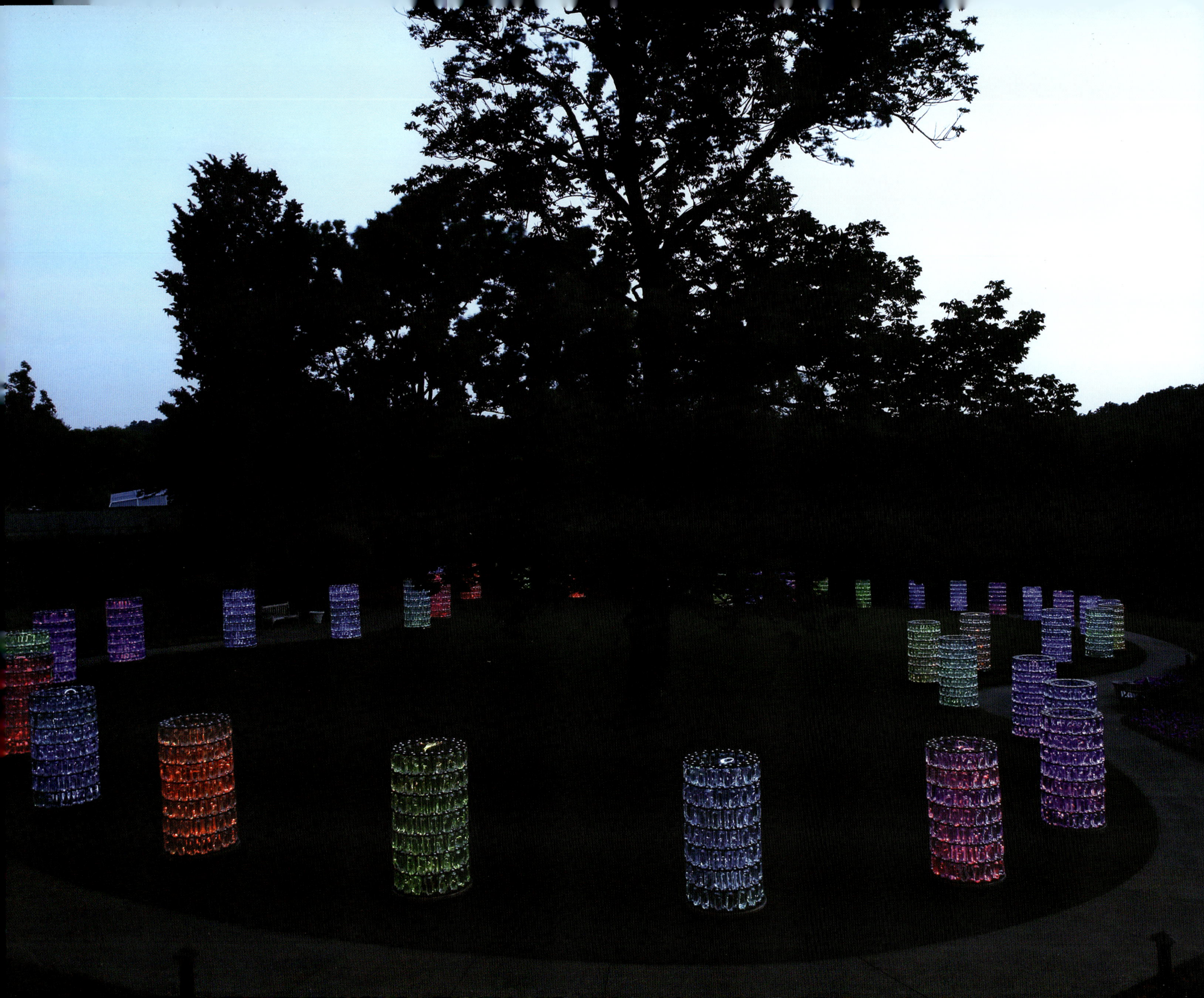

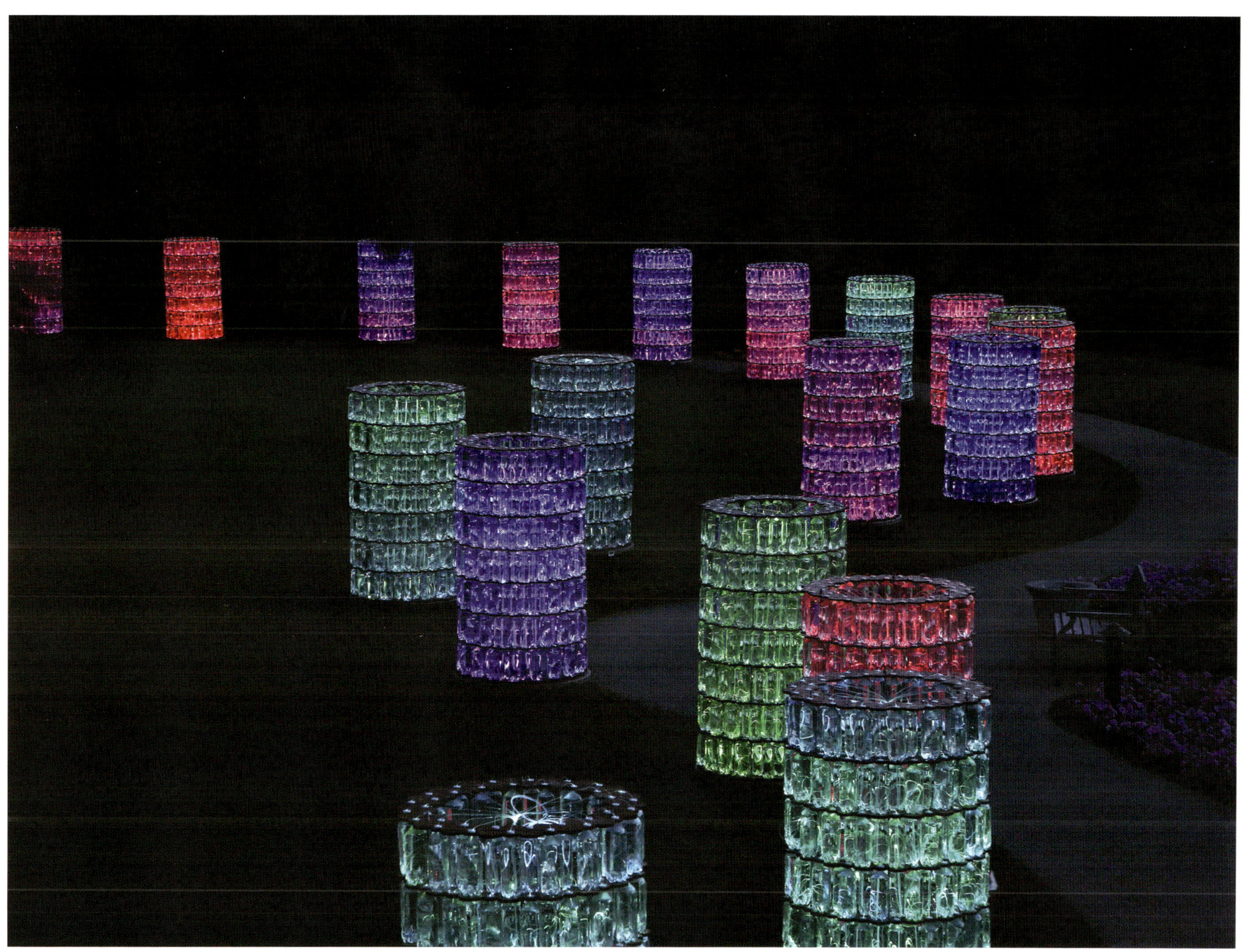

Pages 92–95: Water-Towers, *Cheekwood Botanical Garden and Museum of Art, Tennessee, USA, 2013.*

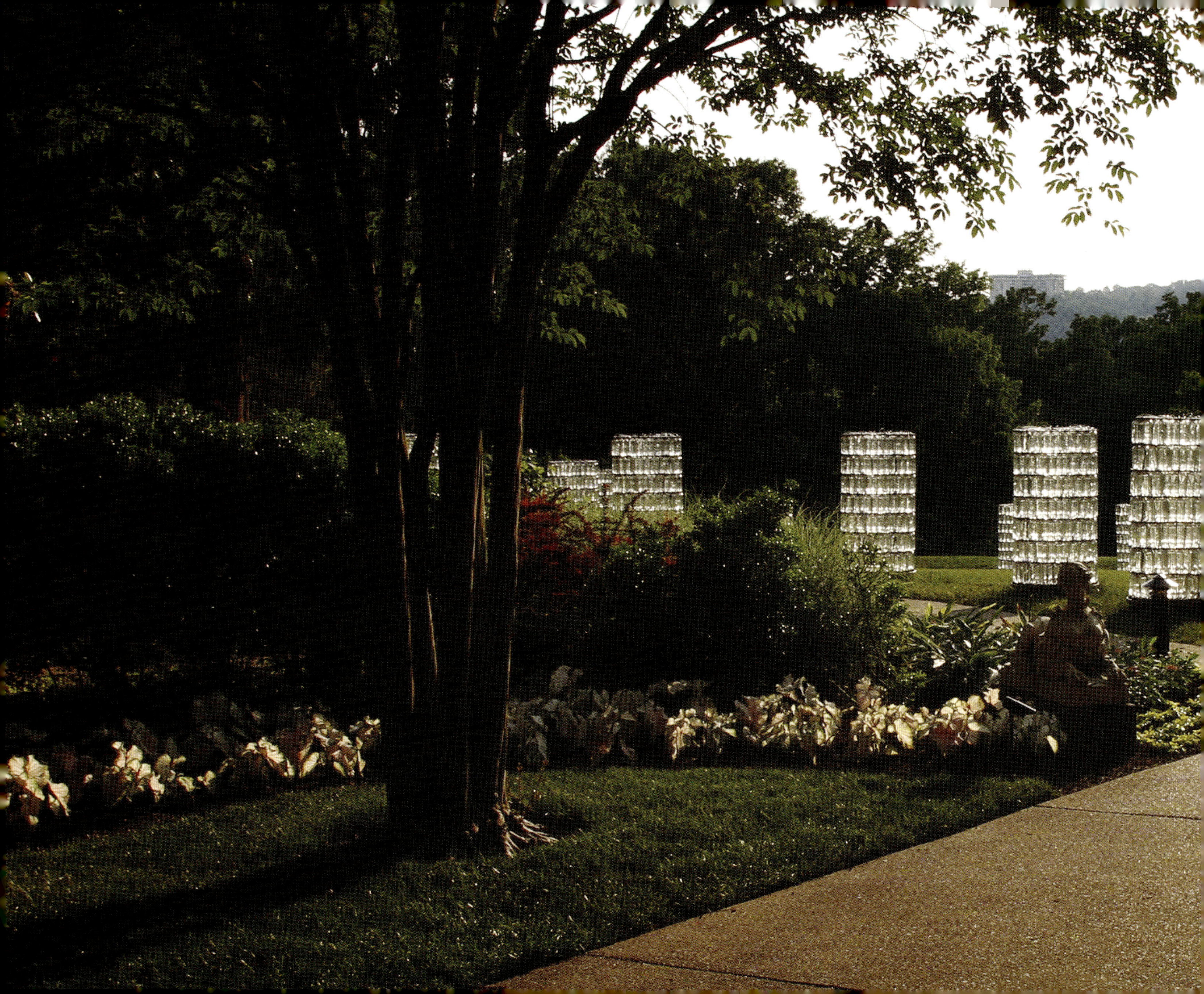

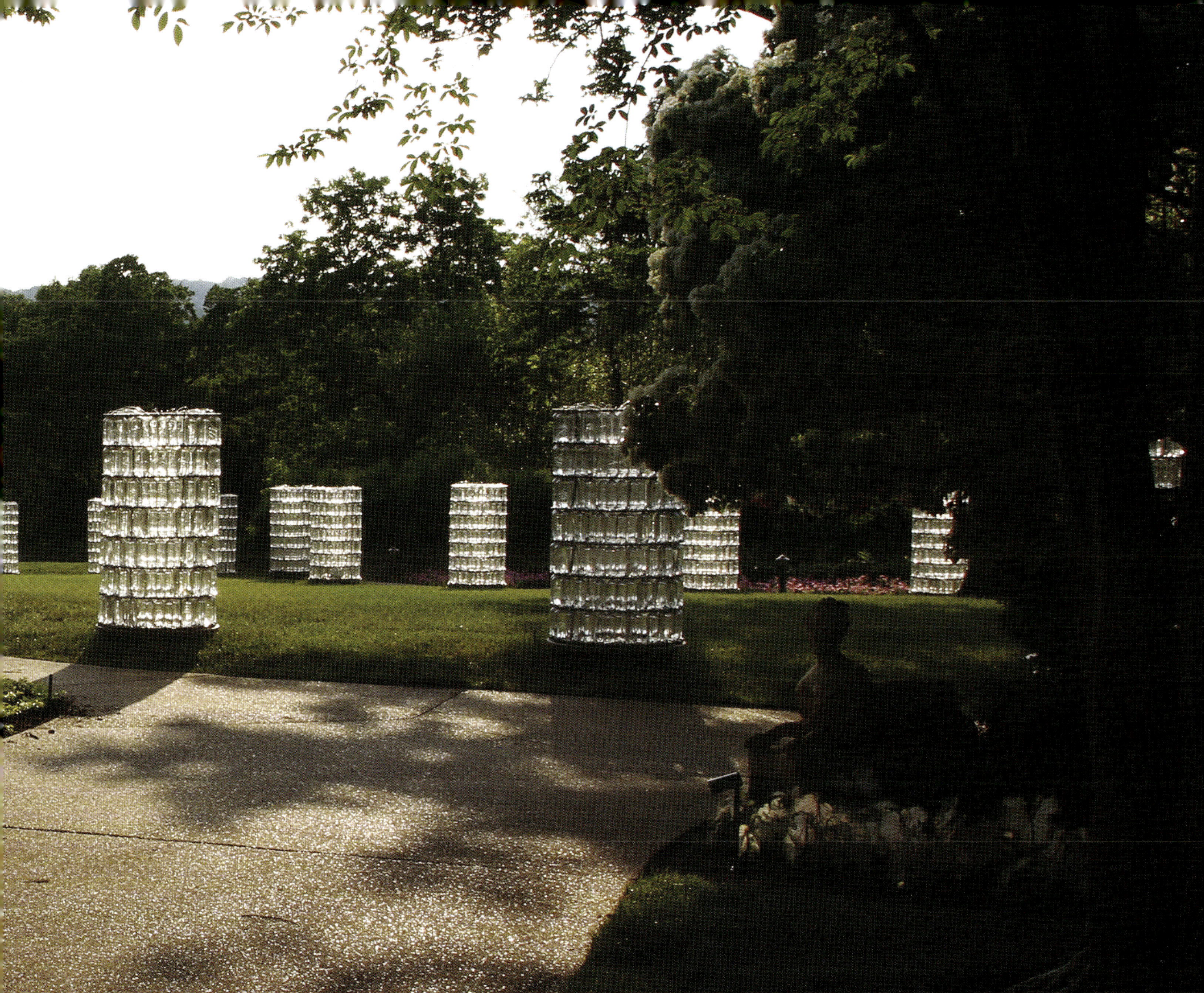

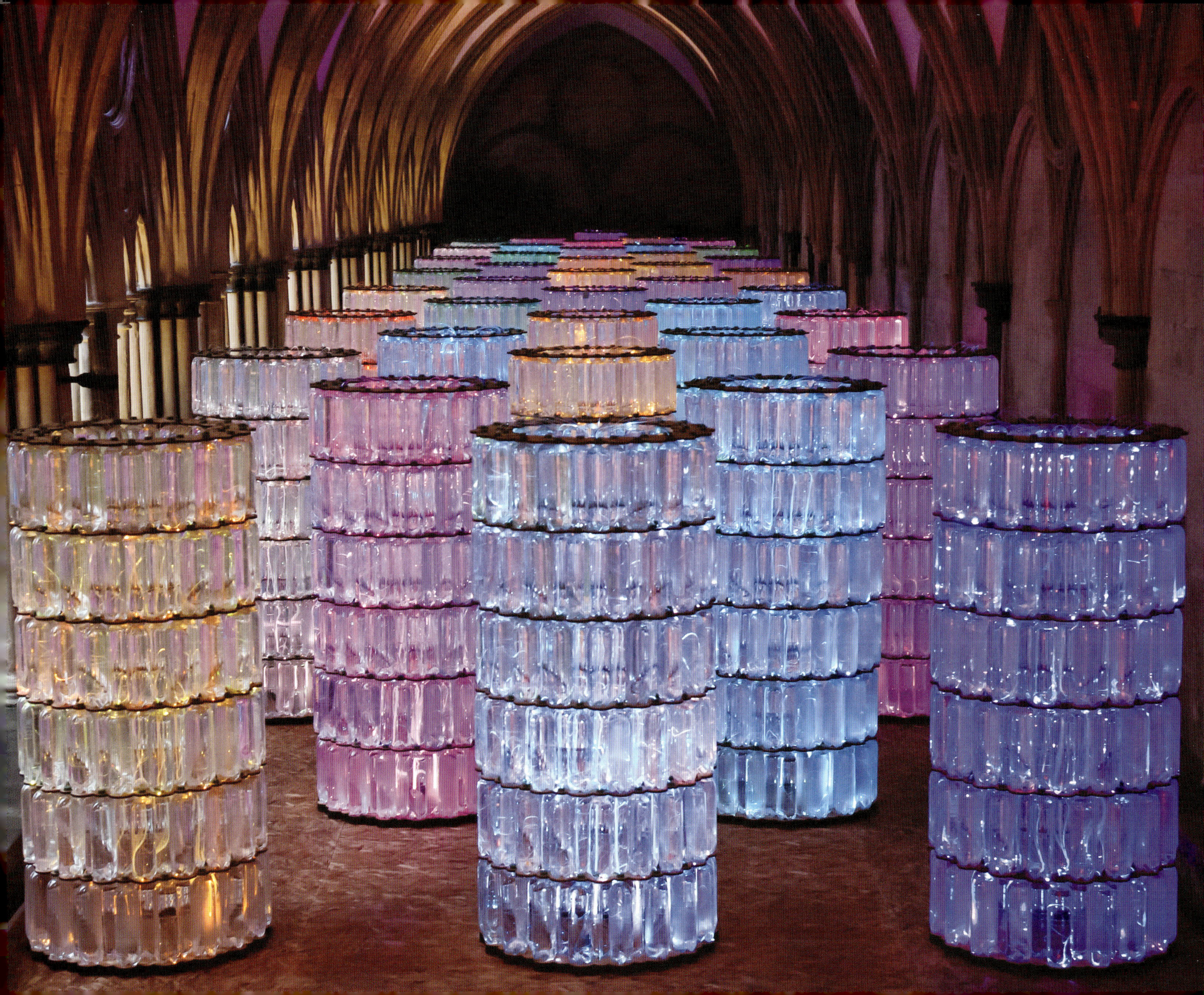

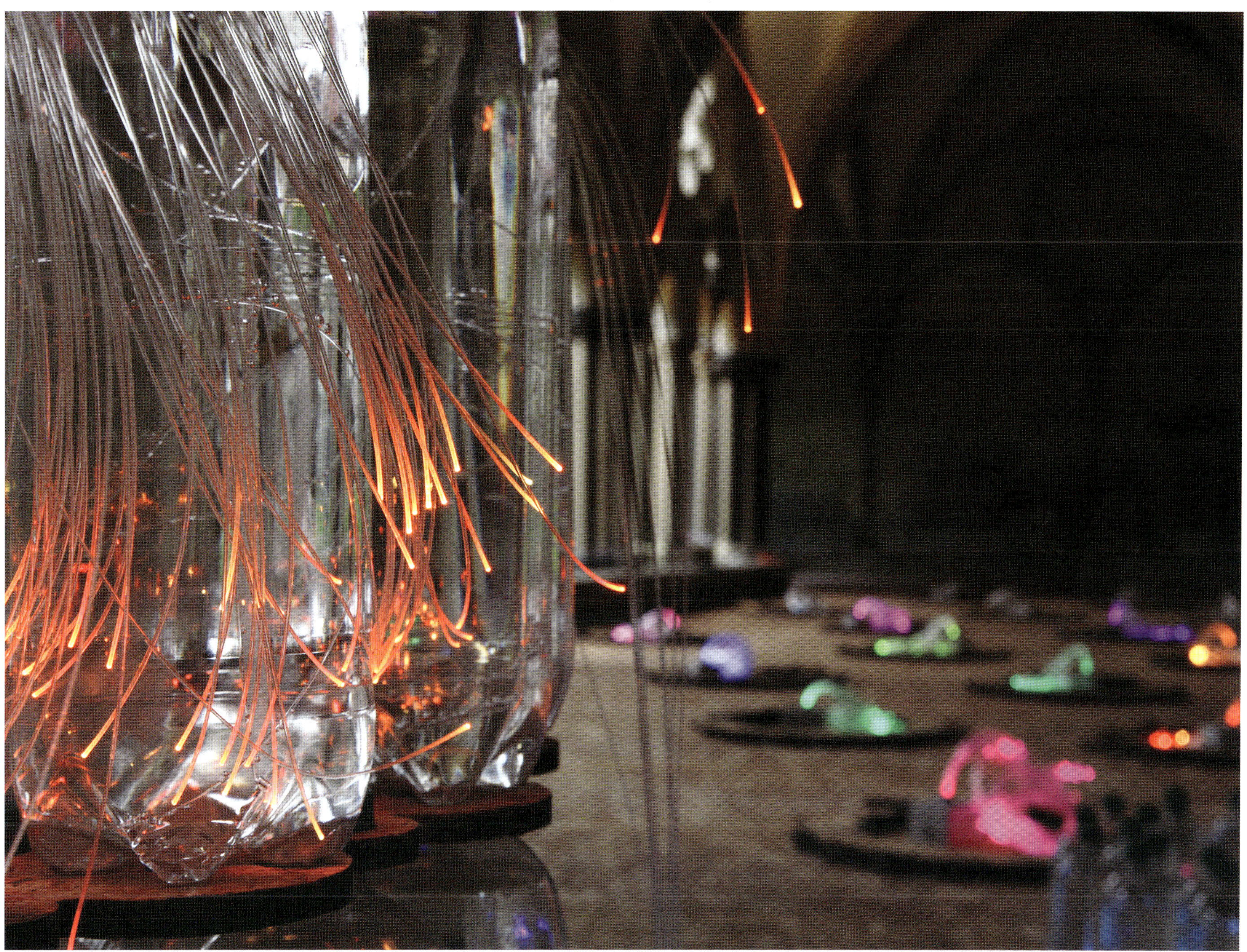

Pages 96–100: Water-Towers, *Salisbury Cathedral, Wiltshire, UK, 2010.*

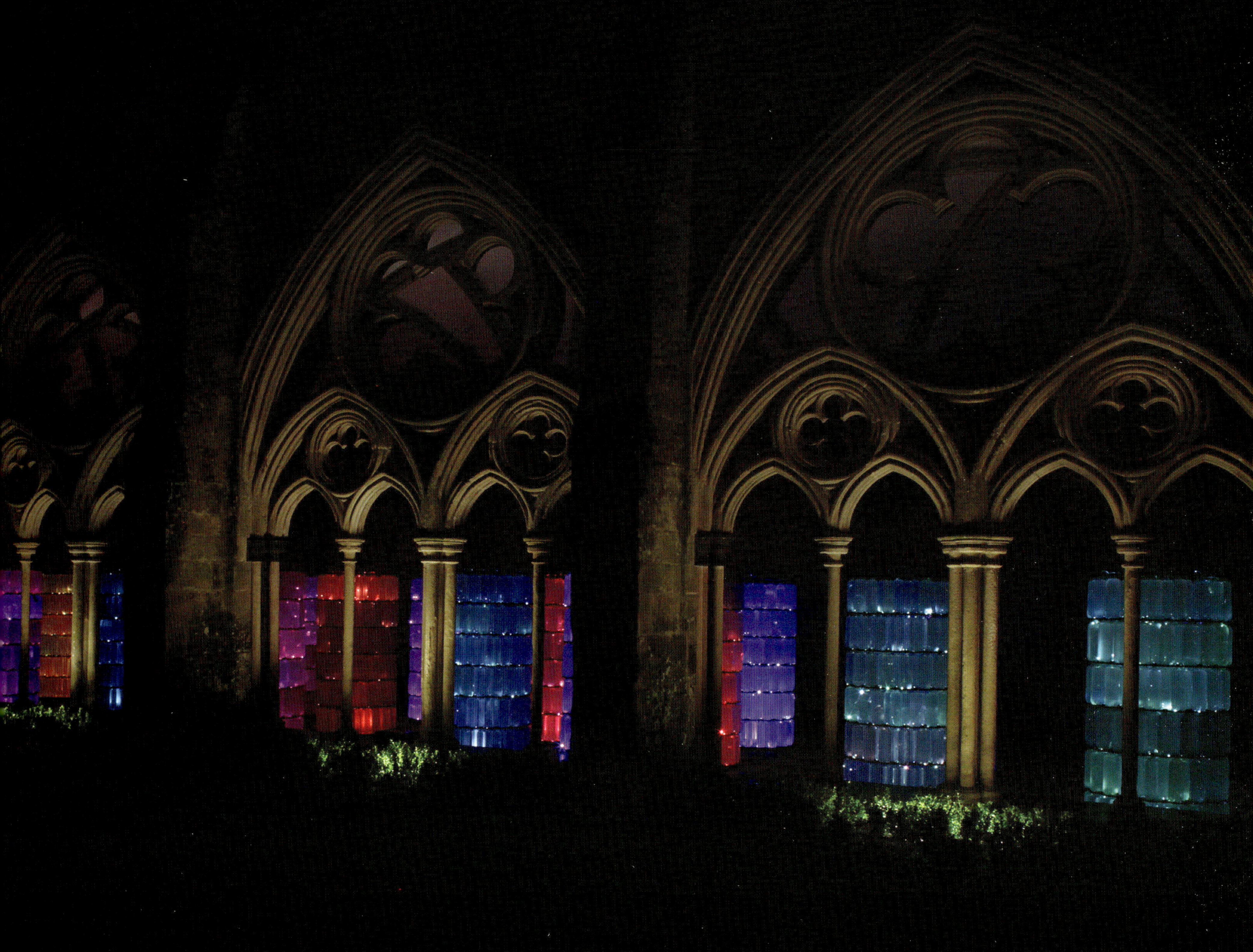

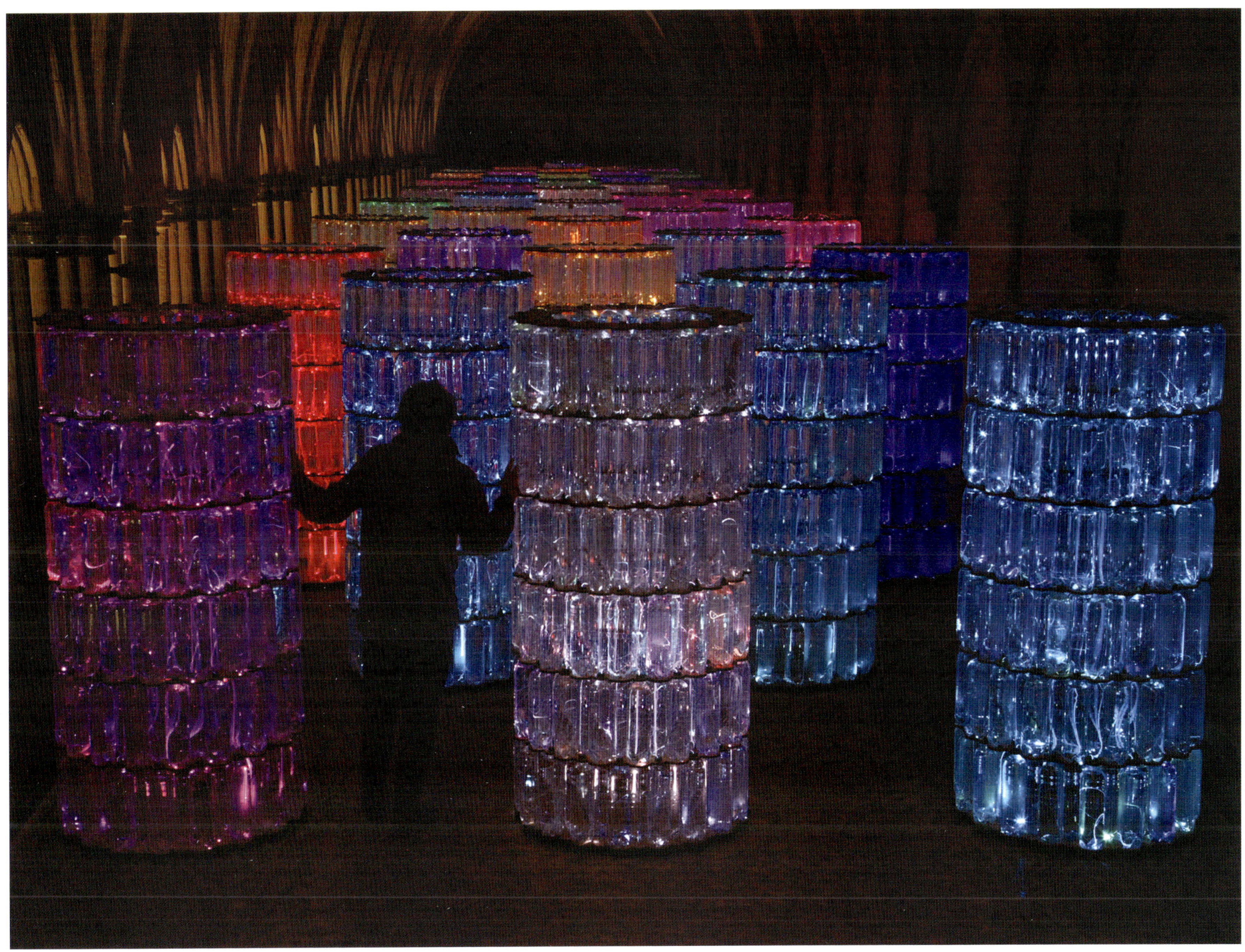

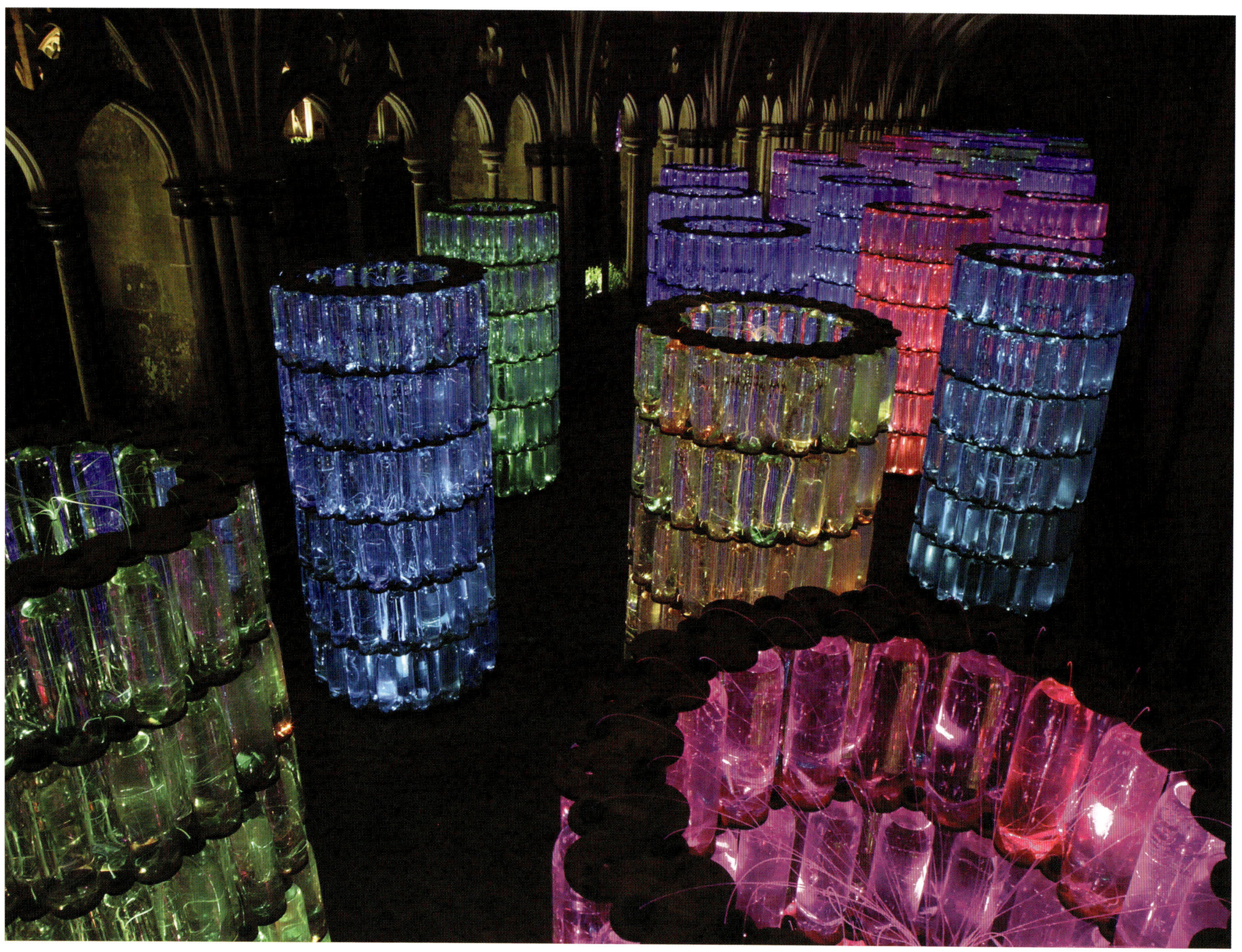

Opposite: Water-Tower *prototype at Long Knoll, Wiltshire, UK, 2010.*

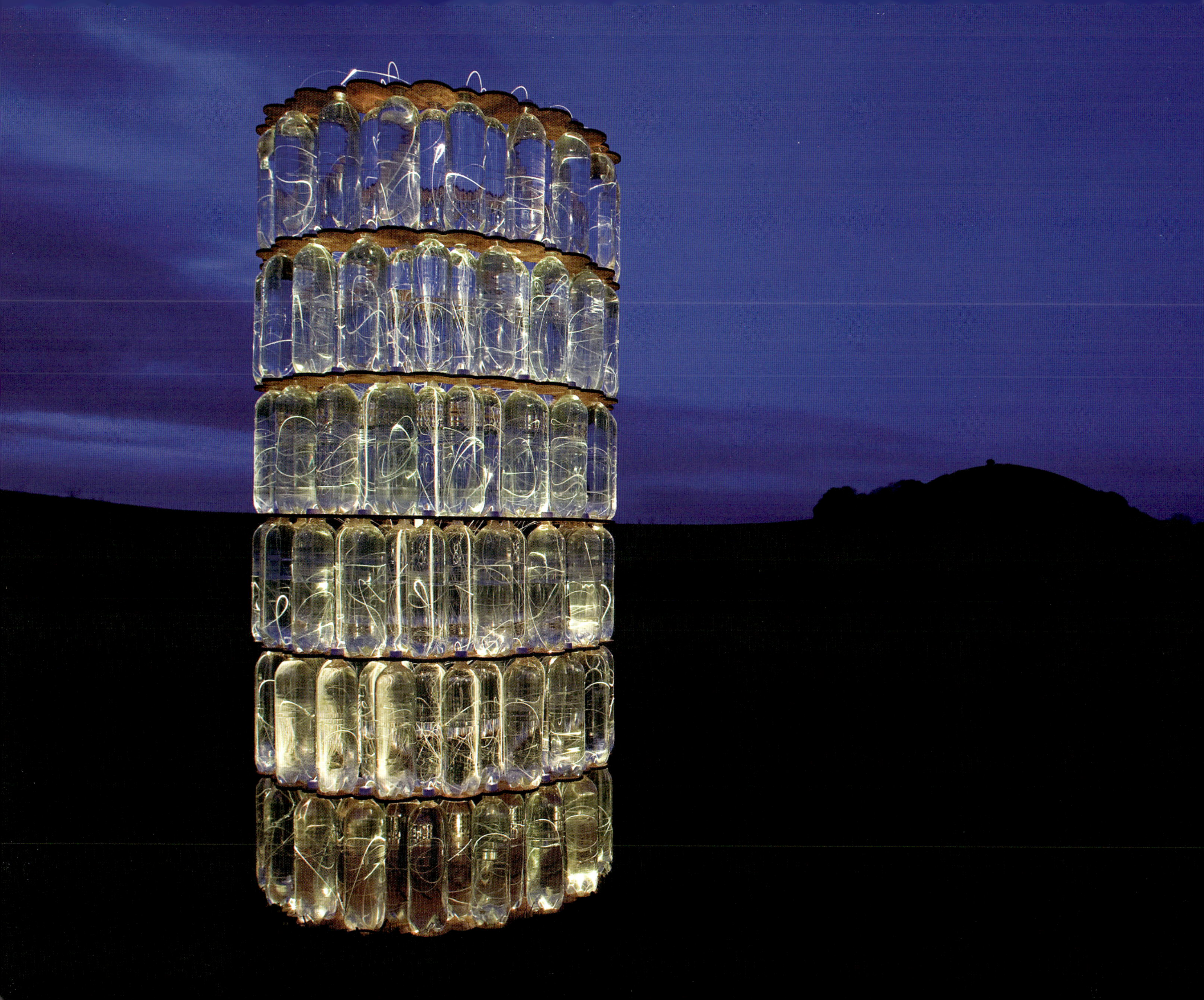

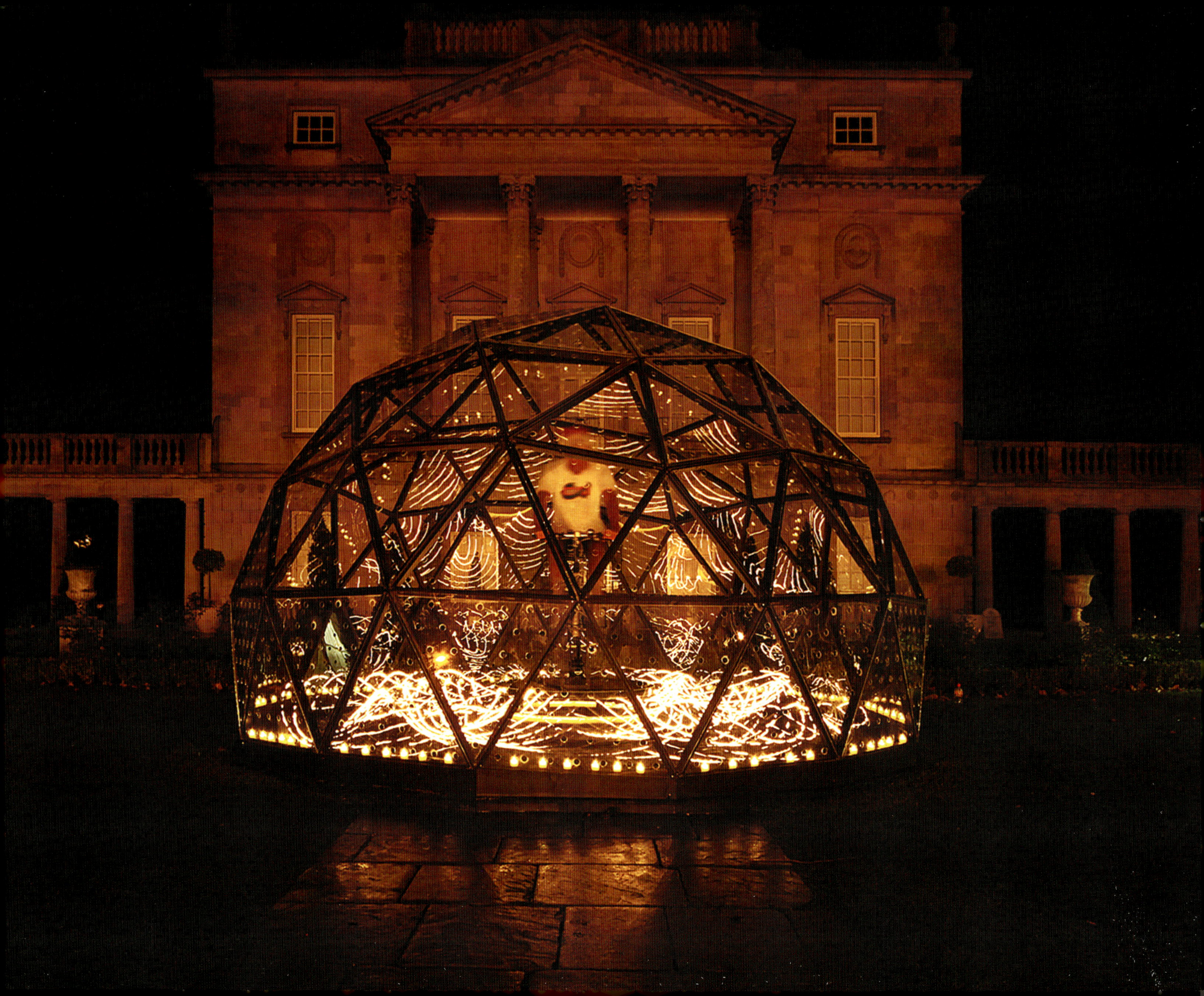

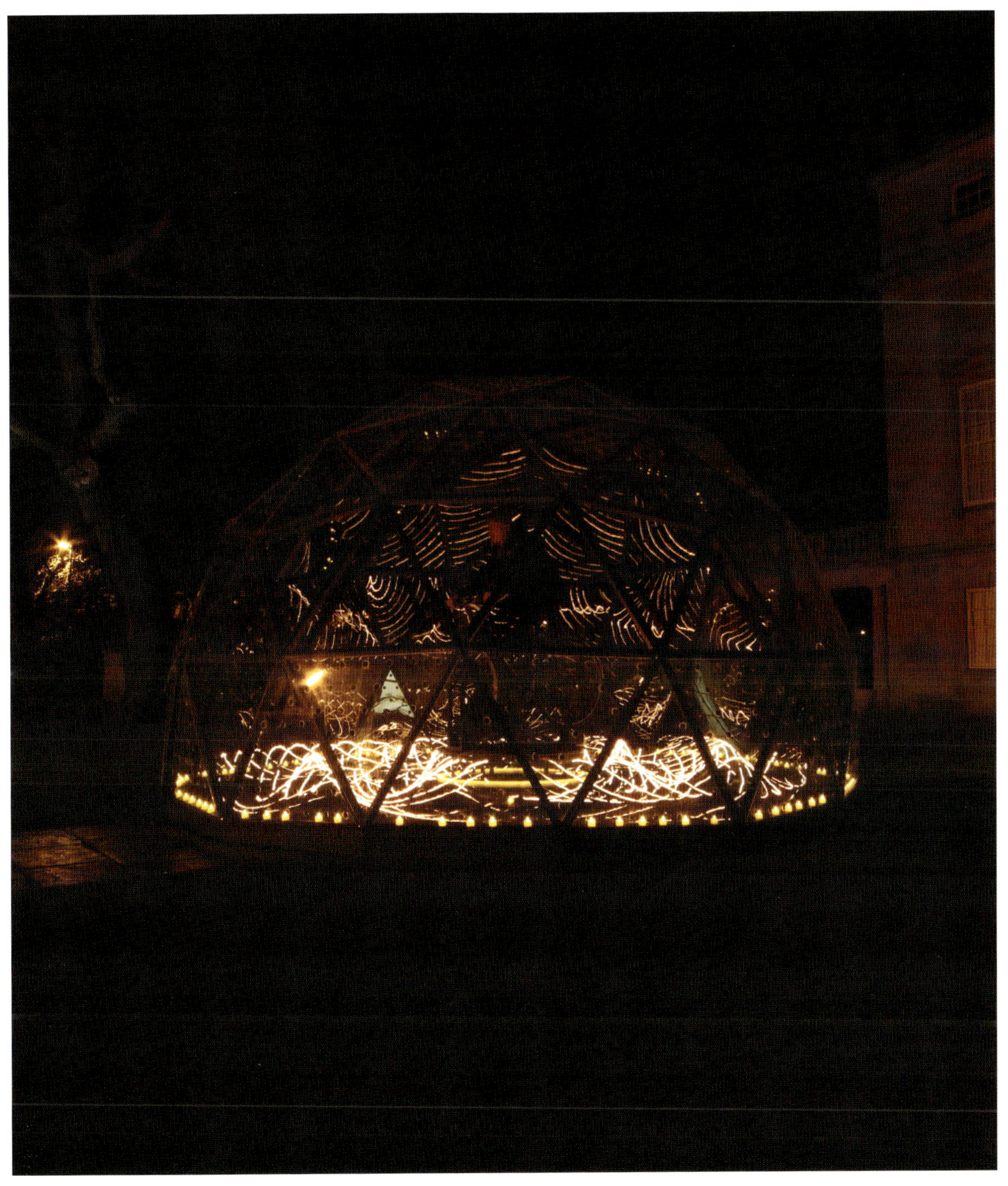

STAR-TURN

I was riding my bicycle in the lanes near my studio one winter afternoon. It was dark and my lights had failed, and I fell off into a ditch full of icy cold cow poop. As I got to my feet, the idea of cycling in a warm, dry, well-lit environment seemed irresistibly attractive. When I got home I started sketching the *Star-Turn* bike.

The design is also an exploration of our cultural obsession with celebrity. This is a tongue-in-cheek bicycle for celebrities, where we can all take our turn to cycle for fifteen minutes of fame. It is supposed to be the ultimate exercise machine, which keeps both muscles and ego in prime condition!

A chance meeting on a train led to a most important venture for *Star-Turn*—the Help For Heroes charity. By the end of the train journey, I felt determined to do my bit to raise funds for this wonderful cause.

Pages 102–05: Star-Turn, *Holburne Museum, Bath, UK, 2011.*

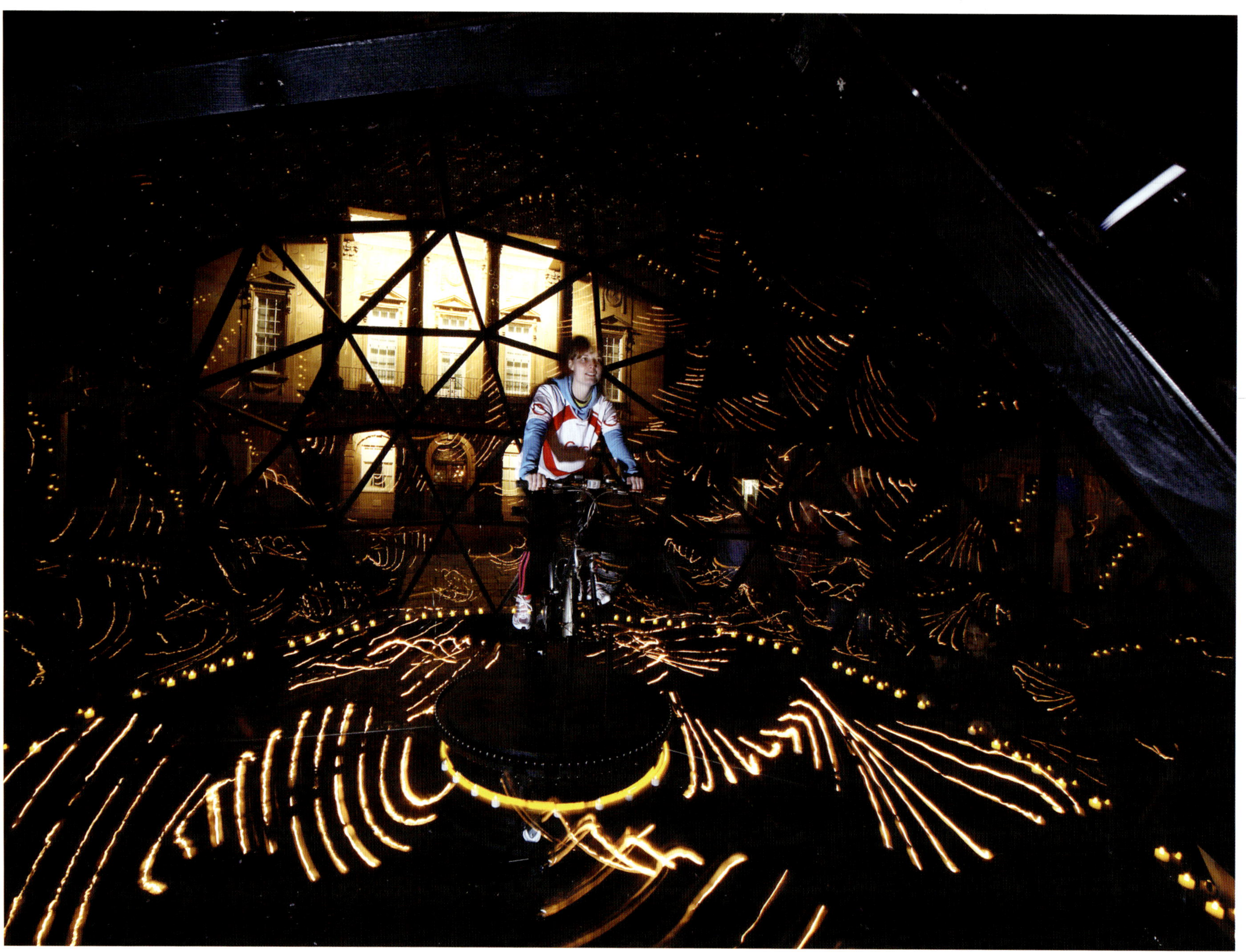

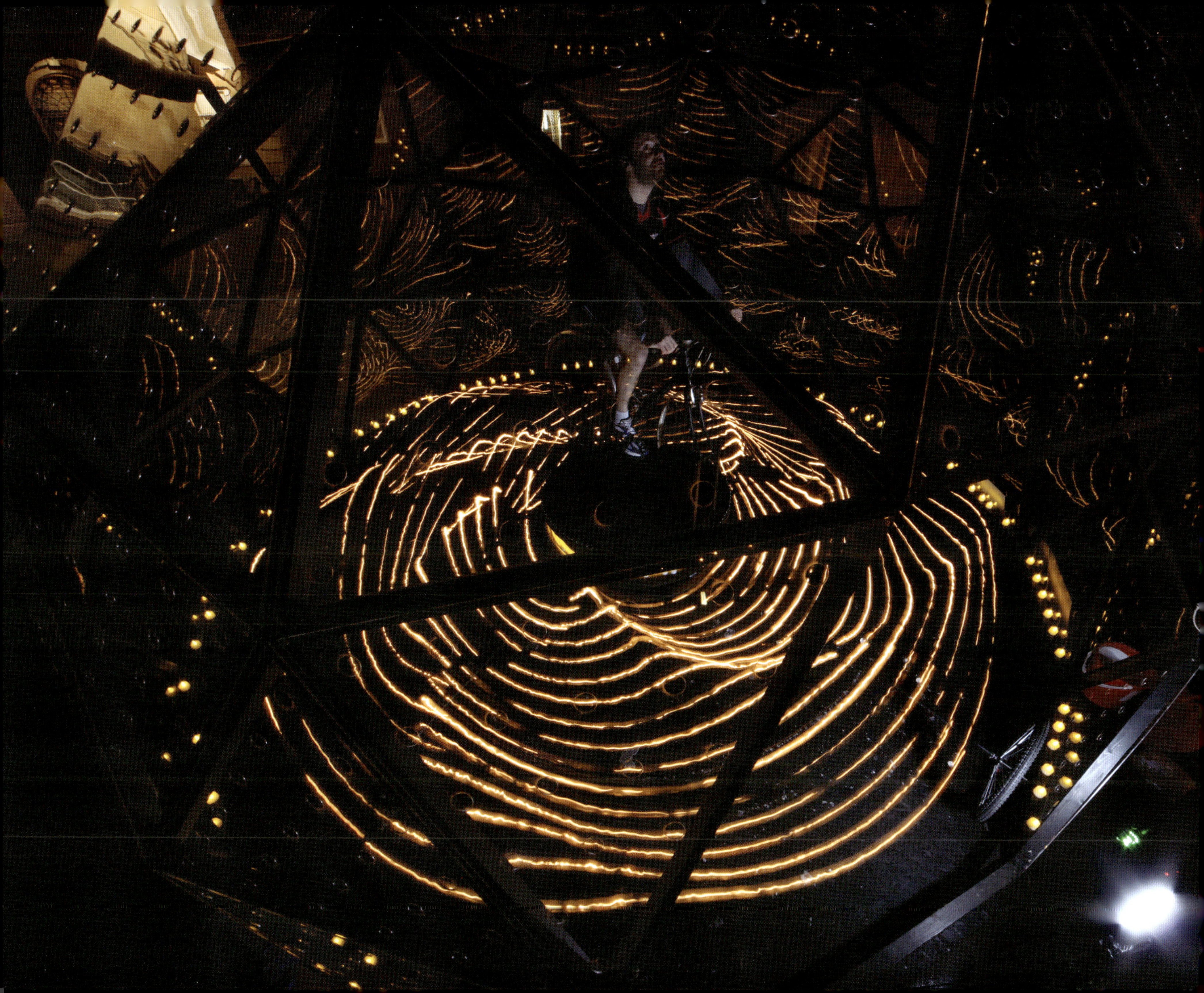

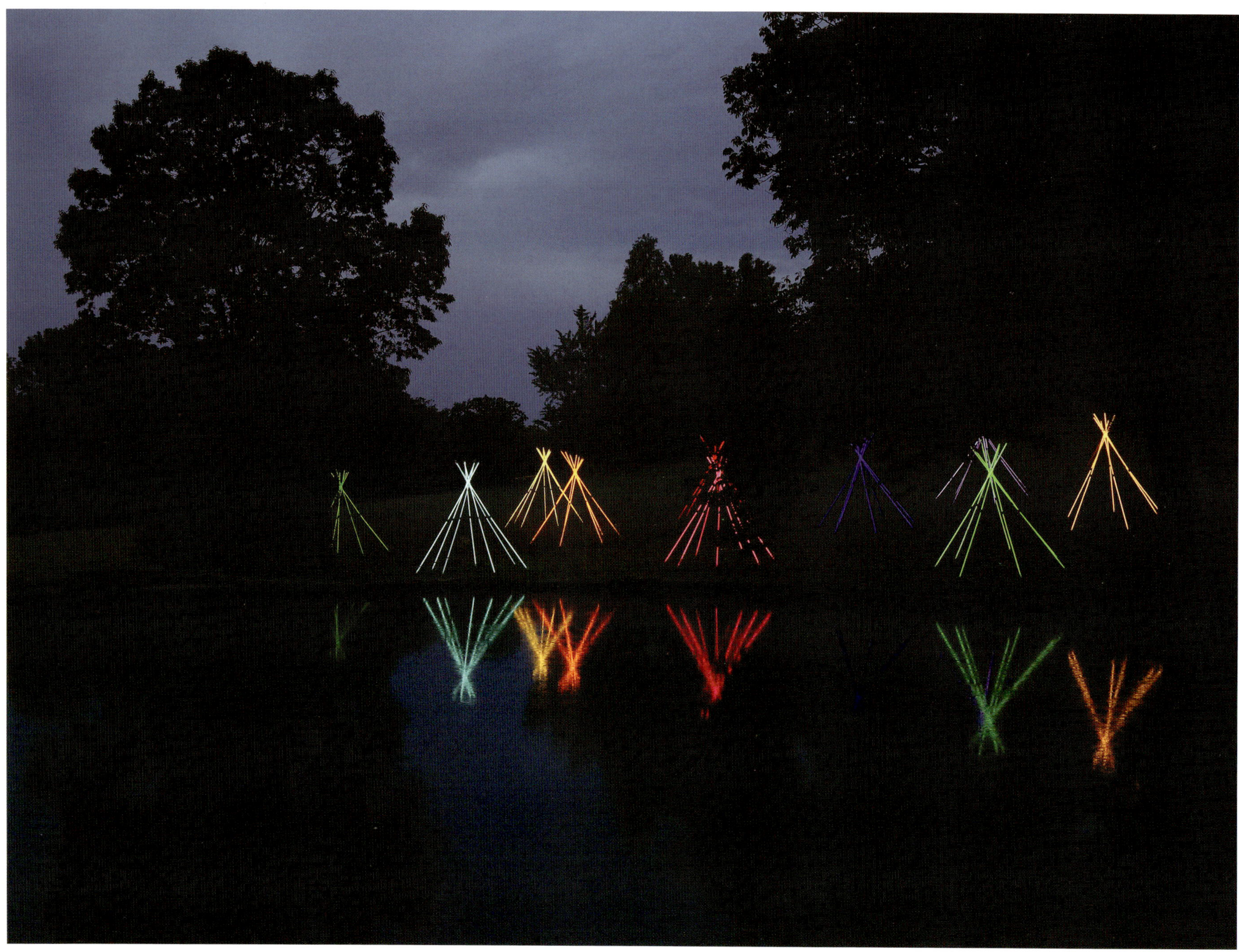

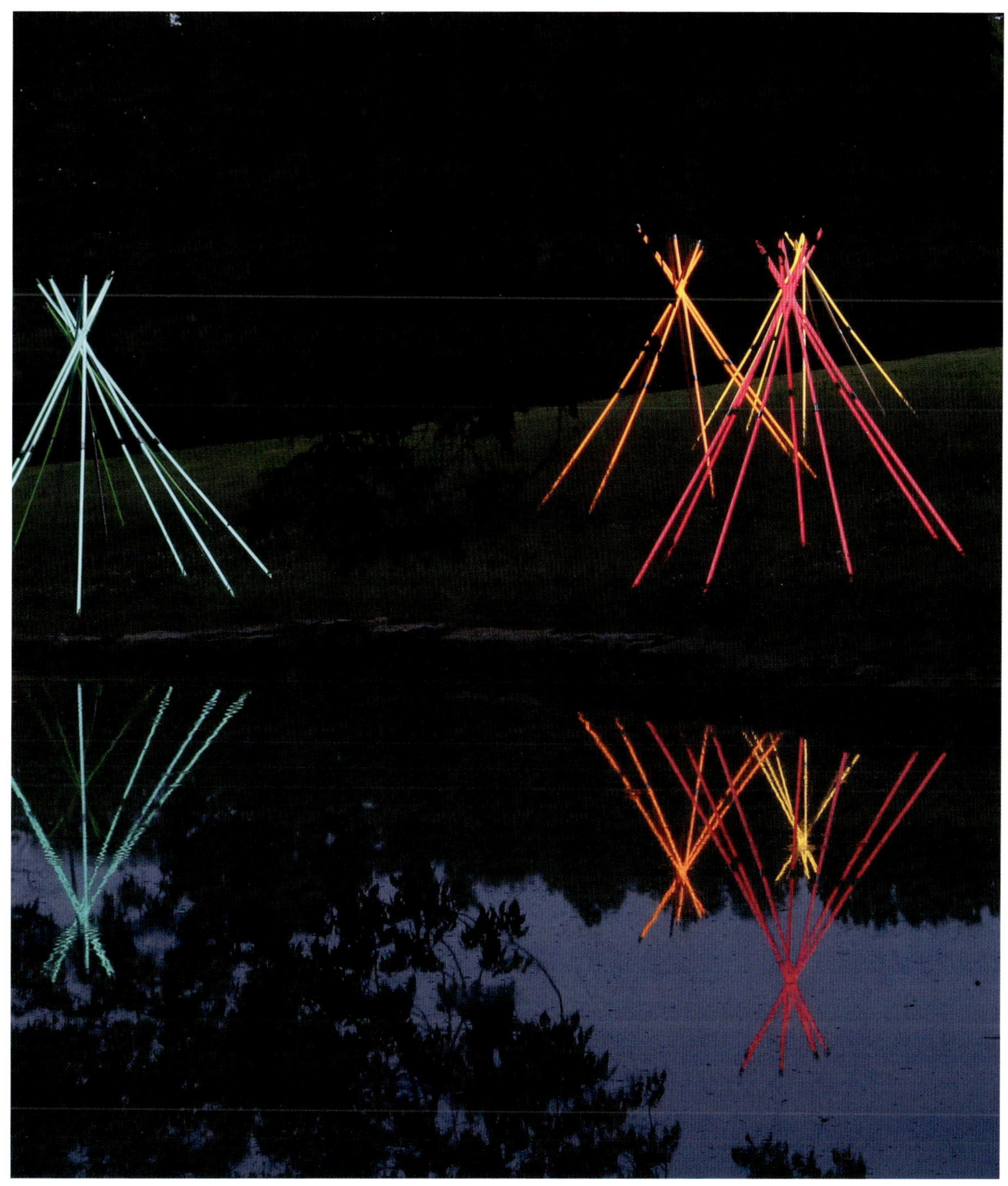

TEPEES

When my family first moved to our current home (a c.1600 Wiltshire farmhouse), my wife, Serena, was keen to keep chickens. Unfortunately, it did not take long for the foxes to discover the unprotected coop.

A local farmer came to the rescue offering a solution in the guise of a device that combined an electric fence system with a redundant fluorescent lighting tube (one that has been spent). A simple combination of a 12-volt car battery and an electric fencer creates a pulse of light when connected to an old fluorescent tube. I had acquired a new lighting technique to play with!

I kept it in the back of my mind for many years, but when I realised that the tubes could be grouped as tepees I was delighted, for the mythic American West as depicted in films and TV had held my imagination when I was a boy in England.

Pages 106–09: Tepees, *Cheekwood Botanical Garden and Museum of Art, Tennessee, USA, 2013.*

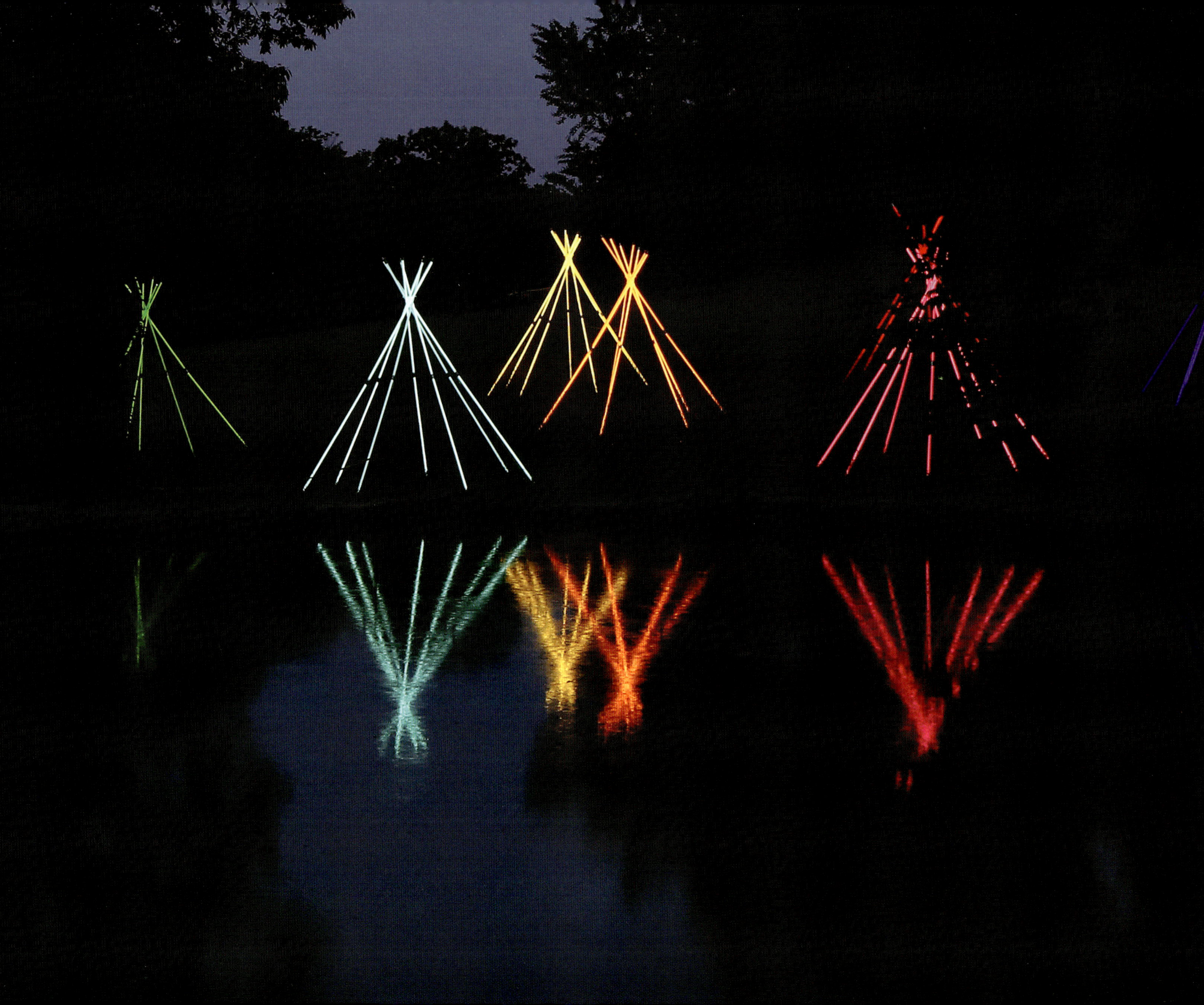

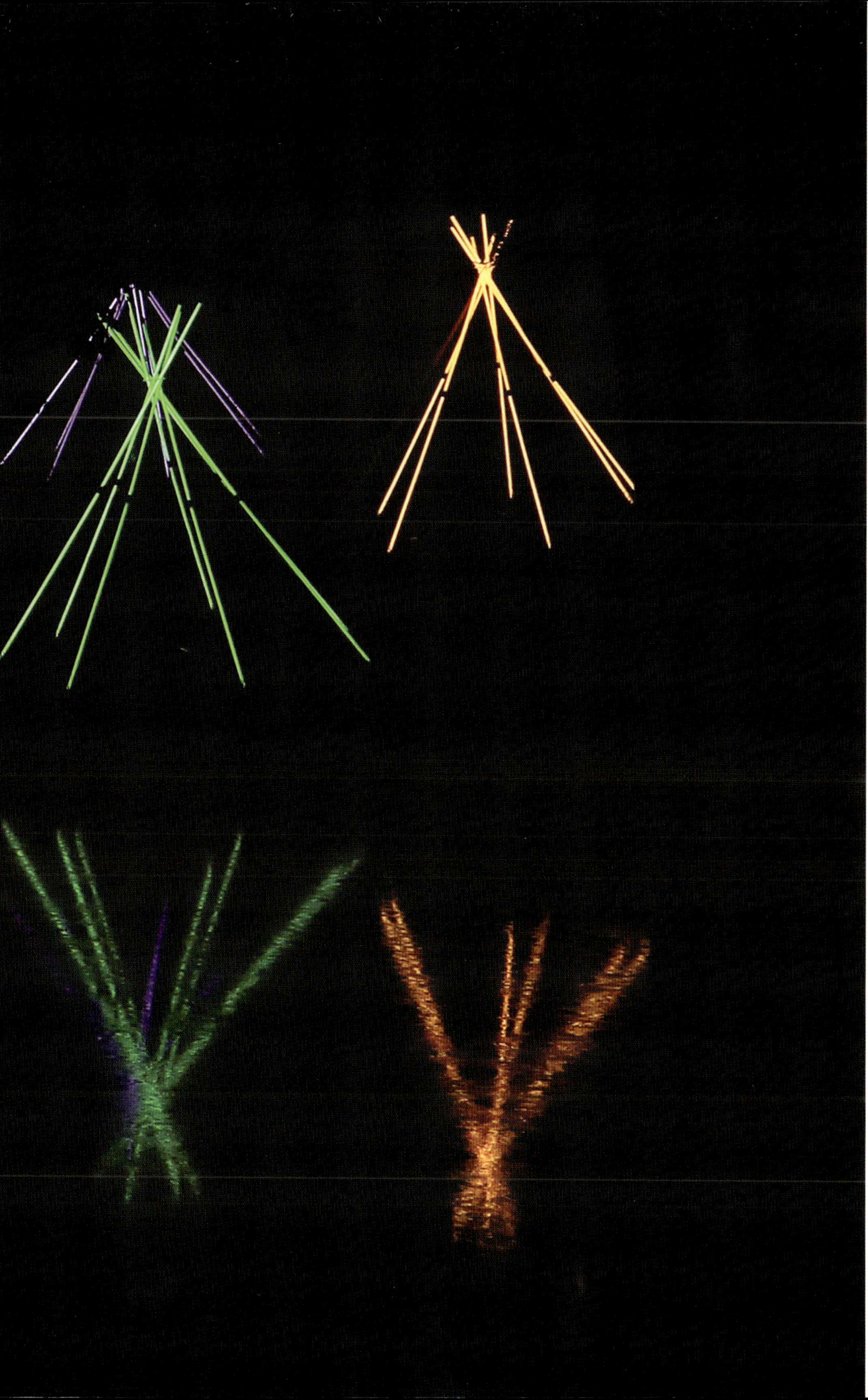

One thing I particularly like about this piece is that it cannot be experienced through photographs in the same way as it can in real time. The flashes of the fluorescent tubes happen so quickly that the eye doesn't see the tepees lit all in a group, only the intermittent flashing tubes of light. But the camera lens captures the entire series of flashes, so the lighted form of the whole installation is revealed.

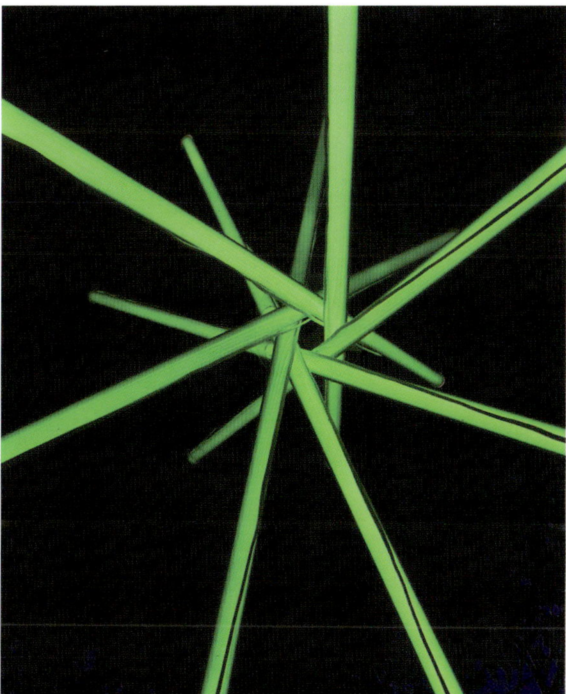

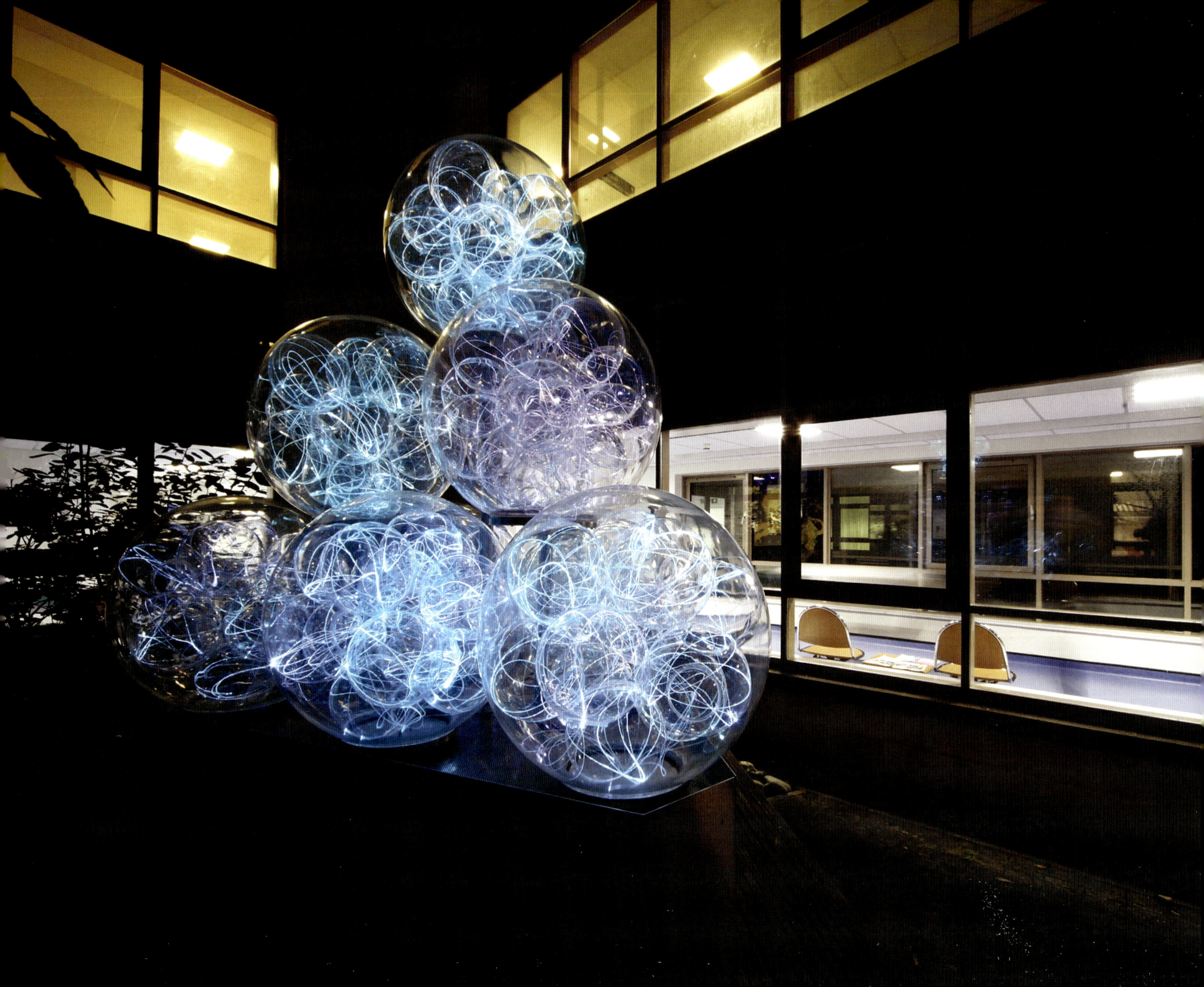

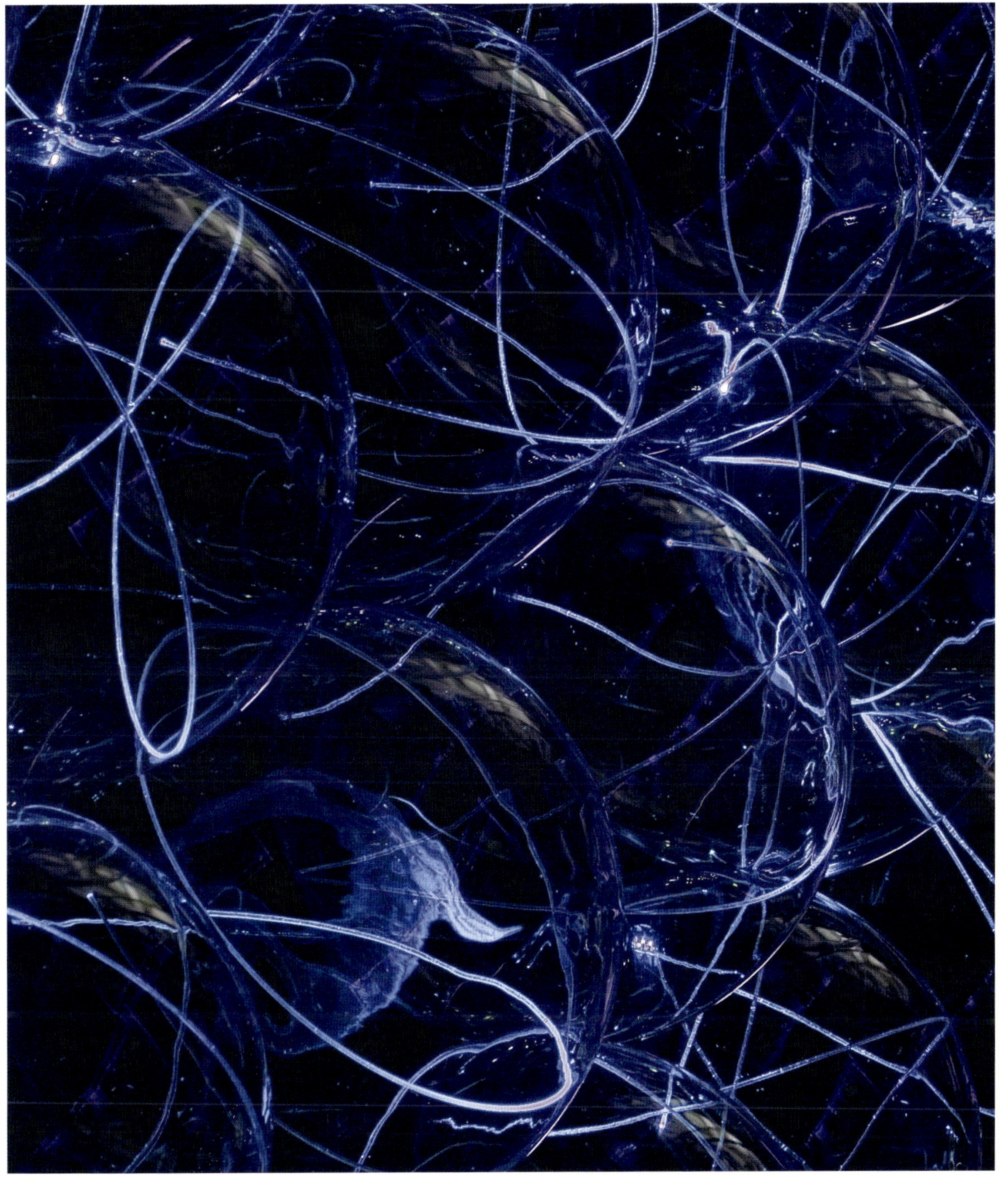

BRASS MONKEYS

"Brass Monkeys" was a phrase we schoolboys used to describe very cold weather, but I didn't know why. Years later, I gleaned those brass triangles that supported stacks of iron cannon balls on sailing ships were called "monkeys," and that in cold weather the metal contracted, causing the balls to fall off. Later on I learnt this was not true, but the saying has stuck with me.

I have created a number of sculptural installations using fibre-optic illumination within spherical forms: *Snowball* (chandelier), *Whizz Pop* (pendant/installation), *Wilma's Comet* (pendant), and *Field of Light* (installation). *Brass Monkeys* is another of my spherical reincarnations. I felt that a three-dimensional pyramid of spheres would create a strong visual statement, but I have to admit the influence of schoolboy humour is ever present.

Opposite and above: Brass Monkeys, *Royal United Hospital, Bath, UK, 2012.*

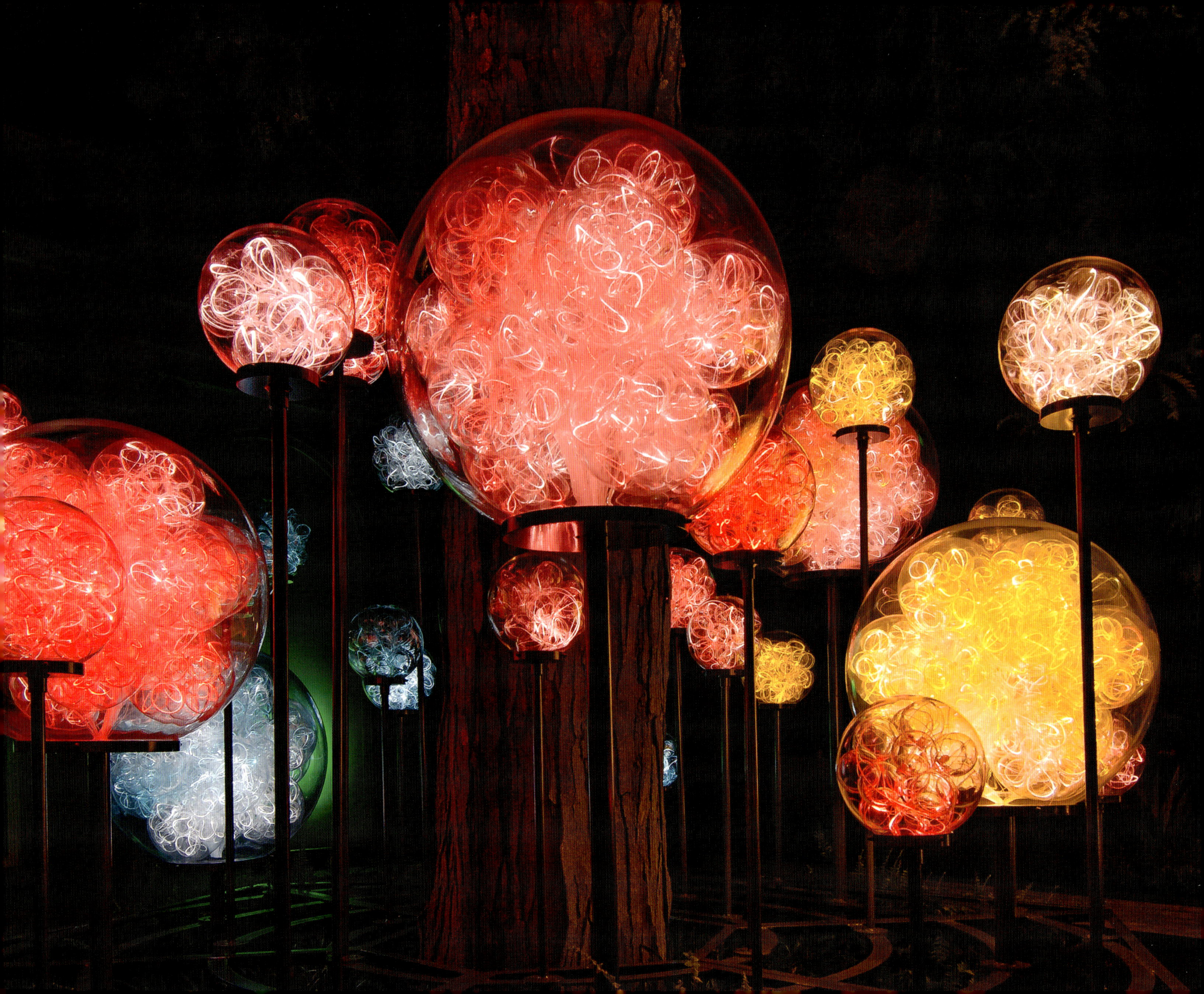

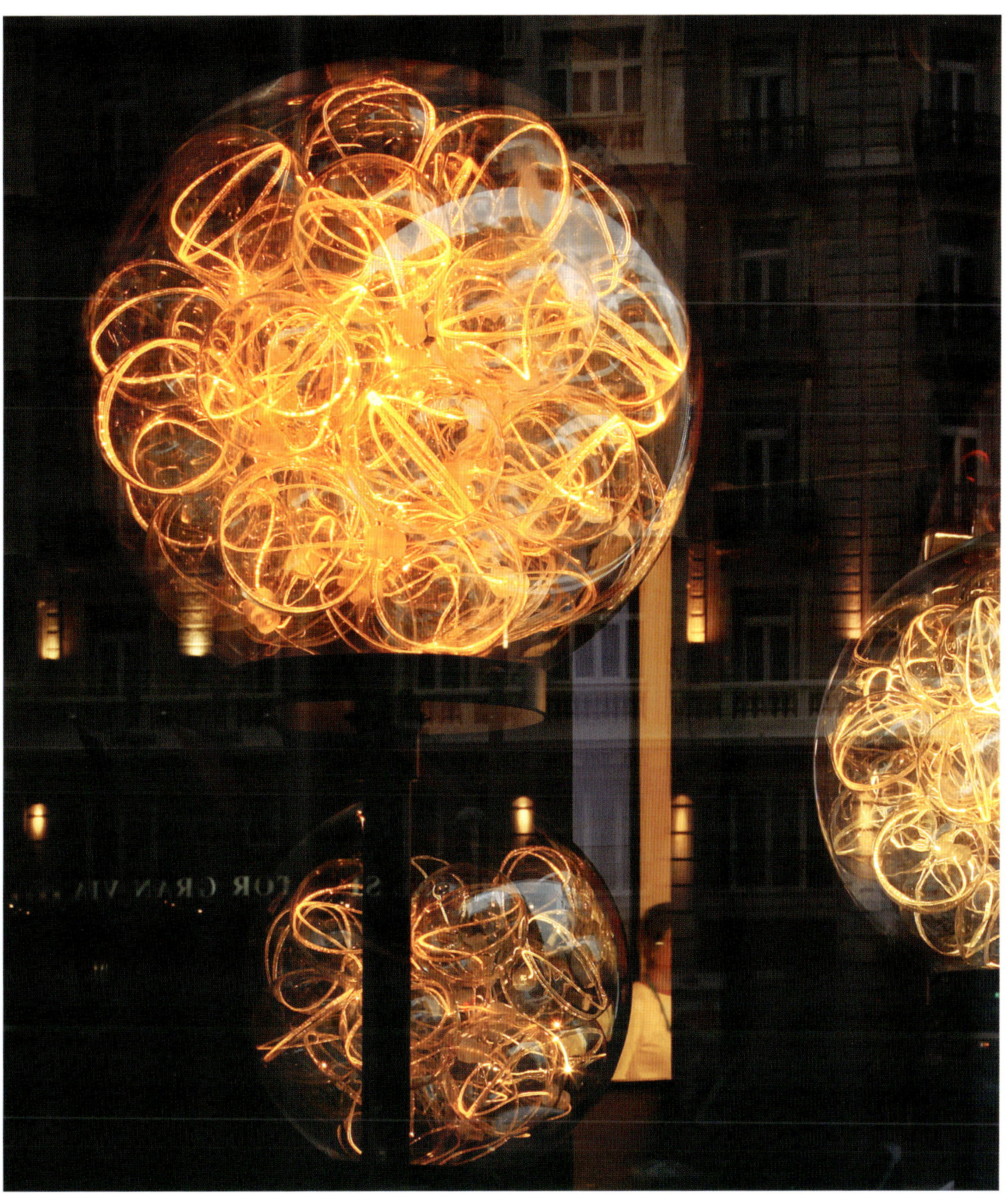

WHIZZ POPS

Twenty-eight years ago, an off-the-cuff remark about my sketchbook and my brain function cut me to the quick. A colleague casually said I had "a butterfly mind." The truth hurt, but it did galvanise me into addressing my cerebral shortcomings.

My solution was simple. To constrain, contain, create, and express my vivid imagination through the medium of light (why I chose light is another story) and let life take its course. Everything I have done since that enlightened day has both a rhyme and a reason.

My sources of inspiration are many and varied, randomly alighted upon (butterfly-like). It has taken me years to perfect my natural capacity for daydreaming into a conscious art. Certain pieces of work are connected by the materials I have to hand. At other times, two seemingly disparate ideas collide and make

Opposite: Whizz Pops, *Longwood Gardens, Pennsylvania, USA, 2012. Above and page 114:* Whizz Pops, *Telefonica, S.A., Madrid, Spain, 2012.*

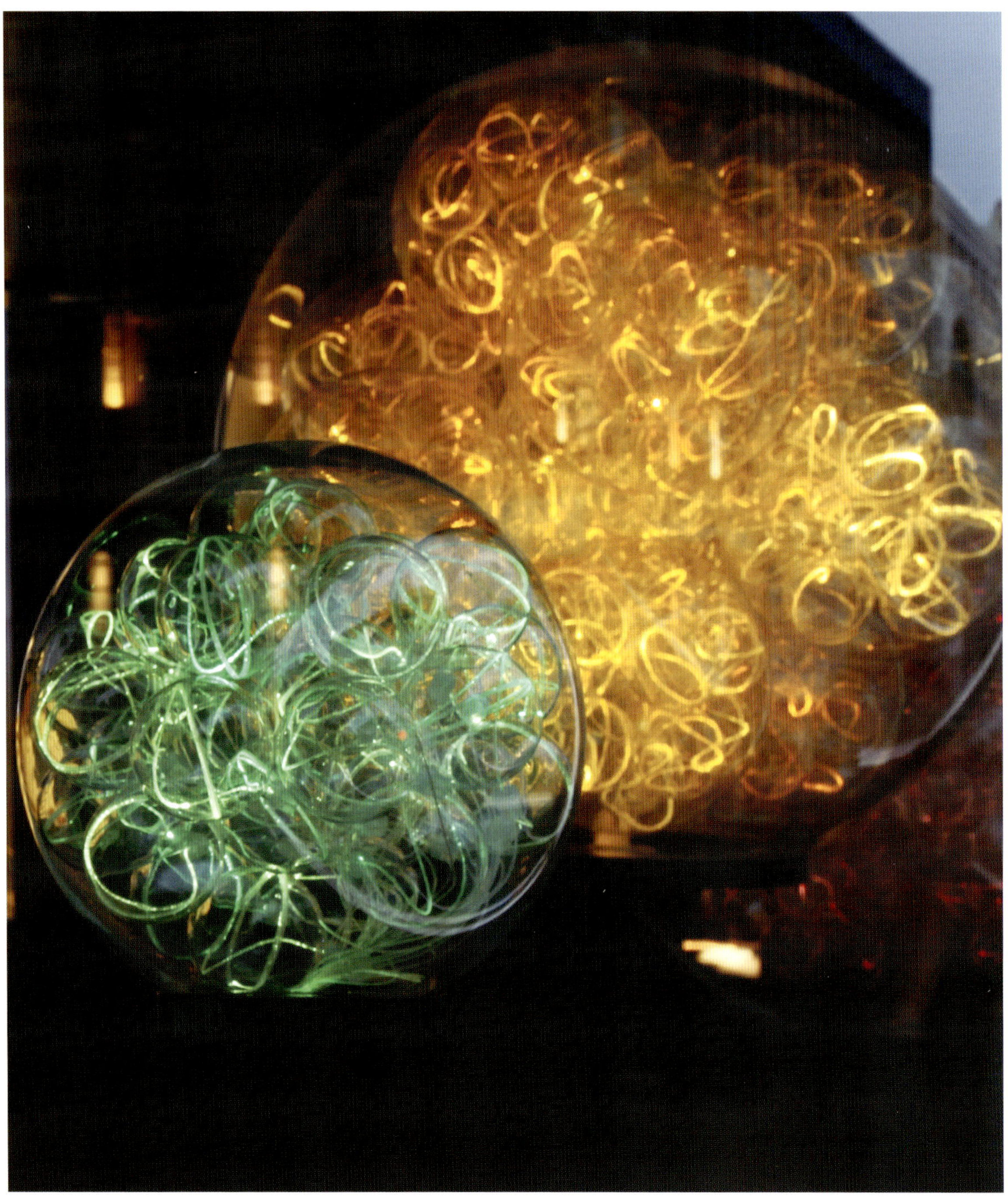

sense. Occasionally, it is a bit of both.

Whizz Pops was not created in a Eureka! moment. It happened because materials were by chance placed side by side in my studio, and they called out to each other. The collision/collusion of glass and acrylic that resulted, although I say it myself, is a winner.

Why do I call it *Whizz Pops*? Roald Dahl's *The BFG* is one of my favourite books that I read to my children, and when I first saw the piece bubbling with light on the workbench, a big magical giant's fluff popped into my butterfly mind.

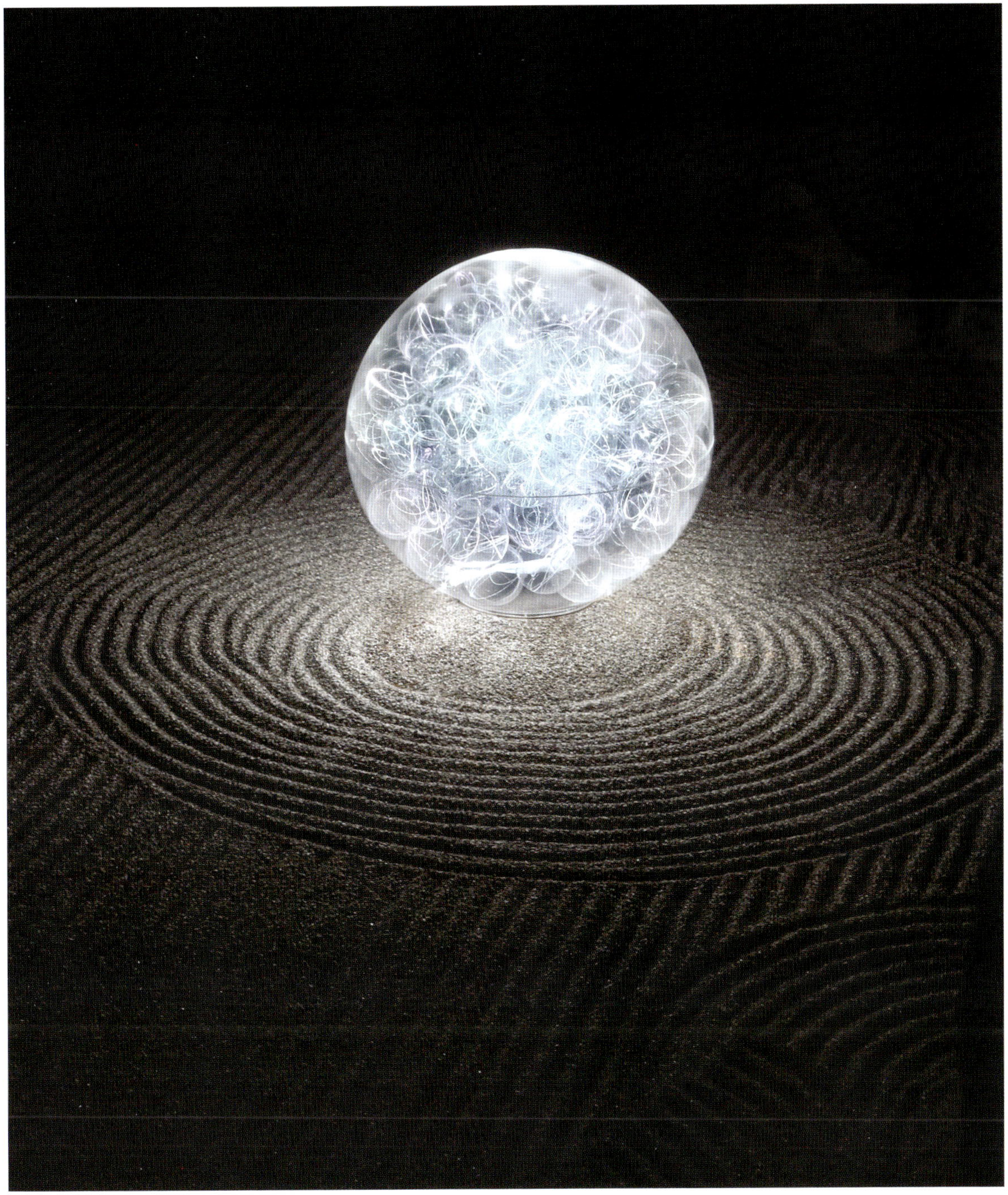

BLUE MOON

During my first visit to Cheekwood, I had an instinctive reaction to the formality of the Japanese gravel lake adjacent to the pavilion. It's an intimate space, set in a valley of rounded hills. Looking at the "lake," I saw the next space for my installation *Blue Moon* to inhabit. The gentle movement of light within the moon plays shadows over the intricately dry raked gravel that surrounds it. My hope was to create a piece that extended the sense of calm within the space.

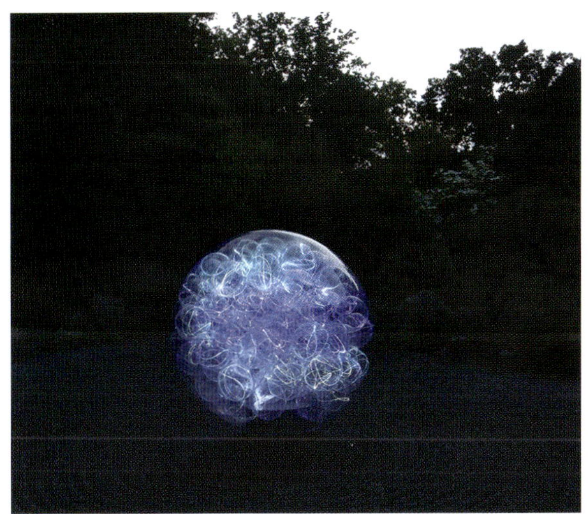

Blue Moon, *Cheekwood Botanical Garden and Museum of Art, Tennessee, USA, 2013.*

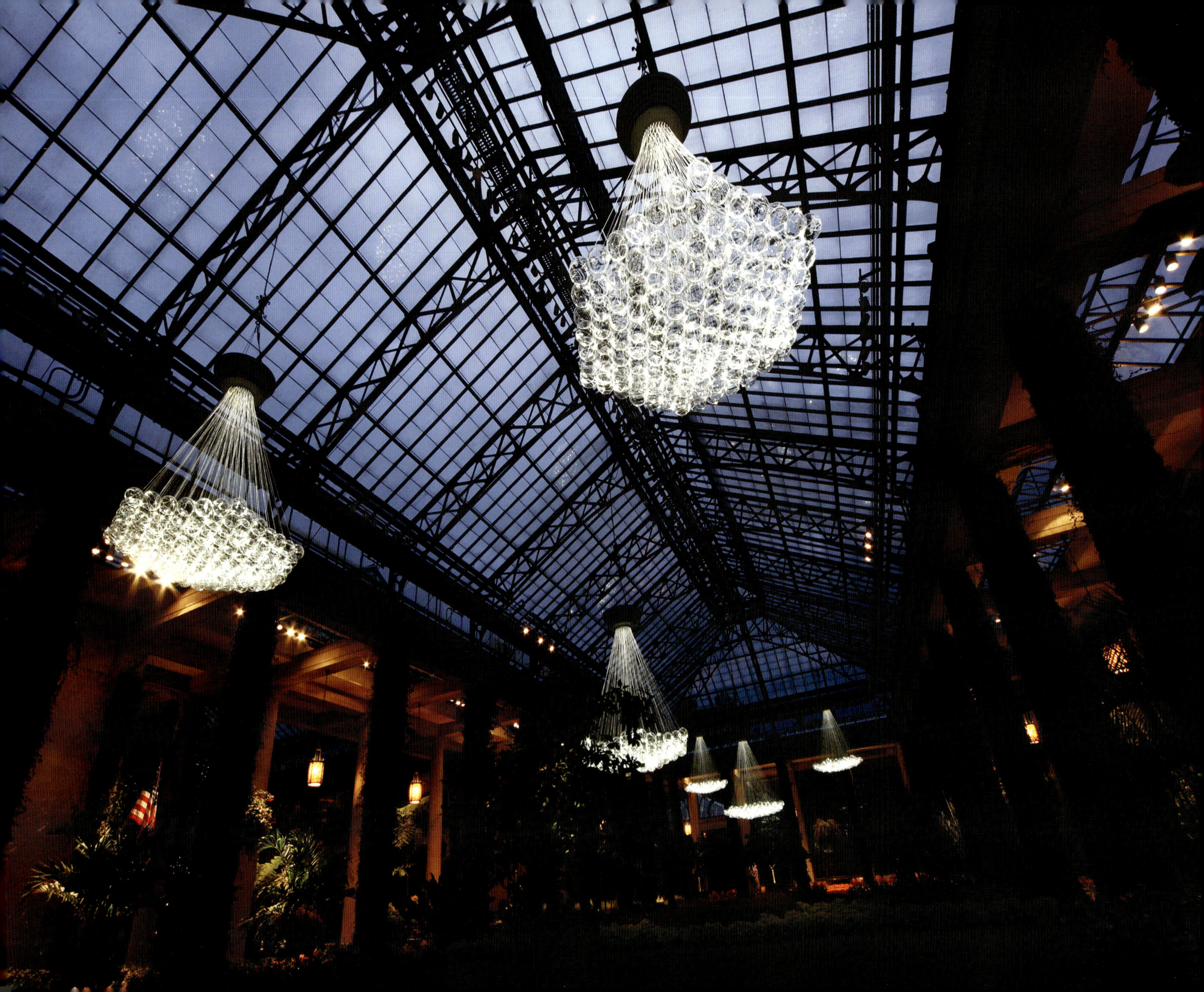

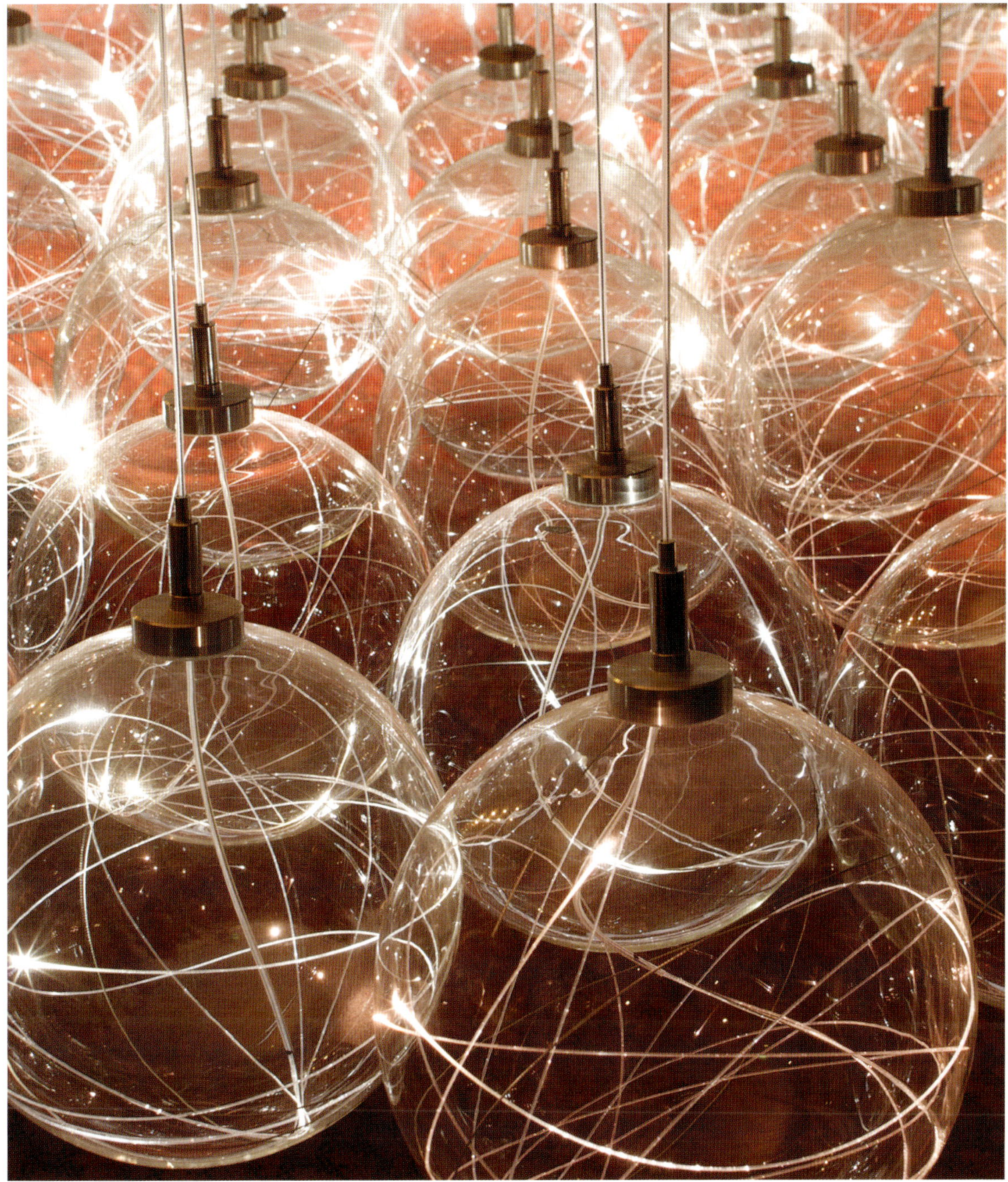

SNOWBALL

The *Snowballs* chandelier design came about partly through luck and partly through the wonderful book illustrations of Raymond Briggs's 1992 classic, *The Snowman*.

The lucky part of the design came to fruition because I was stuck in a traffic jam in front of a shop displaying translucent Christmas decorations (balls for trees). I happened to have a fibre harness for a shower luminaire I was designing on the passenger seat of my car. I simply wondered how the balls would look attached, all clustered together, to the fibre harness. I hopped out of my car and bought all the stock. The design came together within days.

The name came about because the illuminated colours reminded me of the subtle colours in the animated version of Raymond Briggs's book, in particular the scene of the dancing snowmen and women under the soft hues of the Aurora Borealis.

Pages 116–24: Giant Snowballs, *Longwood Gardens, Pennsylvania, USA, 2012.*

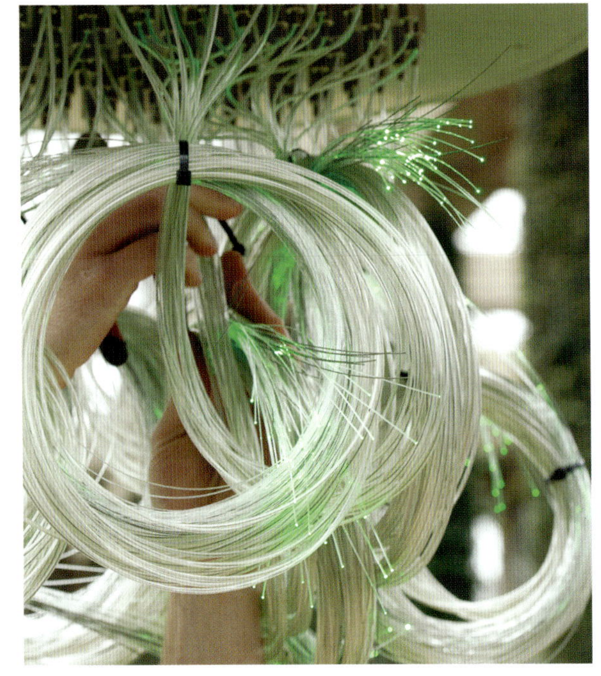

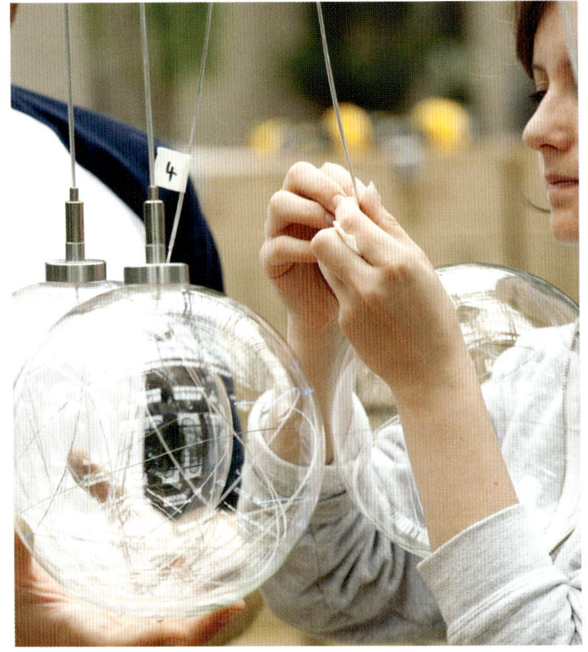

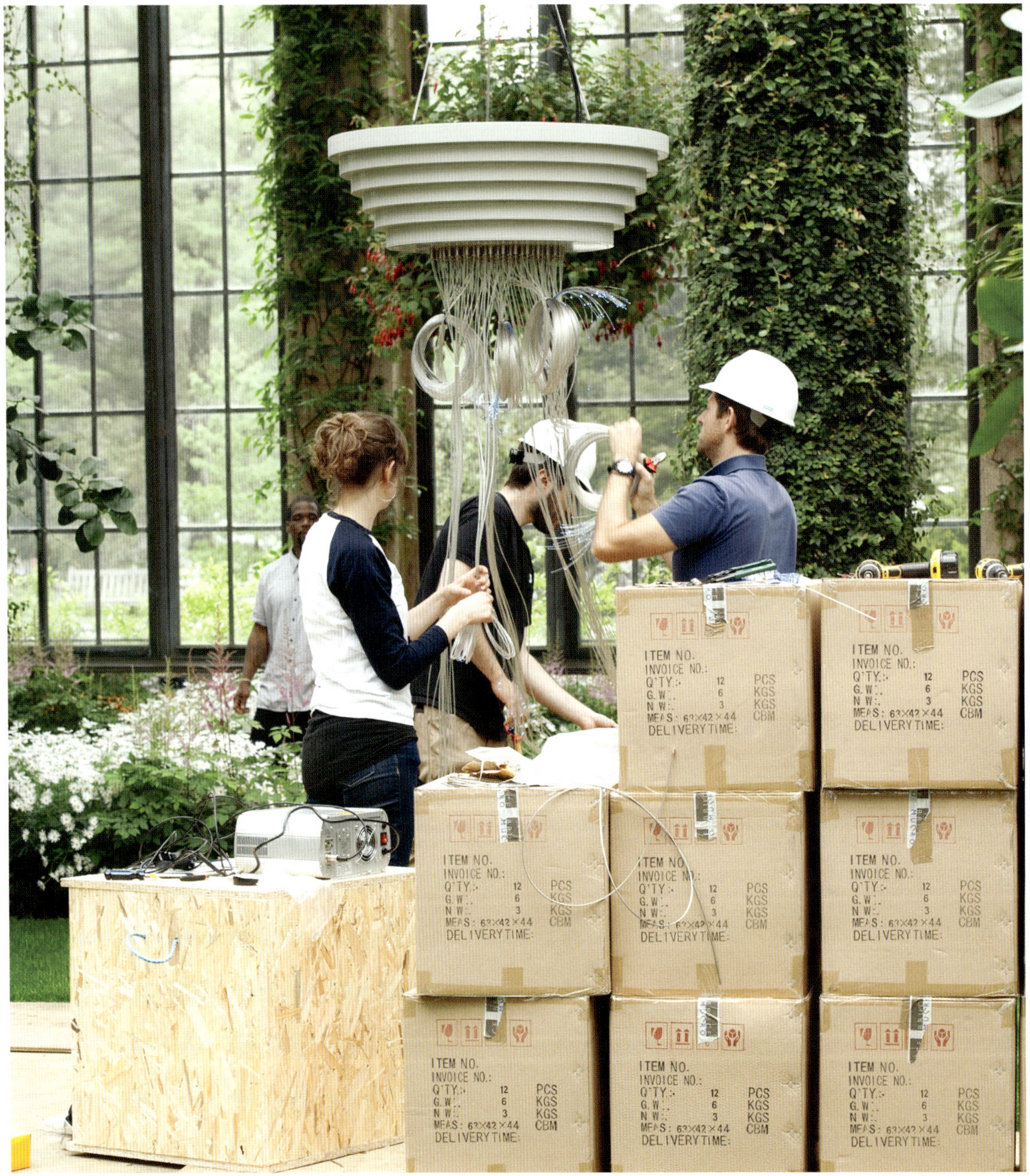

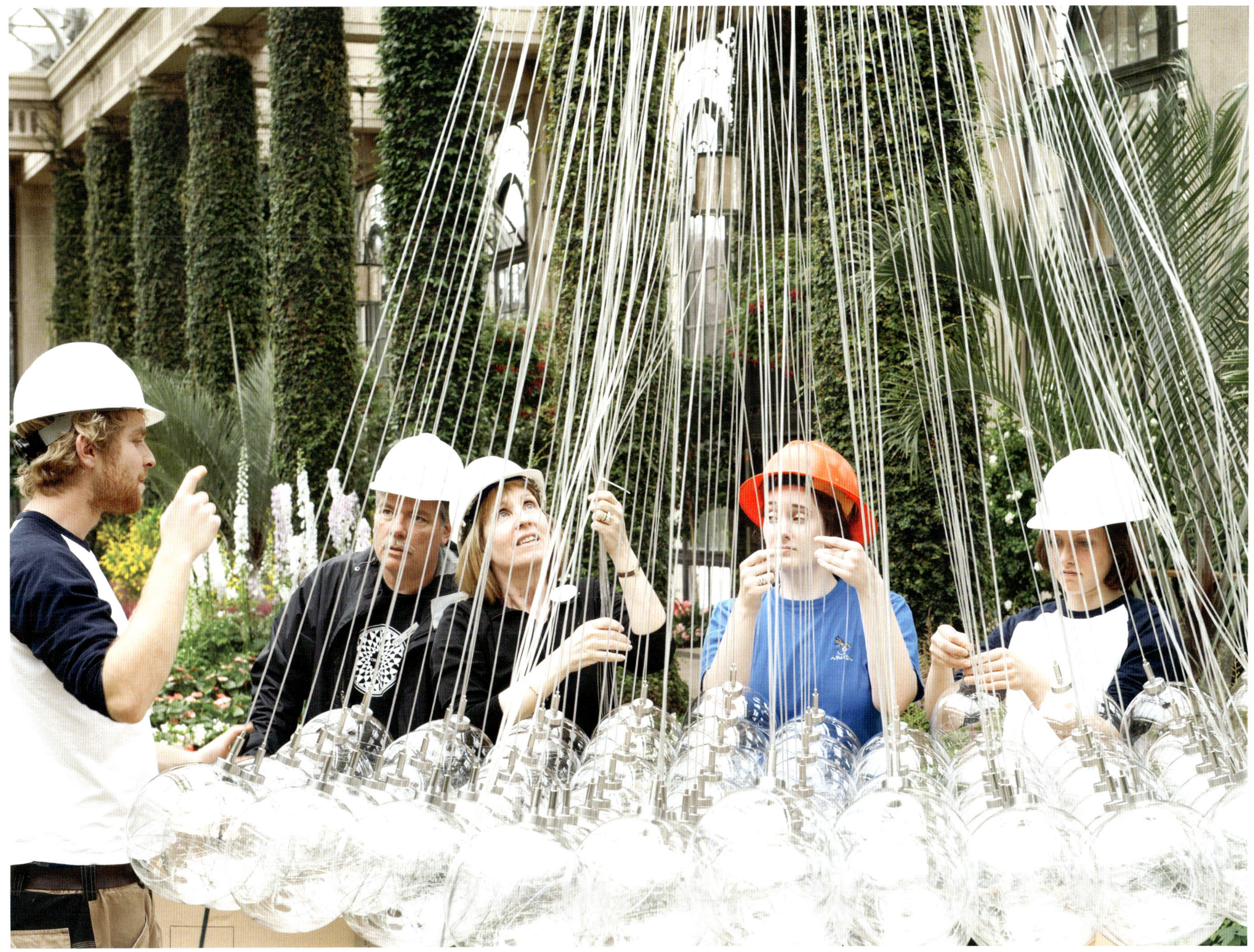

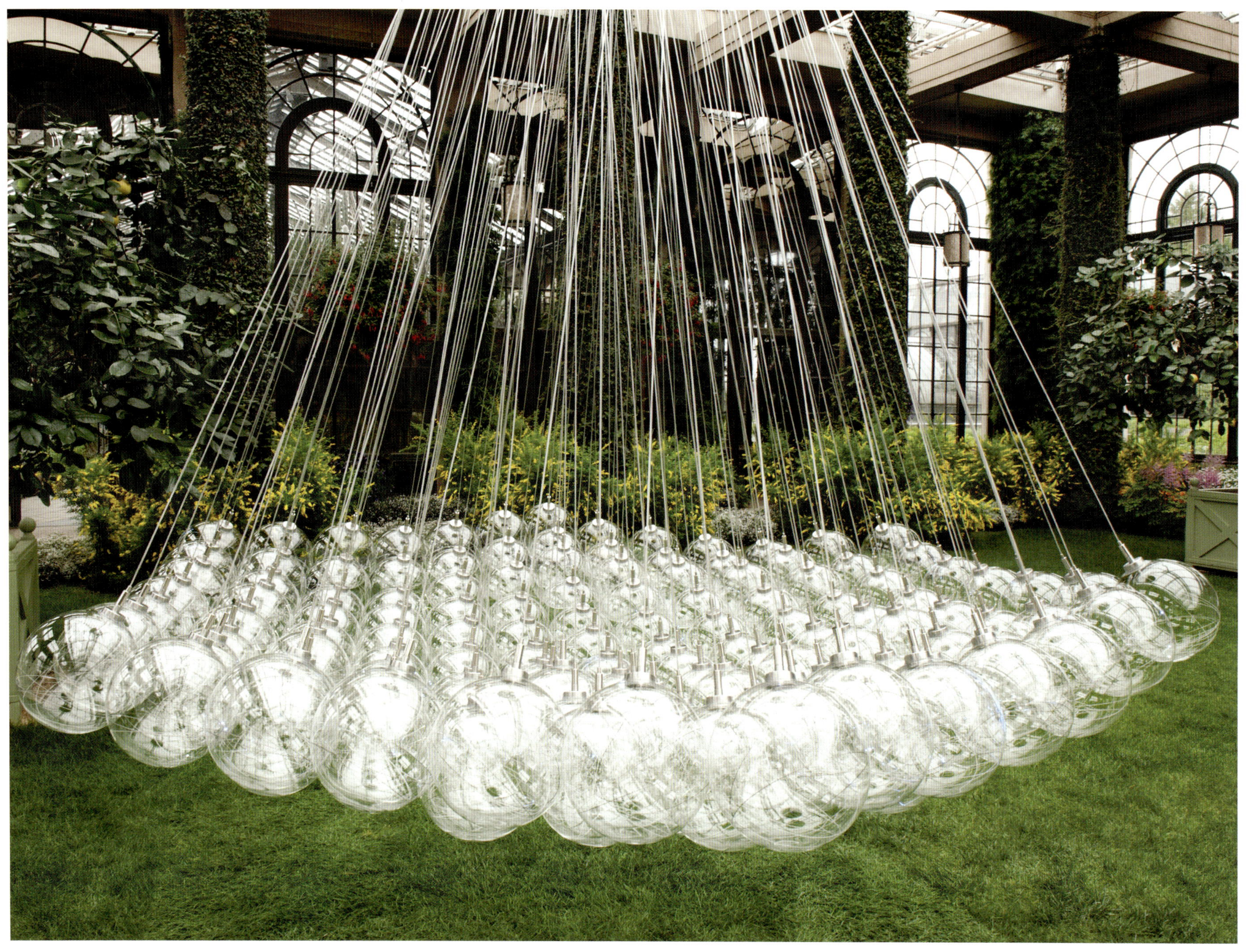

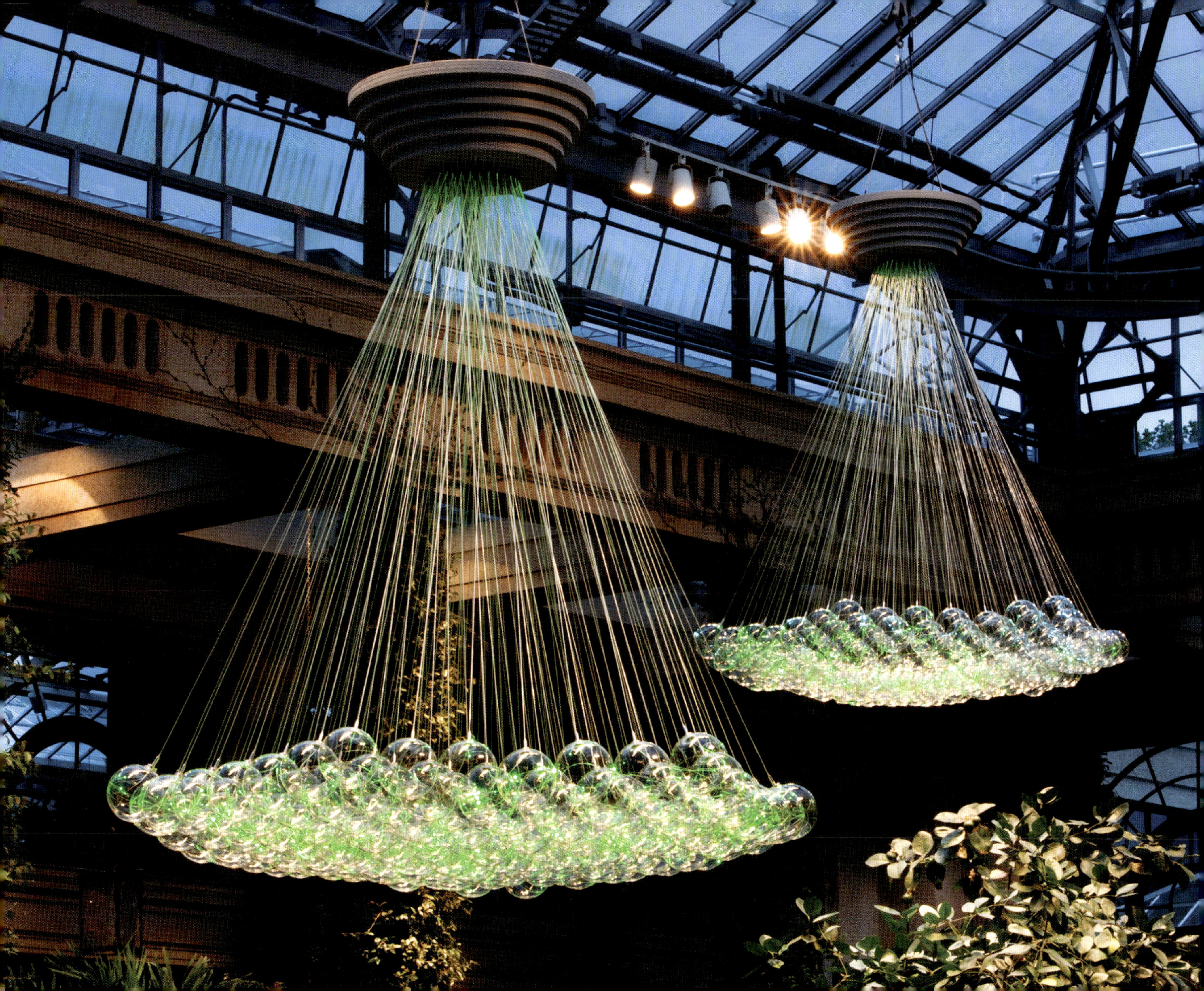

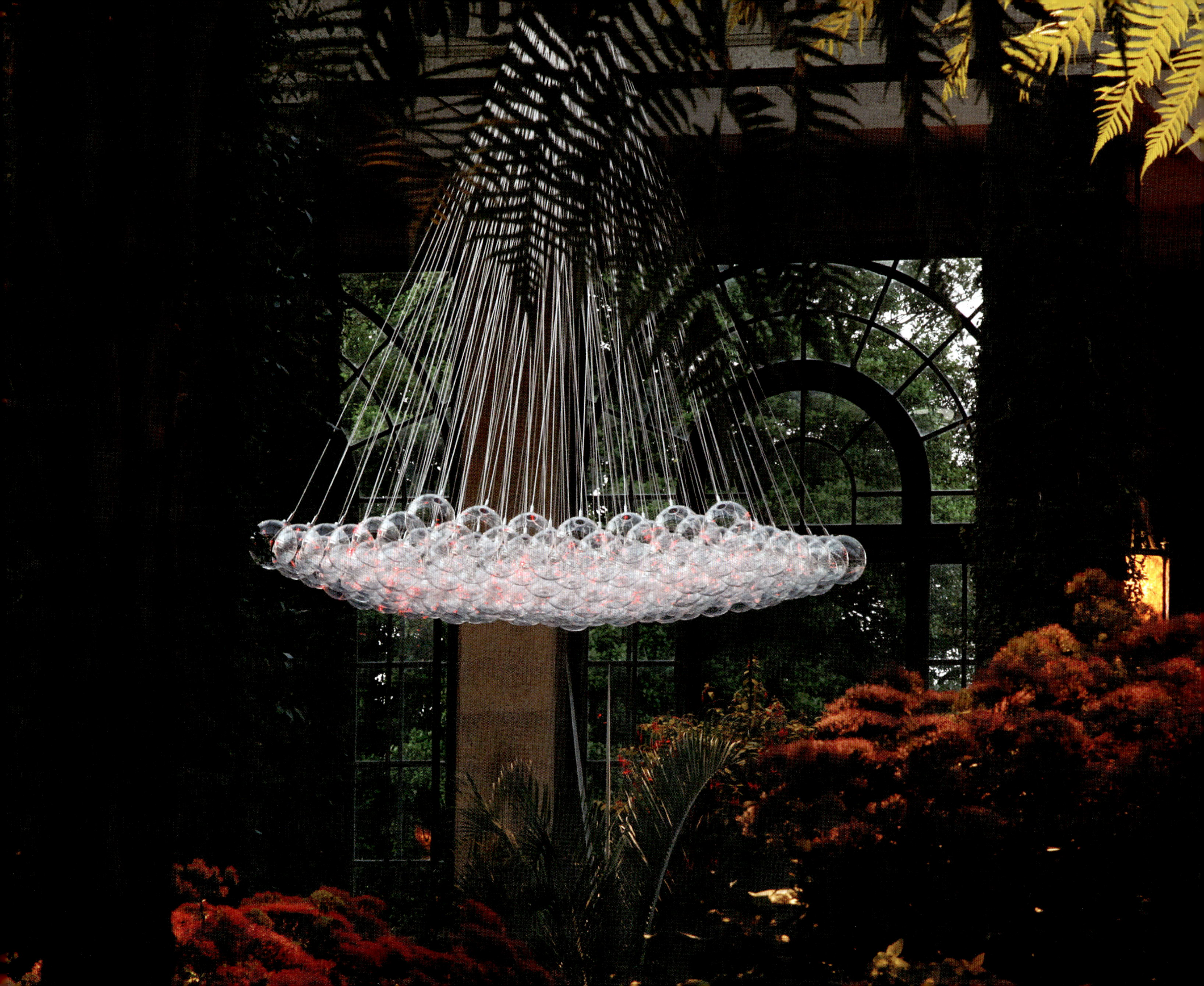

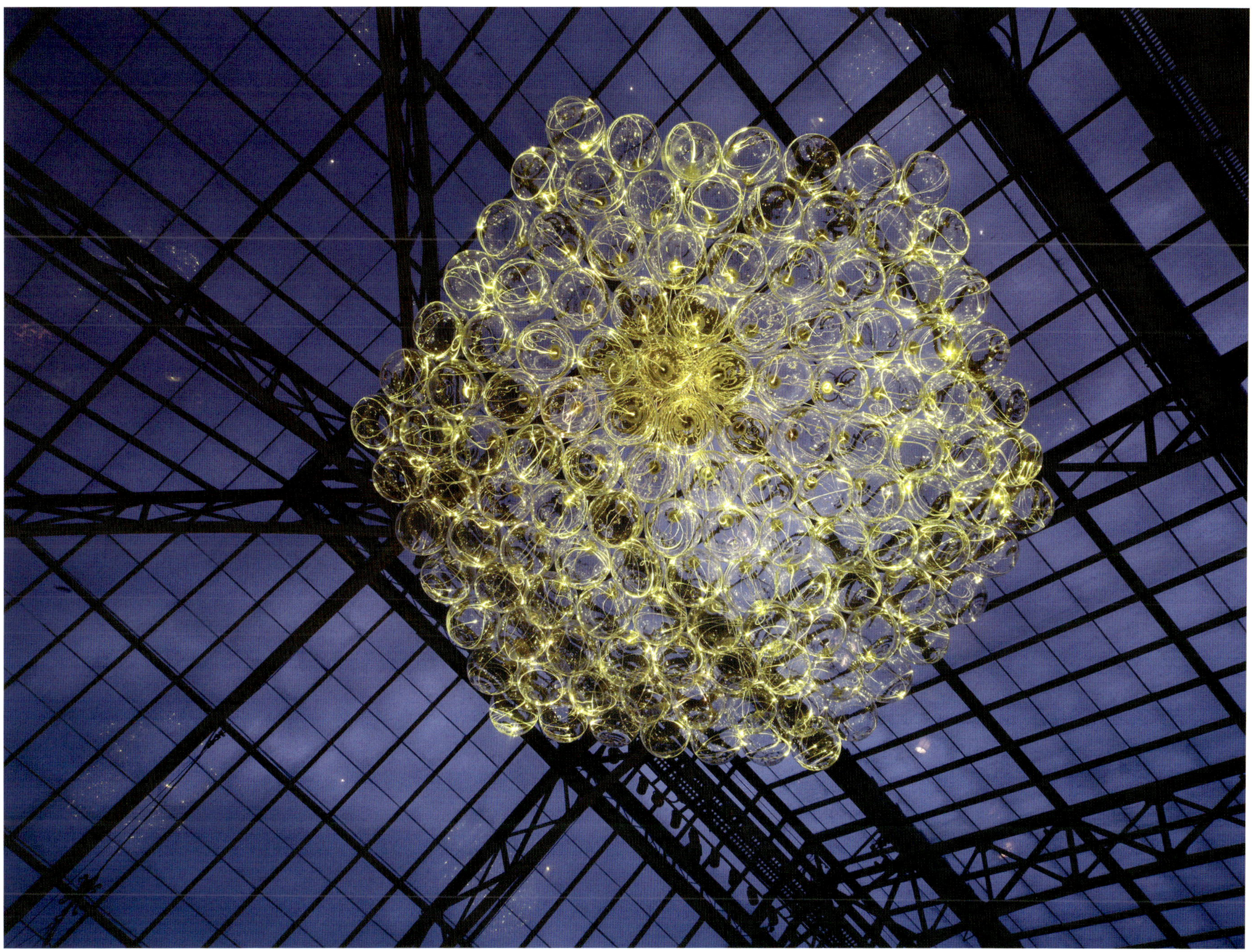

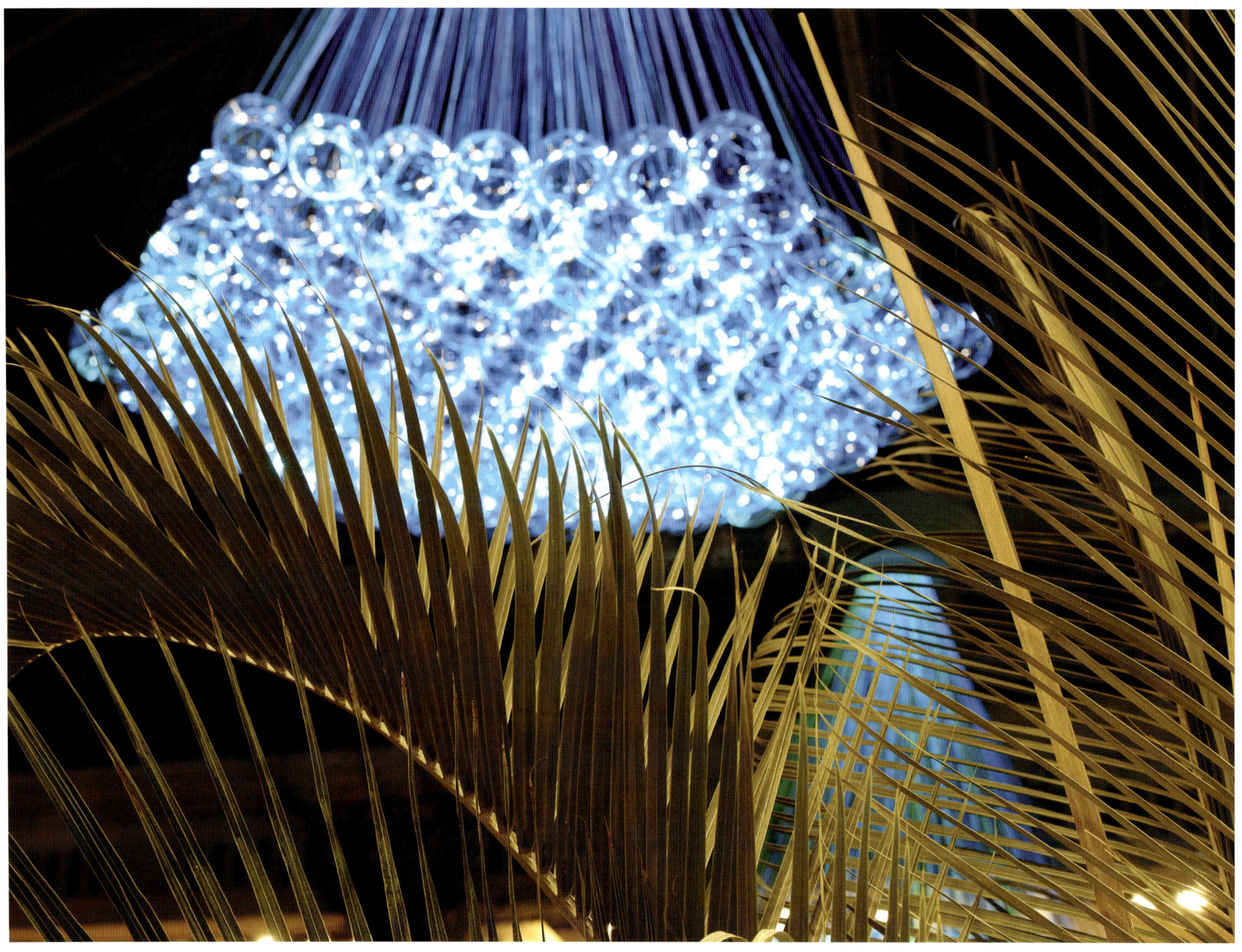

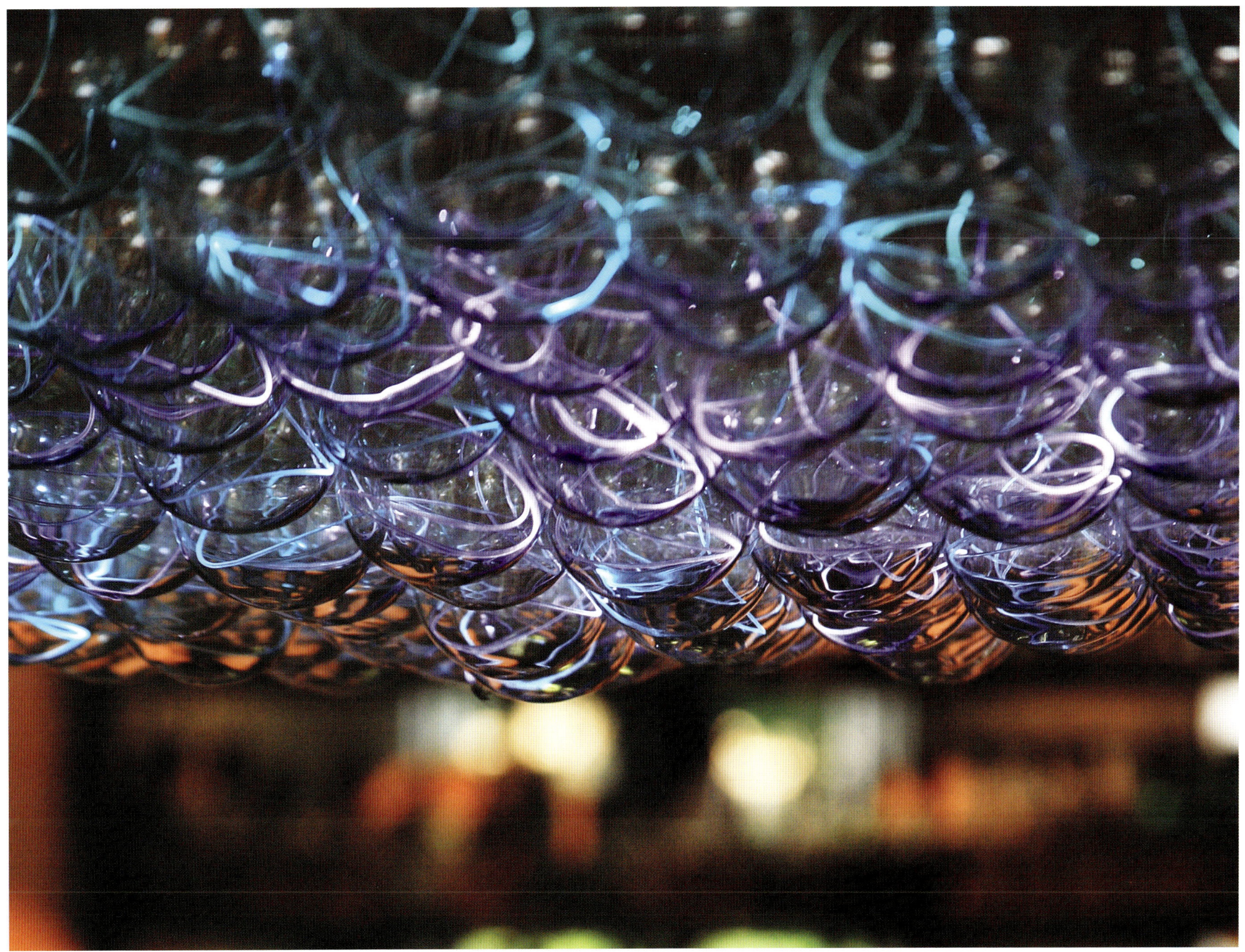

Snowball, *Babington House, Babington, Somerset, UK, 2008.*

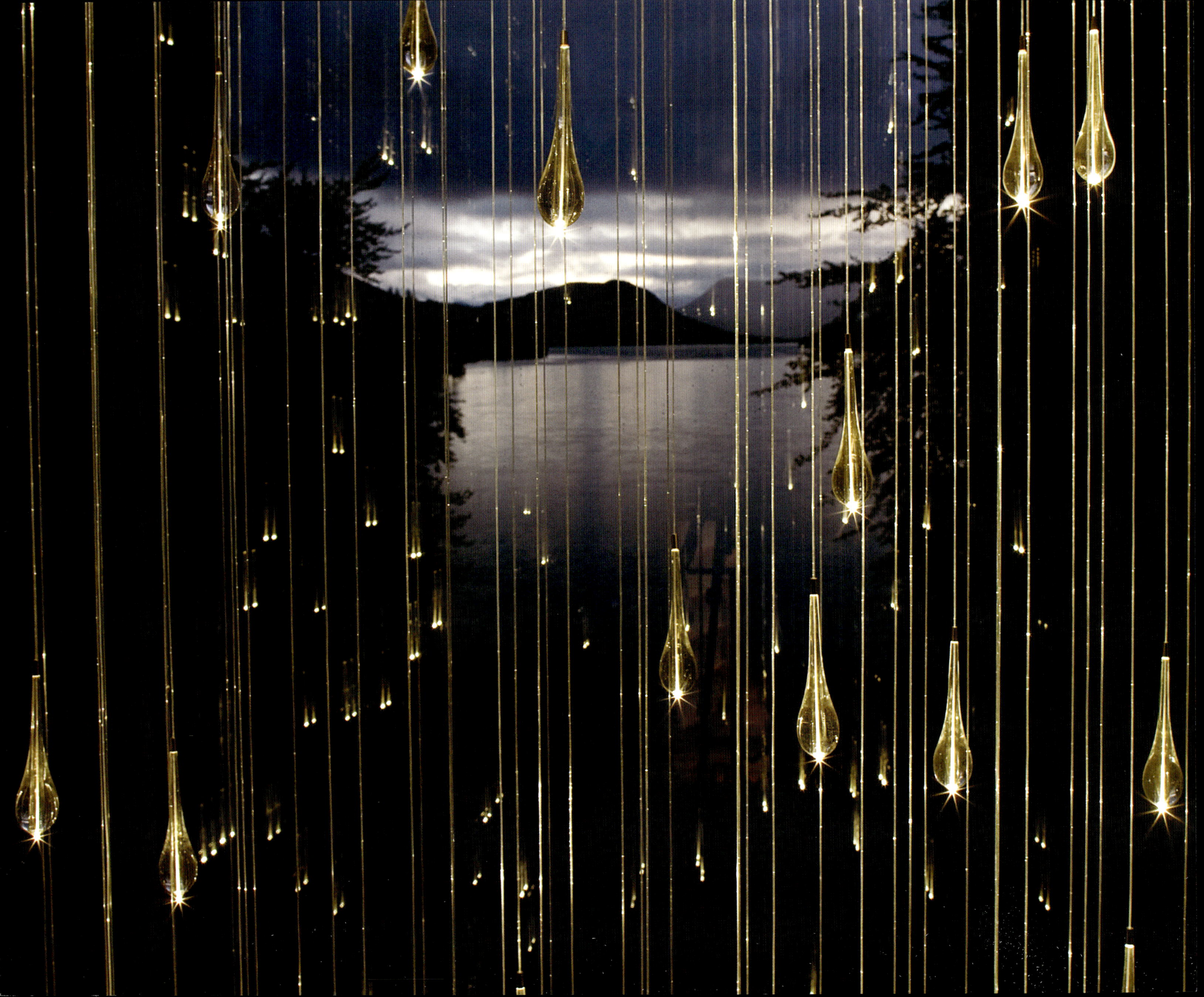

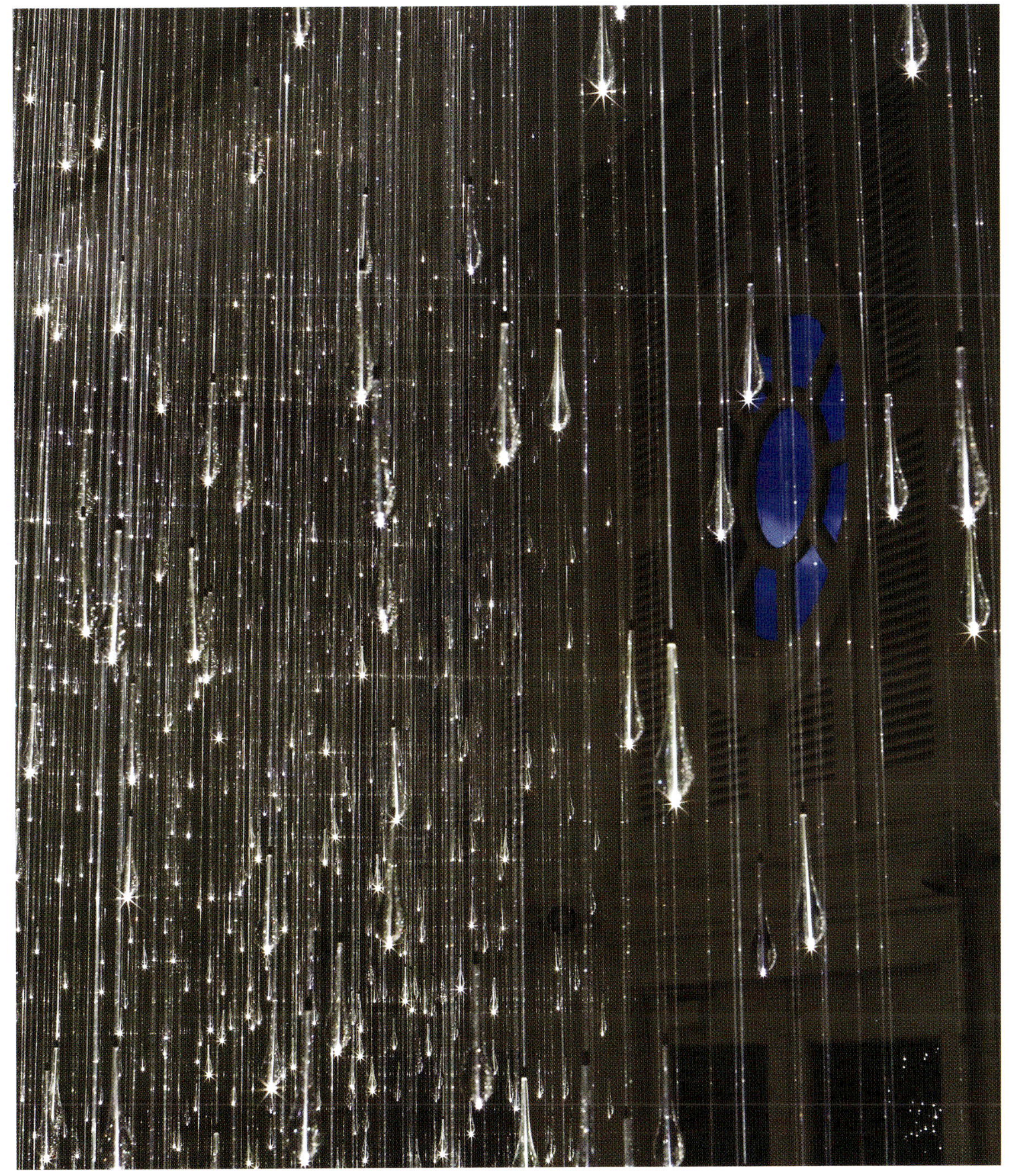

LIGHT SHOWER

In 2008, I was invited to propose lighting designs for a contemporary Highland lodge at the head of Loch Ossian in Scotland. I found myself sitting on a step halfway up the main stairs of the lodge absorbing a magnificent, uninterrupted view of the loch and group of snow-capped mountains beyond. It was raining in squalls against the plate-glass window, which distorted the view with rivulets of water streaming down the panoramic pane. The words "light" and "shower" registered in my mind, and I had my idea.

The original installation now hangs motionless as if suspended in time, overlooking but not interrupting the view of Loch Ossian. By day it catches glimpses of the sunshine, shedding prismatic flecks of light onto the stairs; by night it morphs into what it is: a shower of light.

Opposite: Light Shower, *Loch Ossian, Scotland, 2008. Pages 127–29:* Light Shower, *Cheekwood Botanical Garden and Museum of Art, Tennessee, USA, 2013.*

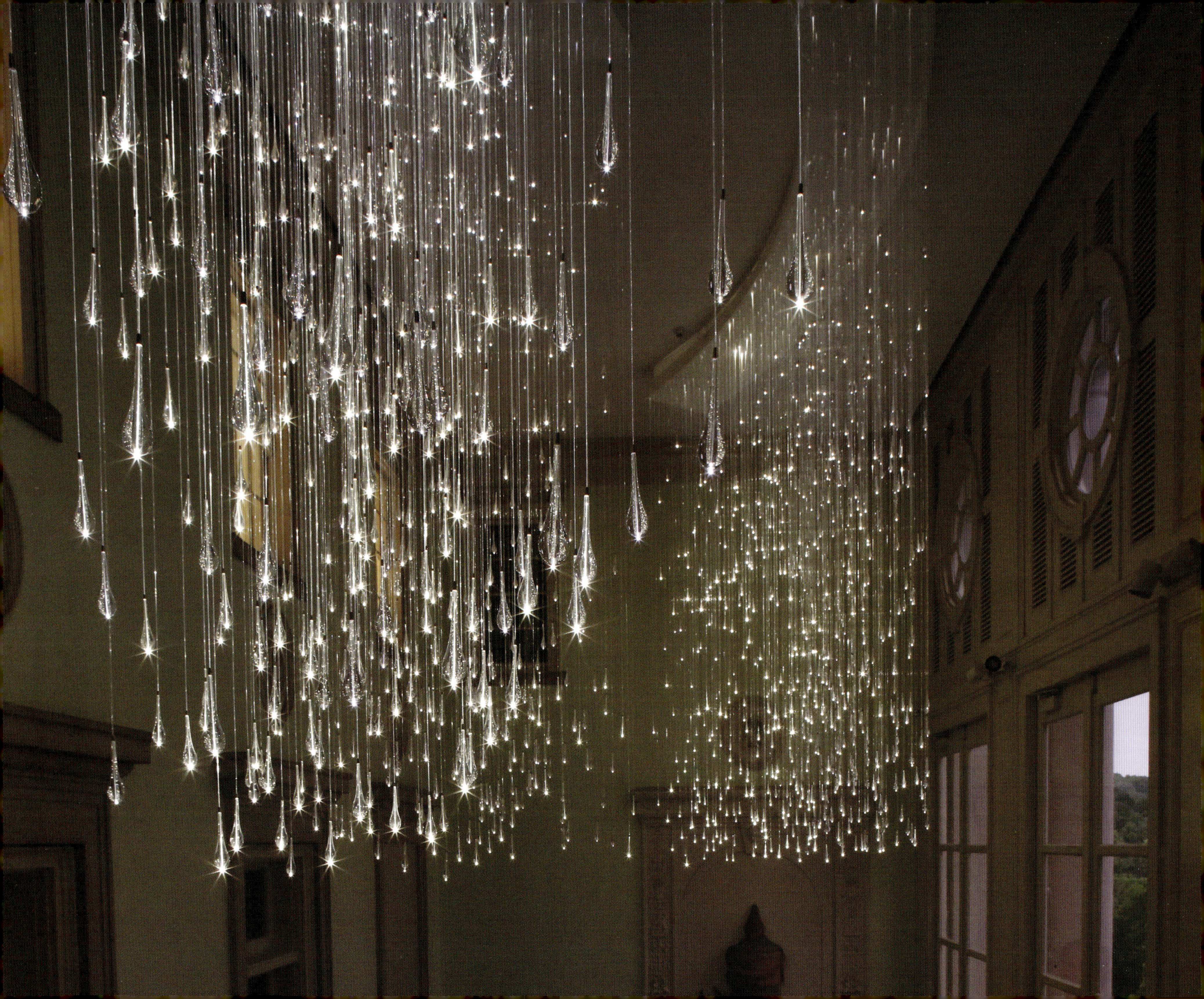

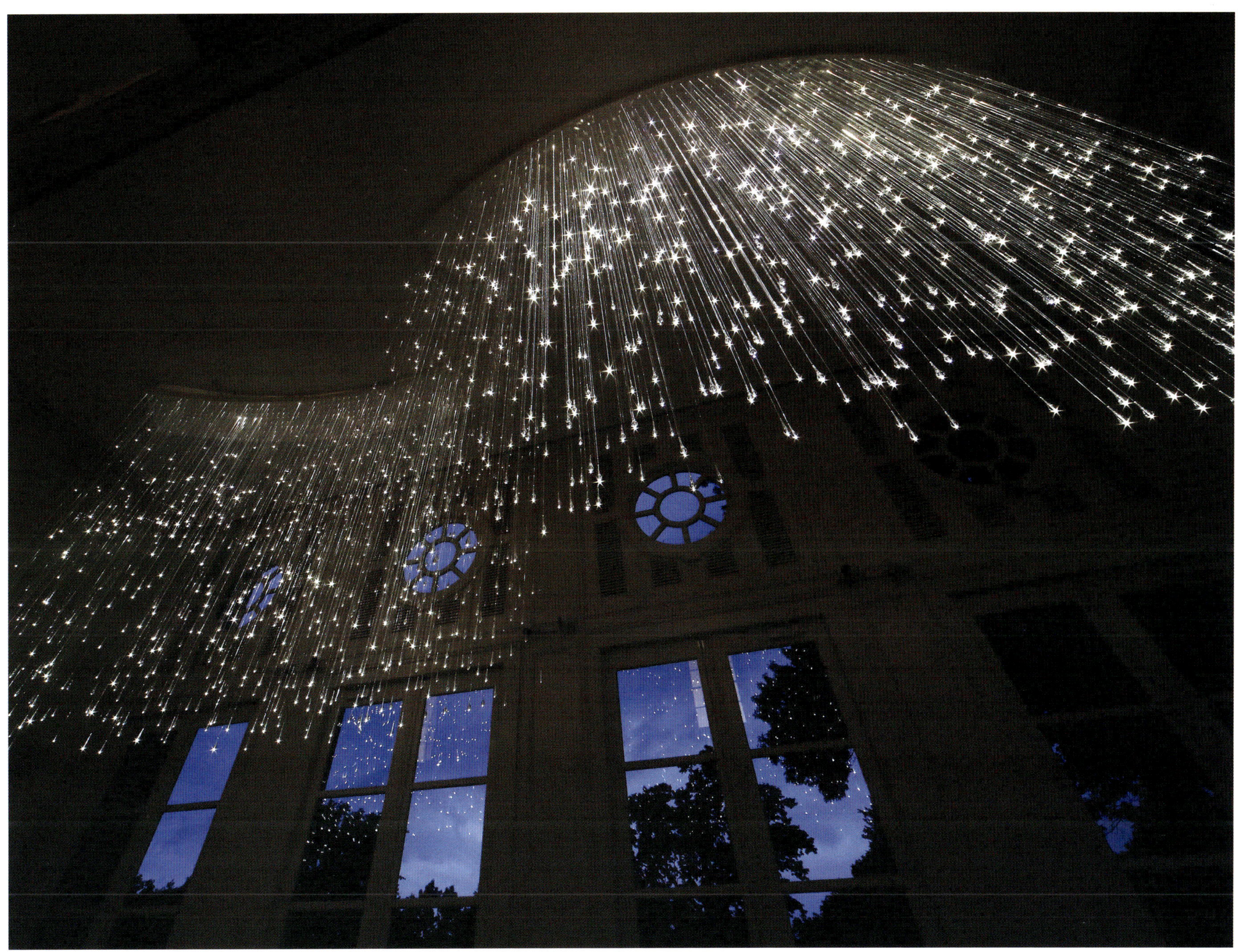

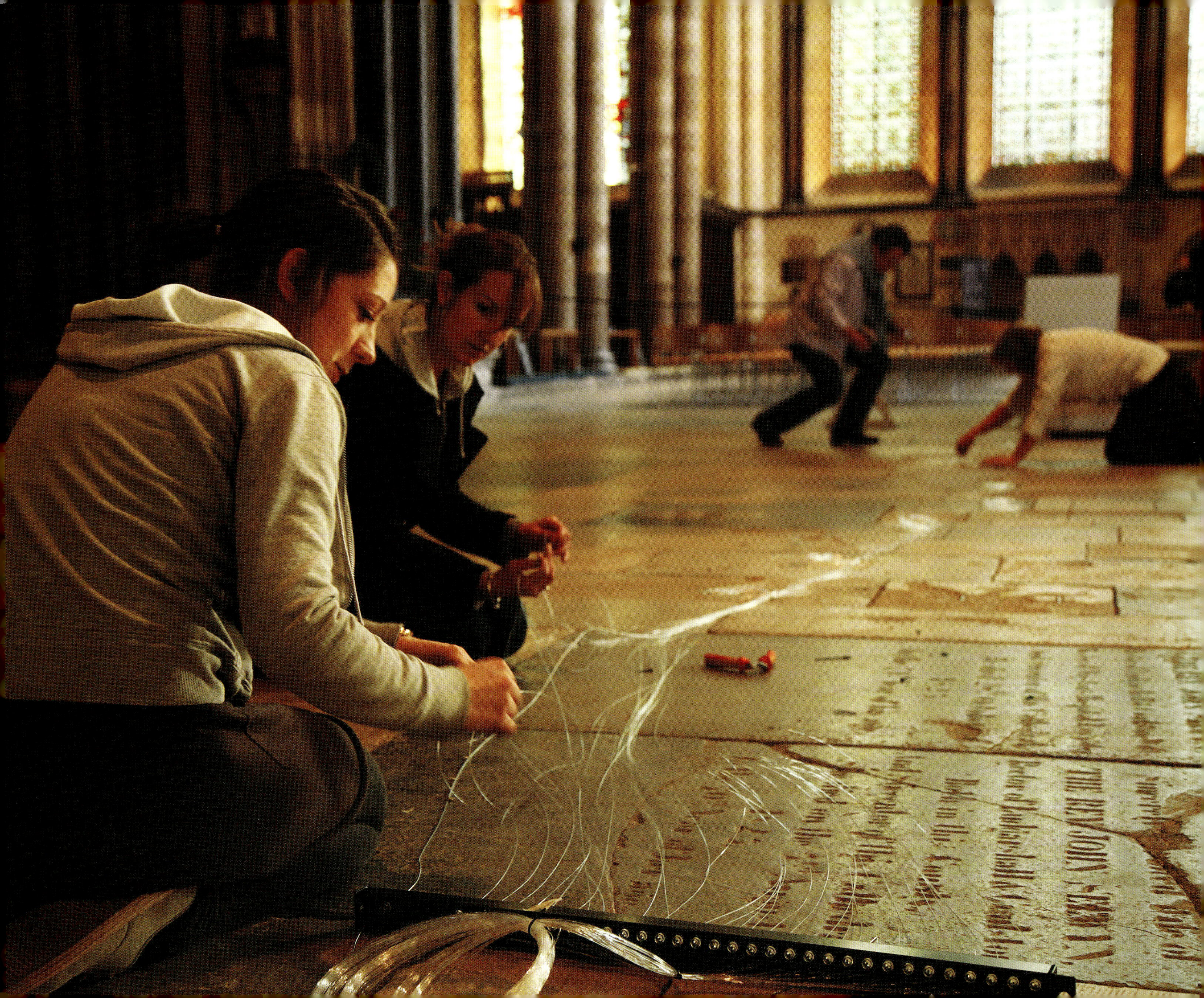

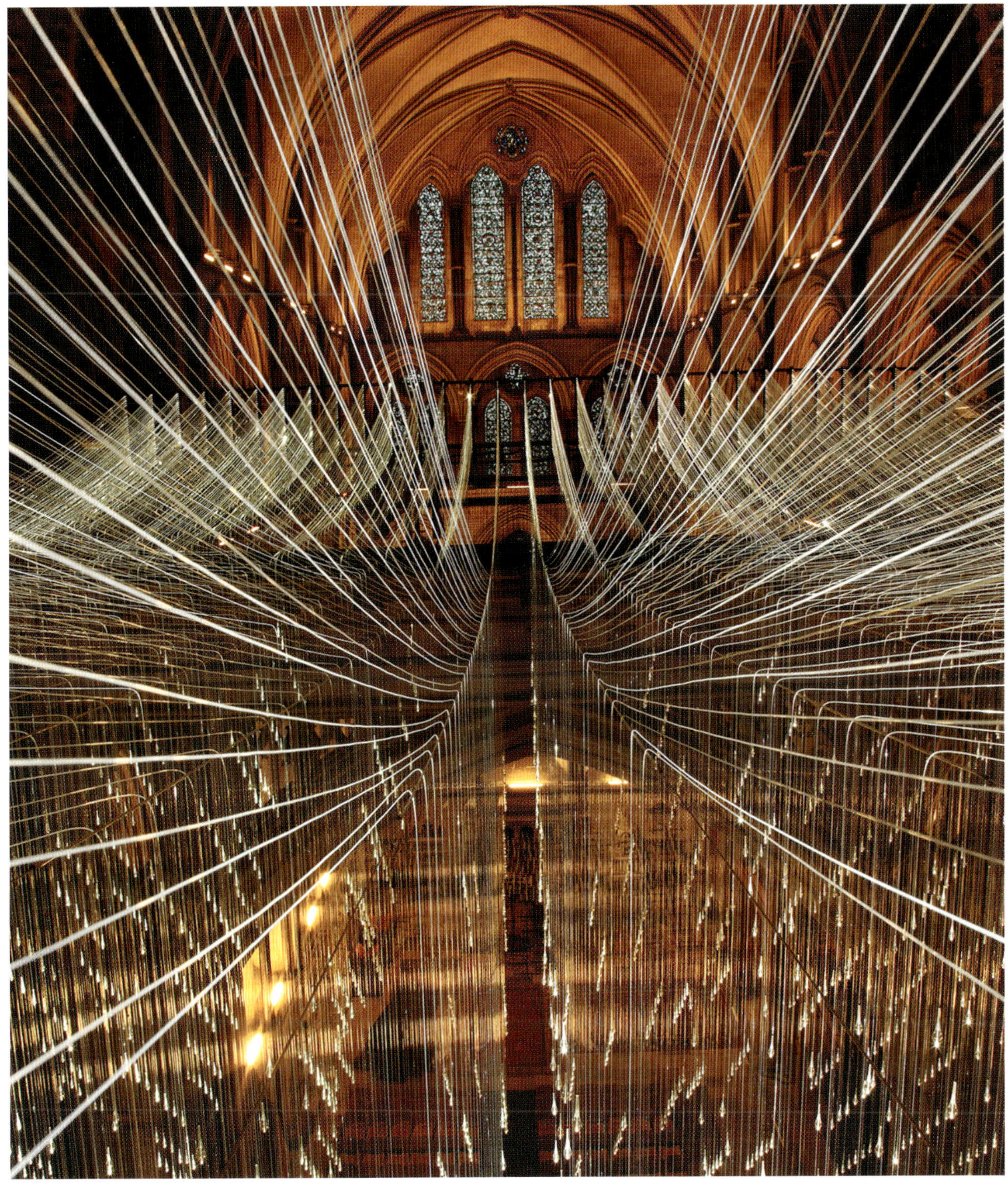

Pages 130–35: Light Shower, *Salisbury Cathedral, Wiltshire, UK, 2010.*

I installed *Light Shower* in the ancient Salisbury Cathedral in late November 2010. It took my team and I five days to install. Though ethereal, *Light Shower* covered a massive area, 10m x 10m x 7m (33 feet x 33 feet x 23 feet). It took 400 man-hours to make it, and 232 man-hours to install. *Light Shower* is made of 1984 strands of optic fibre, each one tipped by a "tear-drop" diffuser, and powered by eight 150-watt metal halide projectors.

Once the testing process was complete, *Light Shower* was switched on for the first time during the Darkness into Light procession to mark the start of Advent at Salisbury Cathedral.

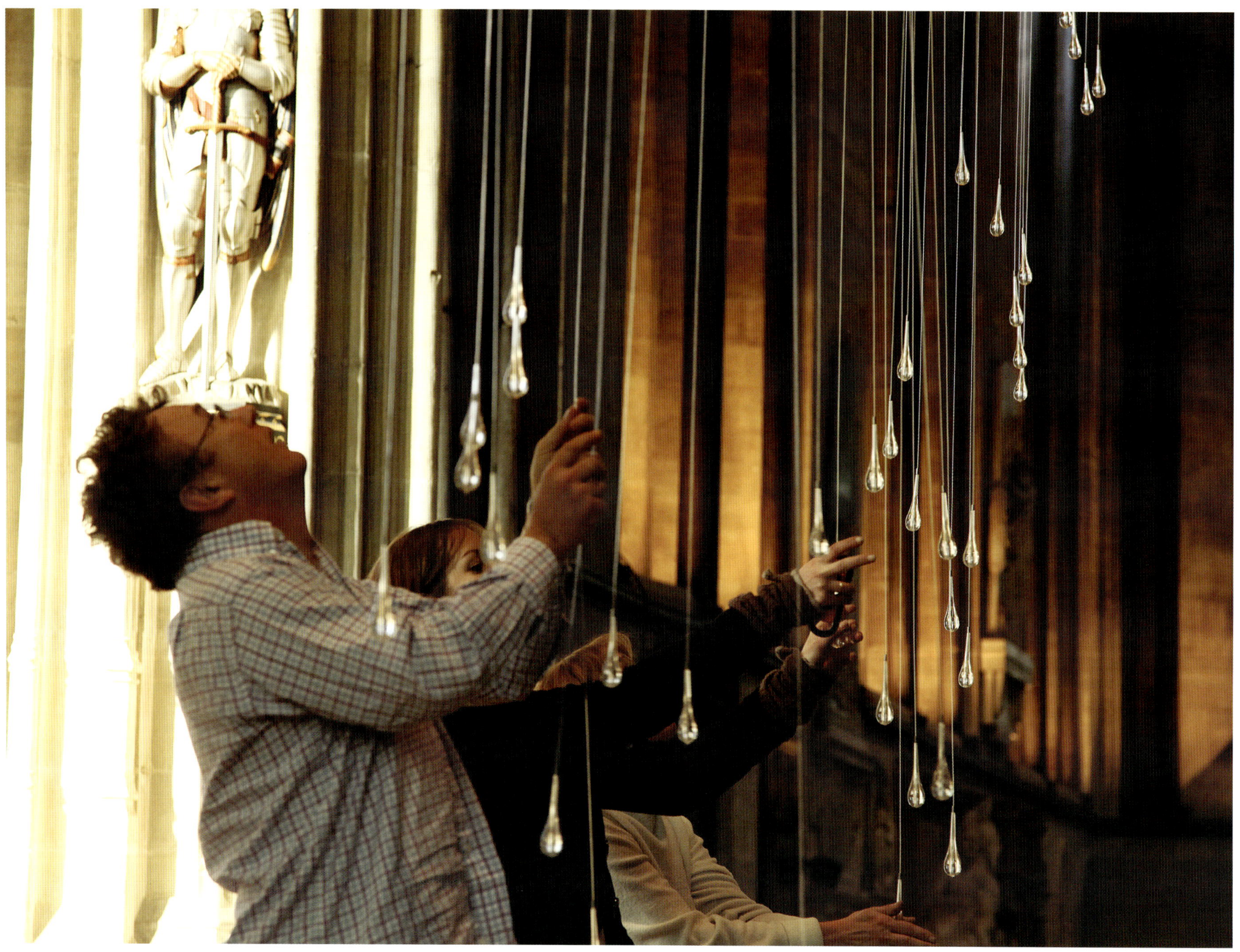

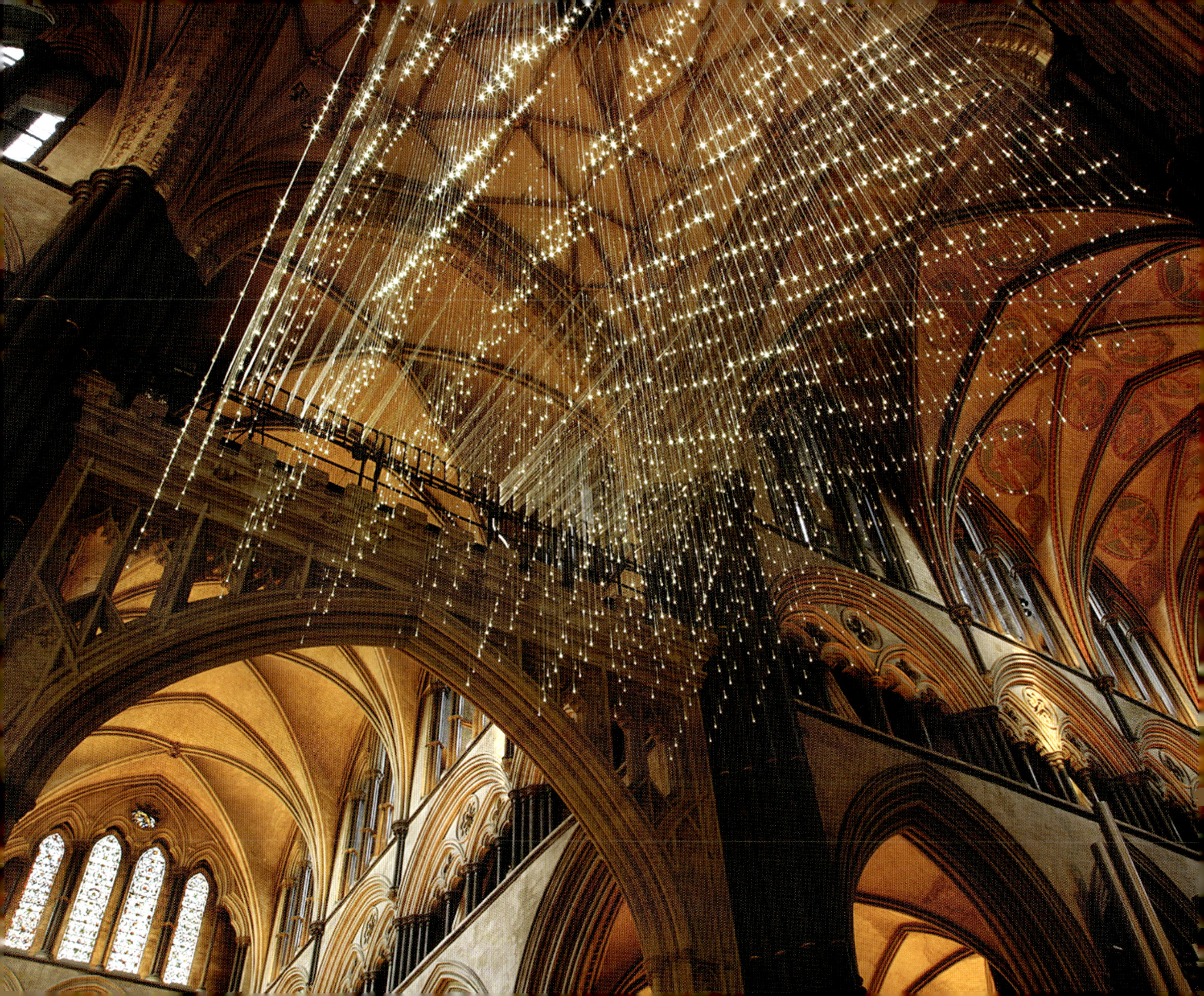

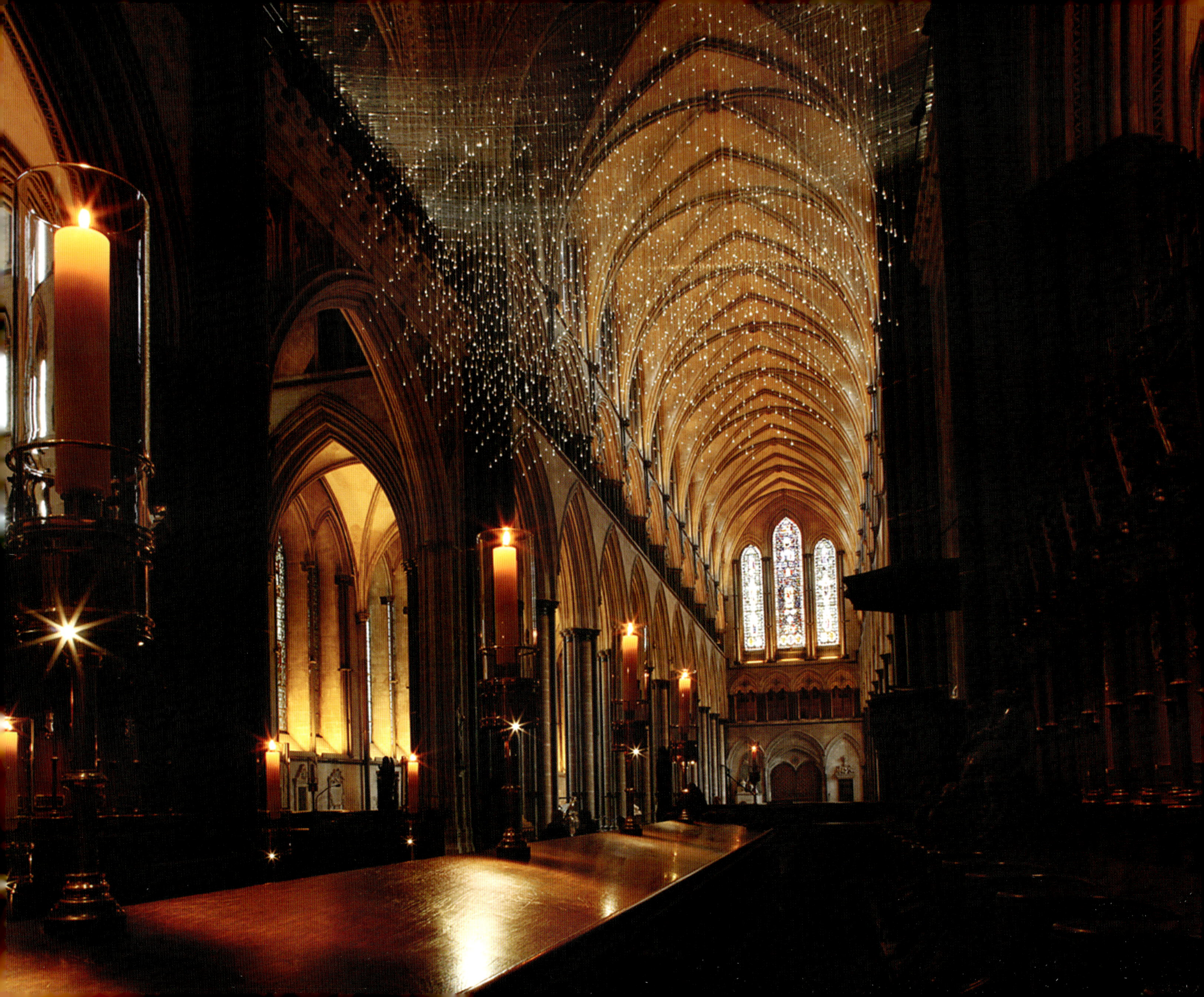

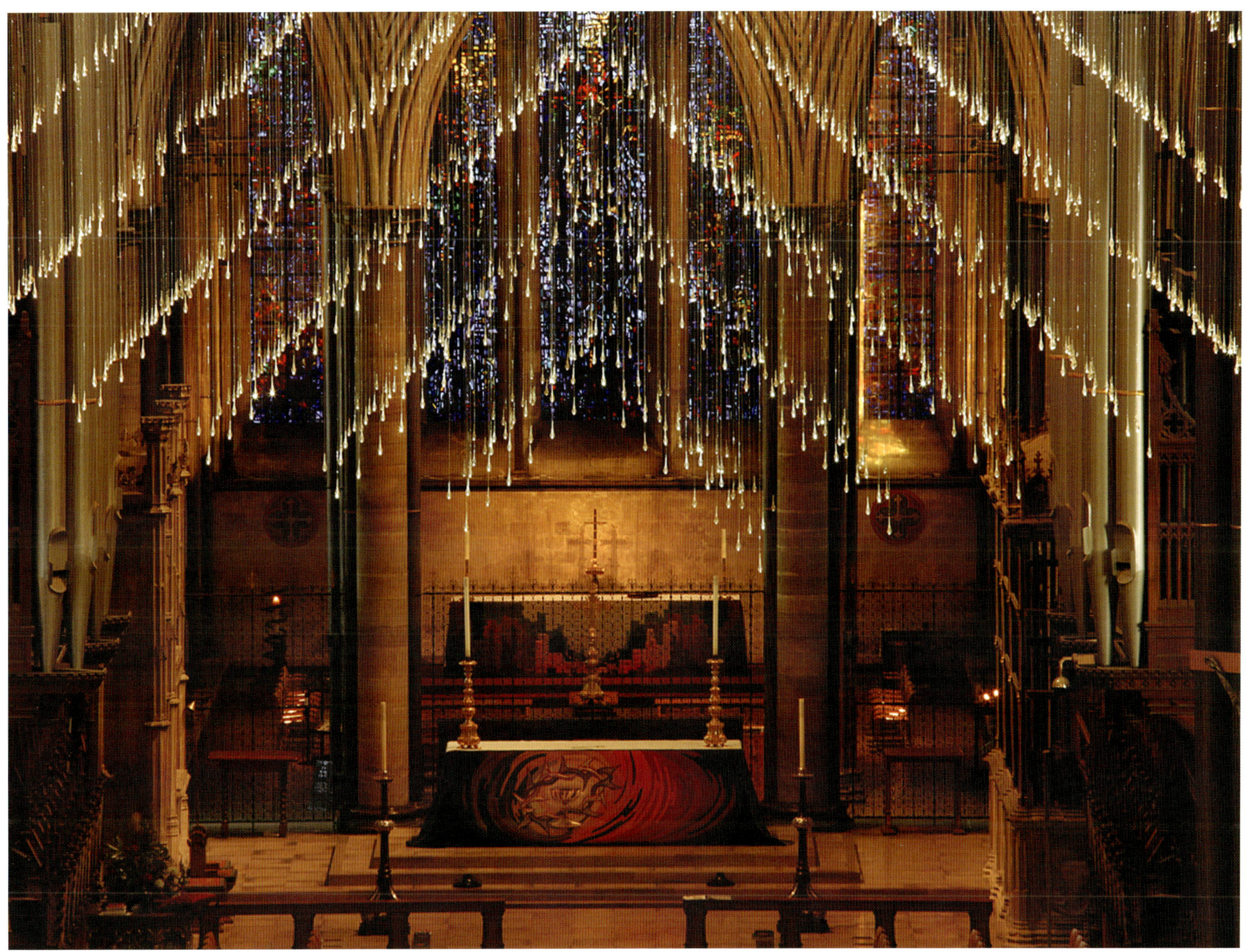

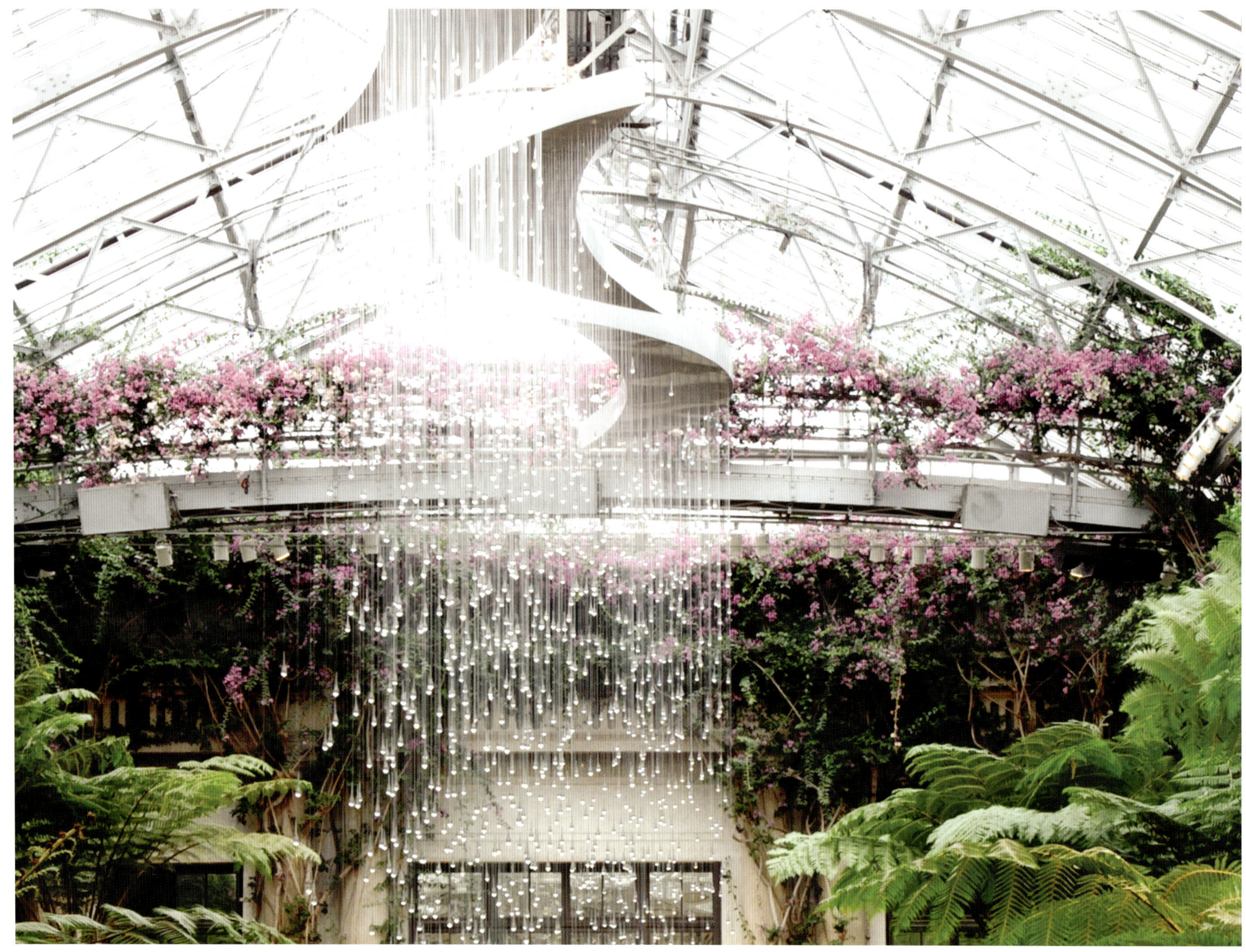

Pages 136–39: Light Shower, *Longwood Gardens, Pennsylvania, USA, 2012.*

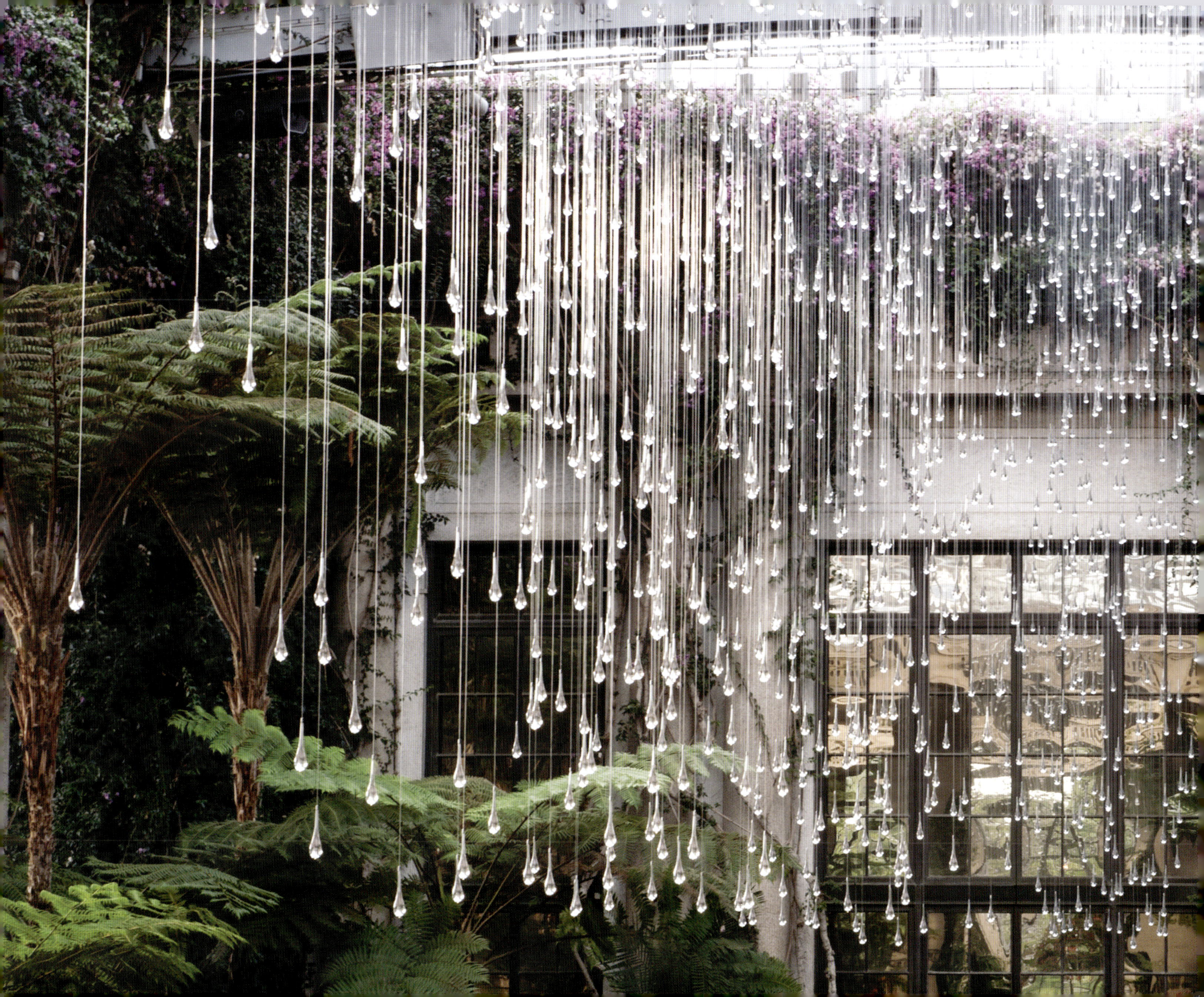

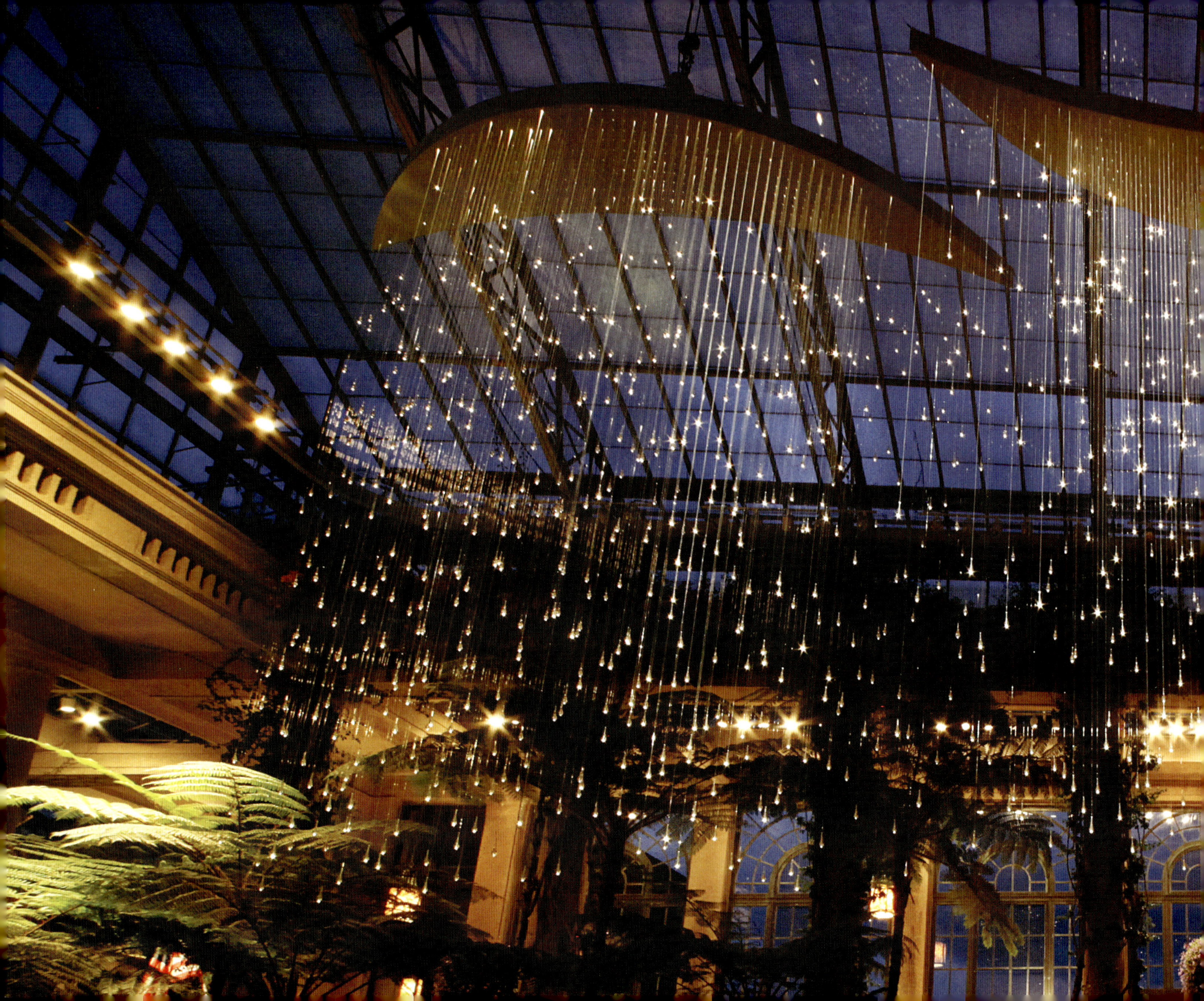

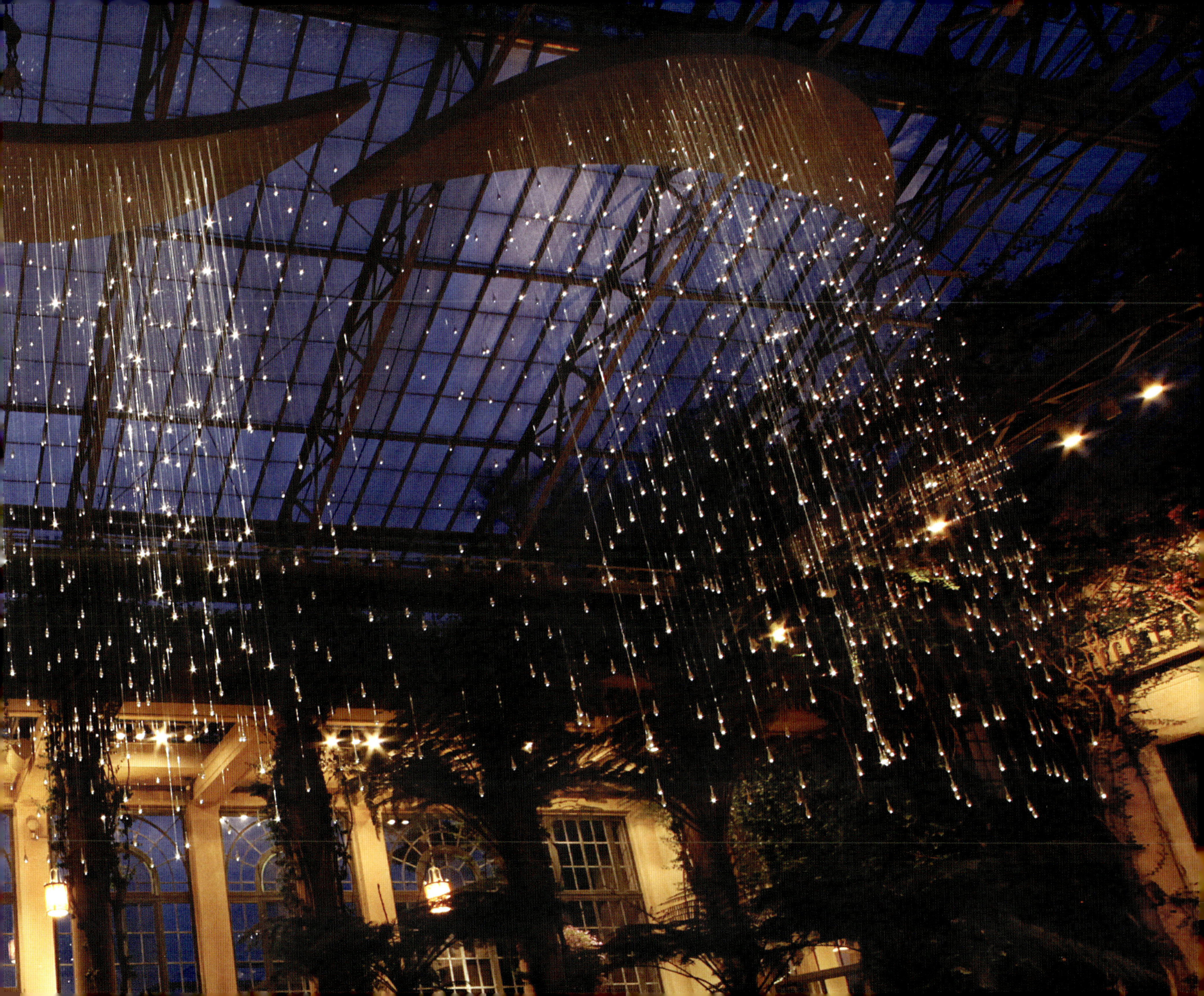

SCULPTURES

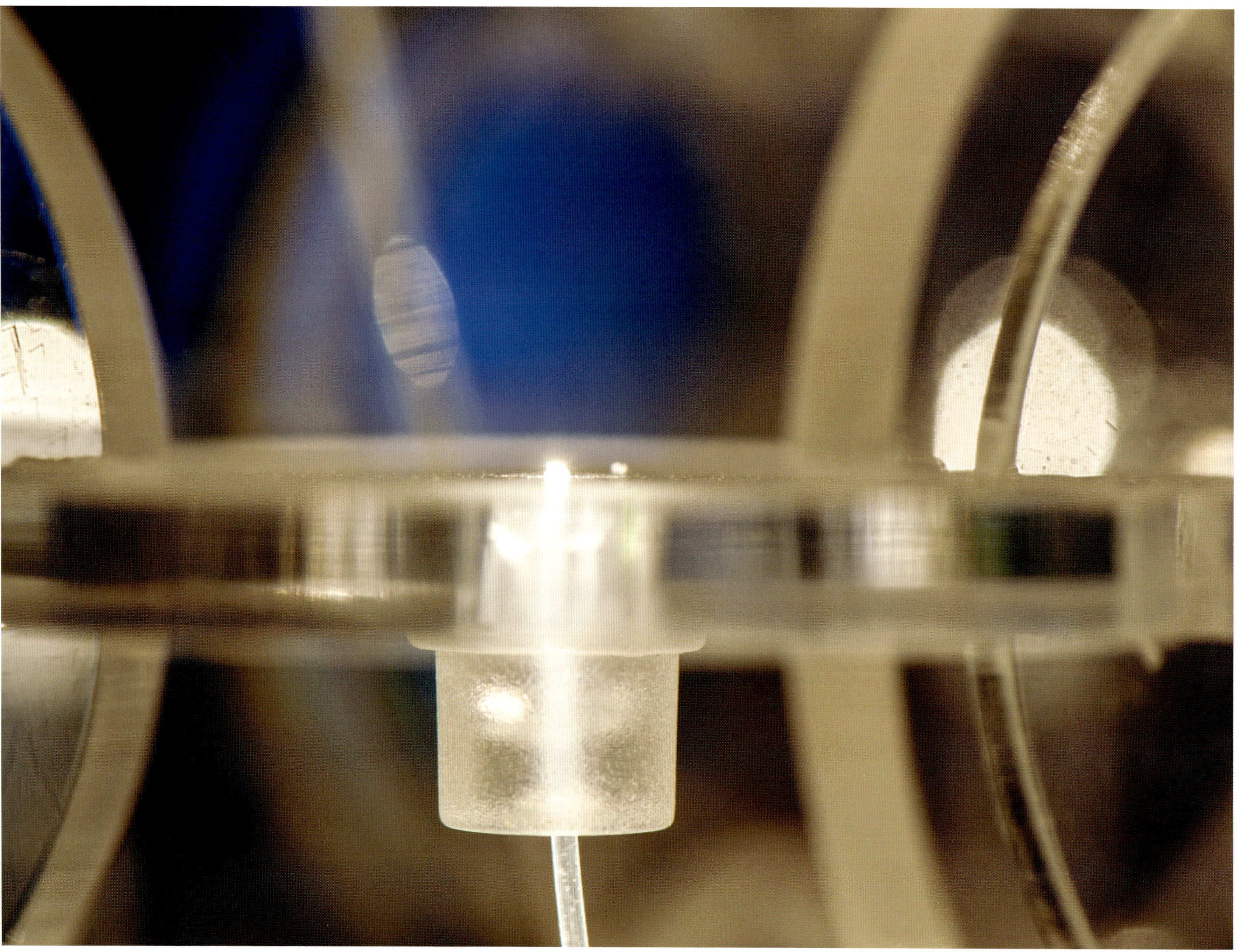

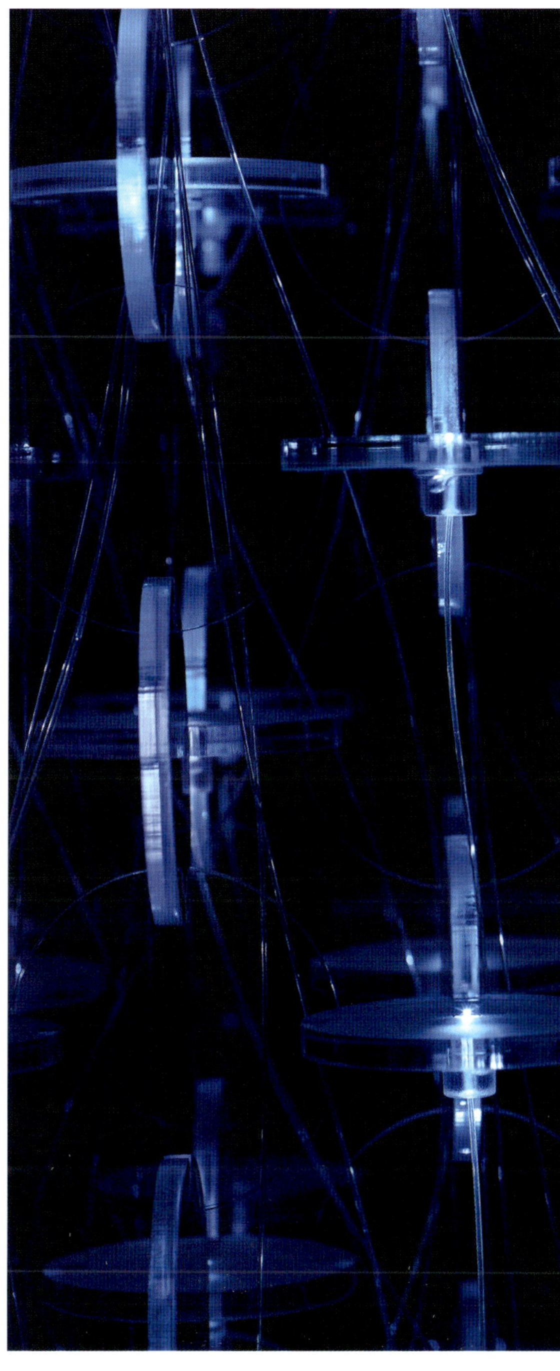

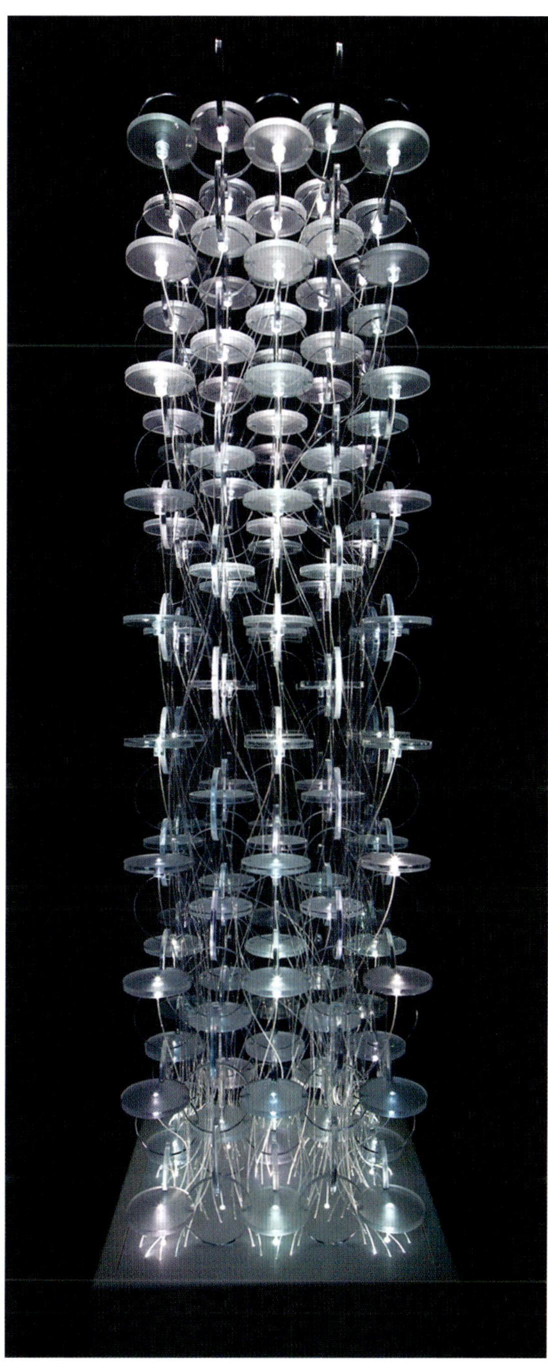

RAPUNZEL'S TOWER

Rapunzel's Tower is a sculptural piece with an architectural focus. Inspired by a natural progression of various ideas and designs that I was experimenting with in 2006, *Rapunzel's Tower* comprises 195 interlocking acrylic horizontal and vertical discs. Each horizontal module is lit by a 1mm fibre-optic cable. The light is located in the base.

The title came to me after creating the piece; the organic feel of the free-flowing fibre-optic strands reminded me of hair, and the modular matrix of the whole construction is a Lilliputian tower.

Rapunzel's Tower, *2006, 430mm (w) x 330mm (w) x 145mm (h) [approx. 17" (w) x 13" (w) x 6" (h)].*

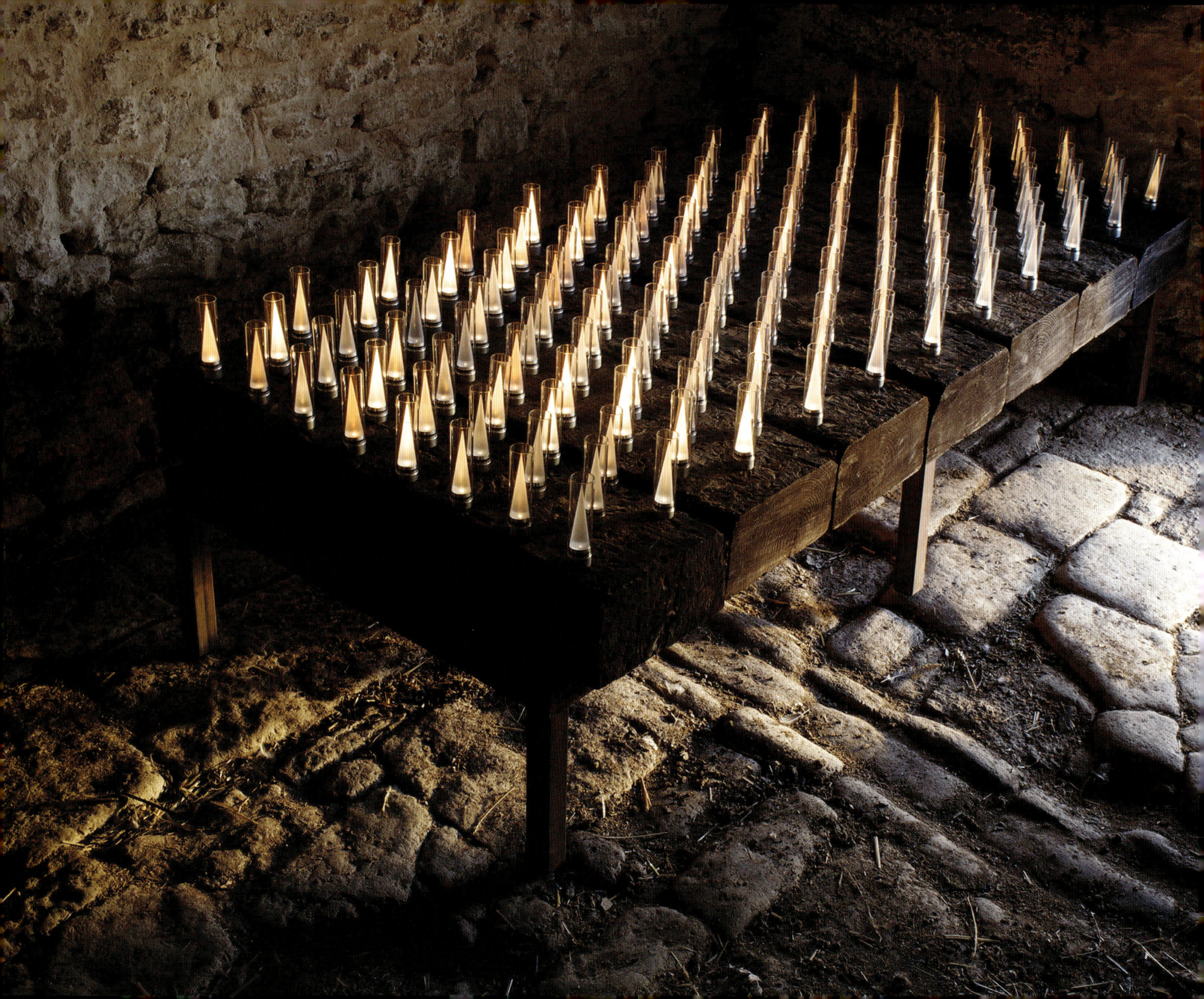

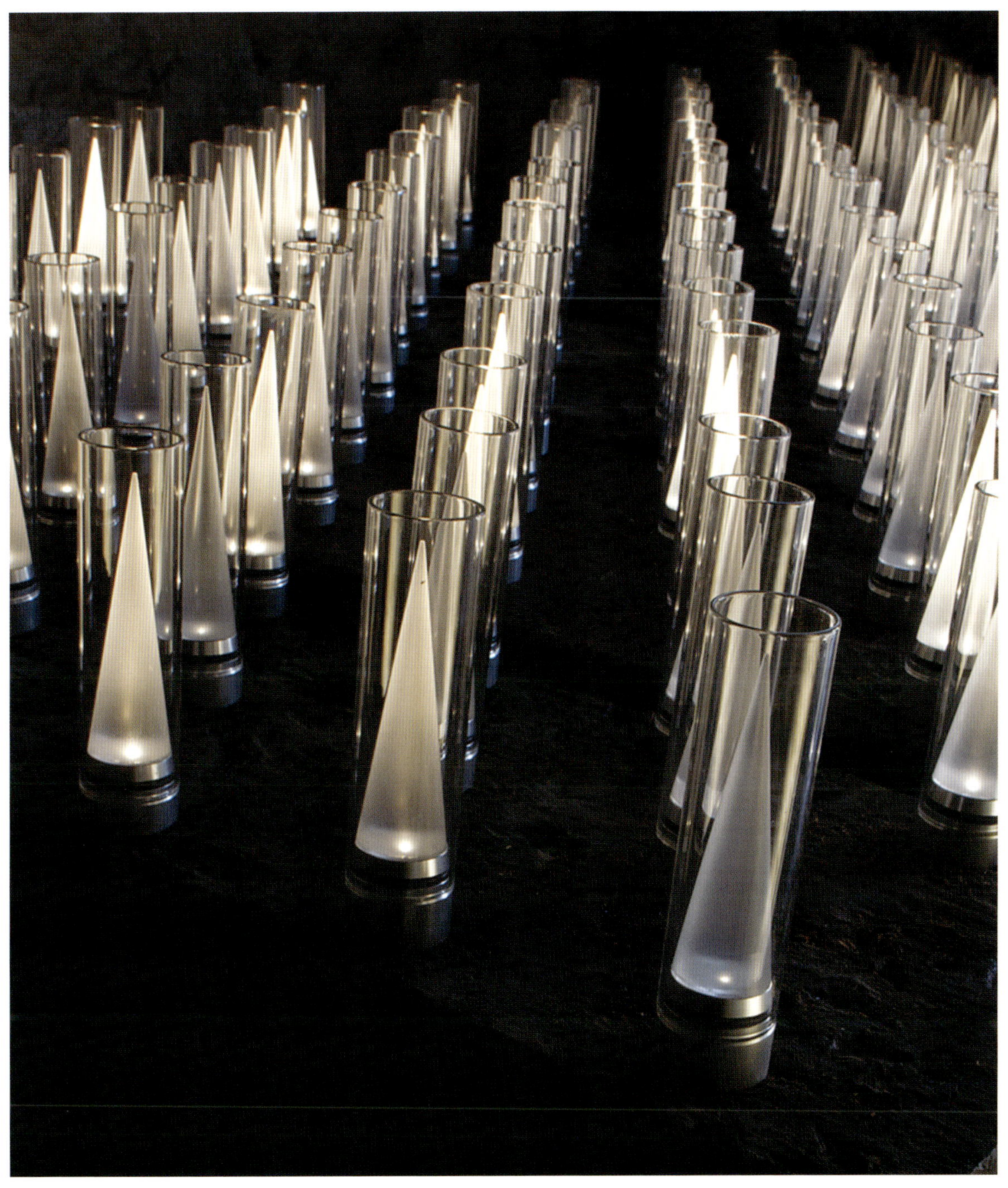

Restless Fakir, *2012, 1750mm (w) x 833mm (d) x 500mm (h) [approx. 69″ (w) x 33″ (d) x 20″ (h)].*

RESTLESS FAKIR

I remember watching, when I was about twelve, on a black-and-white TV, *Carry On Up the Kyber*. I loved the schoolboy humour of the "Carry On" films; and on this occasion, I decided to tape the soundtrack on my portable cassette recorder. One scene that caught my attention was of a skinny little fellow acting as a *fakir* (holy man), who slept on a bed of nails.

The die was cast, and from that moment the very mention of India conjured up, amongst other things, fakirs and beds of nails! The inspiration behind *Restless Fakir*, therefore, is an amalgam of thoughts and ideas, sprinkled with a pinch of schoolboy humour.

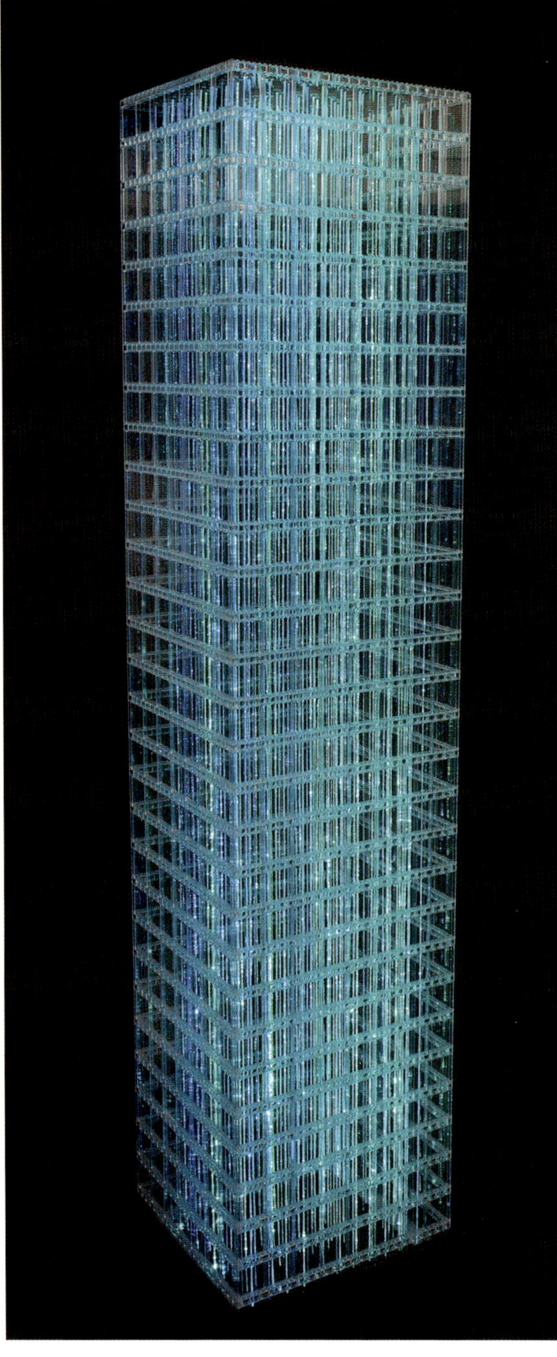

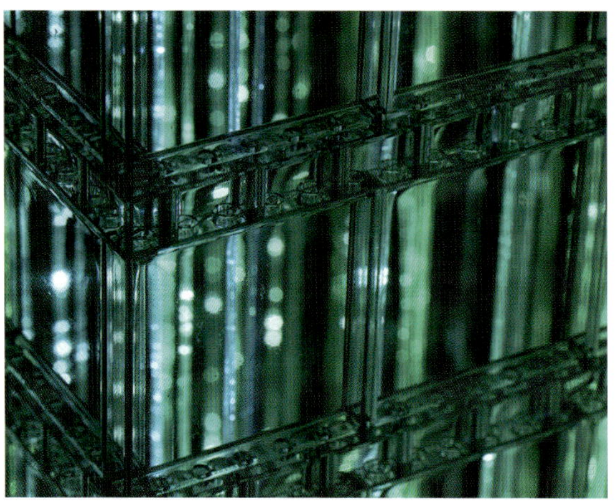

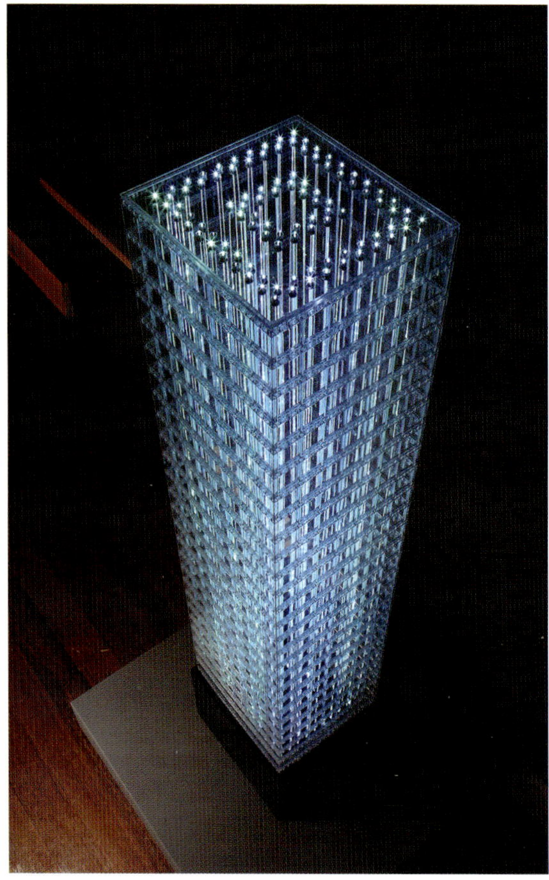

BOOGIE WOOGIE

Boogie Woogie is a lighting installation built with transparent Lego® bricks, fibre optics, and LED projectors. The installation was inspired by a number of ideas that have influenced my work since my childhood. I was particularly excited to be able to work with transparent Lego® bricks, having been a lifelong fan of the product. Many years catalyzed for me to draw together my ideas for this installation.

Boogie Woogie Lights is based on a series of abstracted visual notations that I endlessly scribbled as an art student when listening to music. However, it was my first visit to New York, in 2008, that inspired both the rectangular architectural tower form and the musical style for the installation.

Boogie Woogie Lights is not an intellectual piece, but it is deeply felt.

Boogie Woogie Tower, *2010, 380mm (w) x 405mm (d) x 1980 (h) [approx. 15" (w) x 16" (d) x 78" (h)].*

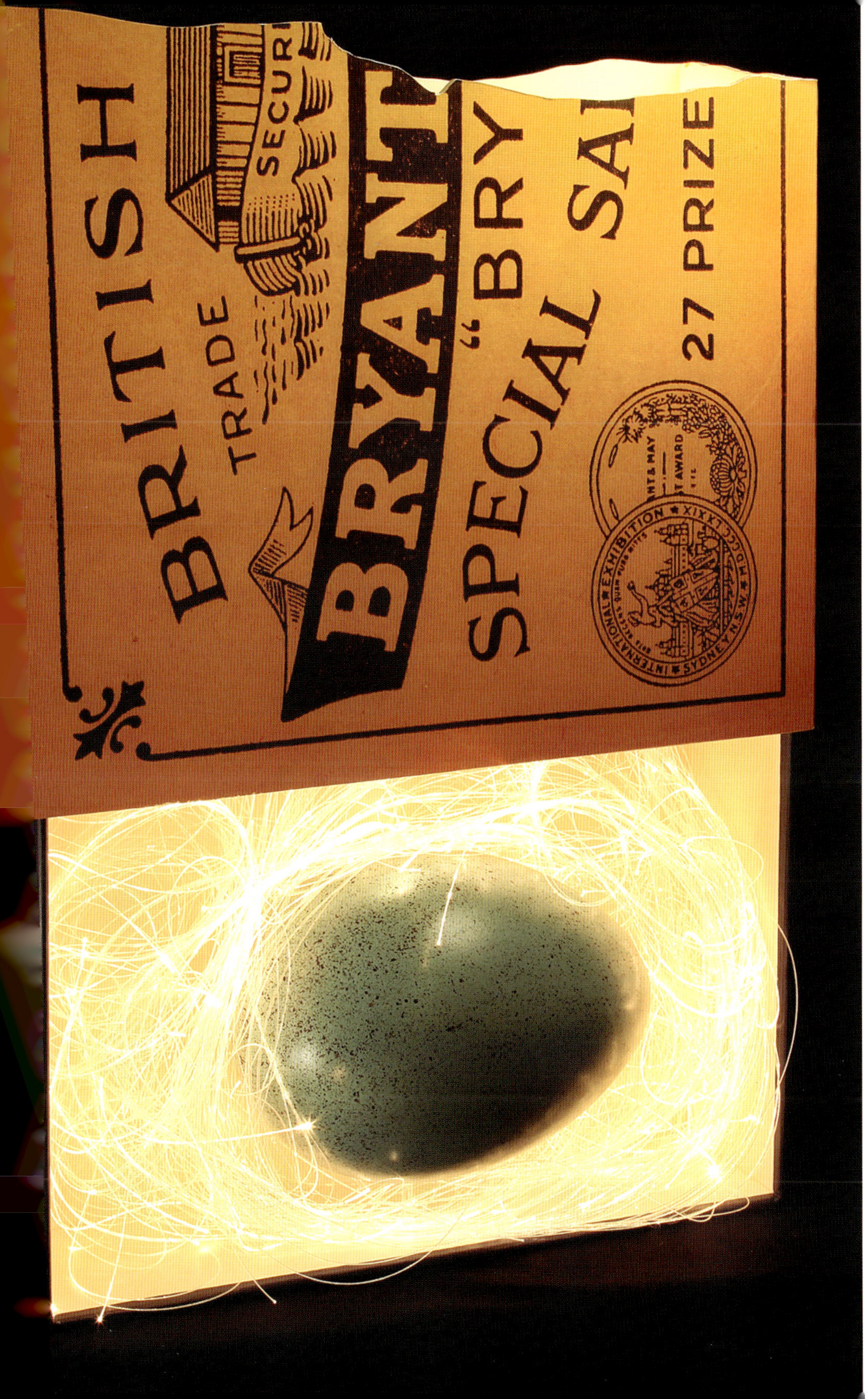

BLACKBIRD

Blackbird was inspired by a childhood memory of collecting bird's eggs that had fallen from their nests. I treated them like priceless jewels, protecting them with empty matchboxes lined with cloudy wads of cotton.

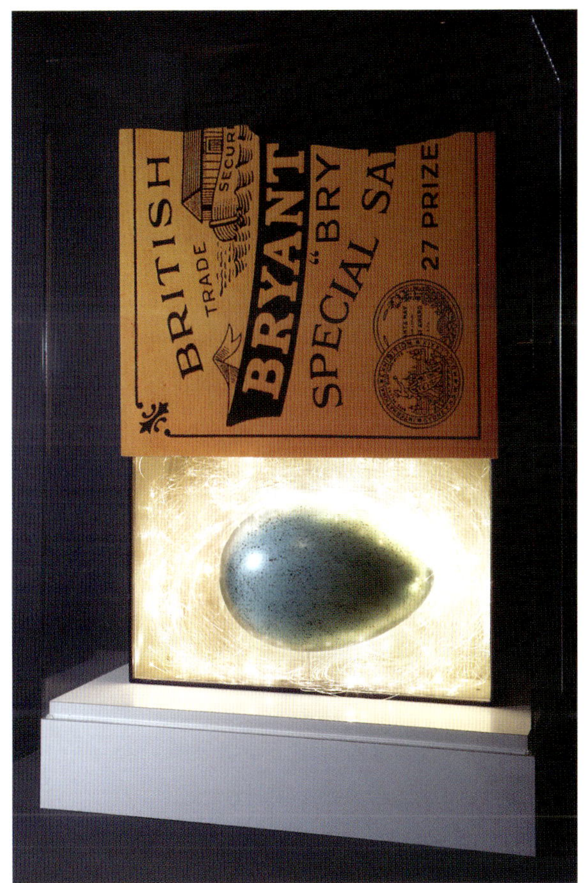

Blackbird, *2012, 860mm (w) x 450mm (d) x 1280mm (h) [approx. 34" (w) x 18" (d) x 50" (h)].*

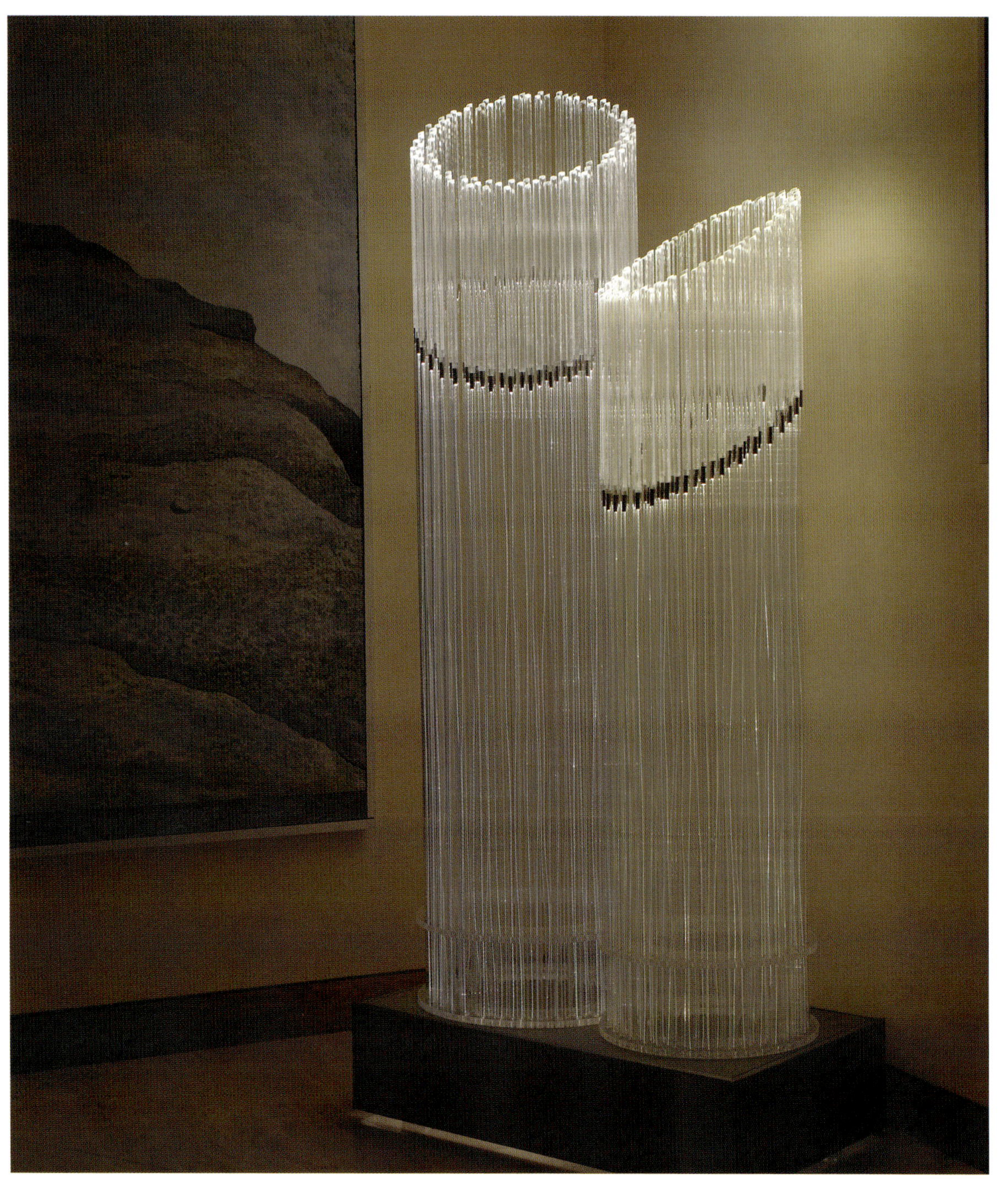

DIAMOND GEEZERS

I created an illuminated light sculpture as a commission to celebrate the landmark sixtieth wedding anniversary of a private client.

I settled on developing the piece around the iconic symbol of the infinity sign, which I feel symbolises the strength and beauty of a successful, long-lasting marriage. *Diamond Geezers* comprises more than 300 individual glass tubes and acrylic rods, arranged in columns to create the impression of two illuminated abstracted figures that stand side by side. The fibre-optic light source is housed in the brushed stainless-steel base.

The two columns of light are tangential with the shorter, the woman, standing next to the taller, the man. The columns lean slightly towards each other to portray the support offered throughout a successful marriage.

Diamond Geezers, *2006, base 800mm (w) x 200 (h) x 400 (d) [approx. 32" (w) x 8" (h) x 16" (d)].*

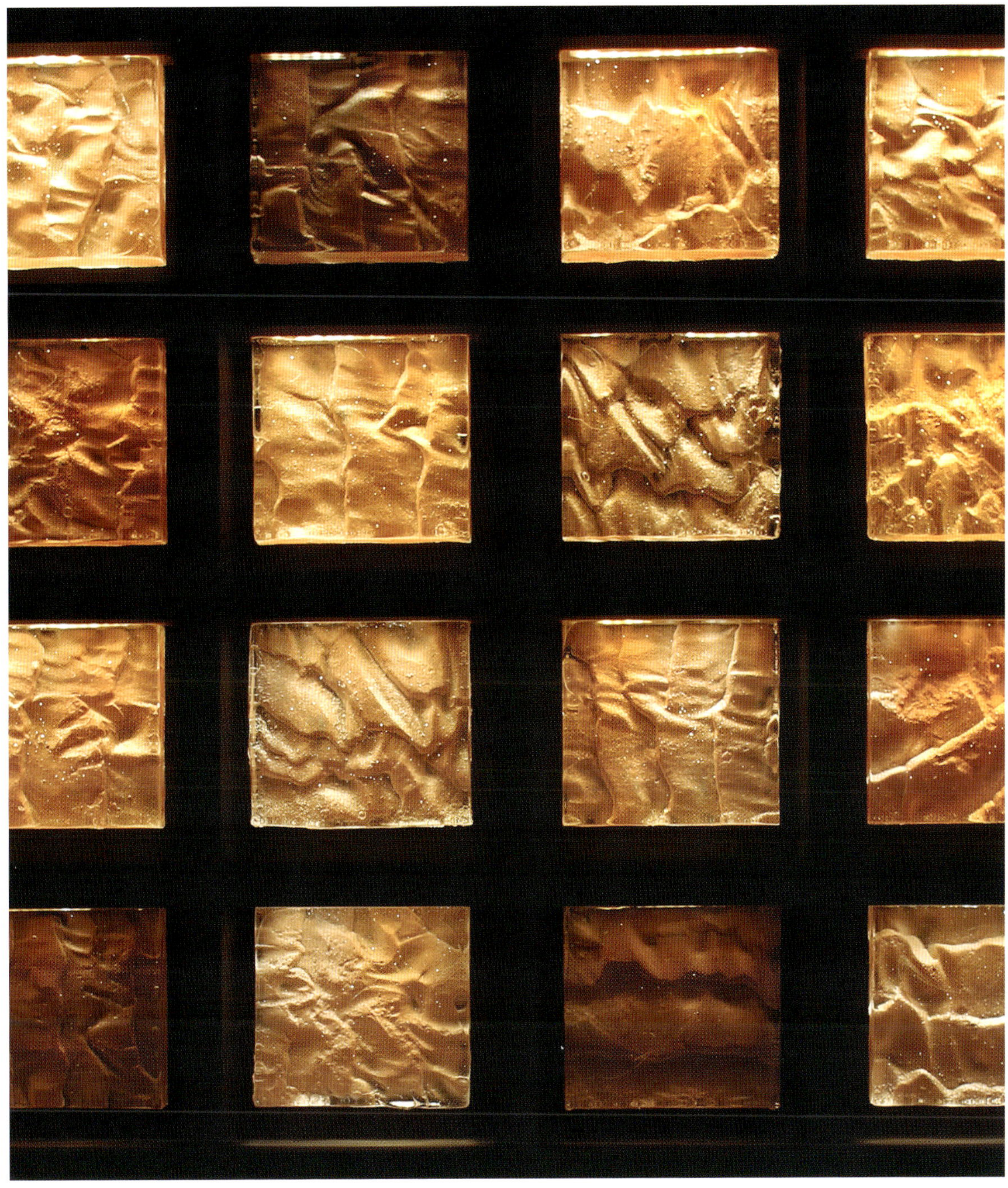

BEACH WITHOUT SAND

In July 1999, I spent a lovely week camping with my wife, Serena, and our children just outside Salcombe in South Devon where I grew up. I have always loved the simple things in life. It is hard to beat sunrise bacon butties, long days at the beach, watching pitch skies for shooting stars, and sleeping under canvas.

In the day our favourite place to visit was Bantham, a wide sandy tidal beach protected by sand dunes at the side of a beautiful river estuary. We had a week of those rare, impossibly clear blue skies and long, balmy summer days. I remember consciously catching myself marvelling at how lucky I was to be so happy; on this occasion I was holding my little girl's hand, ankle deep in a tidal pool looking for crabs and shrimps. *Beach without Sand* is simply my reconstruction of this perfect moment.

Beach without Sand, *2012, 2630mm (w) x 405 (h) x 1525 (d) [approx. 104" (w) x 16" (h) x 60" (d)].*

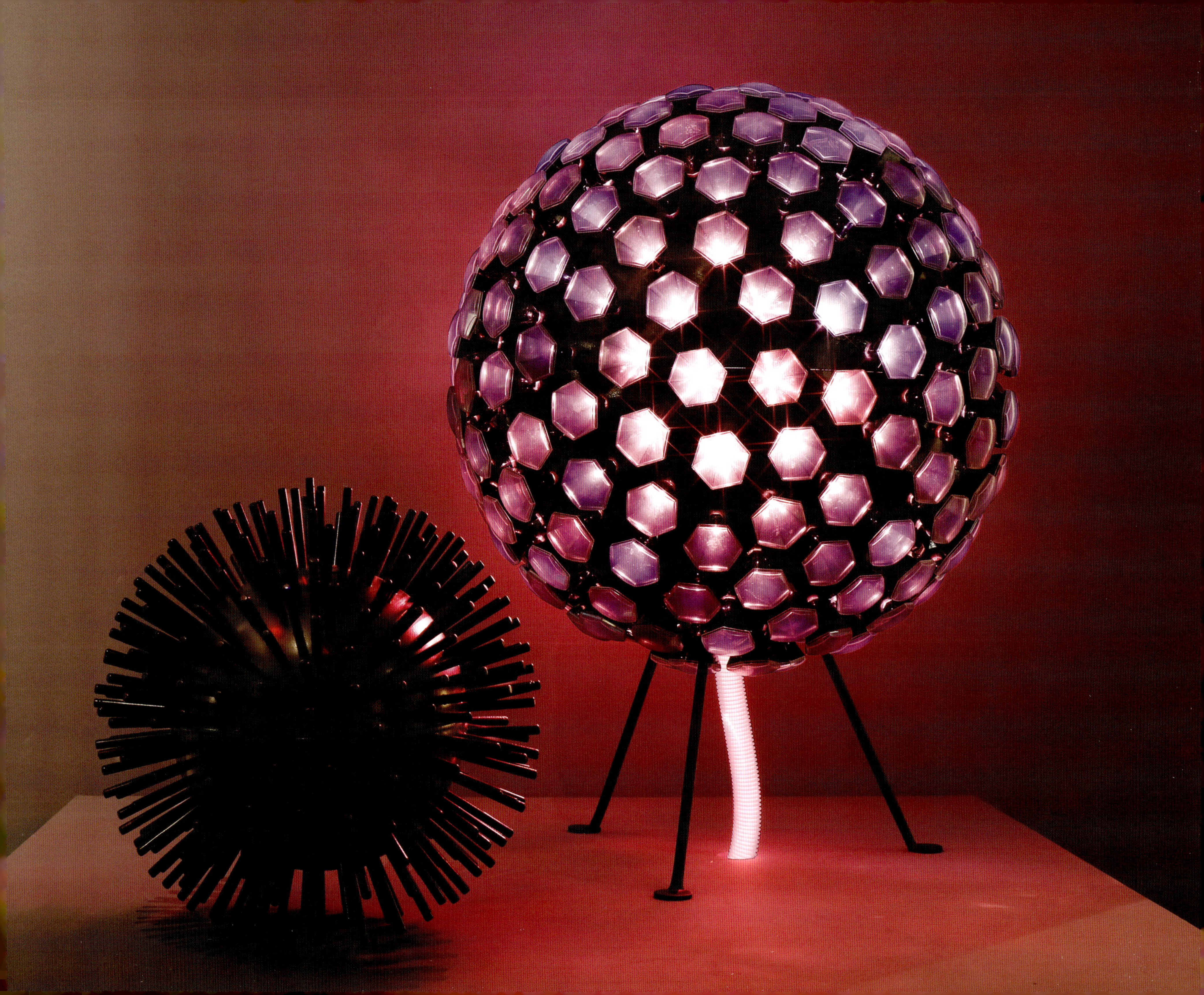

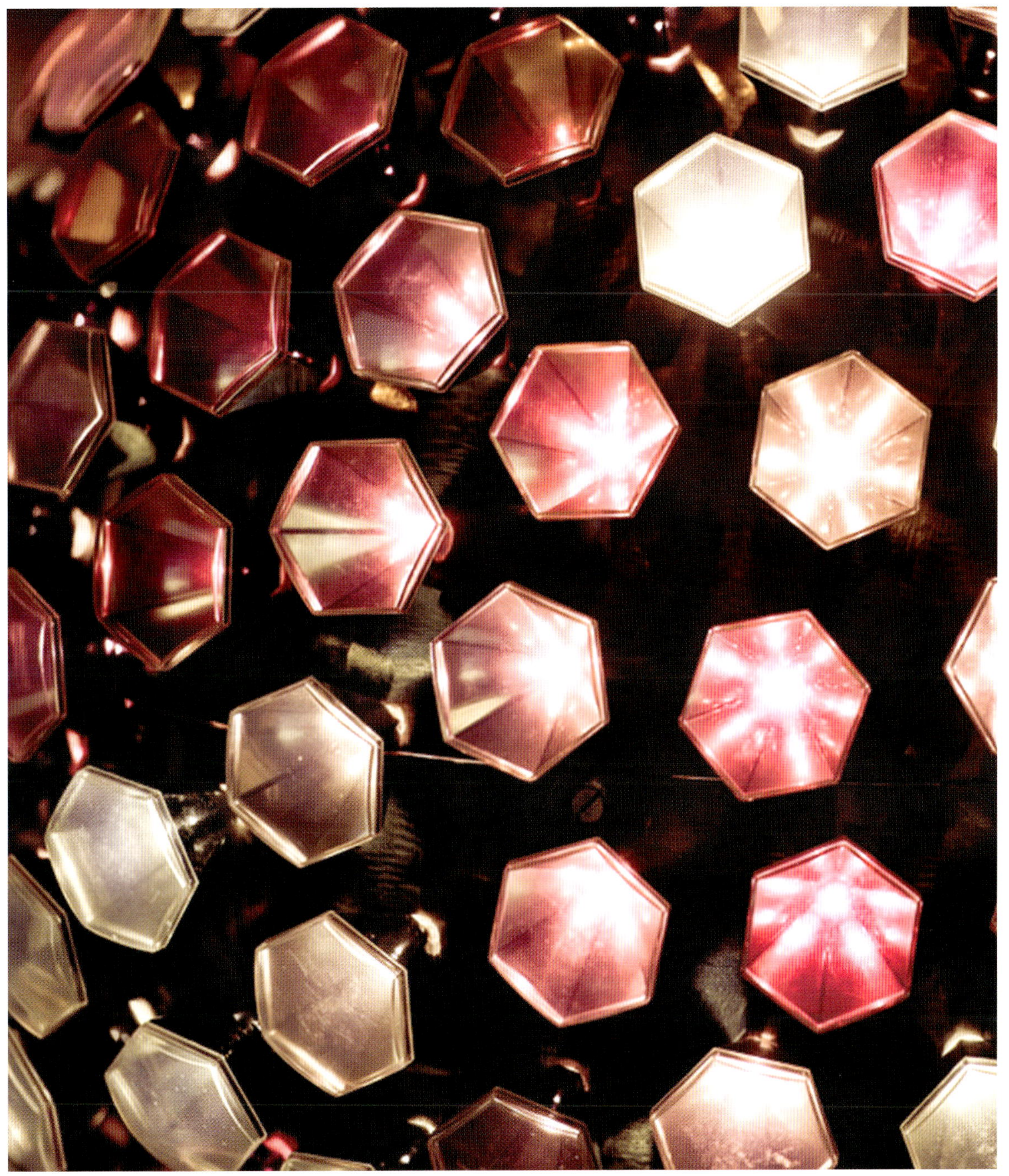

GNASHER'S BIG RASPBERRY

A favourite comic strip character of my childhood was Gnasher, a black mutt with a Methuselah hairstyle. Gnasher had an irreverent character that appealed to my sense of humour. Years later I was fabricating a projector housing for a luminaire, a metal sphere covered in hundreds of metal dowels (secondhand craft-knife handles), and I realised as the piece came together that it looked just like Gnasher.

The main component of the two-part sculpture reminded me of a giant raspberry; and "blowing raspberries" is an expression to describe a rude sound that disrespectful children (and cartoon dogs) directed towards authoritarian adults!

Gnasher's Big Raspberry, *2008, Raspberry: 610mm (w) x 610mm (d) x 825mm (h) [approx. 24" (w) x 24" (d) x 32" (h)]; Gnasher: 440mm (w) x 440mm (d) x 440mm (h) [approx. 17" (w) x 17" (d) x 17" (h)].*

COMMISSIONS

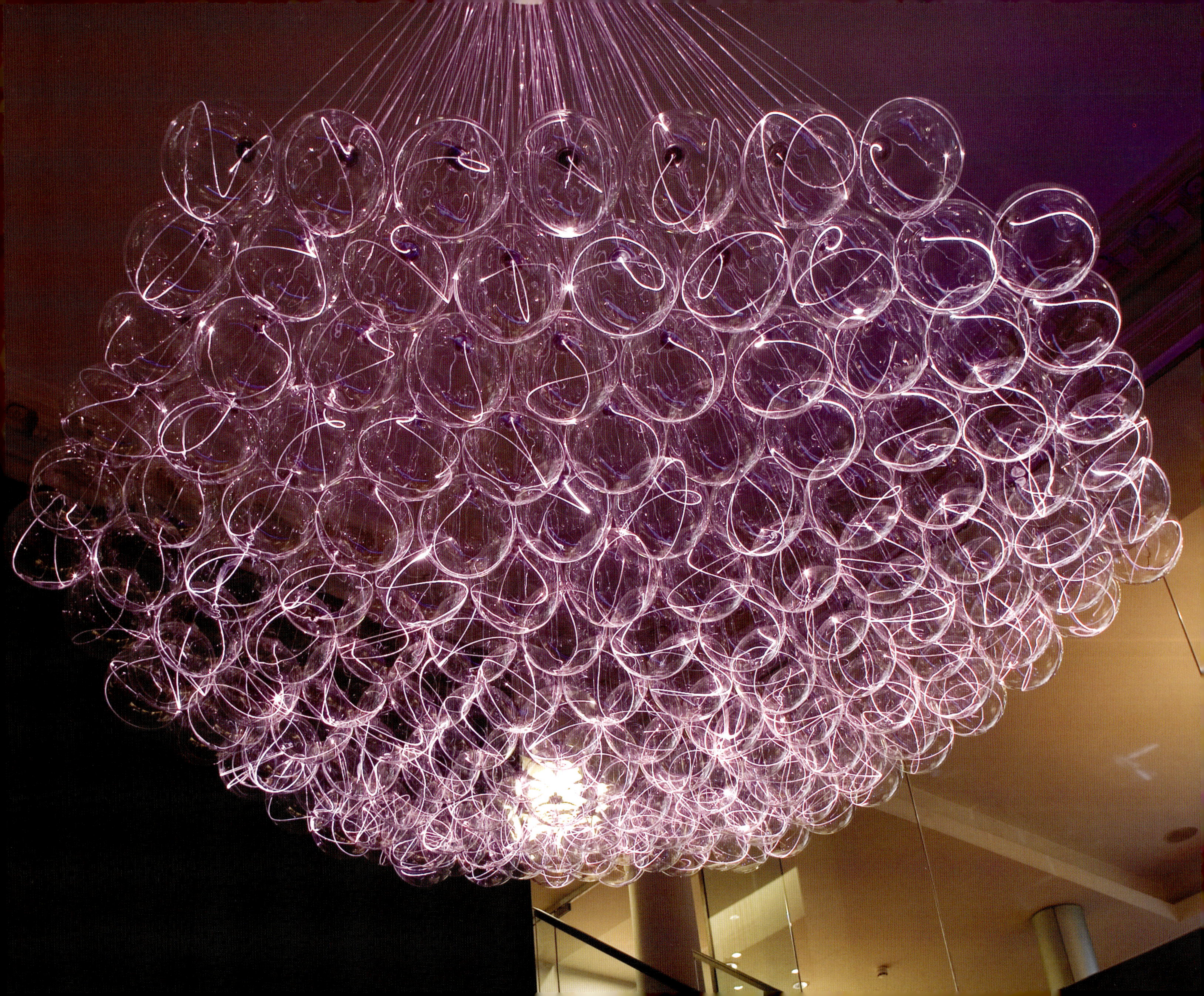

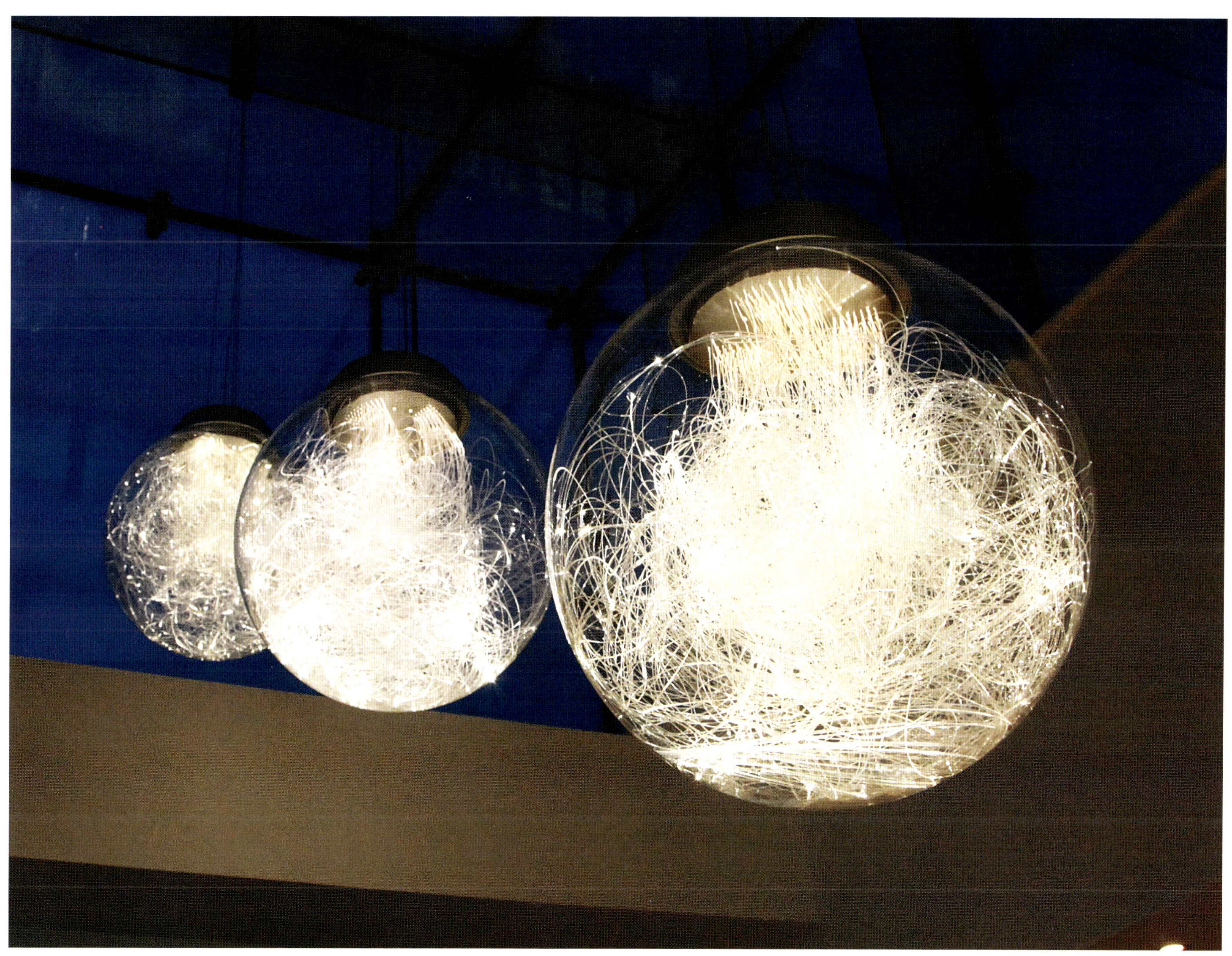

Opposite: Snowball, *64 Knightsbridge, London, UK, 2008. Above:* Wilma's Comet, *Private Residence, London, UK, 2011.*

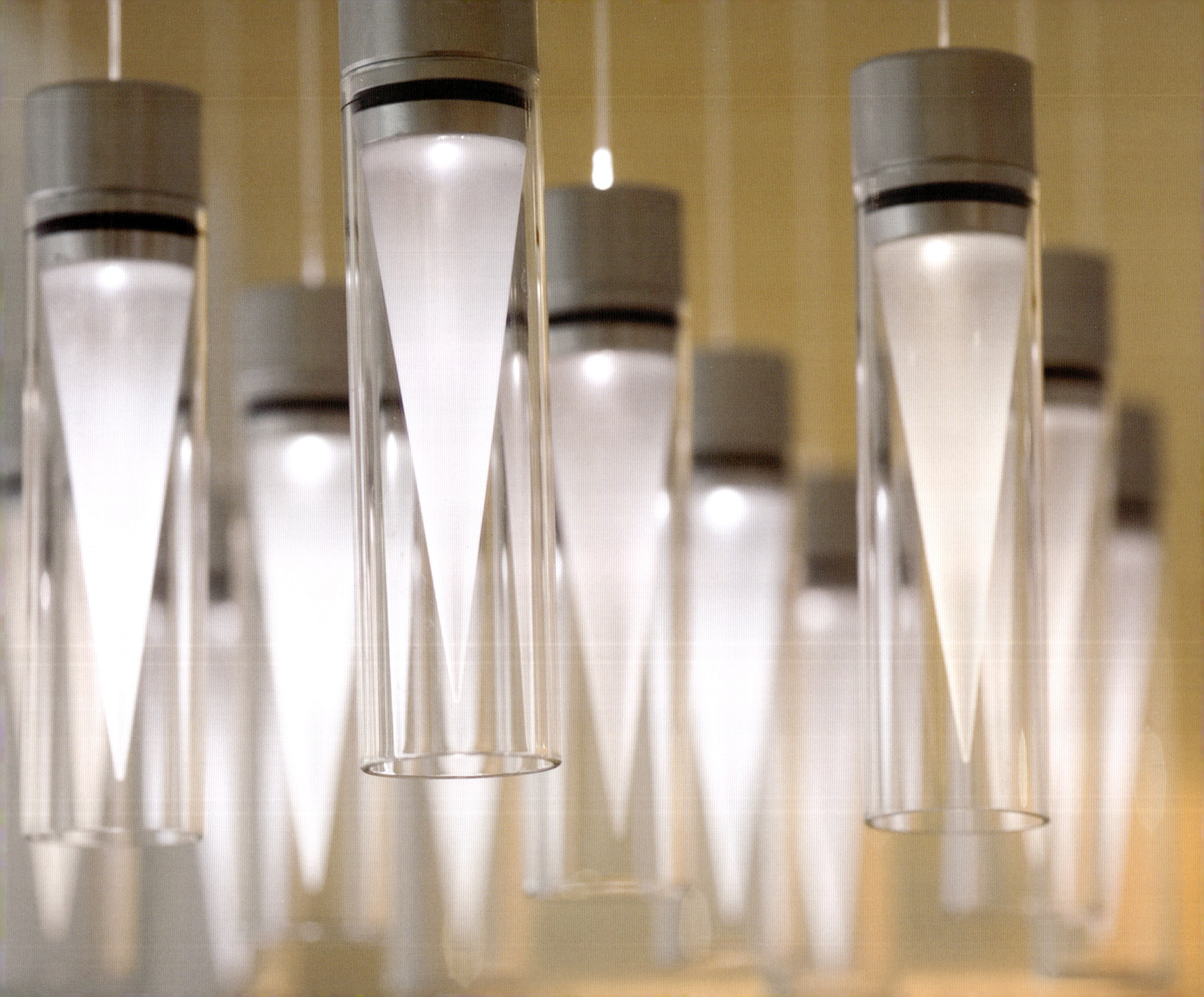

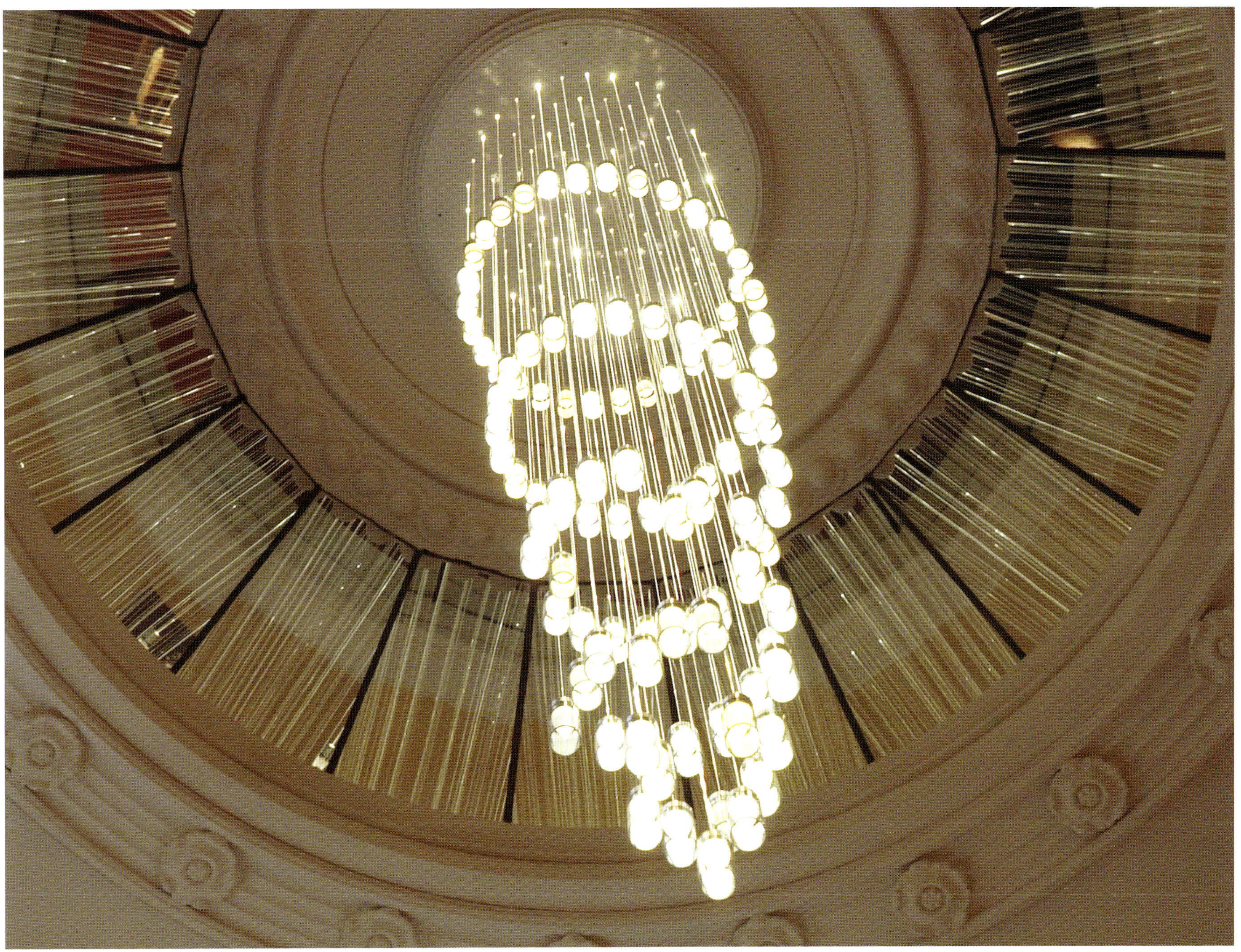

Opposite: Cone Matrix, *Private Residence, Warwickshire, UK, 2008. Above:* Cone Chandelier, *Cotswold House Hotel, Gloucestershire, UK, 2003.*

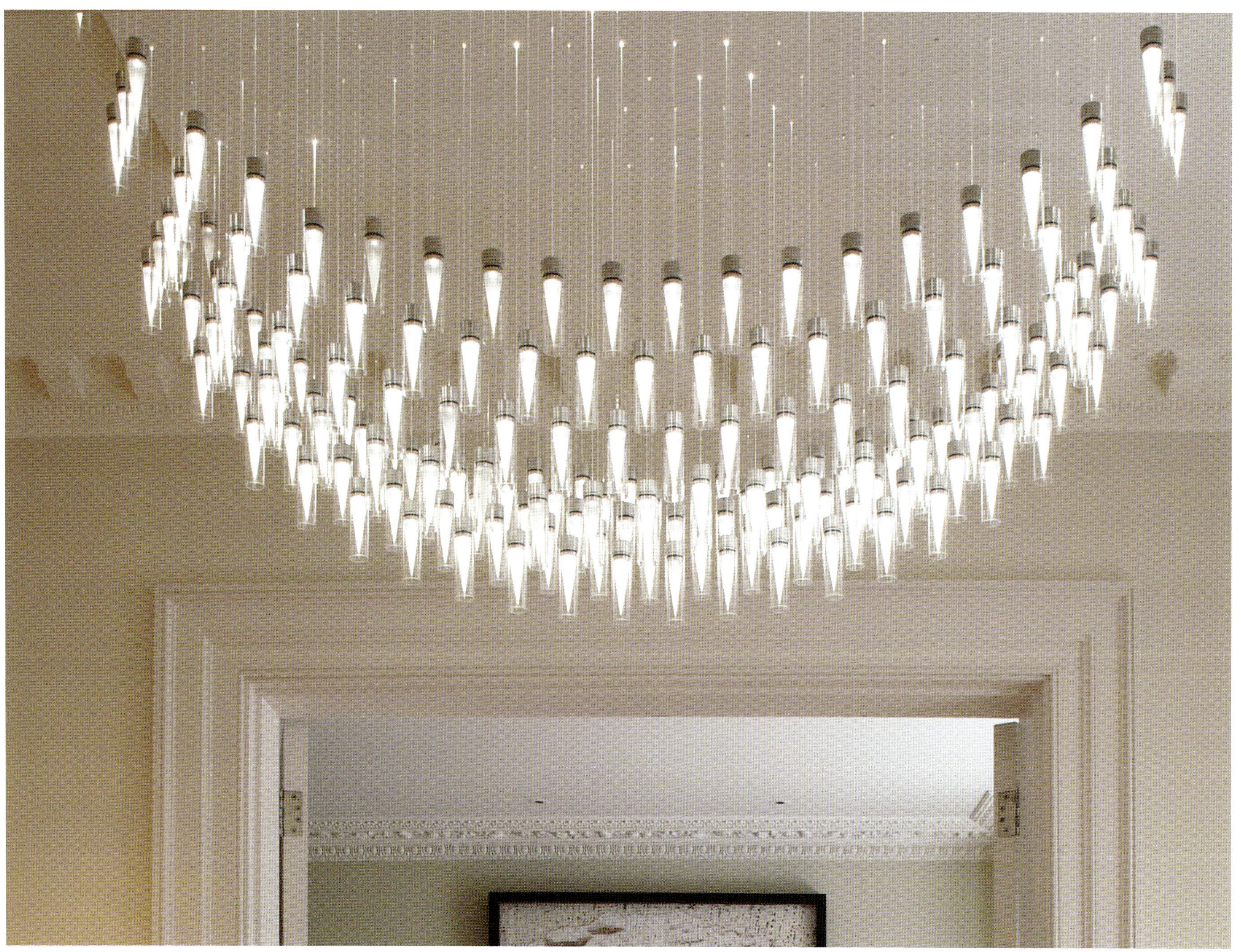

Above: Cone Chandelier, *Private Residence, London, UK, 2005. Opposite:* Cone Matrix, *Private Residence, London, UK, 2003.*

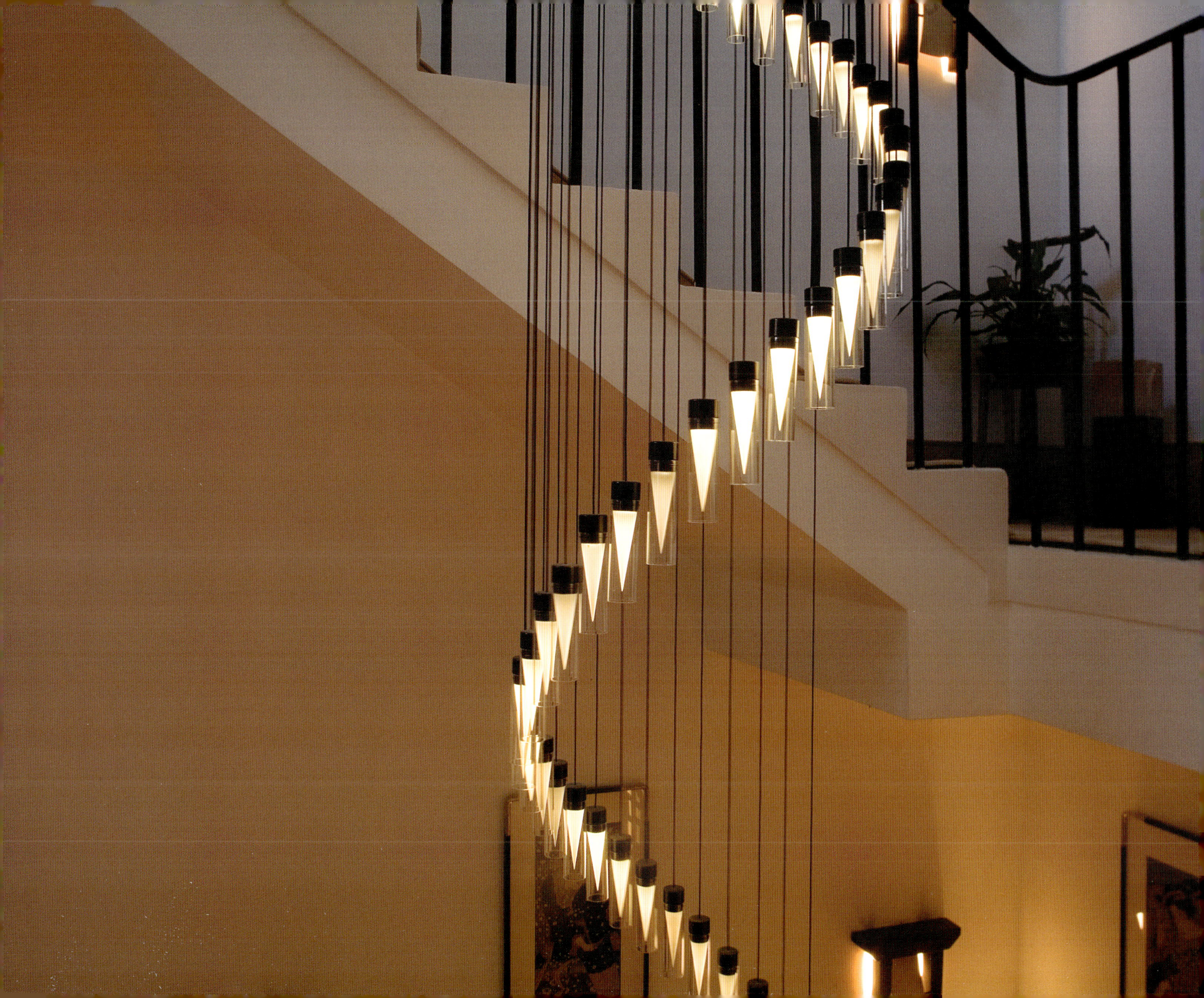

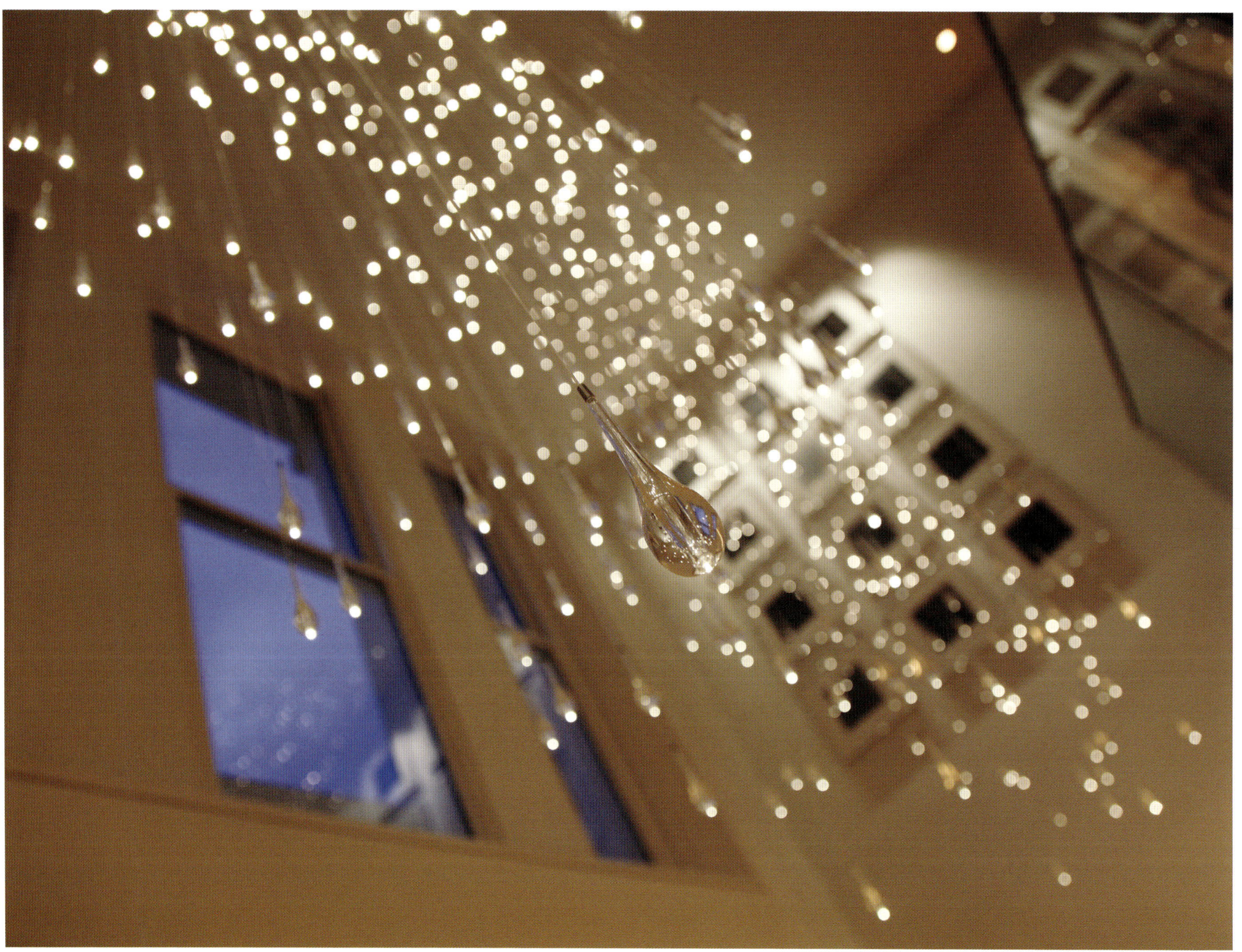

Above: Light Shower, *Private Residence, London, UK, 2009. Opposite:* Light Shower, *Private Residence, London, UK, 2009.*

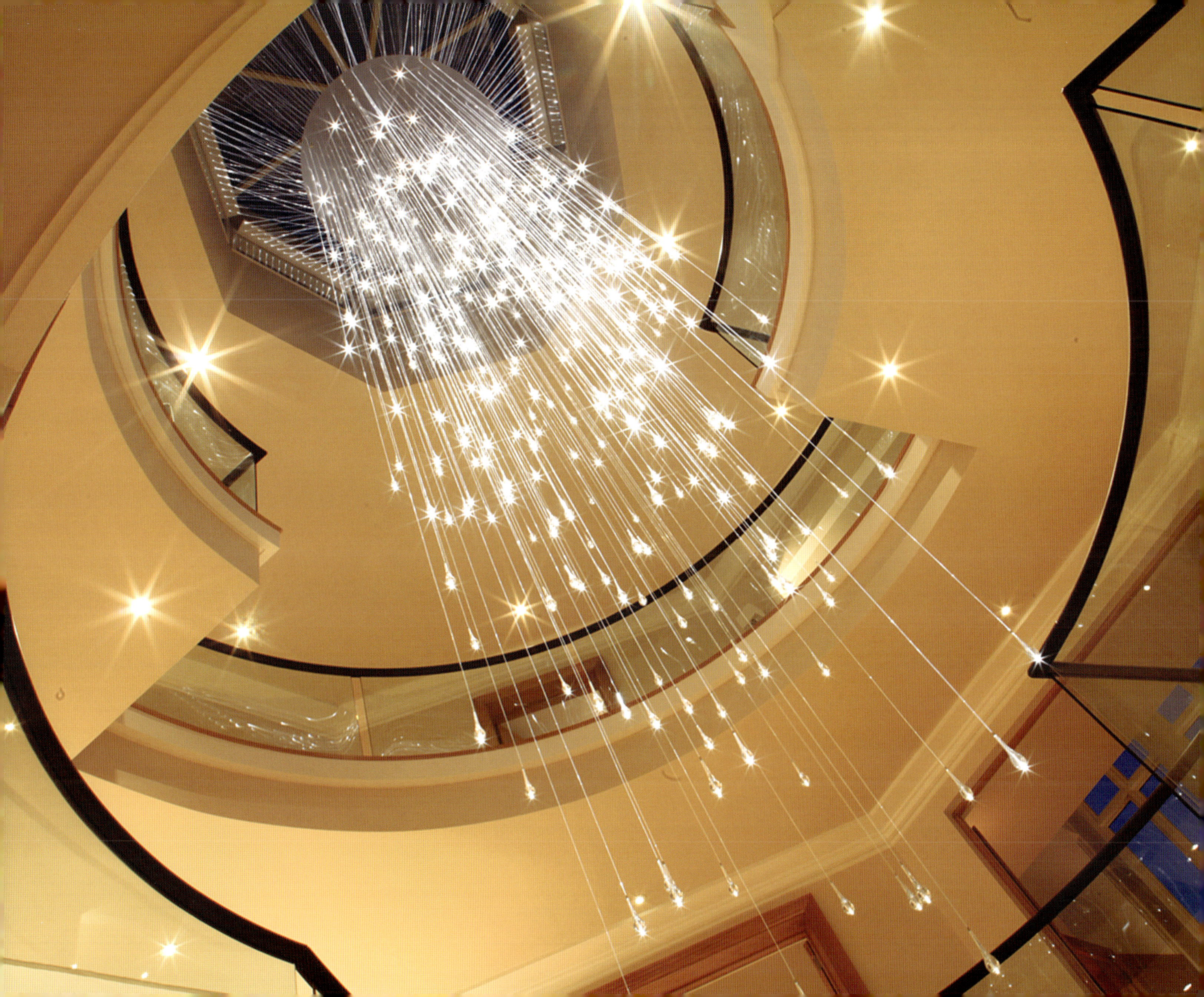

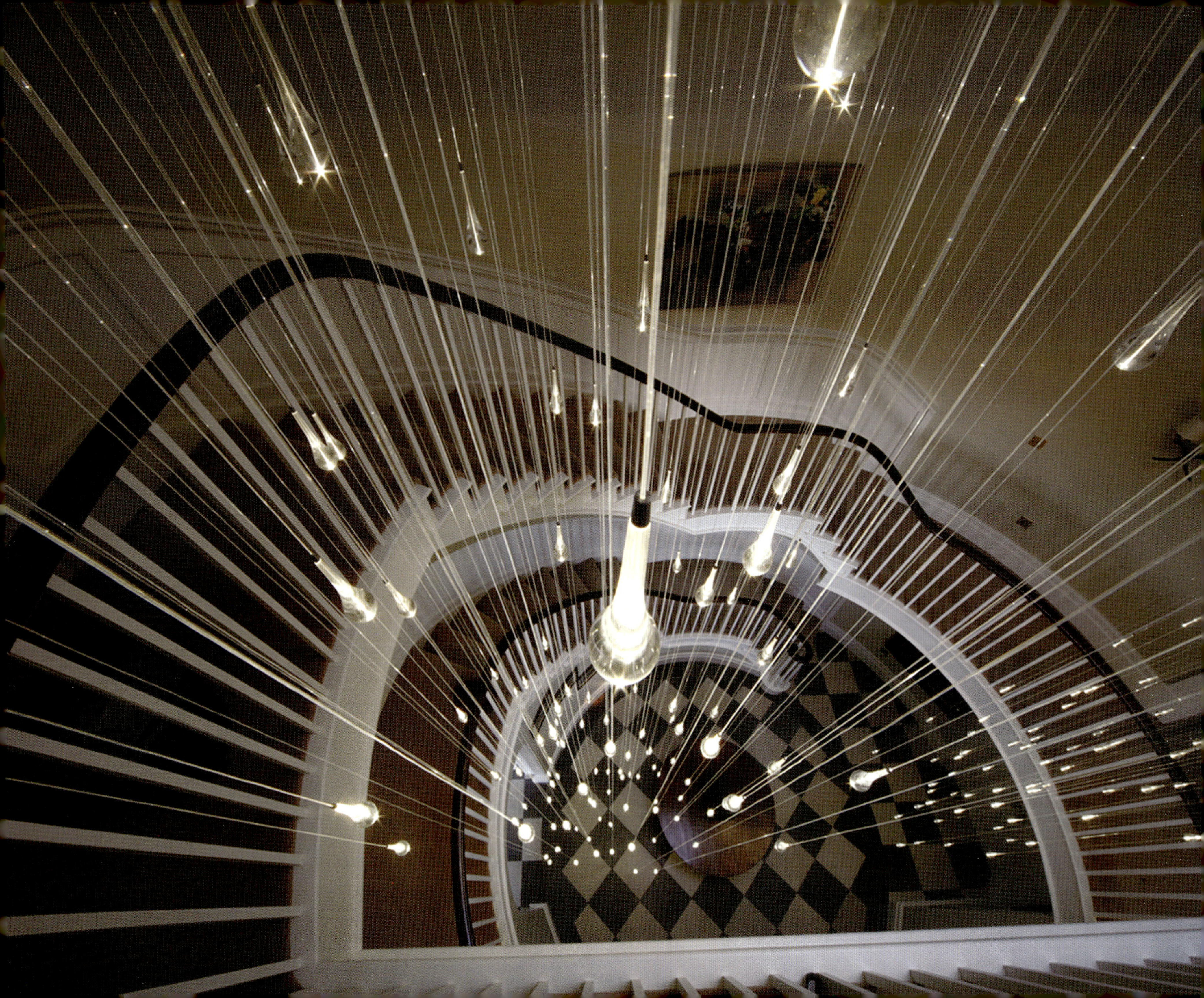

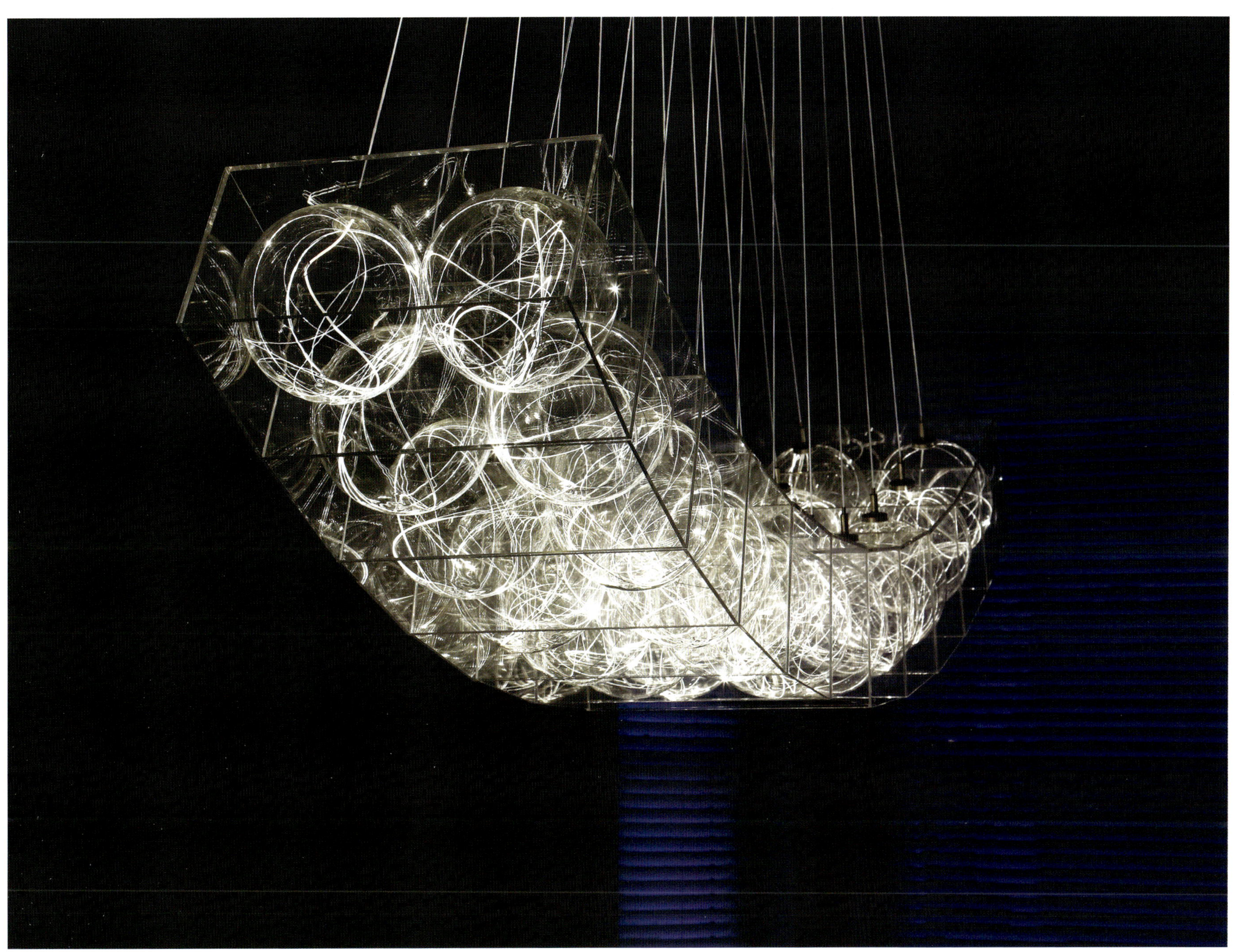

Opposite: Light Shower, *Private Residence, Somerset, UK, 2012. Above:* Swing Low, *Private Residence, London, UK, 2013.*

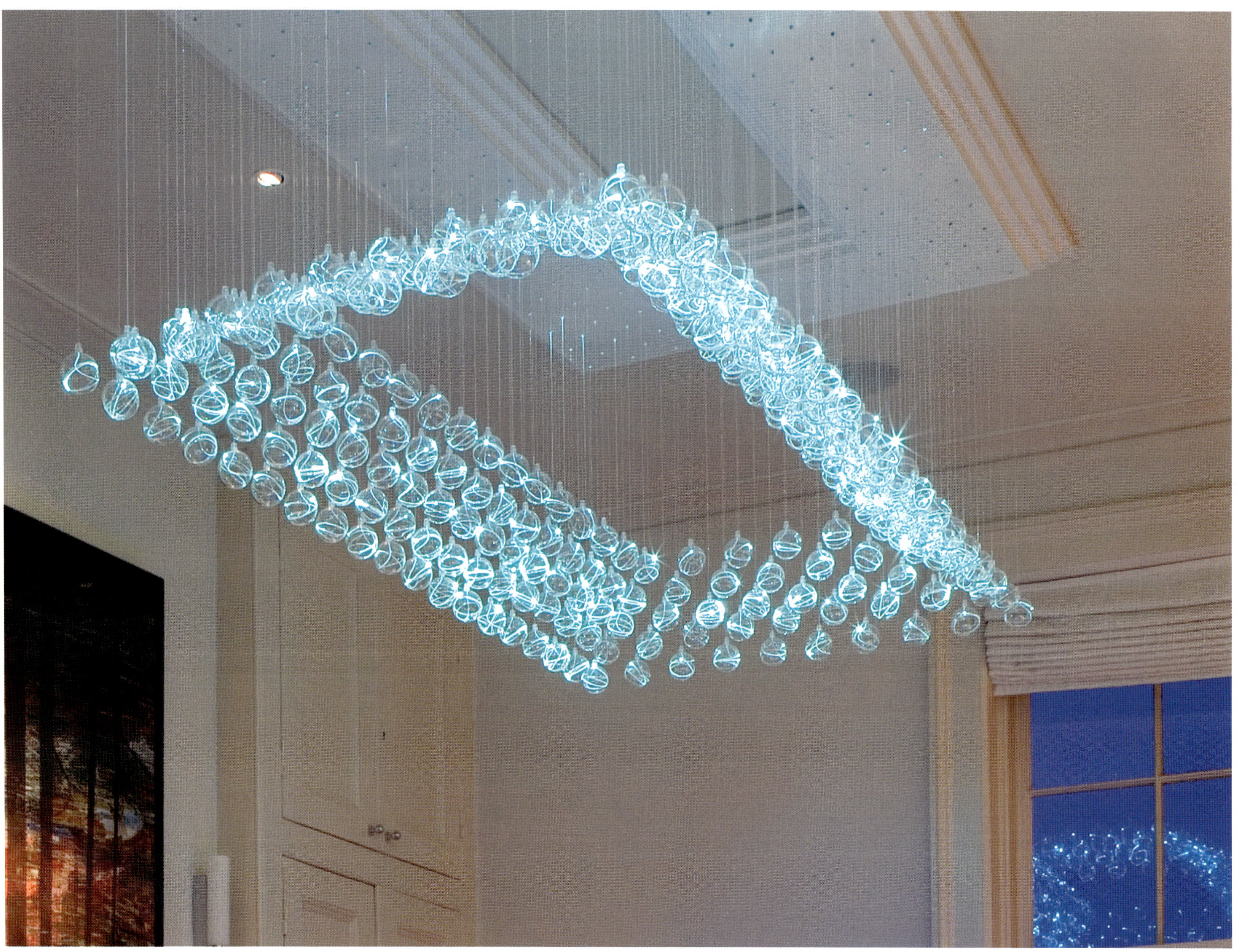

Snowball Canopy, *Private Residence, Gloucestershire, UK, 2008.*

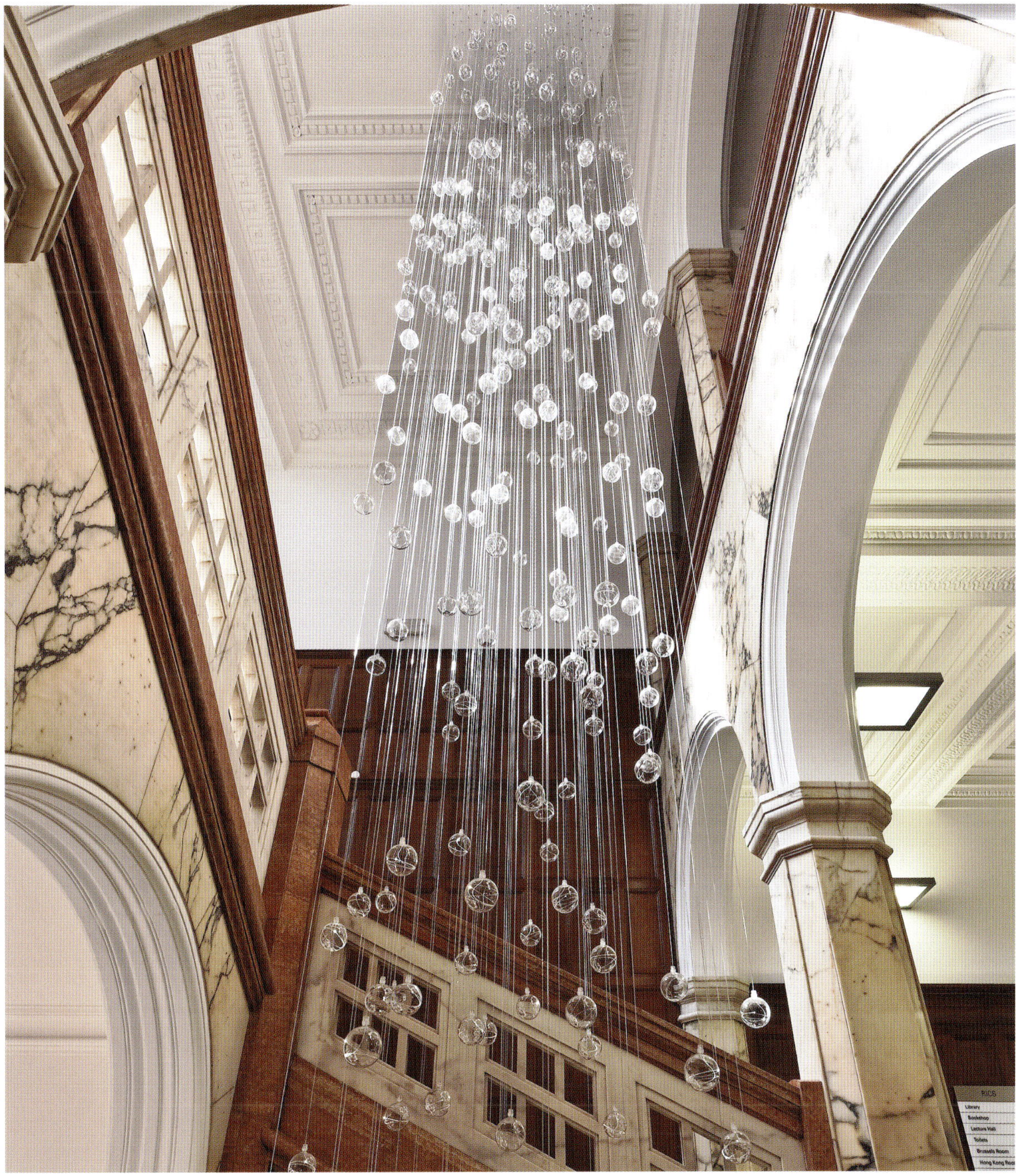

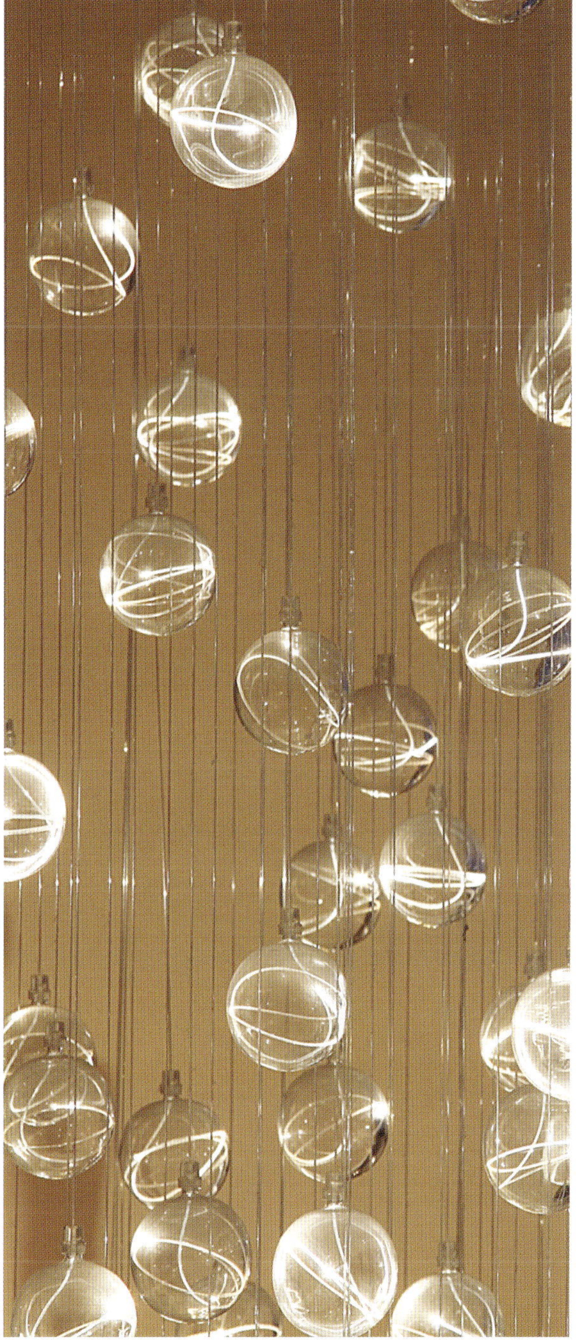

Random Snowball, *Royal Institute of Chartered Surveyors, London, UK, 2009.*

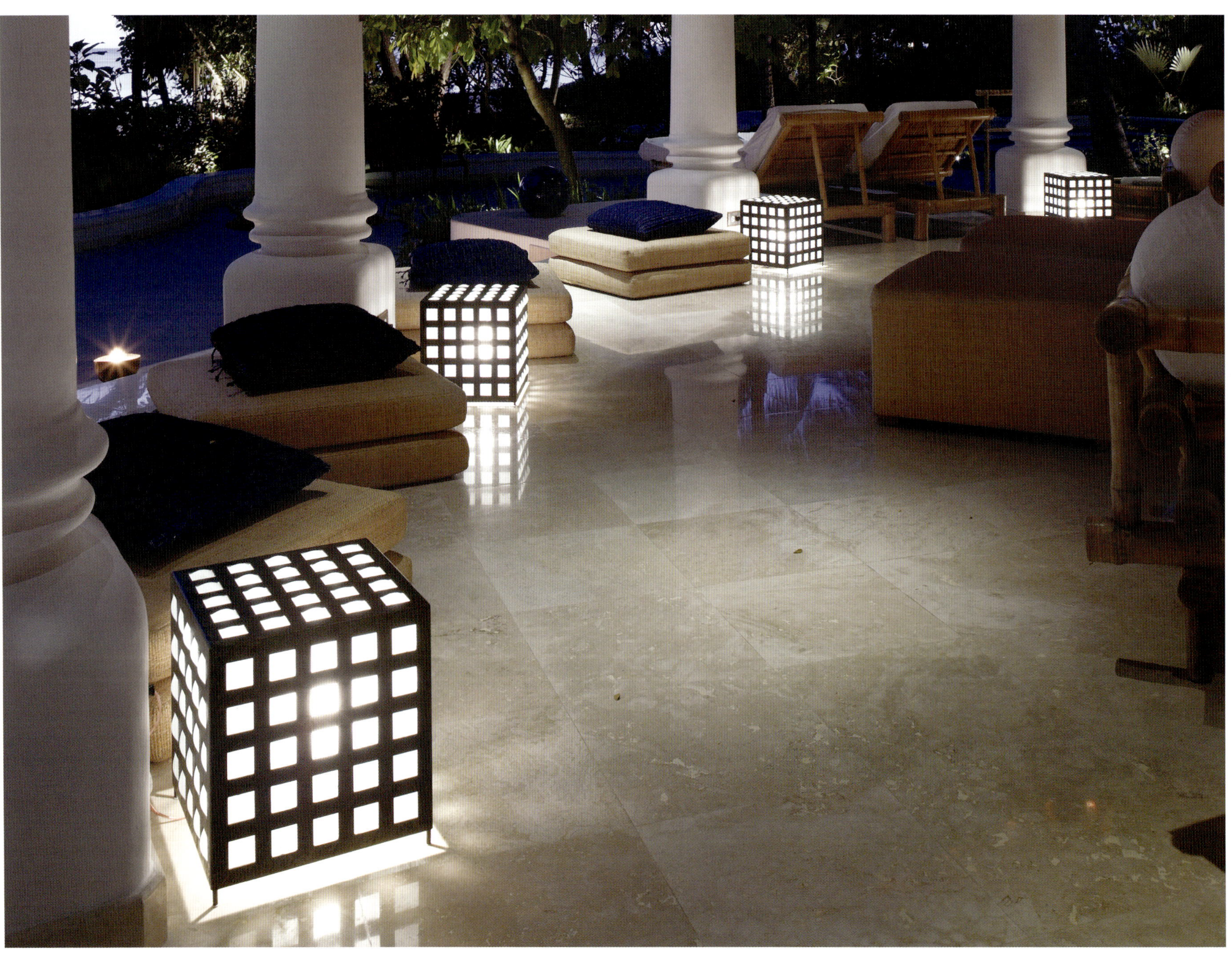

Cube, *Private Residence, Barbados, WI, 2007.*

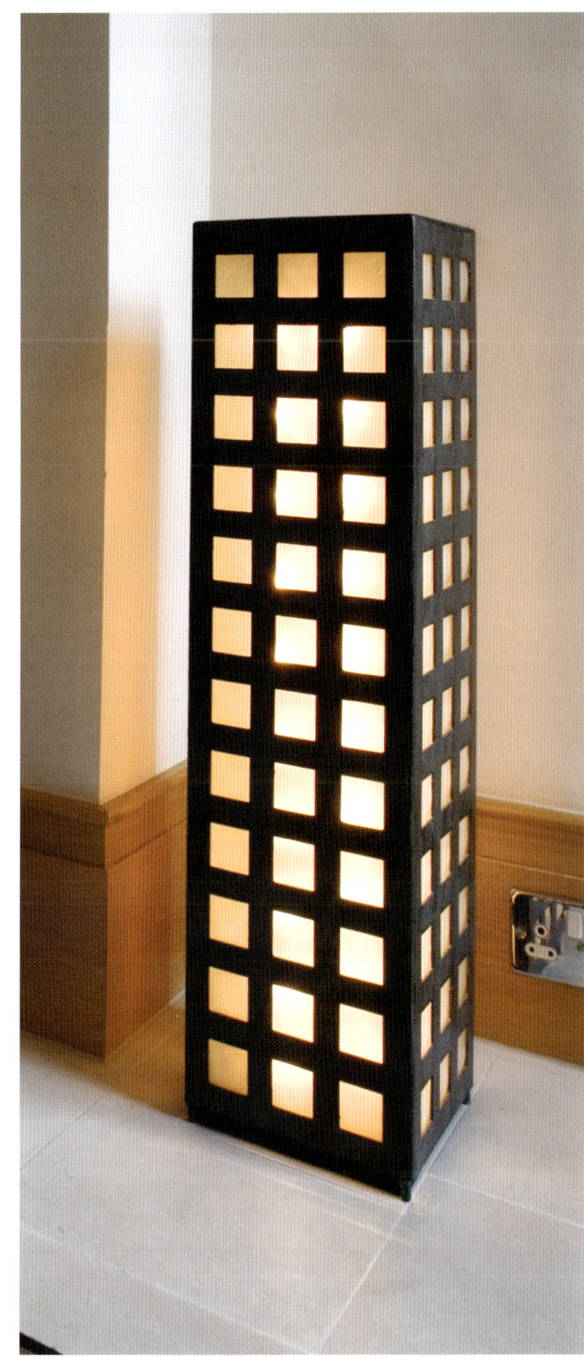

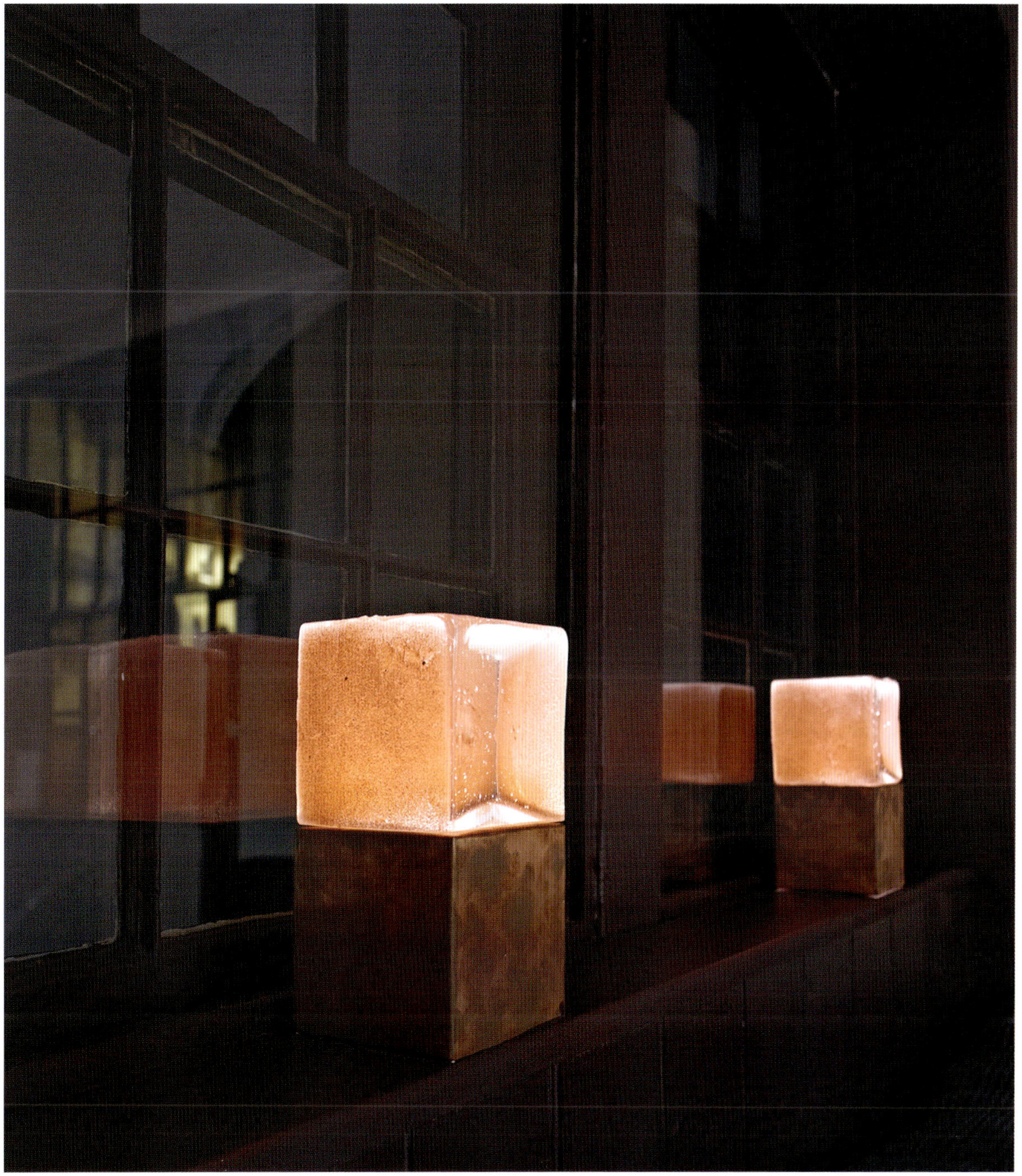

Above left: Cube, *Private Residence, Barbados, WI, 2007. Above right:* Cast Cubes, *The Archangel, Somerset, UK, 2010.*

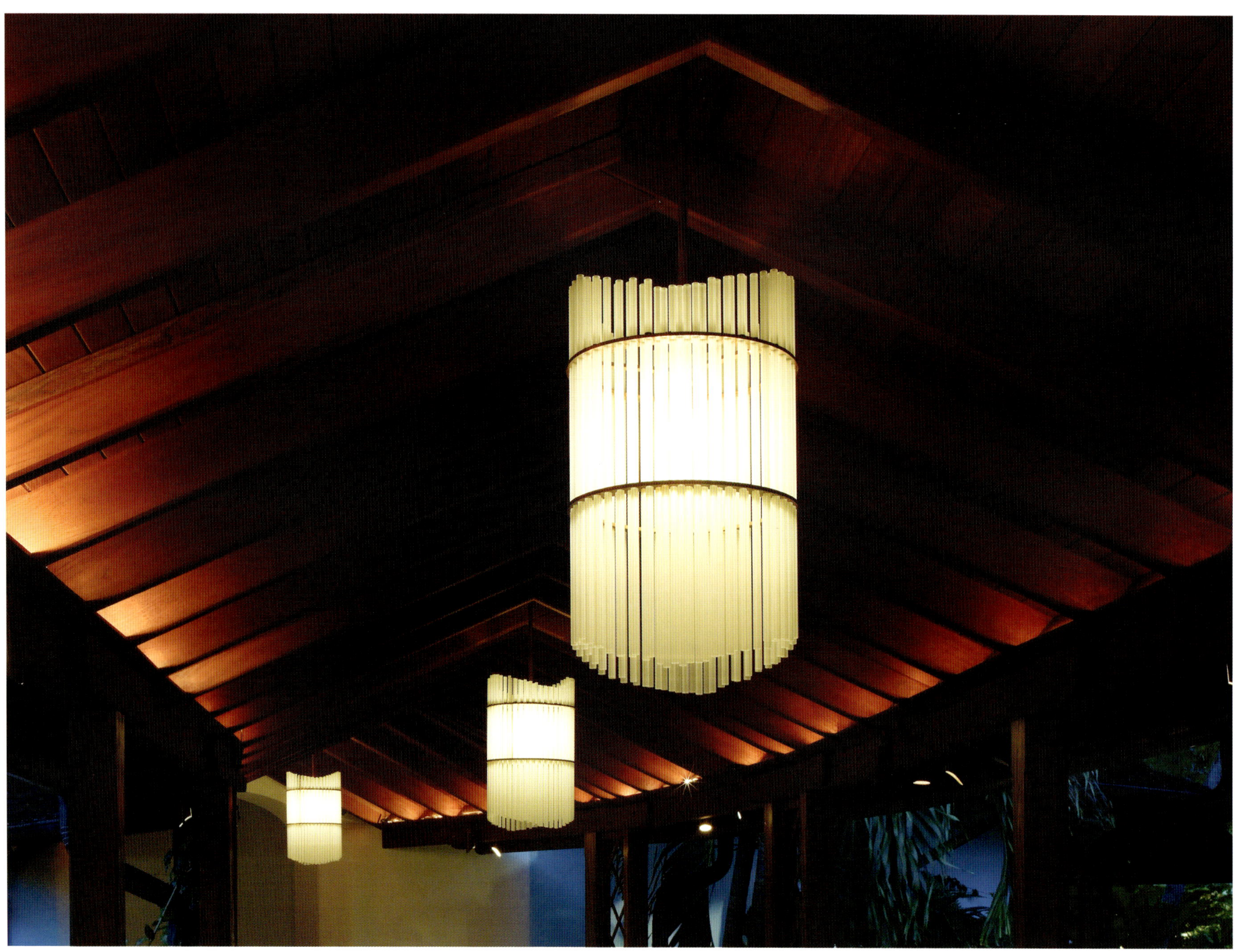

Fluted Lanterns, *Private Residence, Barbados, WI, 2006.*

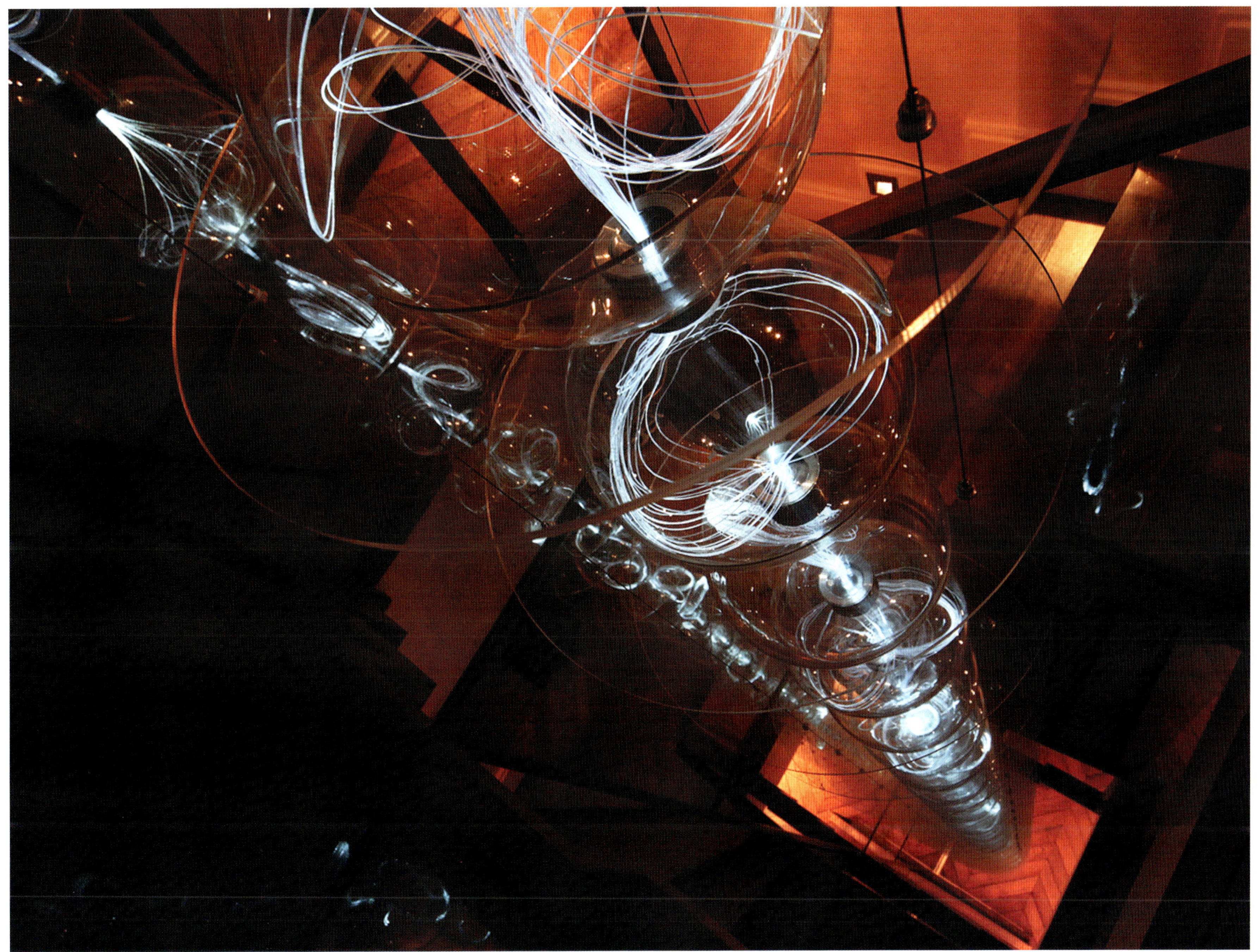

Vandergraph, *Private Residence, London, UK, 2011.*

CHRONOLOGY

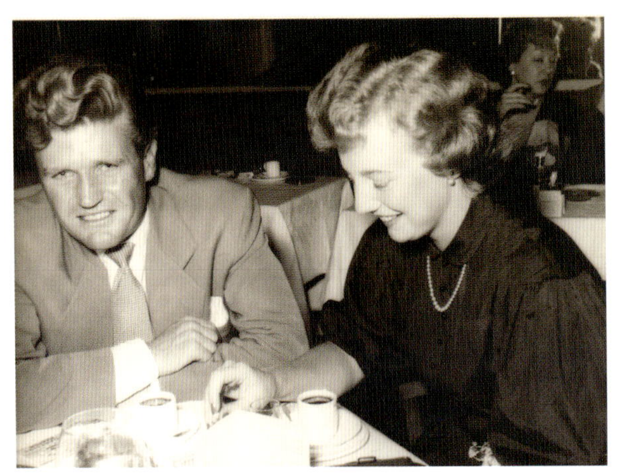

1959

Bruce Beaton St Clair Munro, born on June 2 in London, the youngest of three children born to Judith (née Ames) and Brian Munro. Lives in Harpenden, Hertfordshire, UK, until parents separate and finally divorce in 1965.

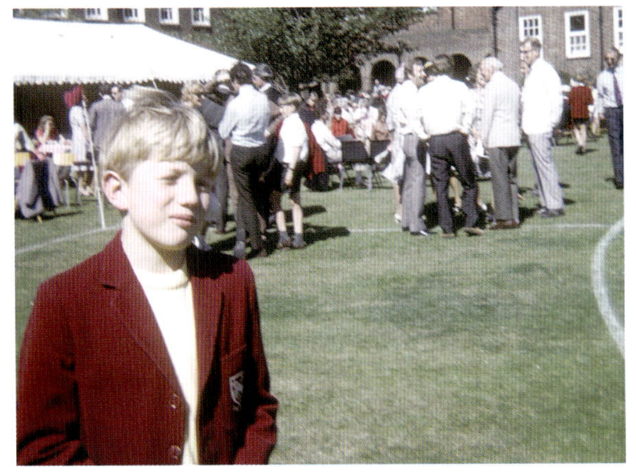

1968

Moves with mother, elder brother, Matthew, and sister, Jane, to "Spinners " cottage, Rayne, Essex. His father moves to Salcombe, Kingsbridge Estuary, South Devon. Munro receives a solid education at the Felsted School, including drawing and painting from life. From the age of nine, art was an important subject for him as he had a natural ability for it and less aptitude for other endeavours. As a youngster, Munro found himself often in trouble for daydreaming.

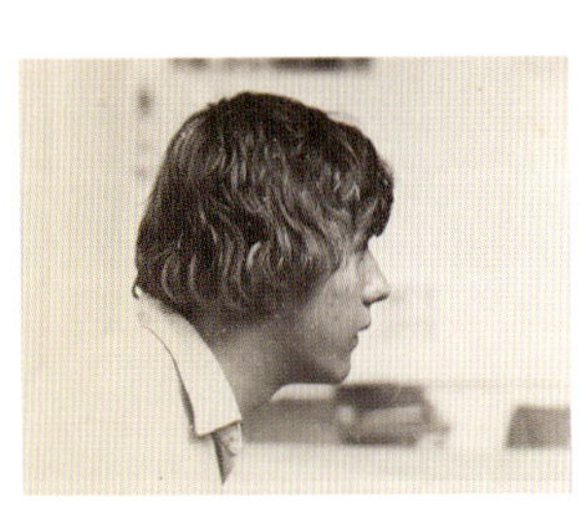

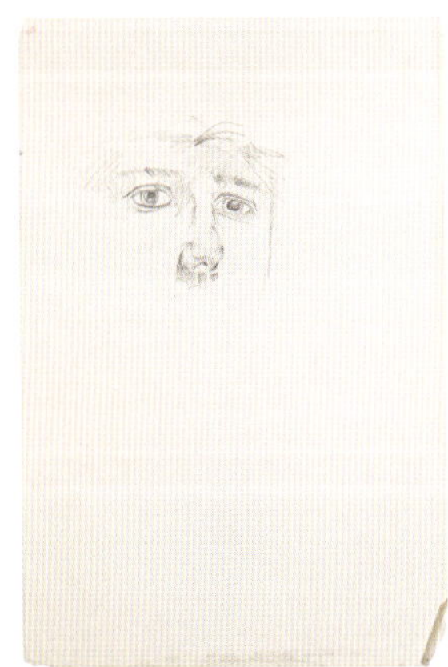

1977

Completes a one-year Foundation course in Art and Design at Braintree Technical College, then commences a degree course at Bristol Polytechnic in Fine Art with a grounding in Art History and a focus on painting. At the end of the first year of this degree, he questions his motivation.

1979

Breaks off his studies for fourteen months and works a multitude of jobs including a *commis* chef, a Christmas employee at Harrods, and an airline courier, until he realises that the practice of art genuinely fills his mind, rather than being a case of settling on art for a career because he is not well suited for other pursuits. Resumes degree in September 1980. Starts to experiment with reaction paintings, based on a personal process of working with paint alone, over the course of hours, in response to an interior monologue of narrative invention.

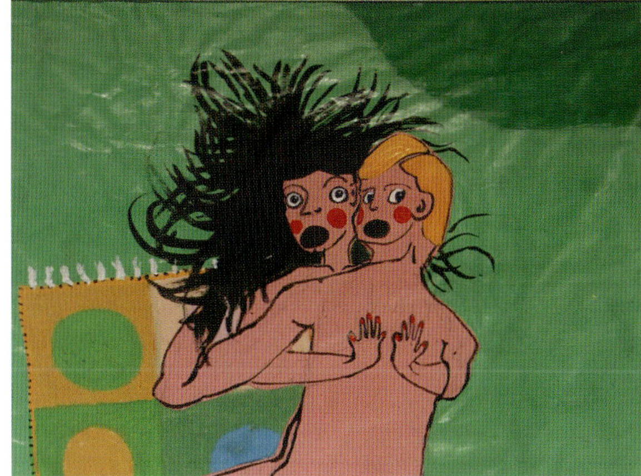

1982

Graduates from Bristol Polytechnic with a bachelor's degree in Fine Art. After much fretting about his potential as an artist, he decides to relax into it and moves to London. Works at Medici Gallery, Grafton Street, a shop dealing in fine art prints and posters. Loves the job as it allows him to look at pictures of art all day. Focuses on moving to warmer climates, as England seems depressing and with few prospects.

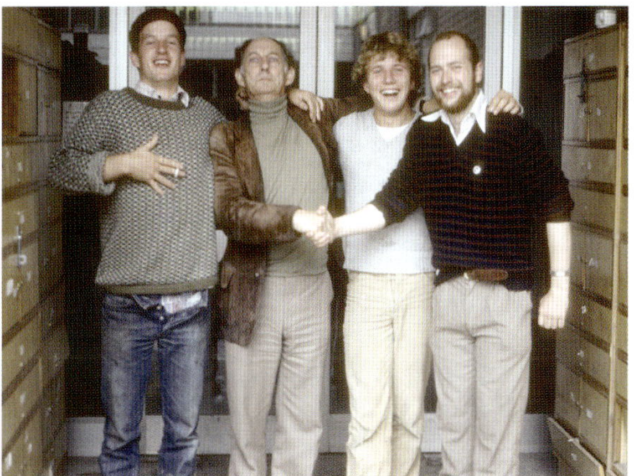

1984

Travels to Sydney, Australia, intending it to be a six-month working holiday. Finds a variety of work as a cook, bricklayer, aerobics instructor, and finally illustrator—with this last, realising that he could make money from his imagination after years of being criticised as a daydreamer.

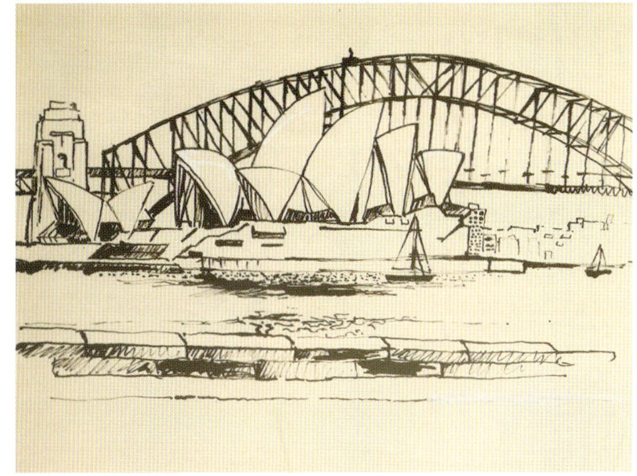

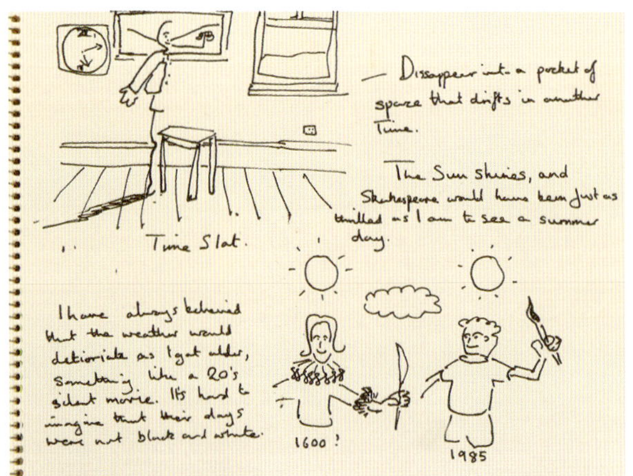

1985

Takes an evening award course with Saatchi and Saatchi and comes across an ultraviolet plastic product whose properties intrigue him. His course tutor, Terry Bunton, writes a brochure that helps him start an illuminated display business, Neo Neon Pty Ltd, for retailers and exhibitions. This includes creating small commercial art jobs and window displays.

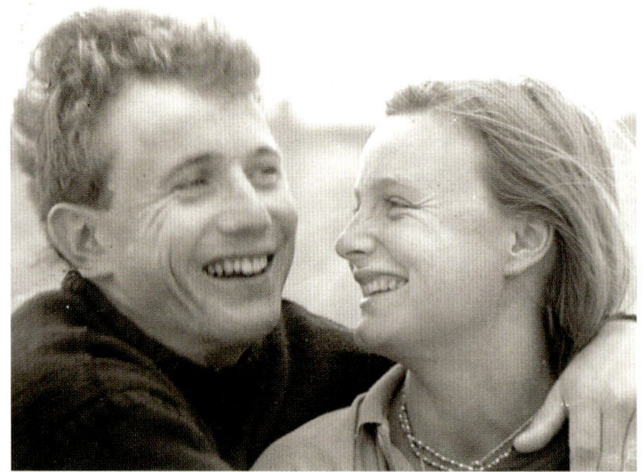

1986

Meets his future wife, Serena Ludovici.

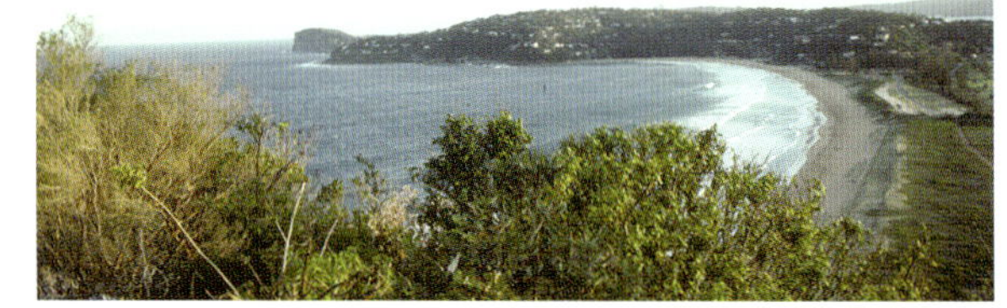

1988

Sells his business to De De Ce Group Pty Ltd and works first as R&D, developing signage products, and then as Head of Production for a new company, De De Ce Signs Pty Ltd, learning about manufacturing and production techniques. Purposely leaves his fine art ambitions out of the equation as he reasons he needs career experience. Moves to Palm Beach, New South Wales, with Serena.

1991

Makes notes in his sketchbooks of moments of condensed connectedness with nature, feeling that these moments of clarity are worthy subject matter to recreate through art. Sets off with fiancée, Serena, on a four-month tour of Australia to explore the natural surroundings.

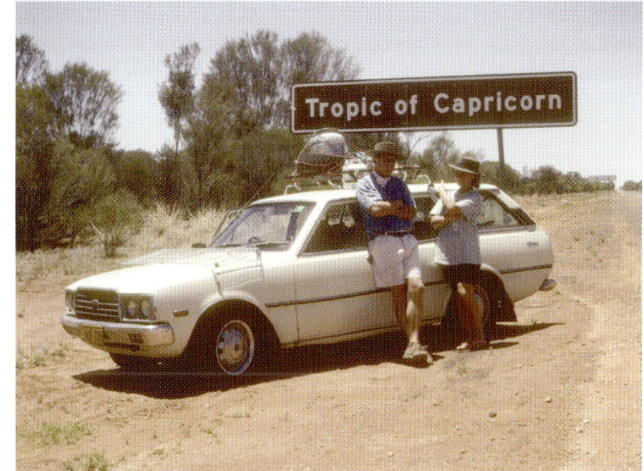

1992

Conceives of an artwork, while camping at Uluru, that would bloom at night like dormant desert seeds responding to rain. Moves back to the UK, initially London, and he and Serena marry. First daughter, Camilla (Millie), is born in December.

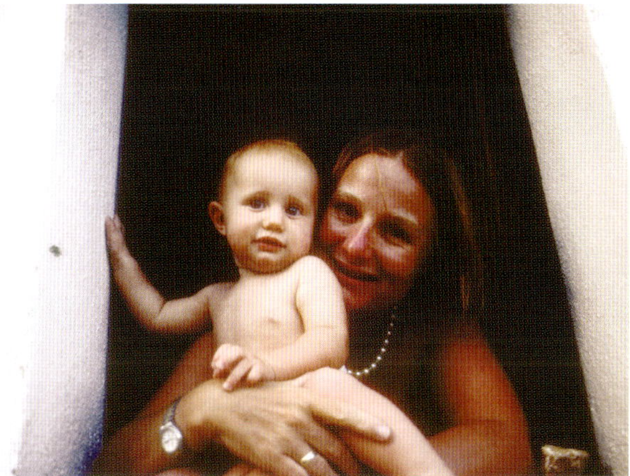

1993

Moves to the country in Dorset, renting an old post office as a studio and intending to make a living as a painter, which proves to be an unrealistic goal. He and Serena consider moving back to Australia as finding work has become very difficult in England.

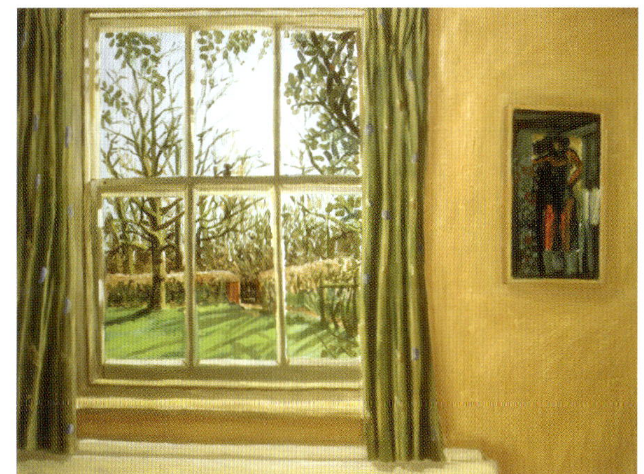

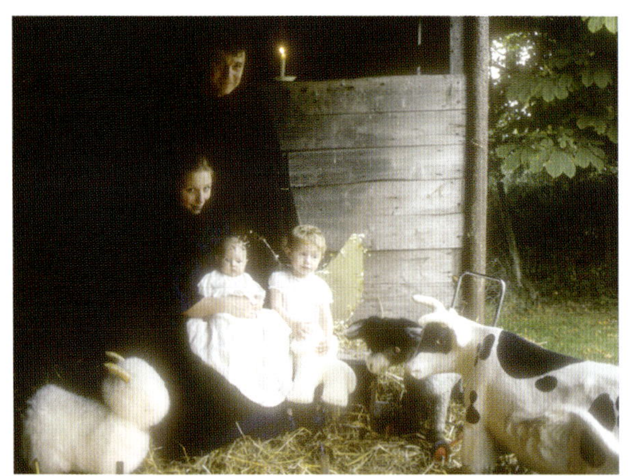

1994

Daughter Florence (Florrie) is born in July. Aware of his family commitments, he purchases a kiln and starts a tile business. The Munros move to Pear Tree Cottage, Somerset.

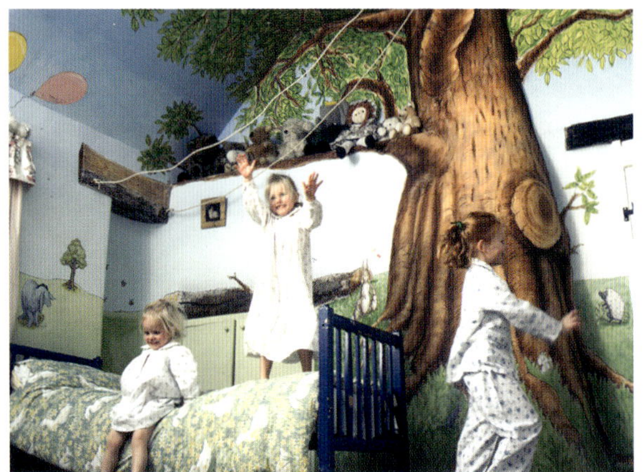

1995

Joins Kevin McCloud design studio to run a specialist paint finishing studio for custom made luminaires. Continues developing his own work at home. Presents first solo exhibition of light works at Round House, Black Swan Gallery, Frome, Somerset.

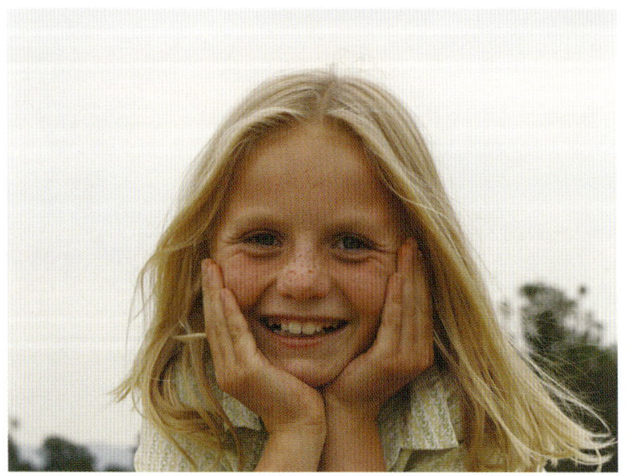

1996

Daughter Isabel (Tink) is born in May. Munro decides to go out on his own, working on mostly residential projects in paint, tile, and lighting. Realises that his light-based inventions are appreciated and begins a series of bespoke designs. Osram names him as its artist lighting advisor for domestic lighting schemes.

1997

Develops his business over the next few years. Receives commissions in UK, France, and Barbados to light houses and gardens. More opportunities arise to create his own pieces.

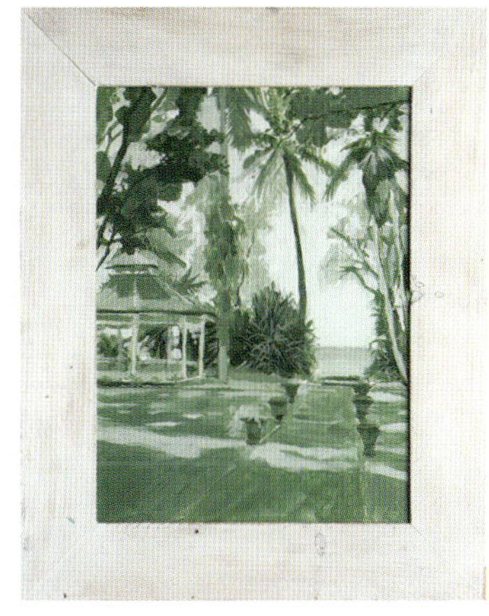

1998

Designs the first *Snowball* chandelier for Babington House, Somerset, UK.

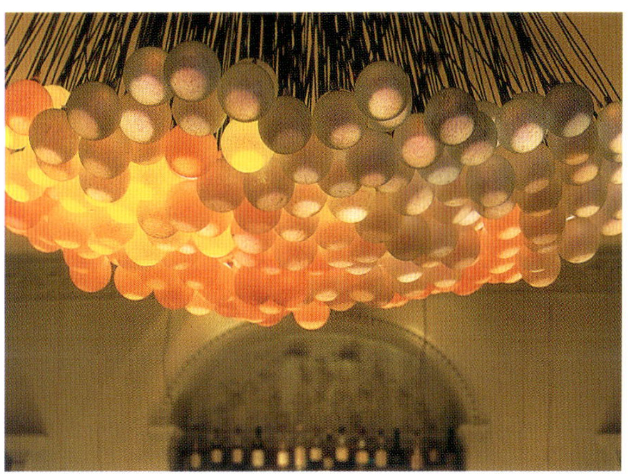

1999

Father dies August 12. As a result, some months after, Munro finds himself beset with anxiety, fear, and a loss of confidence for six months to a year and credits this interlude with an increased sensitivity and capacity for compassion. Begins to think again about simple experiences of connection as valid material to serve as the basis of art.

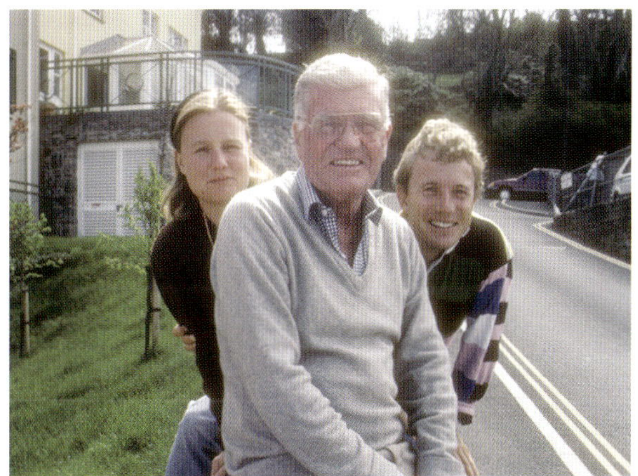

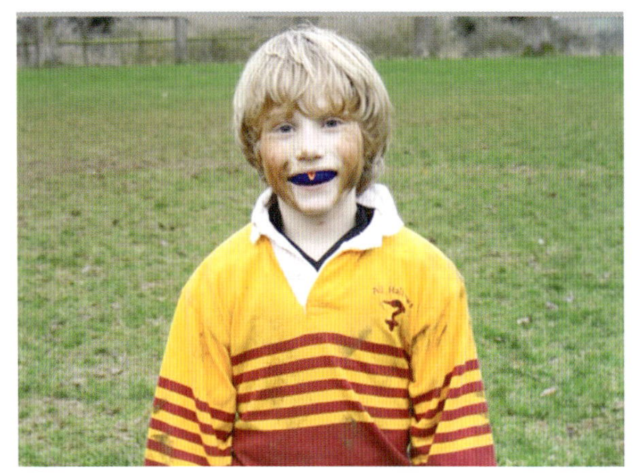

2000

Son, Thomas (Tom), is born in December.

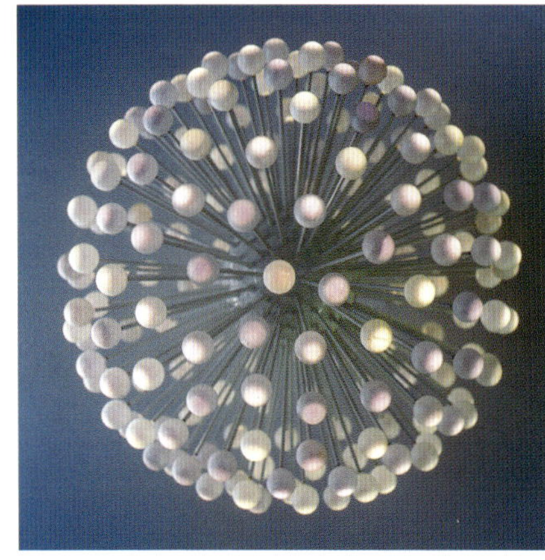

2002

Designs *Sputnik* pendant and is invited to exhibit this and *Snowball* chandelier at Sotheby's contemporary art exhibition, Bond Street, London. *Sputnik* chandelier is purchased by Liberty & Co. for new headquarters on Bond Street. Presents solo exhibition at King's Library Development, Chelsea Harbour. Referencing his past sketchbooks and early ideas, Munro starts to talk freely and to dream about making big pieces inspired by his experiences of emotional clarity, especially the illuminated field from Uluru.

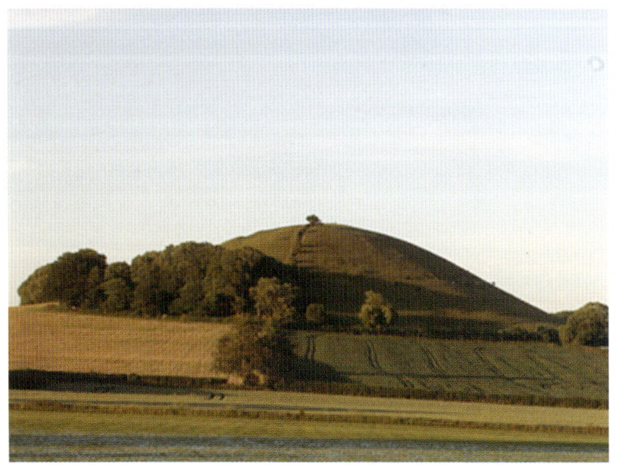

2003

Purchases Long Knoll, a sixteenth-century derelict farmhouse and outbuildings, with a ten-acre large field. Begins to entertain concrete ideas to act on his desires to execute very large outdoor installations in the field behind his house. Looks for low-cost components as an economic necessity and uses components he understands from his lighting design business. Harvey Nichols, Knightsbridge, London, commissions a window display of 10,000 illuminated stems.

2004

Creates a design for the Victoria & Albert Museum's Pirelli Garden as a participant in the "Brilliant" exhibition, using 5,000 of the Harvey Nichols components. Hires two young lads from the nearby village to stake out his first true *Field of Light* at Long Knoll. The costs for this are more than he anticipated, leaving Munro £50,000 in the red. The installation generates interest that sustains him for the next eighteen months. Leaves the illuminated field up for a year, with a sign reading, "Please turn the lights off when you're finished."

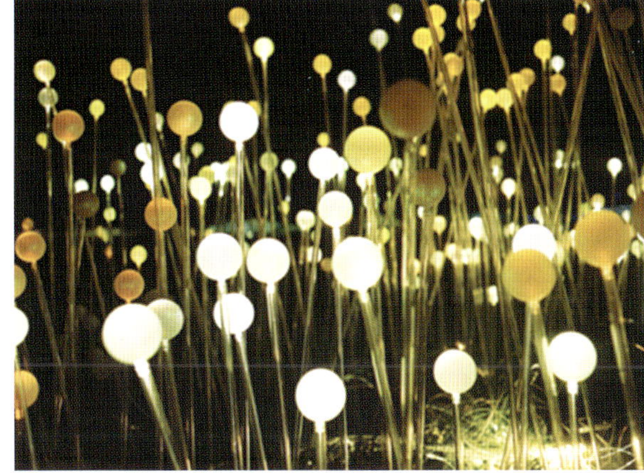

2005

Creates an infrastructure to realise his artistic aspirations with the help of entrepreneur and family friend, James Alexandroff.

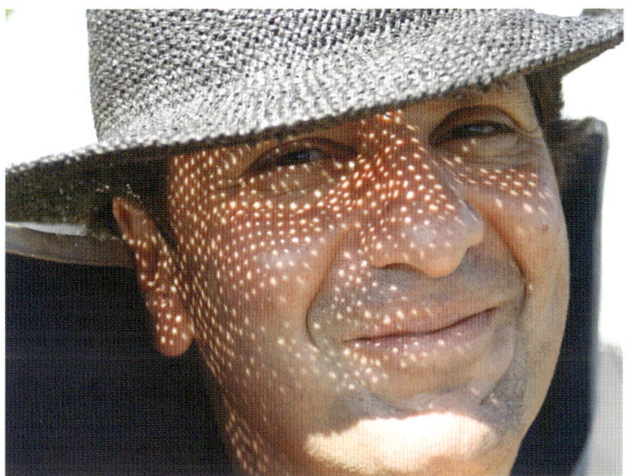

2008

Joins Cameron Macintosh design team to revamp Queens Theatre, London. Creates *Field of Light* for the Eden Project, St Austell, Cornwall. Designs first *Light Shower* for Corrour House, Loch Ossian, Scotland.

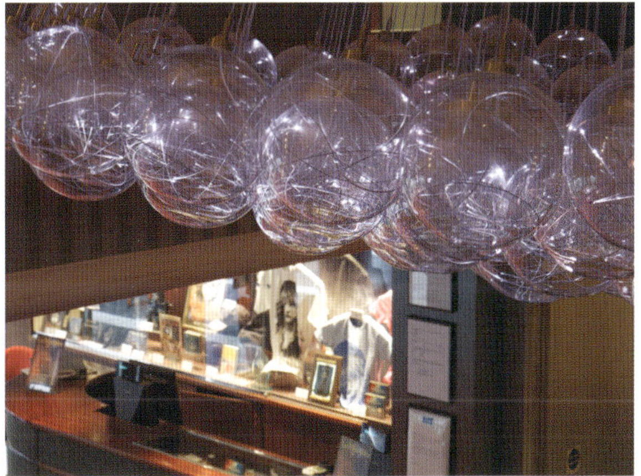

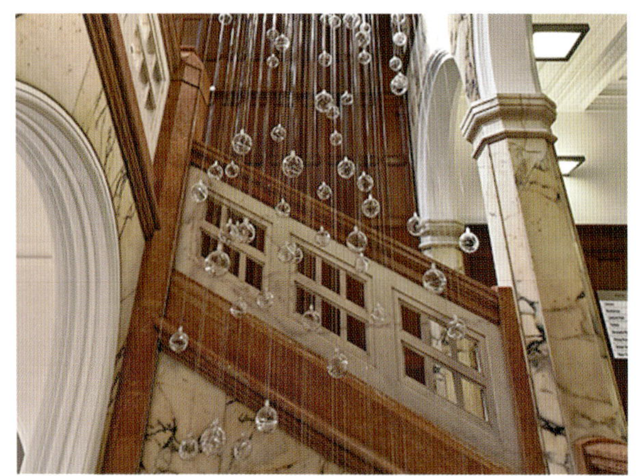

2009

Creates commissioned installation for the Royal Institute of Chartered Surveyors (RICS) in London.

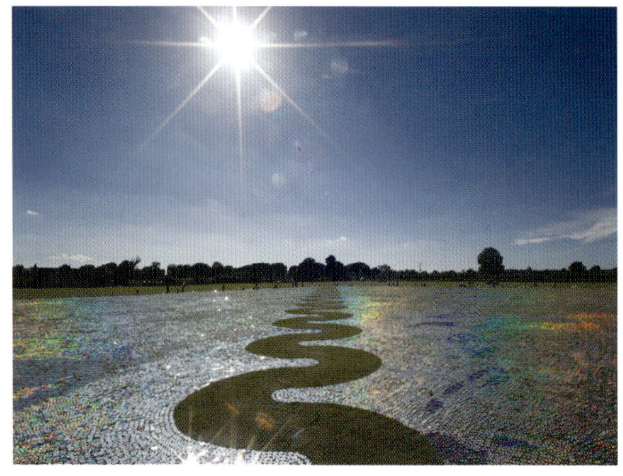

2010

Creates *CDSea* with 600,000 used CDs and the help of 140 friends at Long Knoll. *CDSea* remains on display for three weeks. The artwork was inspired by a remembrance of feeling connected to his father in England through the sea from far-off in Australia. Exhibits *Water-Towers*, based on his fascination with synesthesia (seeing sound in color) and *Light Shower* at Salisbury Cathedral, Wiltshire, UK. Participates in the "Contemplating the Void: Interventions in the Guggenheim Museum" exhibition, New York. Creates bespoke chandelier for the Royal Society, London, UK.

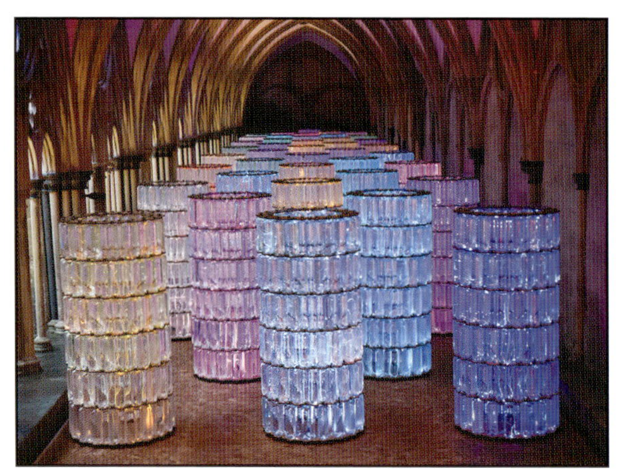

2011

Participates in Biennale Kijkduin, The Hague, Netherlands. Exhibits *Field of Light* at Holburne Museum, Bath, UK, where Munro also creates *Star-Turn* as a fundraiser for Help for Heroes. Opens exhibition sponsored by Bentley Motors at Kensington Palace, London, UK, and exhibition sponsored by JP Morgan at Universities of Glasgow, York, London, and Warwick, UK. Receives FX Product Designer of the Year Award.

2012

Opens first solo US exhibition at Longwood Gardens, Kennett Square, Pennsylvania. Exhibits at Waddesdon Manor, Buckinghamshire, UK; the Oslo Festival of Light, Tjuvholmen, Norway; Pratt Institute, New York, USA; and Telefonica, S.A., Madrid, Spain. Completes bespoke commissions for Royal United Hospital, Bath, UK; Moet Hennessy, UK; Alexander McQueen autumn/winter catwalk, Paris, France.

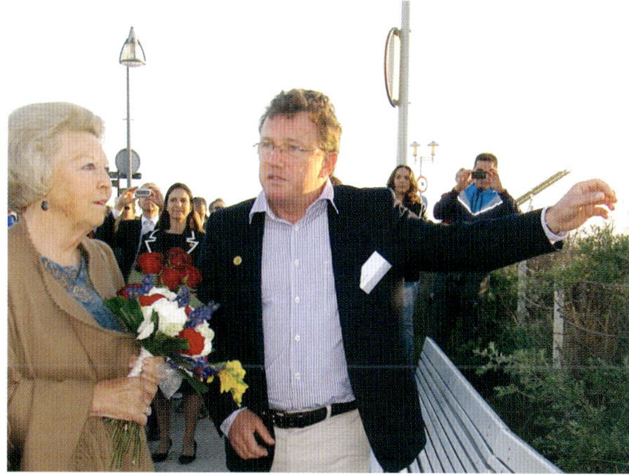

2013

Opens exhibitions at Cheekwood Botanical Garden and Museum of Art, Nashville, Tennessee; Franklin Park Conservatory and Botanical Gardens, Columbus, Ohio; and Waddesdon Manor, Buckinghamshire, UK, where he will have an annual exhibition residency through 2015. Wins American Alliance of Museums (AAM) Excellence in Exhibition Award for *Light: Installations by Bruce Munro* at Longwood Gardens.

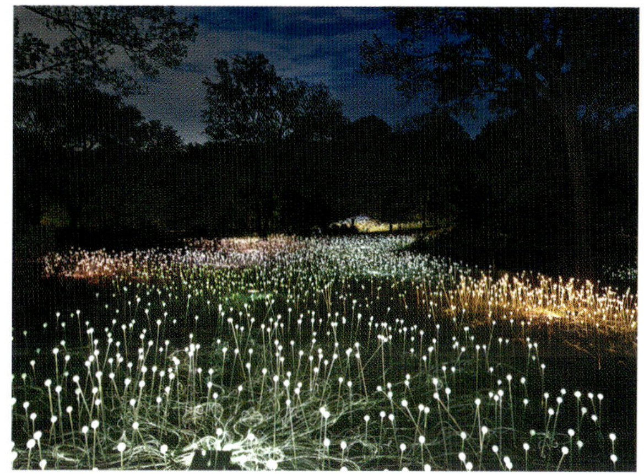

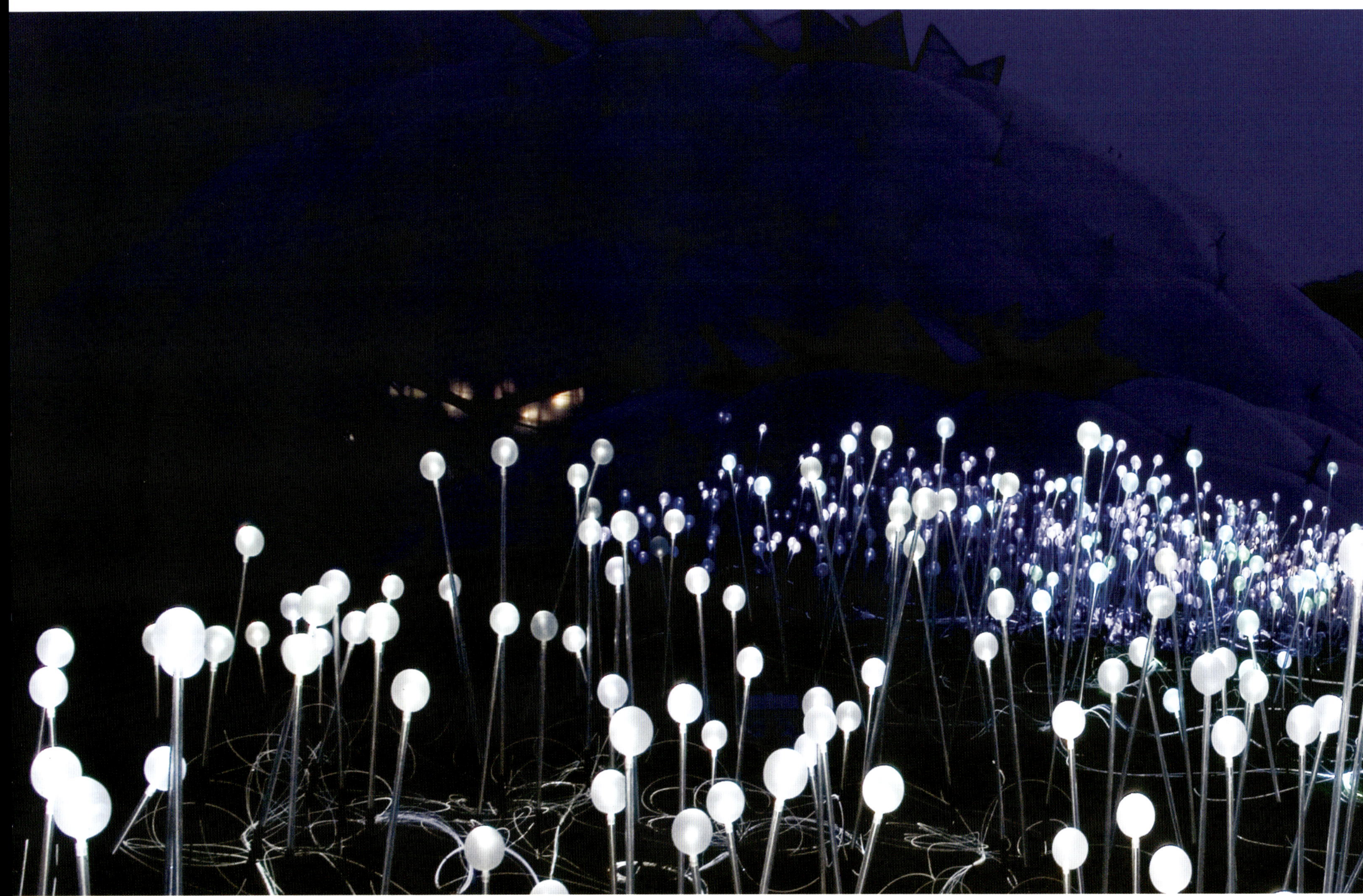

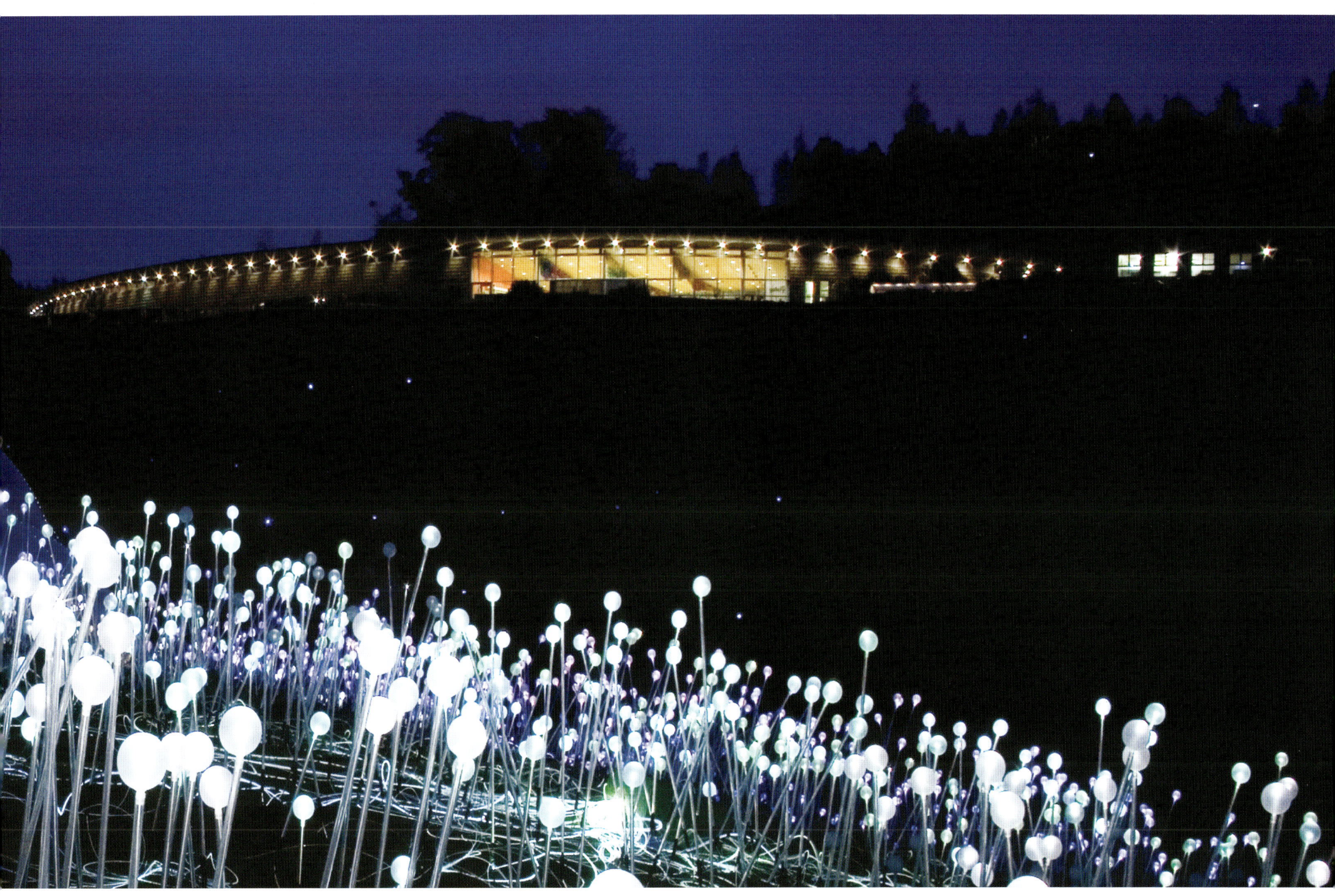

Field of Light, *Eden Project, Cornwall, UK, 2008–2009.*

ACKNOWLEDGMENTS

Too many to thank individually, but all are integral and prove that the sum of the whole rules! My thanks to all the generous patrons and clients who have supported my work, the talented engineers and artisans who make it, the brilliant team at Long Knoll studio, our American colleagues, and the wonderful museums and gardens that give me and my team the opportunity to live the dream.

Bruce Munro

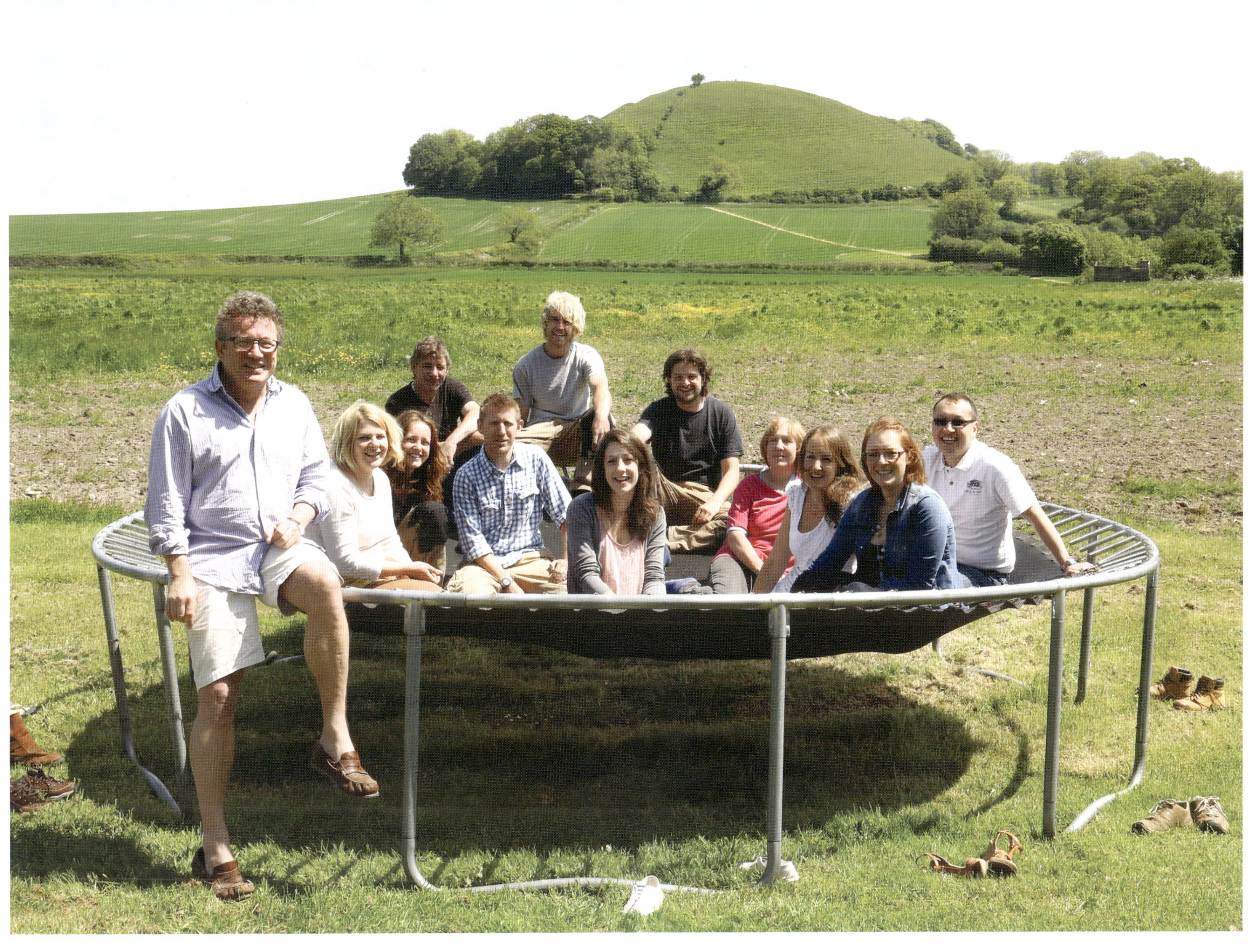

Bruce Munro and team at Long Knoll Field, Wiltshire, UK, 2013. Left to right: Bruce Munro, Catherine Wright, Lauren Entwisle, Adrian Richardson, Ben Burr, Mo Webb, Adele Seaward, Michael Fountain, Tina Whittock, Anna Craddock, Abby Bryant, Ronald Bicker.

PHOTOGRAPHERS

Vincent Evans
xiv

Mark Pickthall
i, iii, iv–v, vii, ix–xii, xvii, xviii, xxi–1, 6–7, 8–9, 10, 12–13, 20–21, 24–25, 26, 30–33, 34–35, 42–61, 65, 68–69, 70–83, 88–95, 97–111, 113–117, 122, 123, 125–135, 138–139, 182–183, 185, 186
All images in Sculptures
All images in Commissions

Hank Davis
4–5, 11, 14–23, 27–29, 62–64, 66–67, 84–87, 118–121, 124, 136, 137

Kyle Dreier
32–35

Chris Newcombe
xxi

Ash Mills
96

John Griggs
112

Bruce Munro
40, 41

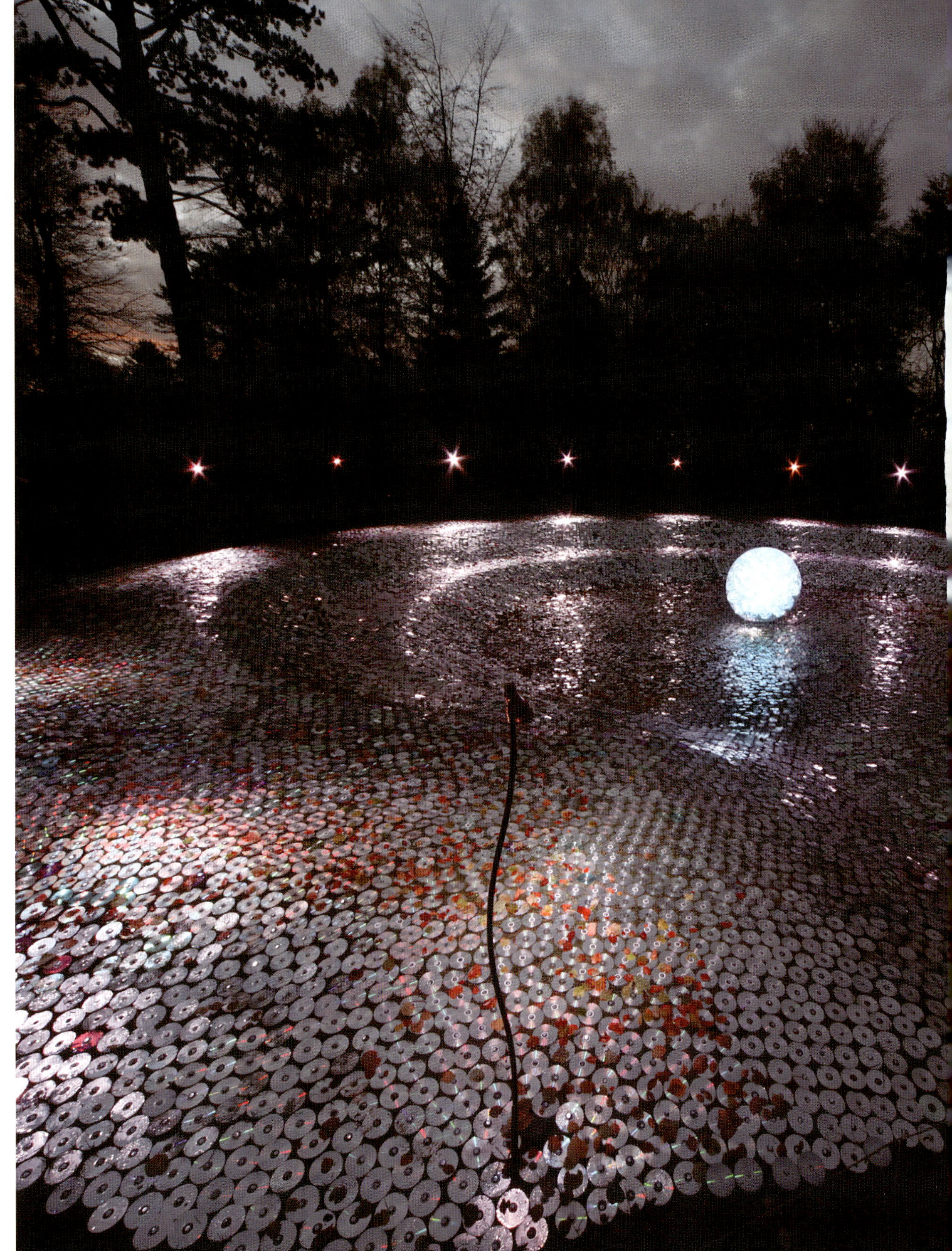